NATIONAL DUTIES

AMERICAN BEGINNINGS, 1500–1900

A Series Edited by Hannah Farber, Stephen Mihm, and Mark Peterson

Also in the series:

Promise to Pay: The Politics and Power of Money in Early America
by Katie A. Moore

Flower, Guns, and Money: Joel Roberts Poinsett and the Paradoxes of American Patriotism
by Lindsay Schakenbach Regele

Banking on Slavery: Financing Southern Expansion in the Antebellum United States
by Sharon Ann Murphy

A Great and Rising Nation: Naval Exploration and Global Empire in the Early US Republic
by Michael A. Verney

Trading Freedom: How Trade with China Defined Early America
by Dael A. Norwood

Wives Not Slaves: Patriarchy and Modernity in the Age of Revolutions
by Kirsten Sword

Accidental Pluralism: America and the Religious Politics of English Expansion, 1497–1662
by Evan Haefeli

The Province of Affliction: Illness and the Making of Early New England
by Ben Mutschler

Puritan Spirits in the Abolitionist Imagination
by Kenyon Gradert

Trading Spaces: The Colonial Marketplace and the Foundations of American Capitalism
by Emma Hart

Urban Dreams, Rural Commonwealth: The Rise of Plantation Society in the Chesapeake
by Paul Musselwhite

Building a Revolutionary State: The Legal Transformation of New York, 1776–1783
by Howard Pashman

A complete list of series titles is available on the University of Chicago Press website.

NATIONAL DUTIES

Custom Houses and the Making of
the American State

GAUTHAM RAO

THE UNIVERSITY OF CHICAGO PRESS
CHICAGO AND LONDON

PUBLICATION OF THIS BOOK HAS BEEN AIDED BY A GRANT FROM THE BEVINGTON FUND.

The University of Chicago Press, Chicago 60637
The University of Chicago Press, Ltd., London
© 2016 by The University of Chicago
All rights reserved. No part of this book may be used or reproduced in any manner whatsoever without written permission, except in the case of brief quotations in critical articles and reviews. For more information, contact the University of Chicago Press, 1427 E. 60th St., Chicago, IL 60637.
Published 2016
Paperback edition 2025

34 33 32 31 30 29 28 27 26 25   1 2 3 4 5

ISBN-13: 978-0-226-36707-1 (cloth)
ISBN-13: 978-0-226-84009-3 (paper)
ISBN-13: 978-0-226-36710-1 (e-book)
DOI: https://doi.org/10.7208/chicago/9780226367101.001.0001

Library of Congress Cataloging-in-Publication Data

Names: Rao, Gautham, author.
Title: National duties : custom houses and the making of the American state / Gautham Rao.
Other titles: American beginnings, 1500–1900.
Description: Chicago ; London : The University of Chicago Press, 2016. | Series: American beginnings, 1500–1900
Identifiers: LCCN 2015037498 | ISBN 9780226367071 (cloth : alk. paper) | ISBN 9780226367101 (e-book)
Subjects: LCSH: Customs administration—United States. | Customs administration—England—Colonies—America. | United States—History—1783–1815.
Classification: LCC HJ6622 .R36 2016 | DDC 3821/.7097309033—dc23
LC record available at http://lccn.loc.gov/2015037498

To
Nerissa Hamilton-vom Baur

CONTENTS

Acknowledgments ix
A Note on Archival Sources xiii

Introduction 1

Part I
Revolution: Philadelphia, 1769

1. Custom Houses, Negotiated Authority, and the Bonds of Empire, 1714–1776 19

Part II
Revenue and Empire: Bermuda Hundred, 1795

2. Political Economy and the Making of the Customs System 53
3. Negotiating Authority in Federalist America, 1789–1800 75

Part III
Revenue and Crisis: Baltimore, 1808

4. Commerce or War? 103
5. Jefferson's Embargo and the Era of Commercial Restrictions, 1807–1815 132

Part IV
Reform: Boston, 1817

6. Dismantling Discretion, 1816–1828 167

Epilogue: Charleston, 1832 197

Abbreviations 201
Notes 203
Index 261

ACKNOWLEDGMENTS

It is a privilege to thank the many people who made this book possible. At the University of Chicago, the late Peter Novick pushed me to get into the history "racket," and Jim Sparrow convinced me to stay in it. Kathleen Conzen taught me how to do research and told me that there was a book to be written about custom houses. Amy Dru Stanley pushed me harder than anyone else, and I am grateful that I continue to benefit from our conversations. I thank Bill Novak for his incredible friendship, camaraderie, and scholarly vision. More than anyone else, Bill pushed me to ask the big questions and propose big answers.

Max Edling and Richard John generously read drafts of the project for years and years and provided incisive comments at every turn. Dan Ernst has been a great critic and friend. As a Samuel I. Golieb Fellow in Legal History at the New York University School of Law, I learned so much from Lauren Benton, Richard Bernstein, Bernard Freamon, and John Phillip Reid. Daniel Hulsebosch and Bill Nelson have been tireless advocates for this project. As a Postdoctoral Fellow in the Program in Early American Economy and Society at the Library Company of Philadelphia, I benefited from the advice of Albrecht Koshnick, Sally Gordon, James N. Green, Daniel Richter, Michelle Craig McDonald, and Roderick McDonald, and especially the incomparable, indefatigable Cathy Matson. At the École des Hautes Études en Sciences Sociales in Paris, I benefited greatly from feedback by Roman Huret, Cecile Vidal, Jean Heffer, Emmanuelle Perez, and especially Nicolas Barreyre. The Hurst Summer Institute at the Institute for Legal Studies at the University of Wisconsin Law School was a life-changing event for me, due in large part to the mentorship of Barbara Welke. The American Society for Legal History is a remarkable community of scholars who have helped me a great deal over the years, especially

Bruce Mann, Maeva Marcus, Chris Tomlins, Mike Grossberg, Sally Hadden, Elizabeth Dale, John Witt, and Holly Brewer.

My colleagues in the Federated Department of History at Rutgers/New Jersey Institute of Technology in Newark helped shape this project at an early stage, especially Stephen Pemberton, Richard Sher, Kyle Riismandel, Kornel Chang, Beryl Satter, Jonathan Lurie, Stuart Gold, Jan Lewis, Whitney Strub, Amita Satyal, Lisa Nocks, and the late Clem Price. Neil Maher was a wonderful mentor and model colleague. Jessica Witte provided extremely helpful administrative assistance. I am also indebted to several NJIT students for their assistance: Taquesha Owens, Franklin Chou, Sandra Moryto, and Marquise Hargrove. Maureen O'Rourke deserves special mention for spending countless hours talking with me about this project and keeping me sane while I was commuting between DC and Newark.

At American University, Sarah Adler, Laura Nitzberg, Kelsi Schagunn, Tracey Livingston, and Lauren Pav were always quick to offer help from the History office. Jordan Grant, Terumi Rafferty-Osaki, Lauren Duval, Amy Langford, and Allison Jobe have been more like colleagues than students. My amazing department chair, Pamela Nadell, has fiercely protected me and supported me at every turn. Dean Peter Starr and the College of Arts and Sciences provided a generous teaching leave and funding, including an Andrew Mellon Fellowship. Michael Brenner, Laura Beers, Allan Lichtman, Richard Breitman, Eileen Findlay, Daniel Kerr, Pedram Partovi, April Shelford, and Alan Kraut read portions of the manuscript and provided excellent suggestions. Lisa Moses Leff and Kate Haulman have gone out of their way as friends, colleagues, and mentors, and I am especially indebted to both.

I cannot possibly do justice to all the wonderful libraries and librarians who have helped this project in innumerable ways. I must, however, acknowledge Clement Ho, Alex Mackintosh, and Martin Shapiro of the American University Library, Patrick Kerwin and the staff at the Manuscript Reading Room of the Library of Congress, The Center for Legislative Archives at the National Archives, Sara Heim and the Historical Society of Pennsylvania, and James N. Green, Cornelia S. King, and the Library Company of Philadelphia.

Mark Peterson, Ed Gray, and especially Stephen Mihm deserve thanks for seeing promise in the project and bringing it into the American Beginnings series. At the University of Chicago Press, it was a joy to work with Robert Devens and Tim Mennel and their super assistants, Nora Devlin and Logan Smith. Caterina MacLean, Katherine Faydash, Marian Rogers, and Ashley Pierce ably helped push the book over the finish line. J. Naomi

Linzer Indexing Services did a wonderful job on the index, and Dennis McClendon and Chicago CartoGraphics valiantly put together the historical maps for the book.

My intellectual and social universe has brought me amazing scholarly connections and friendships. Thank you to Tim Stewart-Winter, Thomas Adams, Stephan Endicott, Arissa Oh, Nate Holdren, Mike Osman, Esther Na, Sadia Shirazi, Nishi Gupta, Sanjay Gupta, Arman Schwartz, Gregory Karelas, Maribel Morey, Cynthia Nicoletti, Kelly Kennington, David Tanenhaus, Matthew Sherman, Ariel Ron, Andrew Wender Cohen, Mark Wilson, Nicholas Parrillo, Michael Willrich, Ajay Mehrotra, Kim Reilly, Tracy Steffes, Kyle Volk, Reuel Schiller, Joanna Grisinger, Abigail Swingen, Dael Norwood, Joseph Adelman, Kenneth Owen, Hannah Farber, Joshua Barkan, Tony Freyer, Chris Desan, and Seth Rockman for their help and encouragement. Karen Tani, Ariel Ron, Christopher Swope, Joshua Stein, Paddy Reilly, Sophia Lee, Christopher Beauchamp, Kevin Arlyck, Serena Mayeri, and Sam Erman deserve special mention for their camaraderie and for helping me with specific chapters and arguments. Alison Lefkovitz gave countless hours of her time to making this project better and countless more tolerating my bad jokes. Finally, special thanks are owed to Jonathan Levy for his part in our sprawling, ongoing conversation about all things history and beyond.

My friends and family continue to be a source of seemingly limitless support. Hilary Conway, Josh Alcorn and Andrea Peterson, Emily and Aric Merolli, and Jenna and Matt Einstein always bring good cheer. The Siddiquis, Clabaults, Plazas, Dedolphs, Swopes, Oblers, and Pranios have welcomed us into a remarkable community on Mansfield Road. I received constant encouragement from Stephen and Zoe Lamb, David Hamilton, and Daphne vom Baur, who also deserves special mention for allowing me to use her beautiful painting for the book's jacket. My aunts, uncles, and cousins—the Swamy, Dwarakanath, Nath, Curtis, Srinivasan, Johnson, Gupta, Pillutla, and Shetty clans—have known me from my earliest days and humored my tweedy conversations at family events. Bharath Nath and Kara Braciale hosted me on several research trips to Worcester and Boston. Nagendra Prasad has always helped me think through complicated aspects of the project. My remarkable siblings, Vikram and Nandini, have helped me in so many ways that I will forever be in their debt. My parents, Jayanth and Hemalatha, will always be my inspiration as scholars, parents, and people.

This book is dedicated to my wife, Nerissa Hamilton-vom Baur, and my two amazing daughters, Saskia and Mirabel. You three are the lights of my life. Sasi and Mira, welcoming you into the world and watching you grow—your smiles, giggles, jokes, hugs, and kisses—have given me my most cherished moments. Nerissa, what a life we've enjoyed together since our paths first crossed in an undergraduate history class in Pick Hall. You have done so much for me. Thank you for encouraging and supporting me from my first days in graduate school through my years on the academic job market. Without your love I'd be nowhere at all. I'd be lost if not for you. And you know it's true.

A NOTE ON ARCHIVAL SOURCES

Spelling and punctuation varies widely in the numerous archival sources used in this study. To provide readers with the most accurate portrayal of these sources, original spelling and punctuation are preserved throughout, unless otherwise noted. Italic for emphasis in archival sources is also preserved.

INTRODUCTION

The story of the creation of the American federal government could concisely be told through the writings of Alexander Hamilton. The first secretary of the treasury's reports on public credit, manufactures, and a national bank are remembered for advocating a muscular federal government capable of taxing, spending, and shaping the nation's destiny. Less known, though, is that the reports were beset by anxiety. Hamilton had no shortage of concerns about the numerous threats facing the young United States. Chief among these problems was a crisis of government revenue. The Articles of Confederation had just spectacularly failed, and the national debt had risen to the dizzying height of $80 million. True, the new Constitution gave Congress the power to tax. And Congress exercised that power by creating a tariff and federal custom houses to collect taxes on imported goods. This customs revenue was to supply the national purse. But Hamilton remained concerned. The problem was the fragile relationship between the federal government and the merchants who paid the customs duties. Above all, Hamilton feared "contravening the sense of the body of the merchants" or violating the merchants' "impressions of what is reasonable and proper."[1]

Hamilton's reputation as a friend of merchants and commerce preceded him, so his concern is not all that surprising. But there was much more to it than this. The merchants were the ones who paid customs duties that were to be the main source of national revenue (see table 1). As Hamilton explained of the federal government, the merchants who paid customs duties had "seconded its operation." *Seconded.* Like deputies of some sort, the merchants had done much to shoulder the burden of building a new American state. In just one short year the United States had begun to build a revenue system from customs duties on merchant capital. A foundation

TABLE 1. Federal Revenue, 1789–1836

Fiscal year	Total revenue (thousands of dollars)	Customs	Internal revenue	Public lands
1789–91	4419	4399	n/a	n/a
1792	3560	3443	209	n/a
1793	4653	4255	338	n/a
1794	5432	4801	274	n/a
1795	6115	5588	338	n/a
1796	8378	6568	475	5
1797	8689	7550	575	84
1798	7900	7106	644	12
1799	7547	6610	779	n/a
1800	10849	9081	809	n/a
1801	12935	10751	1048	168
1802	14996	12438	622	189
1803	11064	10479	215	166
1804	11826	11099	51	488
1805	13561	12936	22	540
1806	15560	14668	20	765
1807	16398	15846	13	466
1808	17061	16364	8	648
1809	7773	7296	4	442
1810	9384	8583	7	697
1811	14424	13313	2	1040
1812	9801	8959	5	710
1813	14340	13225	5	836
1814	11182	5999	1663	1136
1815	15729	7283	4678	1288
1816	47678	36307	5125	1718
1817	33099	26283	2678	1991
1818	21585	17176	955	2607
1819	24603	20284	230	3274
1820	17881	15006	106	1636
1821	14573	13004	69	1213
1822	20232	17590	68	1804

TABLE I. (continued)

Fiscal year	Total revenue (thousands of dollars)	Customs	Internal revenue	Public lands
1823	20541	19088	34	917
1824	19381	17878	35	984
1825	21841	20099	26	1216
1826	25260	23341	22	1394
1827	22966	19712	20	1496
1828	24764	23206	17	1018
1829	24828	22682	15	1517
1830	24844	21922	12	2329
1831	28527	24224	7	3211
1832	31866	28465	12	2623
1833	33948	29033	3	3968
1834	21792	16215	4	4858
1835	25430	19391	10	14758
1836	50827	23410	n/a	24877
Total	830152	682956	22252	89089

Source: John Joseph Wallis, "Federal Government Revenue, by Source: 1789–1939," Table Ea588-593, in *Historical Statistics of the United States, Earliest Times to the Present: Millennial Edition*, ed. Susan B. Carter, Scott Sigmund Gartner, Michael R. Haines, Alan L. Olmstead, Richard Sutch, and Gavin Wright (New York: Cambridge University Press, 2006), http://dx.doi.org/10.1017/ISBN-9780511132971.Ea584-678.

was now in place. The once-distant dreams of national legitimacy, sovereignty, and power were now imaginable. Nurturing the customs revenue system meant taking seriously "the sense of the body of the merchants."[2]

Hamilton's concern suggests that a tax system based on customs duties made the early federal government dependent on merchant capital. The government gained revenue and stability. But the merchants also stood to gain. They had forced their voices onto the pages of Hamilton's report. Now they were poised to shape the nation's political economy. The federal government's dependence on custom duties, then, had empowered the nation's importing merchants. But Hamilton's tidy writings contain only cryptic hints about this reciprocal relationship between the federal government and the merchants who supported it. Things become much clearer on the waterfront, and inside the federal government's custom houses. There, as ships came and went, federal officers collected revenue from and enforced regulations on merchants' imported goods. But how did they do so, what with the federal government's dependence on importing merchants and their capital? Then there was the problem of historical precedent, as only years before, the British Empire had tried but failed to collect revenue from its own custom houses. How would federal officials extend the tentacles of the state into the notoriously volatile Atlantic marketplace? And finally, what would this governance mean for American politics? Although Hamilton and his successors in the Treasury continued to wrestle with these questions for decades, surprisingly few have paid them much attention since. These questions are at the heart of this book.[3]

THE CUSTOM HOUSE FROM ABOVE AND BELOW

The custom house is a new if unsurprising venue for telling the story of the early federal government.[4] Just as *oikos*—ancient Greek for "house"— was the root of the concept of the economy, so the custom house was a pillar of political economy, the early modern science devoted to increasing government wealth and power.[5] In theory, the custom house was the "pulse" of increasingly centralized states where sovereigns enforced trade regulations and collected revenue on imported goods. In the "fiscal-military states" of early modern Europe, sovereigns used customs duties to secure credit, service debt, finance governance, and bankroll military expeditions.[6] The founders of the United States envisioned the new federal government as the center of their own fiscal-military state. And so they too turned to customs duties. Admittedly, there were few alternatives to customs duties, especially because the founders feared that any serious discussion about taxing slaves would alienate the South. But customs duties were also convenient because of how they worked. Merchants paid customs duties on imported goods directly to the government. The merchants recouped their losses by adding the cost of duties to the prices of the imported goods at sale. Most Americans, then, would experience national customs duties only through consumer prices. No federal tax man would cometh. Customs duties left the lightest of footprints on society and seemed to fulfill revolutionary republicanism's ideological promise of limited government.[7]

Despite their importance custom houses were often unremarkable structures. In smaller ports they were rooms in officers' homes, shacks, or apartments. Custom houses in important ports were modest multistory buildings. Inside were two or three officers with a few weighers, gaugers, or carters nearby. Within the custom house a visitor was likely to encounter volumes of federal laws and a small cache of tools, such as hydrometers, chains, scales, and ropes. Here and on the waterfront, customs officers collected revenue and inspected an enormous range of goods, from spirits to linens to slaves (see fig. 1). Their actions produced a remarkable paper archive—accounts, abstracts, letters, tables, statutes, chits, and correspondence shuffled between the Treasury, Congress, courts, and custom houses—that occupies tens of thousands of cubic feet in the U.S. National Archives. This archive is the spine of *National Duties*.[8] The story that

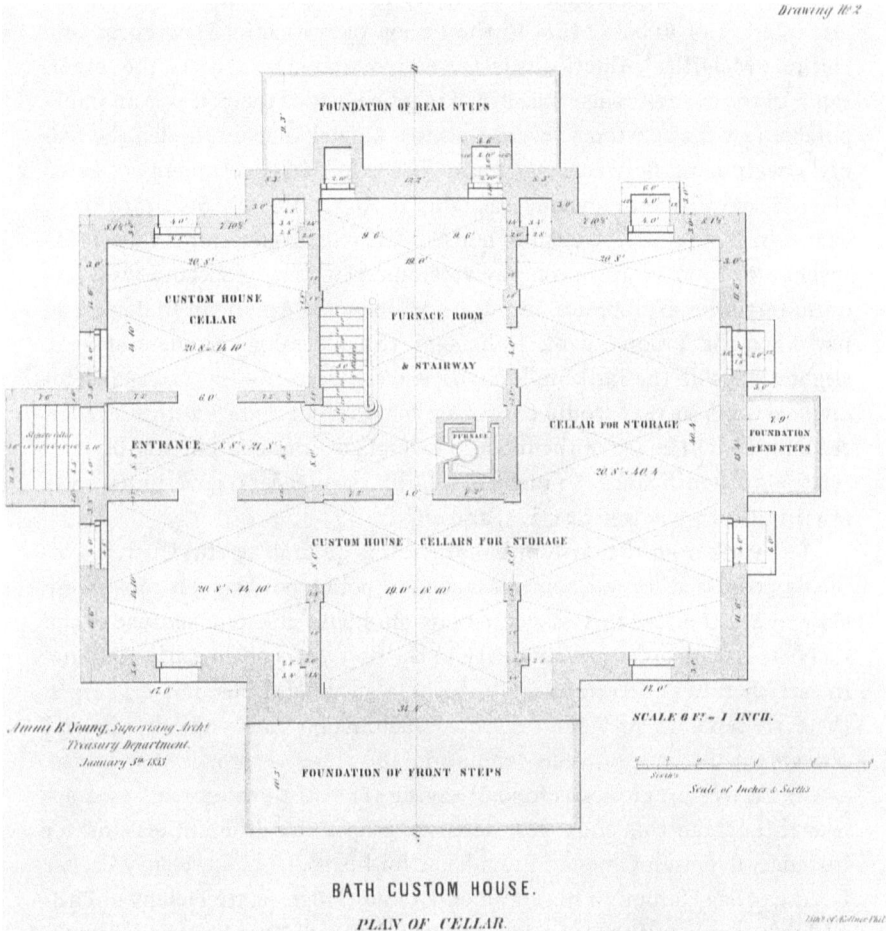

Fig. 1. Cellar floor plan of the Bath, Maine, custom house (1853). Custom houses were not only important in the nation's biggest ports. In Bath, Maine, for instance, the federal government drew up plans for a custom house in which the entire cellar would be a storage area for goods awaiting inspection or seized items subject to prosecution. Library of Congress, Prints and Photographs Division (LC-DIG-ds-04568).

emerges from this archive is a dramatic confrontation between two great revolutions of early modernity—the consumer revolution of the marketplace and the fiscal-military revolution of the state.[9]

On the one hand, when viewed through the lens of high political economy, the history of custom houses in the early republic is a fairly straightforward story about the creation of an active and energetic federal government. Though most Americans never stepped foot within a custom house, few would have disputed its significance. The custom house became the most visible icon of federal governance in American culture, from the architecture of Robert Mills to the fiction of Nathaniel Hawthorne and Herman Melville.[10] Americans in the early republic recognized the importance of the custom house because of what happened there: it was an indisputable fact that customs revenue almost singlehandedly funded the federal government. Between 1789 and 1836 the federal government collected about $830 million in revenue (see table 1). Approximately $682 million of that sum came from the custom houses. The federal government used this revenue to fund its military; pay veterans' pensions; prosecute wars; acquire territory; expropriate, murder, and dislocate American Indians; and pay down the national debt. To be sure, this federal government appears slight alongside the hulking leviathans of modernity—the 11,491 federal civil servants in 1831 would constitute but a minor agency within the bureaucratic archipelago of the modern federal government. But size bore no relation to significance. So understood, this early federal government was anything but weak (see figs. 2, 3, and 4).[11]

The view from the custom house itself is quite different. Customs officials possessed formal commissions and police powers. But most were slow to use coercive tactics against custom-house clientele because of the inchoate nature of federal authority in the first years of the early republic. In fact there was a certain art to being a successful customs officer. In the early republic, presidents selected customs officials and other federal officers on the basis of their reputation and status—"proper characters," as George Washington was fond of saying. The customs officials who appear throughout this book were deemed "proper" for different reasons: for instance, Jeremiah Olney of Providence for his social clout, Henry Packer Dering of Sag Harbor for his commercial knowledge, Sharp Delany of Philadelphia for his military service, and John Lamb of New York for his revolutionary reputation as a Son of Liberty. No matter their particular niche, it was hoped that men of this ilk possessed reputation enough to compensate for the fragility of early federal authority. In short, these officers were expected to gin up federal authority from their own distinction.[12]

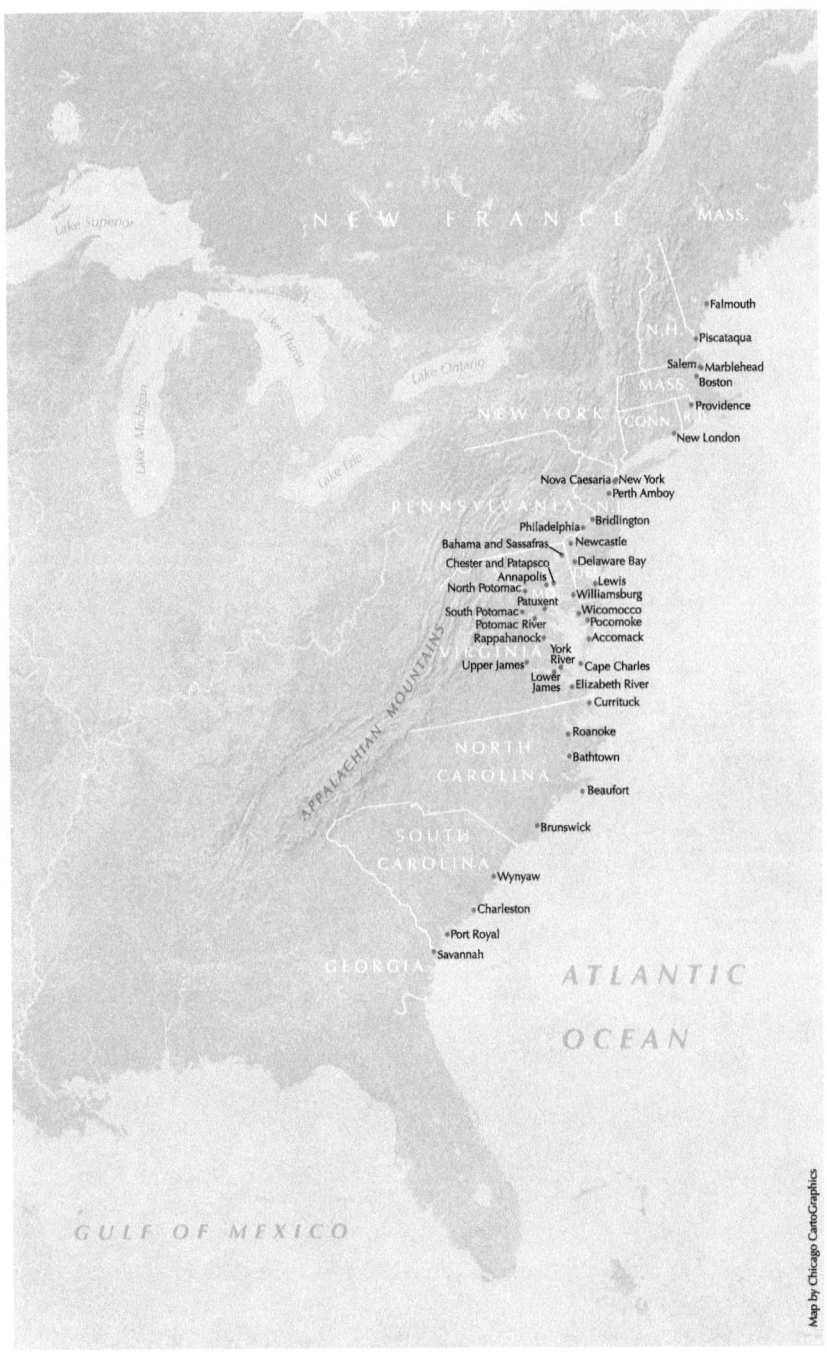

Fig. 2. British imperial custom houses (1760). By the mid-seventeenth century, the British Empire maintained forty custom houses in North America of varying sizes and importance. Chicago CartoGraphics.

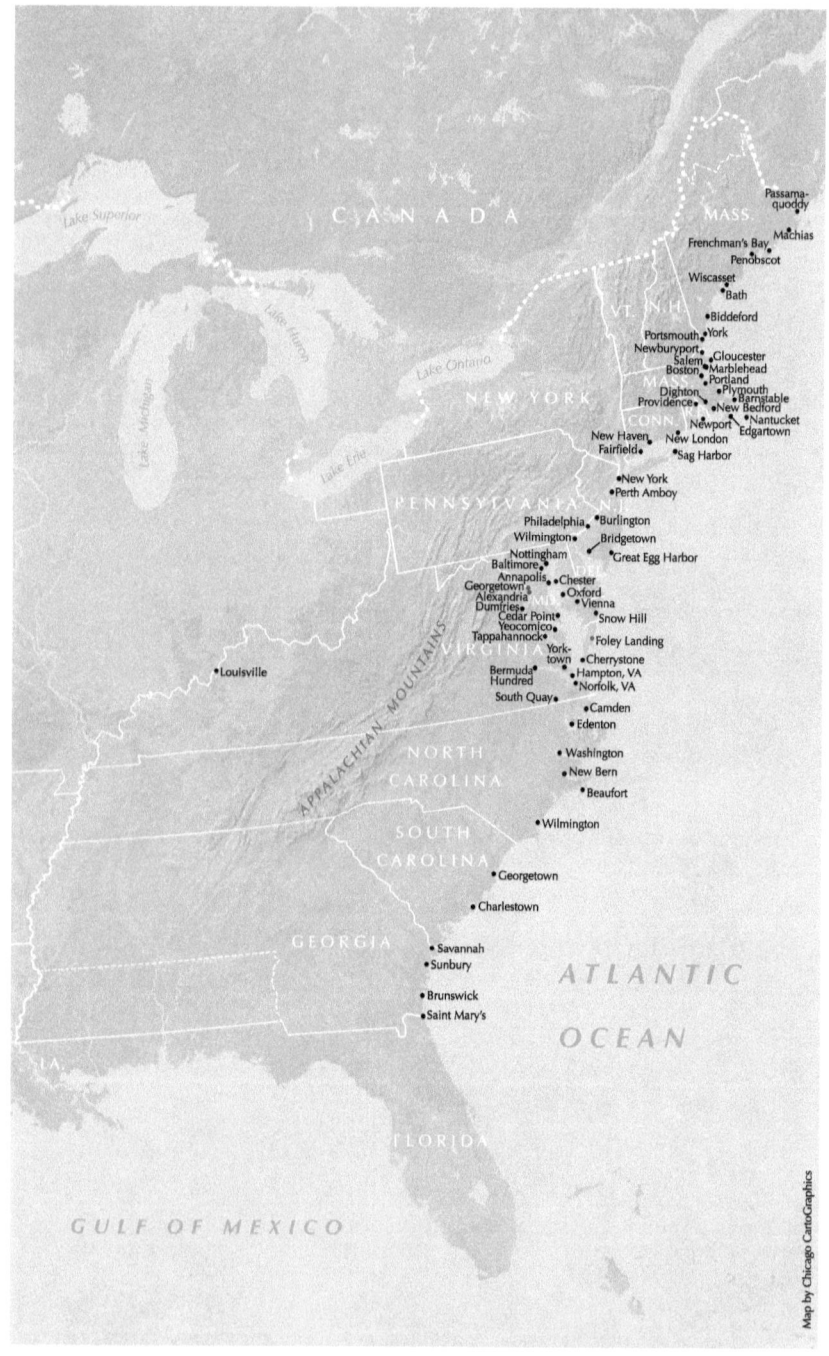

Fig. 3. Federal custom houses (1789). As the new federal government came into existence, Congress apportioned sixty-six custom houses throughout the country. In adding twenty-six facilities to those the British Empire had stationed in North America, Congress hoped to install a federal presence on the nation's coasts that would suffice to deter smuggling and maximize tariff revenue. Chicago CartoGraphics.

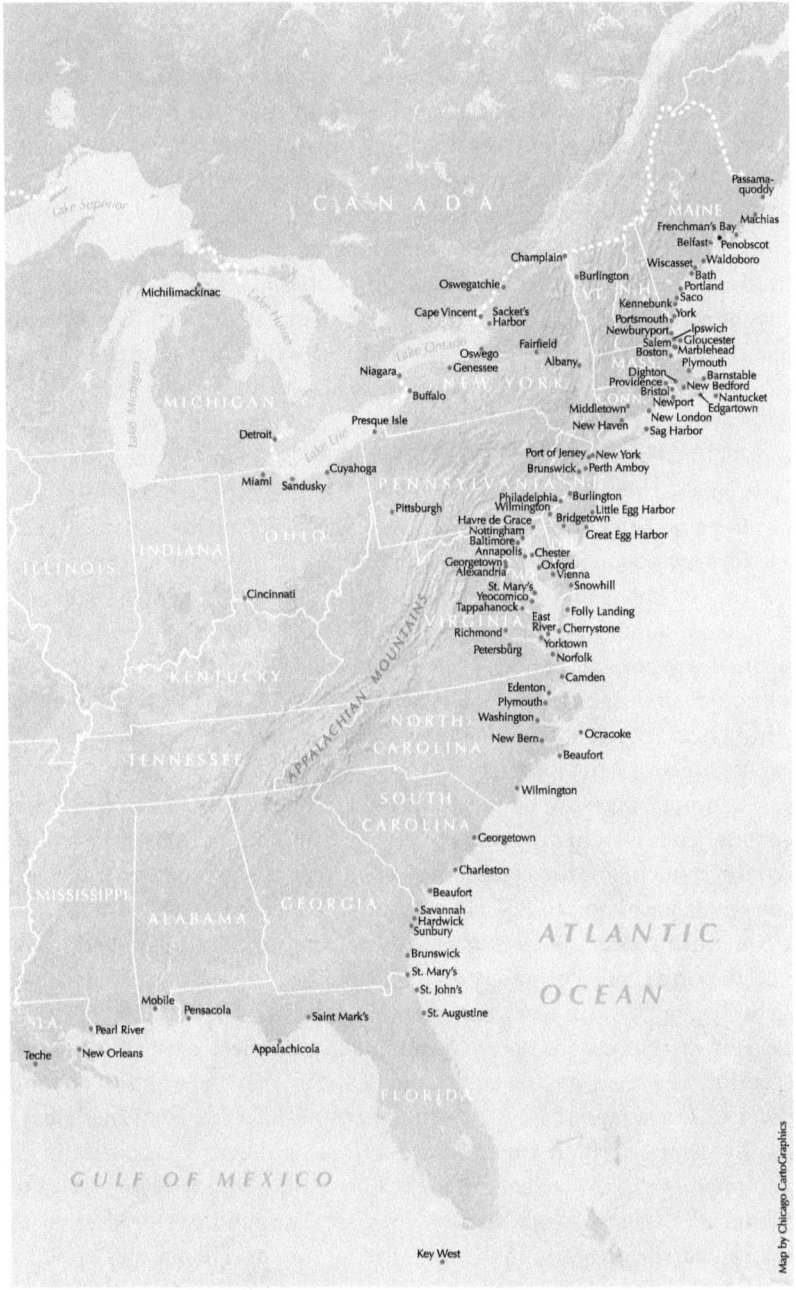

Fig. 4. Federal custom houses (1832). By the Jacksonian era, the number of custom houses had grown significantly to 107. The sharp increase since the founding of the republic reflected the emergence of new river ports in the nation's interior, as well as a renewed ideological commitment to combating smuggling and tax evasion. Chicago CartoGraphics.

The unique power relations of the early modern waterfront made things all the more complicated for the first customs officials. They were few, and their outposts were slight. Against them crashed the tide of the Atlantic market, as North American merchants imported innumerable goods, human chattel, and bewildering webs of credit from abroad. In this moment within the history of capitalism, too, imperial rivalries and global warfare filled the market with both immense wealth and risk.[13] Accordingly, the class of men—variously referred to as merchants, merchant communities, men of the market, and perhaps most aptly, "commercial peoples"—who lived in this roiling world were understood to be important.[14] Leading merchants—for instance, Welcome Arnold and John Brown of Providence, Archibald Gracie of New York, and Stephen Girard of Philadelphia—were distinguished figures in their communities. A great many middling merchants pooled risk, borrowed from one another, vouched for each other, and shipped goods as a group. Sailors and mariners manned the vessels that carried goods and credit across the oceans, and they too held stakes in the commercial marketplace. Together this group plied the trade that supplied government coffers, fueled fads and revelry, and supplied cosmopolitanism and transatlantic political currents. Commerce was more than a thing or a vocation. Commerce was a force, and the American republic was born a commercial society.[15]

The importance of commerce in revolutionary America and the early republic gave merchants social, cultural, and political power.[16] Not unlike the residents of the eighteenth-century English countryside made famous by labor historian E. P. Thompson, the merchants who did business at American custom houses expected that their local norms would influence the ordering of economy and society. They accepted the legitimacy of the federal government's intervention into the marketplace in the institution of the custom house. Many paid the duties that bankrolled the federal government in the early republic.[17] But they expected to have the power to shape how the custom house would function, from the hours it would operate to the manner of inspections, and even to exceptions and exemptions from the letter of the law. Above all, local merchants expected customs officials to align the law with local commerce's need to access and exploit the Atlantic marketplace. And just as Thompson's crowd in eighteenth-century England used protest and violence to mark the limit of free-market logic, so importing merchants in the early United States resorted to the same tools to define the boundaries of the state. Mobs of merchants, sailors, and other waterfront characters had stormed British imperial custom houses during the American Revolution to express anger over British political economy. And the custom-house mob would persist into the first decade of the nineteenth century.[18]

At the custom house, then, importing merchants and commercial interests came to enjoy a privileged position. But this was not patronage, as merchants rarely demanded appointments from customs officials. Nor was this a story of "capture," because, as we shall see, customs officials could and did flout the merchants' interests. "Corruption" is also not a very helpful concept because, while customs officials governed in ways that benefited local commerce, very few of those officials materially profited from their activities.[19] In addition, the modern-day concept of corruption presupposes that the state and the market are distinct and should be distinct. Not only did Americans in the revolutionary era and early republic understand corruption very differently, but a central claim of this book is that when the United States came into existence, the modern liberal belief that the state and the marketplace must be distinct simply did not exist.[20] Quite the opposite, in fact. In classical political economy, it was necessary for the state to tap into merchant capital. Doing so required incorporating merchants and their capital into the fold of the state. In the eighteenth-century British colonies, then, commerce was governance by other means, and merchants executed crucial functions for the state. Overseas commerce extended borders, settled colonies, supplied armies and navies, and circulated credit and information. By 1776, removing commercial influence from governance would have been as unwise as it was impossible. Commerce was crucial to how the British Empire worked.[21]

And it is empire, rather than capture or corruption, that proves most useful in reconciling the custom house of political economic theory with that of the waterfront. Governance at federal custom houses mirrored that of the British imperial custom houses. On the periphery of the eighteenth-century British Atlantic, officeholders negotiated authority with colonial subjects in a variety of ways. At the custom houses, imperial customs agents interpreted the Navigation Acts in ways that benefited and facilitated swashbuckling American merchants.[22] In London, the Board of Trade and the Exchequer tolerated the rash of smuggling, trading with the enemy, and other commercial crimes that were everyday occurrences in North American ports, because the benefits of American commerce far outweighed losses of revenue and dents to the rule of law.[23] Since Great Britain drew most of its revenue from internal excise taxes, it was easy to overlook colonial smuggling. Also, American violations of the Navigation Acts, while occasionally embarrassing, helped weaken Great Britain's main competitors, France and Spain.[24] For this reason colonial customs agents devised a wide-ranging discretion to negotiate their authority with American merchants. A main argument of this book is that federal customs officers did the same after the American Revolution. Empire persisted into the early American republic, then, not only as an intellectual framework for the founders to understand federalism, rights, and citizenship. It persisted in practice, too. The negotiated authority between officeholders and merchants that had helped cohere the British Empire would help sustain the early federal government on its maritime frontier.[25]

The imperial lineage of custom-house governance should suggest the broader possibility of understanding the early federal government as part of an empire. With its center in the nation's capital, this empire had several peripheries beginning with the states themselves and ending on the maritime and western frontiers.[26] Like British imperial governance in North America, federal governance operated through extremely complicated relationships with connected political units. It was also subject to powerful currents from competing empires on its borders.[27] Customs officials were tasked with enforcing revenue and commercial laws in the face of these challenges. They did so by using discretion—the ability to choose which laws they would seek to emphasize, and how they would seek to do so. This discretion was not strictly legal, for it was nowhere to be found in federal law. In fact, Congress would repeatedly assert that customs officials were subordinate to the secretary of the treasury.[28] At the custom houses, however, officers would continue to rely on discretion. They decided which laws to apply, and which laws to ignore; when to make an example out of a lawbreaker, and when to sweep transgressions under the rug. Most often, they used their discretion to align federal revenue and regulatory law with local commercial communities' expectations about how governance should work. This negotiation of authority between officeholders and merchants anchored federal governance at the custom houses during the early republic, just as it had once helped structure British imperial governance in North America.[29]

The subtle negotiations between officers, importing merchants, and other waterfront characters that took place routinely in and around the custom houses are the crux of this book. Yet they are almost impossible to pin down.[30] Only a handful of merchants copped to their attempts to unduly influence the inner workings of the custom house. Likewise, few officers recorded the specific moments when negotiations occurred. Fewer still considered their governing practices negotiations. But over and over in the early republic customs officials interpreted laws generously toward merchants, limited enforcement of purportedly intrusive legislation, and looked the other way when confronted with illicit waterfront activity. When they failed to do so, they inevitably faced abuse, intimidation, shaming campaigns, tax avoidance, violence, riots, and lawsuits from angry merchants. The Treasury Department occasionally intervened, not to rebuke wayward officeholders, as one might expect, but to urge customs officers to take seriously the opinions of the commercial community in which they resided.

The story of the custom houses in the early republic sheds new light on the inner workings of the early American state. Though the idea of a stateless American past has sharply receded, the federal government is generally considered far less significant than states and municipalities, which developed robust coercive powers over spaces, property, persons, families, and local markets.[31] Yet the early federal government was incredibly important. The founders patterned the Constitution on the blueprint of the European fiscal-military state so the federal government would be chiefly oriented outward toward the world, involving itself in issues of commerce, borders, diplomacy, and war.[32] Much is known about how the federal government expropriated and murdered American Indians in the West and Southwest. A great deal is also known about how the federal government acquired territory and subsidized western expansion. Communication and infrastructure policy are also well understood.[33] An examination of how the federal government developed the means to regulate commerce and extract revenue from merchant capital reveals an important dimension of the early American state.

National Duties recovers the lost history of custom houses in the early American republic to explore the persistence and ultimate dissolution of imperial governance in the federal government of the United States between the American Revolution and the Jacksonian era. The argument proceeds chronologically in four parts to illustrate how British imperial custom houses functioned through negotiated authority in colonial America; how early federal customs officials replicated imperial governance by negotiating authority with importing merchants in the first two decades of the early republic; and how imperial governance became a political and moral problem requiring reform in the wake of the Napoleonic Wars.

Americans have always been conflicted about their federal government. Tea parties past and present embody profound ambivalence about taxation, spending, regulation, and coercion by a distant central government. But this ambivalence began long ago. When Alexander Hamilton launched his plea for expansive federal power, he watched as federal customs officials negotiated their authority with the very merchants they were supposed to tax and regulate. Subsequently, Thomas Jefferson and James Madison, so often understood as the intellectual flag bearers for the cause of limited central government, tried to replace older patterns of imperial governance with more centralized control of the custom houses. But there is more than irony here. The story that unfolds in the pages that follow reveals that the history of the early federal government cannot be understood without considering local confrontation and contestation, foreign intrigues and affairs, and perhaps most importantly, Atlantic capitalism itself. That story begins on a shadowy waterfront in 1769, as the American Revolution laid siege to the Philadelphia custom house, and laid bare a crisis of empire.[34]

PART I

Revolution: Philadelphia, 1769

On an October day in 1769, a mob descended on the custom house. The day before, an imperial customs official named John Swift, acting on an informant's tip, seized 5,000 gallons of the colonists' prized Madeira wine, which smugglers had attempted to land without first paying customs duties. It did not take long for the merchants to suss out the informant's identity. A mob quickly materialized near Carpenter's Wharf and caught up with the informant next to the custom house. The informant "was attacked by some Sailors, who were set on him by the merchants. They threw him into the River, dragg'd him out and poured some Buckets of Tar upon his Head, & then Feathered him; they dragged him over the Stones half the length of the Street (the mob still gathering as they went) till they came to the Pillory, the mob pelted him with Stones & mud about four hours, then they brought him to the Custom House."[1] The mob had come calling for John Swift.

Swift had the good sense to flee. But he knew his reprieve would be brief. "I fear it will not end here, for it seems the People have taken into their Heads to mark me out for the next victim of their wrath. I have been guilty of a crime for which I shall never be forgiven—and as I am already condemned, I know not how soon, I may be executed." On the revolutionary Philadelphia waterfront, "the people"—"the merchants," "some Sailors," and other commercial peoples—were judge, jury, and executioner.[2]

But what, exactly, had been Swift's "crime"? He had done none other than his sworn duty to enforce imperial revenue laws at the Philadelphia custom house. Why might this have so incited the mob? In fact, Swift's decision to enforce the law was a marked departure from the usual course of business at the Philadelphia custom house. In the past, Swift and his men had ignored a steady traffic in smuggled goods. But Swift was a conscientious officer nonetheless. He did not have his hand in the till. And unlike those of many of his brother officers, his office was no sinecure. Rather, Swift governed by not taking official notice of smuggling. In this way, Swift kept the peace with the city's powerful West Indies merchants.[3]

Swift was well equipped to manage the fragile relations between Philadelphia's commercial community and the British Empire. He had been born to Londoners of unexceptional stock who moved to the colonies in the early eighteenth century. Swift soon found his calling as a merchant—and a "very successful" one at that. Swift's new fortunes lent him status, which, in turn, secured him political authority. Swift would serve on the Common Council of Philadelphia from 1757 until 1776. Swift was also active in Philadelphia's cultural life as manager and treasurer of the "Philadelphia Assemblies," a dancing society with almost sixty subscribers around 1748.[4]

Swift understood that governing at the custom house required negotiating authority with Philadelphia's merchants. Like so many imperial officials who served in the North American colonies, he had learned to what extent commercial peoples in Philadelphia would permit assertions of the empire's power, and he enforced the law to its limits, but rarely beyond.[5] So Swift and other customs officials accepted undervalued manifests in order to reduce duties owed; shipping papers that were forged, altered, or out-of-date; excuses—even outlandish ones—for undocumented trips to foreign ports, and unreported goods on board vessels; late payments—or sometimes none at all—for the many customs bonds required by law. In return, the commercial peoples of Philadelphia made little trouble on the waterfront. They filled out paperwork, took oaths, provided help in small matters, took out customs bonds, and kept their illicit commerce quiet, however common it may have been. At the Philadelphia custom house, then, routine business was "an ongoing series of negotiations, of reciprocal bargaining" between imperial agents and local commercial peoples.[6]

For several decades, the British Empire had itself benefited from the negotiated authority at the Philadelphia custom house, for reports of calm and quietude testified to the health of the empire. After the Seven Years' War, however, the British Empire sought to strengthen its coercive hand in the colonies, especially at the custom house. George Grenville's ministry dispatched new supervisory officers to tighten customs enforcement and punish lackadaisical customs men. The era of negotiated authority at the custom house thus began to unravel as men like John Swift felt intense pressure to enforce the letter of imperial law. The mob was the result. It stalked John Swift until he left office in 1772. "I am told 'Wo be to the Collector' is wrote upon the Walls of Houses," recalled Swift.[7]

In one of his final letters to the Board of Trade, Swift struggled to take stock of the competing forces—imperial administration and local commerce—that now enveloped the Philadelphia custom house. When the Treasury demanded strict enforcement of the law, it tied Swift's hands to negotiate his authority with Philadelphians. "What can a governor do without the assistance of the govern'd? What can the magistrate do unless they are supported by their fellow citizens? What can the Kings Officers do if they make themselves obnoxious to the people amongst whom they reside?"[8] Without negotiation, Swift lost his legitimacy. The British Empire would not be far behind.

CHAPTER ONE

Custom Houses, Negotiated Authority, and the Bonds of Empire, 1714–1776

On the evening of March 5, 1770, a scrum broke out between royal soldiers and a "motley rabble of saucy boys, negroes and mulattoes, Irish teagues and out landish Jack tars" on King Street in Boston. In the chaos of the moment, one shot was fired, and, quickly afterward, a few more followed. Five colonists were killed. But for Paul Revere, the facts of the Boston Massacre did not speak for themselves. Some needed beautification, especially the protagonists. It would not do for "the American cause to be represented by a huge, half-Native American, half-African American, stave-wielding, street-fighting sailor" like Crispus Attucks. The bad guys also needed a touch-up. Revere arrayed the redcoats in a tidy phalanx and gave each soldier a cold-blooded grimace (fig. 5). He also added two signs to teach distant readers what these murderous soldiers were defending: "Custom House" and, directly above it, "Butcher's Hall." Revere had erased Attucks to dignify the mob. He distinguished the custom house to villainize the enemy.[1]

By the time Revere set to work in 1770, the British imperial custom house had become a backdrop of the gathering revolution. Since 1756, British Treasury officials had been pressuring colonial customs agents to strictly enforce new taxes and commercial regulations. Colonial merchants, sailors, and others fiercely resisted these actions. Their tool of choice was the mob, and from the outbreak of the Seven Years' War to the first shots of the War of Independence, mobs around the custom house were an all-too-frequent sight on the waterfront.[2] Colonists also possessed subtle weapons, such as lawsuits and informal social pressure. "For there was scarce a port in America," recalled Commissioner of Customs Henry Hulton, "where an Officer had endeavoured to make a Seizure, or refused

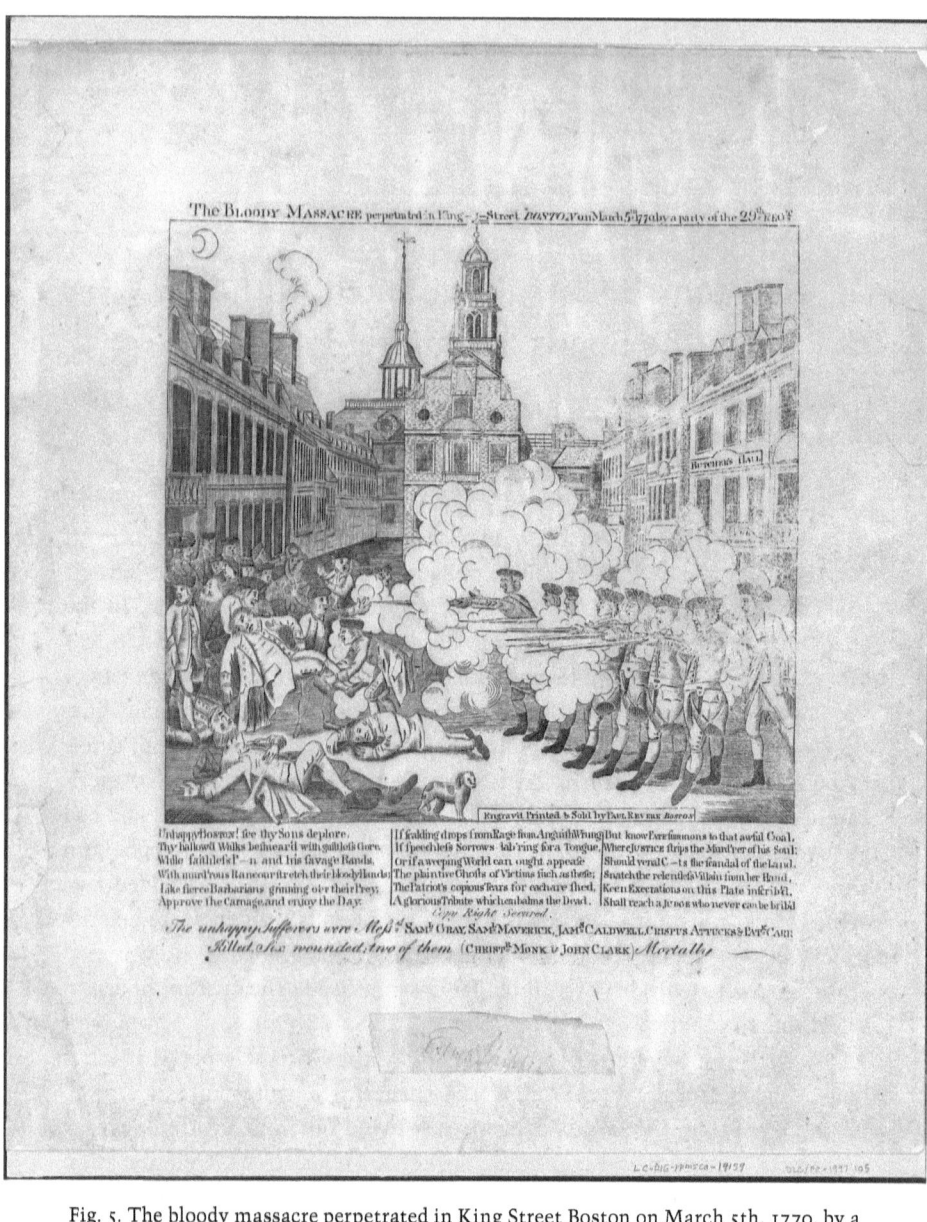

Fig. 5. The bloody massacre perpetrated in King Street Boston on March 5th, 1770, by a party of the 29th Regt. Paul Revere's famous 1770 print of the Boston Massacre portrays British army regulars in front of the Boston custom house firing upon colonists. While scholars have demonstrated that Revere's depiction erased the diversity of the colonists in attendance at the massacre, Revere also awkwardly added the label "Custom House" to ensure that viewers throughout the colonies would correlate British violence with policies of increasing taxing and regulation after the Seven Years' War. Library of Congress, Prints and Photographs Division (LC-DIG-ppmsca-19159).

a complyance with the will of the People that he had not been tarred, & feathered."³

Tar and feathers represented a new tactic, but colonists' other methods for resisting customs officers dated back to the seventeenth century.⁴ Until 1756, however, colonists made only sporadic use of these practices. By and large they did not need them. Prior to the Seven Years' War, customs officials in the colonies, under unremitting pressure from local men of the market, had consistently bent or broken the letter of the Navigation Acts and measures such as the Sugar Act. This lax administration was a universal feature of custom-house governance in eighteenth-century America until the American Revolution. Nor was it an accident. Imperial officials in London were well aware of the smuggling that flourished in North American ports. They knew of the great deal of slack between the laws and regulations of Parliament, the Treasury, the Board of Trade, and the Foreign Office, on the one hand, and on the colonial waterfront, on the other. Whitehall allowed local norms to determine "what were legitimate and what were illegitimate practices" at the custom houses and other imperial institutions.⁵

For managers of empire like Robert Walpole, colonial smuggling ironically strengthened the bonds of empire. The colonial merchants who did business at the imperial custom house sought access to lucrative markets—both legal and illicit—in the West Indies and elsewhere. As they pressured customs officials to allow trade in prohibited goods or with prohibited ports, these colonial merchants consistently violated the basic terms of the British Navigation Acts. But in their pursuit of commercial gain at seemingly any cost, they enlarged the influence of the British Empire. And for metropolitan observers, it was increasingly clear that colonial commerce that ran afoul of the Navigation Acts siphoned supplies and capital from the rival Spanish and French empires. As colonial merchants negotiated the boundaries of custom-house authority in North America, and plied their technically prohibited commerce, they served the expansionist ends of the British Empire.⁶

The American Revolution disrupted the system of custom-house governance that had taken root in the colonies since the Glorious Revolution. Around the time of the Seven Years' War, rival visions of empire called into question the quiet understanding that had structured legal relations between metropolitan authorities and colonial customs officials on the one hand, and colonial customs officials and colonial merchants on the other. As the colonies became viewed as an untapped source of revenue, Treasury and other officials stepped up their calls for colonial customs officials to tighten enforcement of customs and other laws.[7] Parliament also created new forms of oversight and control in the colonies, so customs officials, to say nothing of colonists, more viscerally sensed imperial authority. By 1770, then, when Paul Revere memorialized the Boston Massacre, the custom house had become a universal symbol in the colonies for imperial excess.

The disruption of imperial governance would prove to be brief. By 1789, when the new federal government of the United States began operating its own custom houses, merchants and federal customs officials would again find ways to negotiate the limits and possibilities of the federal government's authority at the custom houses. The founders would of course look to the meaning of the American Revolution to make sense of the world in which they lived. But in imperial customs law and administration during the American Revolution there was also a more specific cautionary tale about how not to govern an empire.[8]

THE FISCAL-MILITARY REVOLUTION AND ITS DISCONTENTS

Empire had preoccupied English monarchs, and had increasingly defined English political culture, since the unification of England and Scotland in 1603. The "fiscal-military revolution" provided a governmental framework to operate and expand the empire. This revolution "radically" increased taxation, drastically enlarged military capacity, and generated a bustling bureaucratic administration "devoted to organizing the fiscal and military activities of the state."[9] The transformation of the English state was particularly noticeable in the realms of taxation and commercial regulation and especially at the custom houses, where the number of employees rose from 1,313 in 1690 to 2,205 in 1782–83. England, now armed with the power to tax, could guarantee revenue to defray the costs of war and expansion.[10]

A key step in building the English fiscal-military state was granting the Treasury central control over revenue collection.[11] In practice, central control meant a hierarchy of bureaus, at the top of which sat the Treasury Board and its subordinate Board of Customs Commissioners. From their perch in the dazzling Long Room atop the London custom house, the commissioners directly supervised prosaic revenue and regulatory activities at English custom houses.[12] Waterfront operations were equally impressive. On busy days, over 800 customs officials swarmed around the London custom house—tidewaiters on board vessels awaiting inspection; inspectors supervising the tidewaiters; watchmen along the quays guarding against unauthorized unlading; hundreds of weighers and gaugers on the wharves handling unloaded commodities; surveyors and landwaiters overseeing activities on the wharves. The customs establishment was also active beyond London. In "outports" such as Bristol, custom houses operated under the supervision of a collector, with up to several dozen subordinate officers. From the Long Room, through London, and along the English coast, this apparatus was "one of the pillars of the mercantilist state."[13]

The chief business of these customs officials was to enforce the Navigation Acts of 1660, 1663, and 1673, which taxed imported goods to discriminate against foreign commerce and protect English commerce.[14] Procedure at the custom house was fairly routine. Each manifest would account for each and every commodity on board a vessel, save for the ship's "stores" of victuals. From the manifest, officials calculated duties and demanded payment of what would become the state's revenue. The manifest and other shipping papers also described the vessel's port of origin and destination. Through these measures, England would guarantee its mercantilist monopoly on shipping by ensuring that vessels remained on their stated course. If a ship's crew violated these rules—or myriad subsidiary rules—customs officials were to place into collection bonds that merchants and ship captains had entered into before setting out to sea.[15]

England's new customs system notched some remarkable achievements in the century following 1690. First, the custom houses collected hundreds of millions in revenue.[16] Likewise, commercial regulations, in tandem with military policy, advanced England's geopolitical interests. The Treasury routinely directed customs agents to be "faithfull & diligent" about preventing trade with France during periods of conflict with France. The custom house was the center of operations for "procuring and pressing seamen" to fill the ranks of England's increasingly powerful navy. Customs officials also inspected vessels to ensure that commodities produced for the export market actually went abroad, and conversely, that goods produced for domestic consumption were not illegally exported. By 1763, the enforcement of these policies contributed to England's dominance in the European struggle for global dominion.[17]

England's new and reformed fiscal-military institutions required a commensurately new cultural infrastructure to structure relations between citizens and the state.[18] This project spanned the long eighteenth century. Prior to the Glorious Revolution, James II pursued a centralized, absolutist state along French lines in which the monarch possessed "absolute sovereignty in his own dominion." His victorious opponents patterned their "centralized and interventionist" state on a Dutch model.[19] The reconstruction of relations between state and citizen during the fiscal-military revolution was nonetheless turbulent, as local populations protected customary norms of equity and justice from the increasingly interventionist state. The poor, for instance, lodged massive resistance against central governmental land policies. As E. P. Thompson explains, government policies triggered "grievances" among the people that "operated within a popular consensus as to what were legitimate and what were illegitimate practices in marketing, milling, baking, etc." Their resistance was "grounded upon a consistent traditional view of social norms and obligations" and "of the proper economic functions of several parties within the community." This was "the moral economy of the poor." If the state committed "an outrage to these moral assumptions," it would provoke "direct action" by the people.[20]

The poor were hardly the only group to assert themselves against the intrusion of central governmental institutions and the liberal rule of law. Waterborne commerce—on rivers within England, or on the high seas abroad—offered a lucrative marketplace in contraband to a wide range of middling laborers, sailors, and merchants. For these smugglers, the state's high duties on popular goods, such as tea, created a "vast world of pilfering and smuggling"—a shadow economy that would expand for much of the eighteenth century.[21] As long as national borders have existed, of course, smuggling has existed in one form or another. But now smuggling took on a newly nefarious character because it constituted a crime, not just against the state, but more directly against the state's revenue. In 1796 one observer spied 2,500 "River Pilferers" in and around London's "docks and arsenals" who plundered 0.75 percent of the state's revenue. Scholars suggest that more was afoot than bands of secretive "pilferers." Rather, the expanded reach of the English fiscal-military state in turn "centralized and concentrated" smuggling operations that had previously been the domain of "petty dealers," merchant sailors, and other men of the lower sort.[22]

Smuggling in eighteenth-century England embodied distinct strands of political culture. On the one hand, some smugglers struck a blow against the increasingly centralized state by committing a "social crime"—in effect a "rebellion"—against the laws of the realm.[23] Some were Jacobites, or supporters of the deposed Stuarts. From Kent and Sussex, these smugglers advanced their material interests while strengthening the Jacobite movement.[24] But smuggling could also serve the state. Smugglers who operated on England's coastal margins helped build the nation's commercial infrastructure and cohere a national marketplace.[25]

No matter the network or sentiments that connected them, communities of smugglers badly outnumbered the small handful of officers who manned England's peripheral custom houses.[26] The vast coastline—with its crags, inlets, and narrows—offered a welcoming geography for smugglers to land their goods. Sympathetic tradesmen and farmers could transport illicit goods to inland markets. Smugglers' mobility also vexed customs enforcement, for when one custom house tightened enforcement on its shores, the smugglers simply found a new mark. When the government imposed itself on one waterfront, the smugglers simply moved to another. The best the Treasury could do was to station vessels called "Revenue-cruisers" at the outports. But the smugglers then turned to "larger, faster, and more heavily armed vessels."[27] Gradually, the smugglers' unrelenting enterprise created a wide gap between the letter and the reality of customs law. For one thing, outports became known for their "informality" in ignoring a vast illicit commerce. To cope with those officials who insisted on enforcing customs laws, smugglers turned to violence. Nor did the smuggling communities think murder too severe a "punishment" to mete out to a particularly incorrigible customs man.[28]

The process that unfolded at custom houses at the early modern British outports was a negotiation between central governmental authority and local commercial communities. The central administration of the emerging English state considered the custom house a bulwark of central authority. But at the custom houses, a very different type of authority interjected itself into the workings of the state. Merchants, seamen, and other interested parties fought for and secured the ability to dictate the terms on which the state's laws would be enforced. Diverse, overlapping political ideologies, from Jacobitism to collective protest, informed their actions. The least common denominator of these ideologies, however, was "opportunism" to participate in the seductive commercial marketplace of credit and commodities. This was the moral economy of the custom house that accompanied the rise of the fiscal-military state in seventeenth- and eighteenth-century England. And it would quietly remain in tow as the custom house found its way to the outer reaches of the British Empire in North America.

PROVINCIALIZING THE FISCAL-MILITARY REVOLUTION

The English fiscal-military revolution was a means to the end of imperial expansion.[29] The English Civil War had largely divided society between those who supported and those who opposed the Stuarts' absolutist vision of the state. Importantly, however, both the Stuarts and the reformers who replaced them shared expansionist aspirations. Thus, throughout the seventeenth century, through the interregnum and revolution, Great Britain charted and stayed true to the path of empire. It was an empire that was primarily maritime and commercial. Oceanic commerce, that is, carried British influence throughout an ever-expanding map of influence and sovereignty.[30]

Commerce had not necessarily motivated the mass migration of English-speaking peoples to North America, but it would soon become a driving force in the growth of colonial prosperity. American colonists quickly discovered that the land they had taken by force and occupied into possession produced a bounty in great demand in Europe and the West Indies. By the mid-seventeenth century, the colonists enjoyed stable, lucrative commercial pathways with the metropole. Southern colonies, such as Virginia, staked their destiny on a single cash crop, tobacco. New England's fisheries yielded tons of codfish, although merchants in the region quickly diversified from fish into other markets. New England merchants also opened new channels of trade with the West Indies, exchanging an array of agricultural goods for plantation products such as rum and molasses. Throughout the colonies, commercial profits went to increasing agricultural production, which, in turn, brought commercial wealth of even greater magnitude.[31]

From the view of the British Empire, though, there was little to be gained if it could not channel the colonies' commercial impulses in directions that benefited the empire. Mercantilist theory mapped out those directions. The colonies' commerce—both sales of colonial productions and purchases of West Indies and manufactured goods—was to be exclusively with Great Britain and other British colonies. The Navigation Acts guarded this mercantilist monopoly by spelling out, in minutiae, the rules about what colonists could or could not buy and sell.[32] A burgeoning central bureaucracy in London instructed colonial customs officials on how to implement the Navigation Acts. Beginning in 1696 the Board of Trade—shorthand for the Lords Commissioners of Trade and Plantations—convened regularly and issued instructions to royal officials in the colonies.[33] The Treasury, too, issued instructions to customs personnel in the colonies. But the Treasury "exerted little pressure on Customs Commissioners" and expected the latter to deal with the details of customs administration.[34]

Royal authority in North American institutions was more fragile than anywhere in England.³⁵ The colonial custom houses were a far cry from the customs establishments in the outports, to say nothing of London. Virginian Robert Pitt built the first custom house in the colonies, a diminutive "brick and timber building," on his personal property. A single room in a merchant's warehouse served as the custom house in Chestertown, Maryland, beginning in 1694. In Rhode Island and Pennsylvania, officials operated custom houses out of their own homes until the mid-1760s. Official outposts of imperial authority thus bore little cultural distinction. Rather, these somewhat anonymous structures blended into the built landscape of colonial commerce.³⁶ Inside, too, metropolitan authority was indistinct. "There was a gap," observes Daniel Hulsebosch, "between the official constitutional theory of colonial governance, and the practice of substantial local autonomy." At the custom houses, North American merchants filled that gap. In emerging ports such as Boston, James City, and St. Mary's City, a burgeoning merchant class shipped fish, lumber, tobacco, and other lucrative commodities to markets near and far without much scrutiny from the few customs agents on the coastline. Customs officials in the colonies routinely cleared vessels purportedly bound for London or Liverpool that never appeared—or rather, that appeared at undeclared and illicit destinations.³⁷

Admittedly, customs officials who acquiesced to the emerging colonial smuggling economy were hardly the class of the service. A Virginia collector, Edward Digges, quit his post after learning that he would earn fees from services rendered, rather than an annual salary. His replacement, Giles Bland, would be executed for his role in Bacon's Rebellion. The collector of the Carolinas in the 1670s, Thomas Miller, appointed himself governor before being overthrown by an armed rebellion, and then tried unsuccessfully for treason. Maryland's customs establishment took its orders not from London but from the colony's proprietor, Lord Baltimore. The one officer who broke this rule, Christopher Rousby, was murdered by one of Lord Baltimore's flacks.³⁸

Yet, as the ordeal of Edward Randolph suggests, conscientious customs agents were met with an unshakable pattern of colonial commercial intransigence. Randolph was of modest Kentish origins. He had failed in several enterprises before being favored by the Lords of the Treasury in 1676 to "look about in the colonies and report back what he could learn of their political, economic, and military strength." Shortly thereafter Randolph received an appointment as a royal customs official for the port of Boston. In 1680, Randolph attempted to seize a vessel named *Expectation* only to be obstructed, threatened, and verbally abused by the ship's crew. Randolph finally seized the *Expectation* with the help of a posse, but a jury acquitted the crew of any wrongdoing. Boston now turned against Randolph to punish him for enforcing the law. Magistrates tripped him up with legal niceties, and locals "harassed mercilessly" custom-house employees or collaborators. This pattern would recur for the remainder of Randolph's stay at the Boston custom house. Of the thirty-six vessels Randolph seized between 1680 and 1682, "all but two were acquitted."[39] Randolph persisted in pursuing "strict methods," however, in the belief that the new authoritarian governor, Edmund Andros, would break the colonists' fever. The Boston merchants now "attack'd from every part." Upon learning of the Glorious Revolution in 1689, Bostonians imprisoned Randolph for eight months and shipped him back to England.[40]

Randolph's New England misadventure ironically justified his third tour of duty in the colonies after the Glorious Revolution. The Glorious Revolution accelerated the spread of central governmental institutions throughout the British Empire. Accordingly, men like Edward Randolph remained valuable for their unique knowledge of the navigation system and its function in the colonies.[41] The Treasury promoted Randolph to surveyor general of the customs and dispatched him to Virginia to oversee the custom houses in the colonies. After a tour of his bailiwick Randolph was appalled. Officials did not "keep adequate books and make proper returns." Colonists used local legal institutions such as the jury to thwart customs officials. Competing waterfront pressures—local merchants, governors' interference, local assemblies' wage regulations, local port regulations—splintered customs agents' official authority.[42]

By 1698, then, English-speaking colonists had begun to provincialize the fiscal-military state, such as it was to be found in North America. Colonists would continue to confront royal, parliamentary, and imperial authority in many different contexts, to be sure, especially through royalist discourses, frontier conflict with Indians, and widespread militia service. Imperial authority was also refracted through the offices of governors and proprietors—and their patronage. But until the 1760s, the modernizing British state was the most distant of the "many legalities" in the North American colonies. By and large, while the Crown remained a "central focus" of colonists' "political culture," it had little bearing on the routine politics and governance of empire.[43] Randolph did not care. He still believed it possible to tighten the coercive bonds between metropole and colonies. In 1698 he introduced new measures at the custom houses to "bring the colonys to Crown which will bring them under his Ma[jesty's] immediate authority."[44] In Annapolis and Pocomoke he replaced absentees with officials who actually resided near the custom houses. Elsewhere he tried to fill vacant posts. He initiated criminal prosecutions up and down the colonies against merchants owing customs duties. Predictably, Randolph's efforts again came to naught. But the greatest indignity awaited Randolph in Bermuda, where Governor Samuel Day jailed him for seven months for attempting to reform custom-house personnel.[45] Randolph's swan song was a bristling exposé of why His Majesty's revenue suffered such "Great Loss" in the colonies: sinecures abounded; in the tobacco colonies customs officials "who were great planters" slanted the laws to their benefit; Delaware and New England customs officials simply ignored mass smuggling. As Randolph saw it, imperial authority at the custom houses had been thrashed to within an inch of its life.[46]

NEGOTIATING EMPIRE, 1704–1756

In the throes of a fiscal-military revolution, England had relied on custom houses to regulate commerce and produce revenue. But by the turn of the eighteenth century, imperial custom houses in North America did neither. As one Virginian complained in 1701, in the proprietary colonies "all the Acts of Navigation, and other statutes against these lawless Practices, are of no Effect." Imperial authorities "are either brib'd or forct into a Connivance." The few who "had the courage to examine into this matter" were "either clappt up in the Logg-house or else forct to run for their lives."[47] Colonial merchants had "forct" customs officials to scrap the letter of the Navigation Acts. This trend would only continue over the next fifty years as salutary neglect and Atlantic market culture further allowed local colonial merchant communities to shape custom-house governance. As colonial trade expanded the influence of the British Empire throughout the Atlantic, however, Robert Walpole and other managers of empire would hesitate to alter the emerging norms of governance at the colonial custom houses. Colonial merchants' insistence on smuggling and trading with prohibited ports belonging to England's rivals may have flouted the spirit of the laws. But it did far more good than harm to the empire.

Colonial merchants' power grab in and around the colonial custom houses was part of a broader reconstitution of political foundations in the eighteenth-century Atlantic world. This binary process of "hydrarchy," as explained by historians Marcus Rediker and Peter Linebaugh, involved the expansion of states and subsequent popular resistance. During the fiscal-military revolution, European states and empires had instituted political economic institutions—like the custom house—from above to channel commerce toward the goals of revenue and expansion. In response, however, those subjected to this revolution, most notably merchant sailors, "organized from below." Colonial merchants were a far cry from merchant sailors and pirates, of course.[48] But colonial merchants resisted nonetheless. They benefited, in fact, from the labor and resistance of merchant sailors and pirates, who made the Atlantic marketplace a liminal space "beyond the line" and reach of the rule of law. Violence and disregard for governmental institutions were central to this "beyond the line" mentality. Men took false oaths; they lied about their cargo and destination; they searched for landings without any traces of official authority; they used false papers to cover illegal transactions.[49] Indeed, the merchants and mariners who subscribed to this reasoning "showed hardly any concern for metropolitan well-being . . . or national correctness." They were happy to trade with England's "enemies" and paid little heed to "charges of treason, or at least want of patriotism."[50]

These developments were reinforced by Great Britain's retreat from the confrontational imperial governance of the era of the Glorious Revolution.[51] In these years, managers of empire such as Robert Walpole and his rival the Duke of Newcastle came to understand colonial customs offices as rewards for party loyalty over and above any significant governance. By distributing offices in the proper manner, they hoped to build an empire of political influence. This influence, in turn, was a formidable instrument—both cudgel and adhesive—in the routine management of domestic political affairs. The preeminence of patronage meant that the men dispatched to colonial offices—lieutenant governors, naval officers, auditors, and others—were inexpert in matters of colonial governance. Moreover, it meant that once in office, these men made decisions based upon their prospective impact on English politics before any serious consideration of colonial ramifications.[52]

The Walpole ministry's emphasis on colonial patronage effectively protected colonial governance, which had once been so problematic, from serious scrutiny. This is perhaps best illustrated by the plummeting stock of the once-formidable managers of colonial affairs: the Board of Trade. Under Walpole, the board became a knowledgeable but oft-ignored vestige of an outdated regime of colonial governance.[53] It knew what was unfolding in the colonies but could do nothing without the patronage power. The ministries were typically attuned to pressing "military and commercial matters," especially reports of French or Spanish encroachments on British North America, but not "ordinary colonial business." To one observer in New York, it appeared that the British Empire had become "shamefully ignorant" of "our own Colonies in America."[54]

Together, shifting Atlantic market culture and British political culture reconstituted the colonial custom houses, transforming them from attempted projections of imperial authority to isolated marchland outposts subject to incredible local, commercial pressure. Thus the regulation of colonial commerce became characterized by an unofficial, but nonetheless ubiquitous pattern: colonists evaded customs laws, and imperial agents did not enforce, or only minimally enforced, customs laws.

The provincialization of the imperial custom houses began during Queen Anne's War (1702–13), when colonial merchants tested the empire's mettle by brazenly trading, in contravention of the navigation laws, with foreign markets—French and Spanish—in the West Indies. Colonial merchants in Boston, New York, and Philadelphia turned to French and Spanish markets because they offered lower prices than British colonial produce in the West Indies. French demand for North American goods also rose dramatically in this period.[55] As early as 1702, the ease with which colonial produce reached foreign markets in the West Indies raised a few eyebrows in England. While the Board of Trade accepted contraband traffic to Spanish colonies—believing it to harm Spain in the long run—it had little patience for illegal commerce with the French West Indies. To police this more pernicious trade, the board devised a punitive bond, to be administered by "the Comm'rs of the Customes" and "their under Officers" in the colonies. Colonial merchants were to refrain from commerce with French subjects, "particularly by way of Curacao and St. Thomas."[56] Despite questions about the program's legality, governors in the colonies received orders to require customs officials to administer the punitive bonds.[57] Little came of the scheme. The board reported in 1705 that even with the bond policy in place, "Illegal Traders" had transformed the colonies into a "receptacle of Goods imported thither from Foreign parts, contrary to Law," in exchange for colonial produce "likewise Contrary to Law Exported to Foreign parts."[58] Even after the Peace of Utrecht in 1713 normalized a commerce that had been illegal at worst, and of dubious legality at best, during a time of war, the board struggled to quash trade with the French. Thus in 1717, the board invoked an obscure 1687 Treaty of Neutrality to prohibit trade with French colonies in the West Indies, while admitting the "impractical" nature of the regulation.[59]

Enforcement had deteriorated at the custom houses. Commissioner of Customs Caleb Heathcote reported no system of "measures" to guide collection of "Revenue ... not only on this Coast but in all other parts of His Majesty's Dominions abroad." The customs laws, he revealed to the Treasury in January 1715, were "neglected & underperformed." In Connecticut, the preponderance of illegal trade prevented Heathcote from making an "effective inspection," but a cursory investigation revealed the "neglect" of imperial officers. Things were much clearer in Rhode Island four years later. Customs officials were not "safe in putting the acts of trade in force" because residents would have them arrested by local authorities, summon a violent mob of "the rabble," or plunder seized goods at an opportune moment. Indeed, "things are wrong on so many accounts, that 'tis not possible for me, to Contract what I have to offer in a narrow Compas."[60] In other words, Heathcote's tour suggested that two sets of pressures, one from above and the other from below, paralyzed enforcement of imperial customs laws. The seat of empire provided but little guidance and even less in the way of resources for customs officials. Meanwhile, in and around the custom houses, colonists used local law and the threat of—and sometimes actual—violence to intimidate officials. The result was an enforcement crisis as customs officials "neglected & underperformed" their duties.

The erosion of imperial authority at the colonial custom house was an open secret in London. After 1715, the attorney general for England and Wales issued opinions in several customs cases that corroborated Heathcote's findings. Rhode Island stood out for the punishments dealt to customs officials who refused to allow merchants to have their way. "The Trading people of the island," wrote Edward Northey in 1718, "do frequently arrest the officers" at the custom house "and put them under very great difficulties and them in Execution by the Laws made there which never had the Kings sanction."[61] Then there was the violence. "Riotous" colonists "armed with axes threatened to kill the officers in case they resisted." Official papers in the custom house were "by Contrivance Burnt and Destroyed" to stymie legal proceedings.[62] It was also impossible to ignore customs officials' malfeasance. Attorney General Thomas Pengelly learned that Maryland customs officials had failed to prosecute overdue bonds for several years. Worse yet, they often had not kept any records. Not that it would have mattered, however. When Surveyor General Maurice Birchfield managed to figure out which merchants owed customs duties, "the partys and Gentlemen of the Country" put up "so many difficulties and Obstacles in the prosecution of the said suits" that "many of them could not be brought on to a conclusion or a hearing."[63]

As the colonial custom houses fell further under the sway of colonial merchant communities, imperial officials would seek to intervene only once, at the behest of London's powerful sugar lobby. In 1732, the sugar lobby presented clear evidence of systematic, unchecked colonial smuggling of sugar from the French West Indies, which the sugar merchants blamed for depressing the prices of their goods. There was no denying that colonial merchants were guilty. In response, Parliament passed the Molasses Act of 1733, which prohibited importation of non-British sugar into any British holding. Customs officials were to seize goods and vessels in violation of the Molasses Act.[64] But the act was a "dead letter" the moment it arrived in the colonies. In 1734 it produced only £330 in the colonies. Between 1738 and 1741, the Molasses Act on average produced £76.[65] The paltry revenue numbers were not due to colonial merchants' newfound probity. Instead, customs officials used their discretion to undermine the act. In Philadelphia, for instance, customs officials did not document any illicit West Indies cargo between 1740 and 1750. In Wilmington, Delaware, customs officials were quick to buy tall tales about the supposedly British provenance of goods that obviously came from the French West Indies. Of course, it was difficult for Wilmington customs officials to weigh and inspect incoming sugar, given that "there is not a pair of scales in the Town with which a Hhd [sic] of sugar can possibly be weighed."[66]

Privately, some imperial agents worried that "enforcement of the several acts for the preservation of the plantation trade . . . would soon become impracticable in America." In colonial New York, for instance, an unmistakable smuggling boom had begun. Lieutenant Governor Cadwallader Colden informed the Board of Trade that "the Custom House officers are not sufficient for preventing such trade & if they were there is so good an understanding between them & the merchants which is evident."[67]

Beyond the Molasses Act of 1733, though, neither Parliament nor British Treasury officials had any interest in disrupting the "good understanding" that had evolved between colonial merchants and customs officials. There was little interest at these levels in the complexities of colonial governance.[68] Importantly, however, this salutary neglect also served the end of imperial expansion. Clearly, it expanded the sphere of English commerce. But more broadly, Walpole and Newcastle proved willing to cede much to the colonies in the way of local self-governance, in exchange for the guarantee of political order and loyalty to the empire. In the seventeenth century, joint stock companies and colonists had done much of the work of settling and ordering the New World colonies. Now the managers of empire turned to their patronage appointments, from governors on down to surveyors and customs collectors, to discover whatever means was necessary to maintain the territorial reach of the empire. In this arrangement of authority, political order outweighed faithful enforcement of the laws.[69]

London's willingness to tolerate the deterioration of the rule of imperial law in the colonies had profound consequences. Above all, this policy of inaction fostered a legal and political pluralism that, as Lauren Benton suggests, facilitated the integration of a vast overseas empire. A regime in which far-flung colonists faced few repercussions for circumventing the reach of imperial authority was a regime that functioned, because, officially or otherwise, it conciliated its subjects.[70] Importantly, then, colonial customs officials' choice to *not* enforce or to *selectively* enforce navigation laws helped create amicable relations between colonies and metropole. Alison Games thus argues that imperial officials in foreign lands who, as these customs officials did, deviated from the letter of the law, used "office to innovate policy." Rigorous enforcement of an unpopular law served only to make London and Whitehall objects of colonial ire. Thus customs officials "never enforced the letter of those laws and permitted much illegal trade." On the other hand, as Hulsebosch argues, "they had to." Imperial agents in the colonies pursued policies and practices that, whatever their parochial effect, ultimately furthered the ends of empire.[71]

CUSTOM HOUSES AND REVOLUTION

Between 1704 and 1756, imperial customs officials in the colonies used their discretion to ever so gently enforce the Navigation Acts in order to facilitate colonial commerce and expand the boundaries of the British Empire. Between 1756 and 1776, however, everything changed. As George Grenville and others in London began to rethink the meaning and significance of the North American colonies, they demanded a new form of governance at the colonial custom houses. Until 1756 the colonies had been understood in chiefly commercial terms, but after 1756 they were contemplated in terms of revenue. The colonies now came to be understood as an untapped, fecund source of revenue to pay down Great Britain's massive national debt after decades of warfare against imperial rivals France and Spain. Customs officials' discretion and subsequent selective enforcement of customs laws had been inadequate to the task of extracting tax revenue from colonial merchants' capital. Now, the home government would seek a new, strict regime of enforcement at the custom houses. Colonial merchants, of course, had taken advantage of decades of salutary neglect to gain significant influence over custom-house governance. They would resolutely resist the British Empire's attempt to reconstitute legal authority at the custom houses. The resulting conflict was a direct precipitant of the American Revolution.[72]

Colonial merchants' nefarious commercial activities during the Seven Years' War helped push Great Britain to rethink its relationship with imperial customs officials and the colonies more broadly. Particularly in the West Indies and in western Europe, the war made already profitable markets all the more lucrative, since armies and navies needed supplies, and marooned civilians would pay extra for life's basic necessities. Colonial merchants in New York and Philadelphia were long accustomed to trading with French and Spanish subjects despite formal legal prohibitions and jumped at the new opportunities. Colonial goods flooded through New Jersey and Rhode Island to Holland. Other merchants used fictitious invoices at the custom houses to prohibited French and Spanish ports in the Leeward Islands and Hispaniola.[73] Likewise, French sugar, rum, and molasses flooded markets in the North American colonies.[74]

Great Britain had tolerated colonial smuggling to the West Indies for several decades, but now began to take a more critical view of things. It was one thing for colonists to smuggle during peacetime, especially if their commerce benefited the empire. During the war, however, this same commerce materially benefited the enemy. Accordingly, William Pitt and others tried to put an end to it "such flagitious Practices." The mighty British navy was enlisted to root out colonial smugglers in the West Indies, leading one colonial merchant to note that many were "being Apprehended for holding a Criminal Correspondence with the French." [75] Governors also received explicit instructions to halt "this dangerous & Ignominious Trade." But the navy had its hands full with wartime hostilities and the governors, who were chiefly political animals, proved unreliable. The burden of enforcement fell upon "the Officers of the Customs."[76] Whitehall's demands on the colonial customs diverged sharply from the sleepy routine of years past. For the first time since the era of Edward Randolph, customs officials, who had grown accustomed to nonfeasance and malfeasance were "to put into *execution* the several Laws and Regulations relative to the Revenue in the said Colonies."[77]

Customs officials in the colonies undoubtedly felt the pressure of the Treasury's attempts to tighten enforcement. Initially, the Treasury's demand for rigor seemed to embolden at least one customs official, New York's Alexander Colden. In May 1756, while making a seizure, a smuggler "offer'd a large Sum . . . not to Seize which I replied all his Estate should not bribe me from my Duty." Colden's "Seizure" subsequently caused "great Noise in Town" because "the Merchts are vastly uneasy as they find bribeing will not do." A year later Colden still sang the same conscientious tune: Parliament's controversial Flour Act of 1757 "will be Strictly Complied with by the Custom House Officers here." In Charleston, a few years later, new collector Daniel Moore rebutted a local committee of leading merchants seeking to soften the custom house's new, rigorous stance. "Charging them with attempting to reform the custom house," Moore "taunted that he in turn would reform the Charleston trade."[78] Philadelphia customs officials began assiduously applying the terms of an old 1696 statute that had long been overlooked. Between June and December of 1761, they forced fifty-six merchants to take out expensive customs bonds for "preventing frauds" to ensure that foods intended for Boston, Halifax, Antigua, and New Providence did not end up in French-controlled markets.[79] Customs seizures and prosecutions would increase in New York, too, and in 1762 the colony's highest court issued a lengthy "note" naming names of smugglers who did illegal business with the French.[80]

During the Seven Years' War, however, colonial customs officials did not fully embrace London's new zeal for custom-house enforcement. It was true that enforcement tightened, but it was equally true that customs officials still found ways to attenuate the letter of the law to benefit local commerce. In Philadelphia, for instance, John Swift went to great lengths to avoid invoking the punitive terms demanded by London. One merchant whose vessel had loaded "without first taking a permit" at the custom house received only a cautionary and explanatory note. Swift extended this caution "as you may possibly be unacquainted with the Laws of the Customs." Swift also warned Philadelphia merchant Charles Pettit that "you entered & gave bond only thirty-eight" hogsheads of sugar, whereas customs officials had detected "forty two." The deputy collector did not seize the goods for this basic violation, but rather hoped Pettit would "please to call on me this afternoon, or favours me with a line respecting this matter" to clear up the apparent confusion. Finally, Swift hesitated to seize even a "seisable" vessel that failed to take out the necessary bonds at the custom house. Instead, the importer "promised to write" an explanation for the custom house's records. Swift's hesitation to compel obedience with commercial restrictions suggests the difficulty of changing a decades-old arrangement of authority at the Philadelphia custom house.[81]

At other custom houses, the home government's new emphasis on custom-house enforcement seems scarcely to have made a mark. New York merchants flocked to New Jersey and Rhode Island "where customs officials were notoriously corrupt and associated in the smuggling business." When Philadelphia merchants found custom-house interference too much to bear, they moved their operation to western Delaware, which was soon swimming in French sugar. As early as 1759, the Board of Trade observed that customs officials in the colonies were simply not heeding demands for strict enforcement.[82] Neither could the British navy help but notice that customs officials often obstructed attempted seizures of contraband goods coming and going from the colonies. Here customs officials' venality was the problem, for when they did seize contraband, they were entitled to a share or "moiety" of the goods. The navy now threatened to cut into their pie. Customs officials fury at the navy's seizure of colonial contraband dovetailed conveniently with colonial merchants' own outrage at the navy's disturbance of the "understanding" that existed in and around the custom house, as Cadwallader Colden had put it some years before. The Royal Navy nonetheless made significant inroads against the illicit West Indies trades, especially in the waters from New England to Halifax.[83]

Colonial merchants also drew upon their authority to influence custom-house government in order to circumscribe Whitehall's new enforcement initiative. They demanded "Indulgence," as Charleston scion Henry Laurens put it.[84] The reality of the situation did not elude those customs officials like Alexander Colden who had once pledged that even "Severe" laws would be "Strictly Complied with by the Custom House Officers here." In fact, Colden's bravado about seizing goods and refusing bribes was only for private consumption. In public, he warned his father, "*This tho' is not to be Spoke of.*" Likewise, even after the king's attorney in New York detected collusive "Practices" between customs officials and merchants, he demurred from launching "a particular accusation."[85] It appeared that "every merchant, & every Mariner" involved in the West Indies trades was wholly united in opposition to the British Empire's attempt to strictly and impartially administer customs laws in the colonies. This rendered virtually impossible the task of prosecuting smugglers. As Carl Ubbelohde has written, "The customs officers and the vice-admiralty court would not dare enforce the King's law if they were accountable to local juries for all their actions."[86]

When colonial merchants found that a custom house went too far in policing contraband trade, the mob quickly materialized. Consider the sad tale of middling merchant George Spencer. As historian Thomas Truxes explains, in 1759 a down-on-his-luck Spencer "began snooping around the warehouses, wharves, and docks along the East River" where he quickly found "fictitious clearances," or customs documents, "provided by New-Haven, New-London, Perth-Amboy," and other customs officials to give legal cover to contraband trade with French colonies. Spencer dished his scoop to New York collector of customs Archibald Kennedy. But Kennedy balked because he knew "rooting out New York City's deeply embedded trade with the enemy would mean taking on the political, economic, and social hierarchy of the city," including the inner workings of Kennedy's own milieu. So Kennedy punted the problem across the Atlantic to request Parliament's intervention.[87] Given the close ties between New York's merchants and Kennedy's custom house, however, it did not take long for word to "spread that an informer was at large." A day later, a merchant and former customs official named George Harison showered Spencer with threats. Then the "Hands of a Mob" got hold of Spencer and dragged him around lower Manhattan amid beatings and volleys of projectiles. A second mob later meted out more of the same. Five years later, the men responsible for setting the mob upon Spencer received a paltry fine of £100 each.[88]

By 1763 imperial officials in London identified their inability to enforce customs regulations in the colonies as a significant moral and legal problem.[89] A movement to reform and centralize colonial customs administration quickly took shape. The case for reform was built on numbers that did not add up. Adam Smith and Jonathan Swift were fond of a saying that "in the arithmetic of the customs two and two, instead of making four, make some times only one." George Grenville and his cabinet discovered similar creative math at the end of the Seven Years' War. Administration of the colonial customs establishment cost £8,000 per year. The cost of British military protection to the colonies was estimated at about £220,000 a year. Customs revenue in the colonies amounted to only £2,000 per year.[90] In the spring and summer of 1763, the Grenville ministry searched for an explanation. By July, they had an answer in a report by the commissioners of customs: "collusive practices" between merchants and customs officials undermined custom houses in North America.[91]

The commissioners of customs 1763 report recommended drastic changes to custom-house governance in the North American colonies, and it became the body of the Sugar Act of the following year. Among the key goals of the Sugar Act was "to make customs enforcement more effective."[92] Customs officials were now to enforce the old, decrepit Molasses Act of 1733 (although duties actually fell) as well as prohibitively high new duties on Madeira, French rum, foreign coffee, pimento, indigo, and sugar. In addition to enforcing new duties, customs officials were directed to take aim at smugglers' tried and tested tools for evading customs duties. The most important of these was the practice of "hovering," in which smugglers stalled their vessels along the coast and exchanged goods with merchants ashore without making entry at the custom house. Finally, the Sugar Act attempted to break the hold of local commercial influence over customs enforcement by dramatically changing the venue of prosecutions. Previously, customs cases would be tried in nearby courtrooms wherein juries were packed with locals sympathetic to apprehended smugglers. The Sugar Act shifted these proceedings to distant imperial Vice-Admiralty Courts, where local commercial influence had no sway. By increasing customs officials' responsibilities, criminalizing common smuggling practices, and reforming the jurisdiction of customs prosecutions, the Sugar Act of 1764 was a full-scale assault on patterns of custom-house governance that had become entrenched in the colonies since the era of the Glorious Revolution.[93]

Discussions about the problem of customs enforcement during the debate over the Sugar Act of 1764 suggested that the home government now regarded the colonies in a new and unflattering light. Before the Seven Years' War, the colonies had been understood in chiefly commercial terms. But Great Britain's imposing national debt in the wake of the war put revenue at the forefront of political economic discussions. It could not help but be noticed that Great Britain's debts stemmed from "the Protection she has afforded her Colonies in times of War." But the colonies had proven unwilling to do their part, it seemed. Decades of "Indulgence" in policy toward the colonies fostered a "Disregard of all Revenue Laws" and "a regular Course" of contraband trade. As the colonists' illicit commerce during the Seven Years' War had made clear, this "Disregard" of the rule of law included materially aiding the enemy. By doing away with this culture of "indulgence" at the custom houses, and by pressing customs officials to collect revenue, the home government hoped to put the colonies in their place. As Grenville's assistant, Thomas Whately, wrote, "Vigorous Measures" like the Sugar Act allowed the Empire "to inforce Obedience to all the Laws." It was time for the colonies "to raise more" for the empire.[94]

The Sugar Act put colonial customs officials in quite a bind. Throughout the colonies, West Indies merchants and others put up a "united front" against customs enforcement. Violence and intimidation were again tools of choice. As customs official Henry Hulton later recalled, "The Officers of the Customs . . . foresaw that they must either offend the Traders by an attention to their duty, or draw on themselves . . . censure of their Superiors, by a neglect of it." If the officials paid "attention to their duty," they faced harsh recriminations from "the Traders." If the officials chose the path of nonfeasance, they faced official rebuke from "their Superiors." By and large, officials chose the former. Thus the Sugar Act could not be and was not enforced. Again Hulton provides a telling explanation: "The Trade had been so long habituated in indulgences, so well practiced in Smugling, and the officers so long used to connivance and neglect, that to establish and enforce regulations for better management, required more authority than . . . Government might chuse to exert." The British Empire simply did not have the "authority" to change the culture of enforcement at the colonial custom houses. As they had for several decades, colonial merchants, however, had power enough to thwart reform.[95]

Even as colonial merchants flaunted their ability to influence customhouse governance in the face of imperial reform efforts, they nonetheless had crossed somewhat of a Rubicon. The punitive measures of the Sugar Act suggested to them that the British Empire no longer cherished the value of their commerce to the functioning of the empire. They felt as if they were "second-class subjects of the crown," explains historian T. H. Breen. Moreover, the end of the Seven Years' War brought a deep depression to colonial commerce. In this dour economic climate, increased duties and tougher customs enforcement seemed downright vindictive.[96] Things worsened considerably after passage of the Stamp Act, which directed among other things that official papers in use at the custom house utilize only stamped paper. This made the custom houses indirect distributors of the reviled stamped paper as of November 1, 1765. As if that did not whip up enough anger among colonial merchants who did business at the custom houses, the stamped paper arrived from England by sea at the custom house, where it was to be guarded. It was inevitable that the custom house would become an important backdrop to colonial agitation about the Stamp Act.[97]

Colonial merchants would use their influence over custom-house governance to subvert the Stamp Act. As usual, violence was part of the "general scheme." As John Hatton, collector of customs in Salem, New Jersey, discovered, even unfounded rumors that an officer "had received the stamp papers" would bring a "Mob of Fellows" to "lay in wait for me." This mob informed Hatton that "if they find any stamp [mutil.] they will burn me & my House."[98] As a prominent Pennsylvanian explained, "the people here are determined never to submit. . . . If those in power at home should think of enforcing it here . . . I can only say that at present we are not more than one degree from open Rebellion." That degree must have seemed terrifyingly close. Brazen Rhode Islanders published the following resolutions in October 1765:

That the C—r of N—shall use none of them [stamps] in his office, upon *pain* of our highest displeasure.

That if he will clear no vessels upon paper without Stamps, that he shall be drove out of town with a high hand.⁹⁹

To the north three months later, officials in the Boston custom house learned that the Sons of Liberty were preparing to descend, but could do little other than put their ears to the ground "for the approaching rumble of the mob." These officials had serious reason for concern, as months earlier, a mob had torn down the house belonging to Customs Comptroller Benjamin Hallowell, along with those belonging to the lieutenant governor and admiralty registrar.¹⁰⁰

Placed in an impossible tug-of-war between colonial merchants and the home government, customs officials devised some clever strategies to stall for time. First, if stamped paper had not arrived from England, or if there was no official stamp distributor nearby, then the Stamp Act was not yet considered to be in force. Philadelphia collector John Swift declared "a suspension of Law in this Province" until the stamped paper arrived. If stamped paper did arrive, customs officials lobbed vague requests for further instructions at various authorities. This bought time in which they did not have to enforce the law. Philadelphia officials went for the broadest possible question, asking, "[How] ought the officers of the customs to act to secure the Revenue of Customs & to preserve the authority given them by the Law?" In New York customs officials claimed to be "at a loss" and requested "Advice and Directions."¹⁰¹

In most ports, however, customs officials eventually caved in to pressure from colonial merchants and permitted ships to clear without the use of stamped paper. They could not rely on delaying tactics indefinitely, because while they helped customs officials save face, such tactics also spelled the de facto closure of the port. No stamped paper meant "there is no Offices yet open," and that, in turn, meant, no business. In Philadelphia the customs officials' stalling tricks caused "a total Stagnation of Business," according to merchant Thomas Clifford. In December 1765, New York customs official Andrew Elliot allowed vessels to clear using unstamped paper—despite the fact that stamped paper had arrived two months before. In Virginia, deference to "the relief of the Trade" brought about a similar decision. Somewhat surprisingly, Surveyor General Charles Stewart came to these officials' defense. He explained to the home government the "dire results" of restraining commerce in the colonies. Eventually, from South Carolina to Massachusetts, imperial officials, including customs officials, backed away from enforcing the provisions of the Stamp Act. It would be repealed in 1766. About a decade later, Henry Hulton recalled that "from that day the Parliament of Great Britain was no longer respected [sic] their right to make Laws binding on the Colonies was denied. The operation of their Acts was resisted, and the independence in general avowed." As Hulton saw it, England should have realized that "the event shewed how erroneous the measure was, of attempting to raise a Revenue in a remote Country, where the powers of Government were weak," and Parliament was "not thoroughly acquainted with the particular local circumstances of the several Provinces." This was the moment for England to "strengthen the hands of Government and support its authority" in the colonies.[102] For Hulton, the Stamp Act debacle highlighted again the stark contrast between the empire wanting powers of compulsion and the colonial merchants' remarkable ability to shape the limits of routine governance at the custom house.

Customs officials like John Swift and Andrew Elliott would receive much of the blame for the downfall of the Stamp Act. In response, Parliament pursued further measures to limit customs officials' discretion by compelling them to enforce the law. The creation of the American Board of Customs in 1767 seemed to address this priority. The commissioners of customs in London informed the Lords of the Treasury "that the oppressions . . . the Officers of the Revenue labour under in America" had "lately grown to such an enormous height, that [it] is become impossible for them to do their duty." Customs officials of course feared "the Outrage of Mobs," but also "Suits, Verdicts & Judgments in the Provincial Courts." Without imperial authority in their support, colonial customs officials were simply overawed by local resistance and pressure. Existing arrangements were inadequate because, as Dora Mae Clark concludes, the office of the commissioners of customs in London was "too far from America to make its authority felt there." The American Board of Customs would represent the commissioners and Parliament's will in the colonies. More importantly, they would directly supervise the operations of the custom houses in North America.[103]

But the American Board of Customs proved ineffective in large part because it addressed the wrong problem with customs governance in the colonies. The problem was not that customs officials were unaware of Treasury instructions or Parliament's will. The problem was that the pressure exerted by colonial merchants—the threats, violence, and other tactics—was more influential in determining how custom officials administered their offices. The American Board of Customs concurred. Shortly after arriving in Boston, it reported that it was "impracticable to enforce the execution of the Revenue Laws, until the hand of government is properly strengthened." [104] The social pressure from below was simply stronger than "the hand of government." In Philadelphia, John Swift explained the dynamic of how customs officials were beholden to local commercial influence. The moment the official parted with the letter of the law, there was no turning back. He concluded, "Once corruption is effected," the officer "must ever do as his corruptors bid him." [105]

Colonists also greeted the board with the same mixture of violence and intimidation that they had long doled out to unaccommodating customs officials. In Rhode Island John Robinson would endure arrest, prosecution, violence, and intimidation. But "he finally took to going about armed." Actions taken by the board also brought new rounds of violence and intimidation. The most famous of these decisions was that made in early March 1770, when the board placed a solider "as a guard at the Custom House" in Boston. The result was the Boston Massacre a few days later on March 5. In the wake of the massacre, furious mobs forced the board to scatter and flee. Henry Hulton took refuge in his home in Brookline, away from the powder keg of revolutionary anger. Or so he thought. In June 1770, a mob tricked its way into Hulton's home, forcing him to defend his family with a sword.[106]

It was around this time that John Swift committed his "crime" of enforcing the law and incurred the wrath of a Philadelphia waterfront mob. But the mobs only appeared when Swift and his brother officers crossed the colonial merchants' expectation of wan enforcement. Otherwise the mob went silent. Swift seems to have learned his lesson. At Swift's custom house, officials ceased making entries for customs duties in February 1772. They were equally casual in canceling custom-house bonds that were crucial to enforcement of the navigation laws. As one investigator noted, officials at the custom house had canceled the bonds with few questions asked. The bonds had "been illegally cancelled at the Custom House by the officers of the Customs for of this Port of New York, to the great Detriment of his Majesty, and the impoverishing the Crown." After "a Conversation . . . with the Collector of his Majesty's Customs here," this official had "but little Hopes these Things will be amended for the Future."[107]

Even if customs officials were willing to risk being attacked or ostracized to enforce the will of the home government, they could not rely on much support from other officers, prosecutors, and even judges. When the mob seized John Hatton outside Swift's Philadelphia custom house, colonial officials were "witnesses to a scene of such cruelty & none of them put a stop to it." Judges and others hesitated to act because, like the colonists they were supposed to police and prosecute, they disapproved of "the oppressive nature of those laws," as Attorney General of Pennsylvania James Allen confided to his diary in May 1772.[108] But they also took seriously the local commercial forces that pressured customs officials as a legitimate source of law. In these years, most prominent judges and prosecutors understood that constitutionalism emanated from London "transatlantically" as well as from several layers of local authority in the colonies. Though roughly compatible, these two broad sources of legal authority could come into conflict when imperial power encroached upon colonial liberties.[109] This was precisely the case with the infamous writs of assistance. Here constitutional theory and popular resistance enjoyed a convenient alliance. The writs, which were to be issued to customs officials for their tenure in office, allowed search of private property in search of smuggled goods. The Board of Customs believed that the writs were vital to the effective enforcement of customs laws. But judges in most colonies did not issue writs of assistance because they deferred to local law, under which there was no provision for general warrants or searches. As John Swift explained of the Pennsylvania Supreme Court, "They say there is no Law that authorizes them to grant standing Writs." Chief Justice William Allen later confided to Swift that he "would not do that upon any consideration." Ultimately, as John Phillip Reid documents, only judges in Massachusetts, New Hampshire, and New York issued the despised writs. In New York the writ of assistance quickly fell into disuse, in New Hampshire it "may not have been used" at all, and in Massachusetts it was used but thrice.[110]

The disintegration of the rule of imperial law in the early 1770s marked the effective end of the colonial customs service as it had operated since the Glorious Revolution. Yet is most likely that neither writs of assistance nor any personnel reform short of the militarization of customs would have accomplished the goal of the strict and rigorous enforcement of the Navigation Acts.[111] John Swift understood why. And it was precisely in this context and in what would be his swan song that he offered these comments to his superiors in London: "The officers of the customs are but few & they have to contend with the whole Body of merchts: many of whom think it no crime to cheat the King of his Duties." "What can a governor do without the assistance of the govern'd?"[112]

COMMERCE AND GOVERNANCE

In April 1773, the Liberty Boys in New York City cowed Collector of Customs Andrew Elliot into handing over "the keys to the customhouse." Though perhaps less literally, colonial obstruction throughout the colonies had shuttered the custom houses, shut down the ports, and eventually vanquished British rule in North America.[113] It is not difficult to imagine why Americans ever since have understood the American Revolution to have been a massive tax revolt or protest against central governance itself. But this is not quite correct. For one thing, at almost no juncture did Americans protest the idea of customs duties on their commerce. By and large, they also accepted the legal and ideological validity of the Navigation Acts to channel commerce for the benefit of the British Empire.[114] On the one hand, revolts against customs enforcement in the 1760s and 1770s were targeted against seemingly extortionate plots to increase revenue. Yet, just as important, they were expressions of discontent, not about the existence of coercive central governmental laws, but about the manner in which those laws were enforced. For decades, commercially oriented colonists, to say nothing of customs officials, had become accustomed to influence custom-house governance through discrete negotiations over the meaning and reach of laws. In 1763, however, the managers of empire in London tried to reform custom-house governance by preventing any further negotiations of imperial authority.

But what appeared to be obstruction to the British and to modern-day observers was governance to the colonists who took to the mob. After all, ever since the British Empire transplanted custom houses to North American shores, merchants, sailors, and other waterfront denizen used violence to make their will known to imperial customs officials. In short, because they had grown accustomed to the power to influence custom-house governance, colonial merchants and their fellow travelers legitimately believed they had a stake, if not a voice, in how the custom houses would go about enforcing laws.

In fact, their waterfront power over imperial customs administration aligned neatly with the colonists' own attempts to regulate Atlantic commerce during the Revolution. Thrice during the revolutionary era, in the aftermath of the Stamp, Townshend, and Tea acts, colonists used "extralegal structures" to "discourage the purchase of British manufactures." According to Breen, the nonimportation and nonintercourse movements broadened the base of the colonists' coalescing, imaginable national polity. Regulating what people could buy or not buy, in other words, helped cohere the Revolution.[115] Those merchants caught up in the moment were unable to distinguish between protest and political economy. Thomas Clifford of Philadelphia repeatedly used the term "shackled" to describe colonists' actions in preventing the purchase of British goods. The carceral metaphor was apt, for the colonists' enforcement of commitments to forgo certain forms of commerce was no less a market restriction than the British Navigation Acts.[116] Indeed, colonial enforcement had had a center that enumerated prohibited goods, and officers on the periphery who went door to door and demanded that individuals swear an oath in agreement. And just as the Board of Customs had once met in the Long Room atop the London custom house to decide policy toward colonial commerce, so New York merchants in 1764 "assembled in the Long Room of Burn's tavern" and decided to restrict British imports.[117]

Enforcement of the Non-Importation and Non-Intercourse agreements overlapped with merchants' and sailors' tried and tested tools of popular pressure against customs officials. For decades, imperial customs officials were ostracized and isolated for too rigorously enforcing the law. The committees that enforced the Non-Importation and Non-Intercourse agreements used "shaming mechanisms" against transgressors. Violence, of course, was the most powerful tool wielded against imperial customs officials when more subtle attempts at influence failed. Colonial committee members were not shy of using the awful and painful spectacle of tarring and feathering against colonial merchants who purchased British goods in spite of the Non-Importation and Non-Intercourse agreements. In Philadelphia, a self-constituted "Committee of Tarring and Feathering" took shape: "To our Care are committed all Offenders against the Rights of America; and hapless is he, whose evil Destiny has doomed him to suffer at our Hands."[118]

Ultimately, the colonial Non-Importation and Non-Intercourse agreements failed because they demanded the same, inflexible brand of rigorous enforcement that had sparked the revolutionary troubles at the custom houses to begin with. There was little room for negotiating the limits and possibilities of political authority and legal coercion within a regime that demanded total compliance. So the merchants involved in overseas commerce, at least some of them, did as they had done since time immemorial and skirted the new regulations. The irony of the situation was not lost on the Philadelphia firm of James & Drinker, which noted that in the upside-down world of the boycotts, "no injunction is intended to be laid on the Smuggler while the hands of the fair Trader is to be tied."[119] But the colonial committees should not have been surprised, because by the mid-seventeenth century if there was one thing about the market that Americans should have understood it was its irresistible pull. That pull had influenced decades of negotiated authority at the imperial custom houses, sparked revolutionary fury about imperial reform, and complicated colonial plans at channeling commerce toward their revolutionary political ends. And the undeniable power of the market would need to be accounted for, no matter what type of government emerged from the American Revolution.

PART II

Revenue and Empire: Bermuda Hundred, 1795

The world had suddenly stopped making sense to William Heth, the federal government's collector of customs for the port of Bermuda Hundred in central Virginia. Heth was a comfortable landowner and slaveowner and a man of distinction. During the Revolutionary War he had been a colonel in the Virginia line, and afterward he directed the Virginia chapter of the Society of the Cincinnati. He also pressed Virginia's claims for wartime compensation.[1] Given his status, Heth was an easy choice for the important position of collector of customs under the new federal government. President George Washington and Secretary of the Treasury Alexander Hamilton favored such men of rank to bear the burden of collecting the nation's revenue and superintending the nation's overseas commerce. It was not only that Heth and others of his elite ilk understood the stakes of office holding; it was also that they felt a calling to lead. Through the prism of distinction and respect enjoyed by men like Heth, Hamilton and Washington wished to project the authority of the new federal government. Heth's reputation gave him, and by extension the federal government, credit with which to forge a relationship with the people. Heth's credit would buttress the nation's credit.[2]

But something had gone horribly awry in the small but significant port of Bermuda Hundred. In 1795, Heth's authority collapsed as the "importing merchants" of Bermuda Hundred engaged in open revolt in and around the custom house. Not unlike John Swift three decades before, Heth had incurred the wrath of the importing merchants by enforcing the letter of the law. In 1789 the first Congress passed several laws to institute the customs revenue and regulation system. Heth studied these laws and applied every provision at his disposal. He prosecuted small boats "without any name" on the hull or whose names had letters "of all sizes." Importing merchants were equally shocked to be punished for lacking proper papers. There were many other peccadilloes that were admittedly "trifling," conceded Heth. But what else was he to do? Washington and Hamilton had entrusted him with the responsibility of sustaining federal authority, collecting revenue, and enforcing regulations. He believed that government could function only by "strict observance" of "the letter of the laws." Any deviation from this course posed a "hazard to which the revenue will forever later be exposed."[3]

But no other custom house in Virginia followed Heth's example. Such "infractions" were "thought unworthy of notice in any other district but this," noted Heth. Importing merchants in central Virginia retaliated against Heth by racing to the bottom: they purposefully bypassed Bermuda Hundred and instead did business at more understanding, neighboring custom houses. By midyear, not a single "dollar of new duties" had been "secured here," lamented Heth. He had given "offence to important Merchants" by being "considered as being 'too strict,'" and now the merchants plotted to make his office "too disagreeable to hold."[4] Heth was surprised at how quickly his situation had soured, for just a few years before, things had been quiet and orderly at his custom house. Heth's small group of inspectors—Frederick Batte, Richard and Charles Eppes, Peter Wilkinson, Andrew Torburn, and John Fitzgerald—seemed loyal and generally trustworthy.[5] He kept neat accounts that reveal steady revenue collection of up to several thousand dollars a month. In fact, he was collecting so much in customs duties that highway robbers had taken note, prompting Heth to warn local merchants "to be cautious how they travel with money to pay their duties." There were "villains" along "the road to the collector's office."[6]

So what went wrong at Bermuda Hundred? In short, the world had passed William Heth by. In Bermuda Hundred and elsewhere in the United States, the Federalist political economy embodied by the custom house had grown unpopular. Likewise, elite control of political authority, already under siege during the age of revolution, was eroding too fast for Heth to comprehend. A third dynamic, specific to the unique location of the custom house astride the Atlantic marketplace on the one hand, and the state on the other, was also at play. Throughout the country, customs officials faced unrelenting pressure from importing merchants and others who had business at the custom house to interpret federal customs law to benefit and protect local commerce. And the customs men, whose legitimacy rested on reputation, used discretion—which had no foundation in the law—to respond in kind. In the early 1790s, pressure from importing merchants slackened customs enforcement and ensured that the custom house served commerce at least as much as it did the work of the state. Everywhere, it seems, except Bermuda Hundred.

Heth believed he had uncovered a scandal of national proportions. But he was stunned to learn from Secretary of the Treasury Oliver Wolcott that he, William Heth, the archetypal elite republican officeholder, was in the wrong. The Treasury well knew how commerce had encroached on the custom houses throughout the country, and more to the point, the Treasury sanctioned this means of negotiating authority. "The laws are certainly rules which you ought to follow," but "it is certain that the officers must take some liberties, now & then with the more formal directions . . . or they will never fulfill the intention." Another danger of following the strict letter of the law, explained Wolcott, was that what was good for one custom house might prove thorny for another. "There are shades of difference in the execution of the Laws," he allowed. Finally, concluded Wolcott, Heth had fundamentally misunderstood what federal authority meant for the ruling Federalists. It had nothing to do with forcibly instilling a respect for the rule of law. Rather, "if the [customs] duties are fairly collected, & in a manner to preserve method & system in the public accounts, the great object is answered," wrote Wolcott. If commercial pressure pushed customs officials to slacken the letter of the law, and if the custom houses became influenced by merchants' expectations, that was a small price to pay for the "great object" of a stable, secure national revenue.[7]

CHAPTER TWO

Political Economy and the Making of the Customs System

After the Revolution, Americans puzzled over how to build a capable federal government that stayed true to republican ideals. Republicanism had already matured from a revolutionary emphasis on individual virtue, selfless service to the commonweal, and local self-government to a postcolonial search for balance between public power and individual rights.[1] For a small cadre of statesmen and political economists led by Alexander Hamilton and Robert Morris, the survival of the American republican experiment required a central government that, above all, could successfully collect revenue. This group—variously referred to as Nationalists or Federalists—relentlessly pursued a new federal government with the power to tax before achieving their goal with the Constitution of 1787. In the months that followed, the power to tax would translate to a national customs revenue system.[2]

Hamilton and Morris turned to customs duties because they wanted to pattern the new federal government on the blueprint of the British state. Others saw customs duties as the most expedient way to solve the United States' revenue crisis under the Articles of Confederation. Though Robert Morris repeatedly lost battles to create a national impost in the early 1780s, his efforts legitimized the basic principle of extracting tax revenue from merchant capital. By the time of the Constitutional Convention, the once "perverse" concept of a capable central government had gained currency.[3] A second, more complicated debate after the convention ensued about the precise details of the customs system. Again, Great Britain was the model. Congress's flurry of customs statutes in 1789—the tariff, the Enrollment Act, the Registering Act, and the Collection Act—effectively Americanized the British Navigation Acts.[4]

Where the framers of the United States customs system deviated from the British model, however, was with personnel. Here George Washington's influence was profound. Though it was important for Washington's customs officers to share the Federalist vision of a capable and energetic government, they need not have been party men. Rather, because he believed collecting customs revenue to be so important, Washington turned to many with experience as impost duty collectors under the states. He also solicited customs officers with every possible mark of distinction—local status, military experience, commercial backgrounds, and officialdom. He expected these officers to use their reputation and status to legitimize fledgling federal authority. Washington explained: "So necessary is it, at this crisis, to conciliate the good will of the People: and so impossible is it, in my judgment, to build the edifice of public happiness, but upon their affections."[5]

THE REVENUE PROBLEM, 1774–1787

The United States was born into debt. As the War of Independence dragged on, the country's dire revenue situation made misers out of every committee in the Continental Congress charged with provisioning the Continental Army.[6] Desperation soon set in. In May 1780, two starving Connecticut regiments contemplated mutiny. Failed uprisings within the ranks two months later shook the Continental Army to the core.[7]

Among the most trenchant critics of Congress's handling of finances was General George Washington's aide-de-campe, Alexander Hamilton. In fact, by 1779 a rumor was circulating that Hamilton was so disillusioned that he had called for a military overthrow of Congress.[8] The rumor quickly died. But it seemed plausible because of Hamilton's well-known and public criticism of Congress's performance.[9] On the whole Hamilton believed that Congress's lack of central governmental authority and institutions limited its capabilities.[10] To be sure, Hamilton knew that Congress had been downright clever in finding ways to finance the war—securing loans, requisitioning tax revenue from the states, and issuing paper money.[11] Yet Hamilton believed these measures had landed the United States in a fiscal crisis. The biggest disaster was the paper money system, in which Congress printed bills of credit to stimulate spending until a later date when Congress would redeem the bills with revenue from unspecified "taxes." Deflation sank the value the bills to dangerous depths in 1779 before Congress abandoned the scheme shortly afterward.[12] Without paper money, Congress was grateful for $10 million in loans from Dutch bankers and the French and Spanish treasuries. Without the ability to pay off these loans, however, Congress lost its line of credit abroad.[13]

In a treatise-like letter on political economy from late 1779 or early 1780, Hamilton called for a new central government that would emulate European states by borrowing heavily to finance war. France, England, the United Provinces, Russia, Prussia, Denmark, and Sweden, among others, had borrowed to bankroll military activities in no way dissimilar to the War of Independence. For Hamilton it was obvious that the United States, too, should have procured a more substantial "foreign loan."[14] The European method of using tax revenue to service loans was equally attractive. Moreover, the ability to raise revenue by taxation would convince creditors to continue to lend to the United States.[15] Finally Hamilton called for a "Bank of the United States"—essentially an American version of the Bank of England—to loan money to the government and issue money.[16] Hamilton's comprehensive proposal of loans, taxes, and a national bank echoed a model of European fiscal statecraft that went back to the era of Jean-Baptiste Colbert.[17]

Hamilton believed that the creation of these fiscal-military institutions would transform American society. Above all, these institutions would give the state the cultural power to sow "confidence" among the people, and specifically, among the wealthy. Wan congressional administration had provoked a negative "opinion, a want of confidence," among hearts and minds in the marketplace. Winning over public opinion was well nigh impossible with a government that lacked any semblance of central authority. Hamilton's program would suffer from no such defects. The proposed national bank, in particular, could "unite the interest and credit of rich individuals with those of the state," and could in turn "accomplish the restoration of public credit, and establish a permanent fund for the future exigencies of government."[18]

But the main obstacle to Hamilton's program in late 1779 was "a want of power in Congress." Hamilton's solution was another hallmark of the great European states and empires: central governance. If the United States government was to have any real authority it must operate from the center of society. Hamilton believed that the United States had already created a central authority—by declaring war, printing money, and engaging in diplomacy—which had subsequently gone dormant.[19] Awakening this central governmentality required explicitly granting the federal government exclusive if vital tasks: military policy, the "power of the purse," and the taxing and regulation of commerce.[20] But creating or resurrecting these central government powers was only half of the story, and the other half dealt with the vexing issue of administration. The Continental Congress, Hamilton believed, merely "attempts to play the executive," what with its labyrinthine structure and division of labor. By contrast, the central government imagined by Hamilton could "act with sufficient decision, or with system" through its bureaus, each manned by armies of clerks and auditors. The "single man" in charge of each bureau would use his executive authority to ensure that government worked with "more zeal and attention."[21]

After his unceremonious departure from Washington's side in February 1781, Hamilton took to print to publicize his vision for a new American state. Between July and August of the same year, he penned four entries of the *Continentalist*, which was published in the *New York Packet, and the American Advertiser*, to curry support for reforming "the powers of the Confederation."[22] Congress was already thinking along the same lines, especially Representative Robert Morris of Pennsylvania. Morris, a merchant of significant means, had watched the debacle of Congress from within, as chairman of the Secret Committee that managed much of Congress's materiel procurement, between 1775 and 1778. In February 1781, Congress commissioned Morris to serve as Superintendent of the Office of Finance, or, as he would come to be known, as financier of the United States. The creation of the position alone signaled a thaw in sentiments toward the European model of statecraft, for the best-known examples of effective financiering were "*Colbert*, under Louis *XIV* and Mr. *Neckar*," according to political economist Pelatiah Webster.[23] Webster here referenced Jean-Baptiste Colbert and the Swiss-born financier of France, Jacques Necker. Necker had reshaped a creaky French tax system with an eye to collecting sufficient revenue to make interest payments on national debts to facilitate further loans to the French state.[24] Between Hamilton's quill and Morris's promotion, momentum seemed to be gathering for a reconstitution of central government.

As superintendent of finance, Morris's main task was to restore public credit. He proposed a financing scheme that mirrored developments in Stuart England and ancien régime France: to make the national debt into a securitized or funded debt for investors to purchase, and to which the government would make only interest payments during the war.[25] For Morris, one key to this mechanism was customs revenue. European revenue systems from the previous several centuries had established customs or impost duties as among the most reliable forms of taxation—although there was significant skepticism about their efficiency.[26] Moreover, almost all of the colonial governments had used imposts in one way or another.[27] The impost was so common because it offered "several advantages over other kinds of taxes." First, it centralized tax collection at a single point—the custom house. There would be no tax collectors roaming through the town and countryside, harassing families for payment. Second, merchants and merchants alone paid the taxes—in essence "advancing" revenue to the government—and then recouped their loss by passing along the tax to consumers. The government reaped revenue from commerce, and merchants recovered their profits through commerce. The impost, in other words, was a creature of commerce.[28]

However, Morris would never get his impost. In 1780, James Madison was among those who recommended that the states adopt a duty of 2.5 percent on imports and exports and give Congress the power to appoint officers to collect this revenue.[29] But in 1782 Rhode Island thwarted the national impost to protect its own revenue system that depended on a state impost. New York then followed suit.[30] Having lost this battle over the impost, Morris opened up a cultural front to sway public opinion in his favor. In Europe, while the modern state had achieved the capability to reach into everyday life in subtle, even obscure ways, it also sought to exert control over the production of knowledge, especially to influence the hearts and minds of the citizenry. Colbert had once been the "information master," with a bevy of humanists to call upon to assemble data and compose works to bolster the state's reputation. Robert Walpole had employed a team of bards to serve as the "antidote" to Whig rhetorical excesses. Jacques Necker preferred trendy prints for circulating the majesty of the state and its ministries.[31] Morris lacked the resources of his counterparts, but he did have a powerful propagandist at his disposal. In September 1781, Morris "sent for Thos. Paine Esqr. Author of Pamphlet called Common Sense and several other and proposed that for the Service of the Country he should write and publish such Pieces respecting the propriety, Necessity and Utility of Taxation." Paine, who had fallen on hard times, accepted the position for an annual salary of $800 with the promise to keep silent about the arrangement.[32]

Morris's public campaign to build support for the impost failed, but it nonetheless promoted the necessity for a more energetic central government during a moment of political crisis. Even in recalcitrant Rhode Island, the issue sparked a debate in the *Providence Gazette* over whether the people desired "a strong nationality" through the impost or whether the proposal was merely the Stamp Act in disguise, and whether "customs officers [were to] be introduced from without" or whether they were to be local officeholders. Virginia, too, would hinder the adoption of a national impost in 1783. Nonetheless, a majority of legislators in that state embraced the theory of "a rigorous, state-centered mercantilist system" when they adopted the Virginia Port Bill of 1784. In New York, Governor George Clinton created a formidable state impost at the expense of the national purse. Yet the debate over control of this branch of taxation served as the catalyst for Hamilton's *Continentalist* essays, and transformed the state assembly into a rhetorical laboratory of American statecraft.[33]

The need for a national impost was heightened by Morris's inability to coax the states into forking over long-promised tax revenue to the federal government. Beginning with the first congressional requisition of 1781, states were to produce several million dollars each. With no power to compel the states to comply, however, the federal government could not depend on this revenue source. [34] In the 1780s, in fact, the requisition system yielded only $5.1 million of the expected $13.7 million, or roughly 37 percent. Some states that attempted to aggressively collect the taxes faced disaster. In Connecticut, citizens refused en masse to pay the requisitions, while in New Hampshire and Massachusetts individuals took to arms.[35]

Alexander Hamilton witnessed the sorry demise of the requisition system firsthand, as the federal government's requisition collector for New York. With no actual power to collect taxes from New Yorkers, Hamilton besieged New York Treasurer Comfort Sands and the state legislature for help but received nothing but empty assurances. In late August 1782, Hamilton announced his resignation.[36] But in his short tenure as a requisition collector he learned a great deal about how taxation worked in practice. New York had plenty of wealth that should have translated to tax revenue. New York's problem, however, lay in the institutions that existed to collect the taxes: state supervisors, county assessors, and local tax collectors were all elected offices. This meant that electoral politics, and the local attitude toward taxation, influenced the degree to which taxes would be collected. As Hamilton observed to Morris, "If the collector happens to be a zealous man and lives in a zealous neighbourhood the taxes are collected; if either of these requisites is wanting the collection languishes or intirely fails." The power to tax was useless unless the officers that collected the tax operated beyond the reach of the "neighbourhood."[37]

In the next few years Hamilton continued to trumpet the need for the impost and an empowered central government in the Continental Congress and the New York Assembly. In Congress between November 1782 and July 1783 Hamilton involved himself in legislative committees relating to the impost, national finance, and other means to "cement the union," though he enjoyed little success.[38] Before departing Congress to return to private life, Hamilton authored a resolution demanding a "Convention to Amend the Articles of Confederation." Among his key points was an argument for a national impost, "because duties on commerce, when moderate, are one of the agreeable and productive species."[39] After winning election to the New York legislature in 1786, Hamilton continued to hammer away at the necessity of the impost. Yet he faced a formidable opponent in the figure of Governor Clinton, who opposed losing New York's lucrative state impost revenue to the central government. It was only when Hamilton reached the Constitutional Convention—accompanied by Clintonite handlers—that his vision of a national impost began to have any real chance of reaching fruition.[40] For the first time since the war, Hamilton had an audience with men interested in advancing the state of "continental politics," as Hamilton had once called it.[41]

At the Constitutional Convention Hamilton contemplated the obstacles that stood in the way of his vision for a new federal government. "The English model was the only good one on this subject," he began, during his first address to the convention on June 18, 1787. The British monarchy and Parliament governed because their authority circulated in everyday life. The federal government lacked this reach. Americans' political identities were anchored to their states because of local and family ties as well as the tangible government services that the states provided. In 1787 the federal government amounted to nothing more than debt, obscure policy debates, and more debt. It lacked any kind of esprit de corps. The states also possessed a rule of law, but there was no such thing as yet as federal law. And when states faced an insurrectionary challenge to the rule of law, they possessed ample civil and military means to respond. This was not the case for the federal government.[42]

Administering this new federal government posed even greater challenges. The main concern was the relationship between the center of government and officeholders on the periphery. Hamilton confronted this problem of command in a "plan" that he presented to the convention shortly after his opening address.

> I Its practicability to be examined—
> Immense extent unfavourable to representation—
> Vast expence
> Double setts of officers—
> Difficulty of judging local circumstances—

> Distance has a physical effect upon mens minds—
> Difficulty of drawing proper characters from home—
> —Execution of laws feeble at a distance from government—particularly in the collection of revenue—
> Sentiment of Obedience }
> Opinion   }[43]

The "Immense extent" of the continent made it "unfavourable to representation" by federal officers. Overcoming this dilemma by appointing many officers would be a "Vast expence." What about conflicts between state and federal officers? If the national government and the states employed tax collectors, and both "setts of" officials coerced the people, would not the people object that they were being unduly taxed? And given that Americans political identities were chiefly local, it was imaginable that they would prioritize paying local taxes while ignoring their national taxes.[44] Distance worsened these already formidable problems. On the periphery, the "Execution of laws [was] feeble at a distance from government ," especially when it came to "the collection of revenue." This was due in part to the character of the officers who might represent the central government. Situated as it was so far from the daily routine of governing, the central government would struggle to enlist "proper characters." Had Hamilton desired to elicit a collective chuckle from his fellow delegates, he might have added supporting testimony from Whately, Grenville, Townsend, and the others who had most recently attempted to collect customs taxes from a great distance from the North American waterfront. Indeed, as Hamilton had identified, something happened to central governmental laws and institutions as they migrated to peripheries: "Distance has a physical effect upon mens minds."[45]

After the convention Hamilton became more bullish about the new federal government in the pages of the storied *Federalist*. He clearly believed that the state of emergency caused by Shays' Rebellion underscored his argument like nothing else could, so he invoked the specter of Daniel Shays from the start. Hamilton exhorted: "Let the inconveniences felt everywhere from a lax and ill administration of government, let the revolt of a part of the States of North Carolina, the late menacing disturbances in Pennsylvania, and the actual insurrections and rebellions in Massachusetts, declare——!"[46] He was quick to point to the need for this new government to corral revenue by collecting duties on commerce, both to defray the cost of the military and the "civil list," and to spur investor confidence and facilitate access to loans.[47]

In the *Federalist*, Hamilton also offered concrete arguments in favor of a customs revenue system. Here he was able to draw on familiar points from the impost wars of the 1780s. Indirect taxes on imported goods were far preferable to "unwelcome" taxes on real property. It was not a land tax—it would not tax plantations; it was not a property tax—it would not tax slaves.[48] Also, because the impost tapped into the market, the market would have its say about the impost. "If duties are too high, they lessen the consumption; the collection is eluded; and the product to the treasury is not so great as when they are confined within proper and moderate bounds." Likewise, excessively high duties "would serve to beget a general spirit of smuggling" that injured "the fair trader, and eventually . . . the revenue itself."[49] Again, Great Britain provided an instructive example, for it had become "opulent" while paying "taxes of the indirect kind, from imposts and excises."[50] Hamilton also offered a second familiar argument about the geography and political economy of taxation. With a customs system, taxation occurred within the walls of the custom house, away from public scrutiny. Federal taxation would thus be a distant experience for most Americans. "The operations of the national government . . . falling less immediately under the observation of the mass of citizens," Hamilton writes in "Number XVII," "the benefits derived from it will chiefly be perceived and attended to by speculative men." Here was a central government that would operate "out of sight," as historian Brian Balogh has aptly put it.[51]

Hamilton's arguments in the *Federalist* for a customs revenue system marked the culmination of a transformation in American political economy during the 1780s. By 1788, a new Constitution, and with it a new federal government, were poised to take effect. Hamilton had been instrumental in changing the way the nation's leaders understood central government. He would now come to play a pivotal role in putting the central government into practice.

"FILLING UP THE BLANKS" OF THE POWER TO LAY AND COLLECT DUTIES

Article I, Section 8 of the new Constitution gave Congress the power to "lay Duties" and "Imposts."[52] But it quickly became clear to the first Congress that few people, if anyone, knew what this meant. James Madison,

Hamilton's ally—at least for the moment—was to shepherd the impost law through Congress. But neither Madison nor any of his colleagues knew how to do so. So they hastily repackaged the old, proposed 1783 impost as a "temporary system" and urged quick passage. But it was, quite literally, too punctured with "blanks" to hold water:

> On rum, per gallon,—of a dollar; on all other spirituous liquors—; on molasses—; on Madeira wine—; on all other wines—; on common bohea teas per lb.—; on all other teas—; on pepper—; on brown sugars—; on loaf sugars—; on all other sugars—; on cocoa and coffee—; on all other articles—per cent. on their value at the time and place of importation.[53]

Yet, as Congress moved "that the blanks be filled up," Madison's formidable powers of persuasion were quickly overwhelmed by a torrent of parochialism and sectionalism.[54] The question of enforcement was also vexing. Jeremiah Wadsworth, who would soon be responsible for collecting customs duties for the port of New London, Connecticut, warned of a particularly high duty on liquor that "it never can be collected." What was to stop the American merchant from ignoring the impost altogether? [55]

Madison and his allies argued that an impost could work for the federal government because it had previously worked for the states. Pennsylvania and Virginia tinkered with their imposts a dozen times or more between 1780 and 1787. New York, Maryland, Massachusetts, and Connecticut had also relied on the impost.[56] Pennsylvania's impost seemed the most successful because state officials collected duties on about 800,000 gallons of alcohol. Massachusetts saw a "dramatic rise" in revenue between 1782 and 1784. And in 1789 Boston impost officials successfully collected duties from 422 vessels. The impost seemed to be the best available tool to generate revenue, both in theory and in recent practice.[57]

At least in some states, administration of the impost provoked vigorous legal defenses of the power to tax and regulate commerce.[58] In 1784 the Maryland legislature centralized the state's impost collection "to prevent frauds in the customs." A year later the Virginia legislature, concerned with lackluster collection of duties, "authorized any citizen to seize a vessel that failed to enter legally and pay duties."[59] Judge Edward Shippen of the Philadelphia Court of Common Pleas offered the strongest pronouncement of this sensibility. In an early 1787 impost case, Shippen used his charge to a jury to explain, "The truth is, that revenue laws are of a harsher nature than any others, and necessarily so; for, the devices of ingenious men, render it indispensable for the Legislature to meet their illicit practices with severer penalties." A Philadelphia jury agreed and condemned the *Anna*.[60] In New York, too, the Court of Admiralty seems to have closely guarded the state's revenue interest in strictly enforcing the letter of the 1784 revenue law. The twenty-seven impost-related seizures that appeared before the court between 1785 and 1788 resulted in twenty-three condemnations. Importing merchants like John B. Riolz, who wrongly assumed that they "might with safety" expect to bend rules, or be allowed lenience, quickly learned otherwise. It was "a bad business," concluded Riolz's attorney, Alexander Hamilton.[61]

But could federal customs officers perform as ably as their state counterparts? Again the experience of the Revolution was difficult to ignore. Massachusetts' representative Fisher Ames recalled "the opposition of our people to the British acts of Parliament" before warning, "If the same opinion is entertained with respect to our ordinances, that they will be defeated in a similar manner."[62] In short, what was to guarantee that federal customs officials would not face the same hostility as had imperial customs officers at the height of the Revolution? If history posed a hoary philosophical problem for customs enforcement, geography suggested a new, more concrete crisis. Thomas Tudor Tucker of South Carolina put it best. "We have an extensive sea-coast, accessible at a thousand points, and upon all this coast there are but few custom-houses where officers can be stationed," warned Tucker. Congress could choose to create so great "a number of custom-houses, on those parts of the coast most assailable," but this would be so costly that it would undermine the entire rationale of the impost.[63]

Since the United States could not station federal agents everywhere, would people obey? According to Ames, the one and only way the customs laws would work was if they were supported by the merchants—if "the merchants are to associate, and form a phalanx in our support," and if the merchants' "private honor is to be called in aid of public measures." Even supposing that "the most respectable merchants will disdain to smuggle," did not the law place the United States at the mercy of the "inferior characters, I care not what you call them, infamous parricides, ready to defraud your revenue by evasion, or any other means in their power"?[64] To collect revenue the federal government would have to rely on the "support" of the very class it was taxing and regulating. Republicanism allowed this to seem feasible. Madison believed that customs laws would illustrate to "the citizens of America" that "their individual interest is connected with the public." Virtuous citizens would understand "the necessity of a due collection of the revenue" and would "give all the assistance in the execution of the law that is in their power," according to Connecticut's Roger Sherman. "The mercantile part of the people," Sherman concluded, "will submit themselves . . . and use their influence to aid the collection." Finally, Alexander White of Virginia confronted the problematic legacy of revolutionary agitation at the imperial custom houses by invoking the people's unity in enforcing the revolutionary Non-Importation movements. Then, the people had selflessly forsaken material splendor and profits for the greater good. "Something like this," he was sure, "may be expected to take place now."[65]

As Congress placed its faith in "the mercantile part of the people" to support the customs system, it moved to a more grueling debate about specific items and rates of duty. It was not the first Congress's most shining moment. A few obstructionists stood above the fray. Senator Arthur Lee of Virginia resorted to histrionics—"so tremendous an accent, and so forlorn an aspect, as would have excited even Stoics to laughter," according to William Maclay—until his demands were addressed. Pierce Butler of South Carolina took his seat in the Senate "and flamed like a Meteor" with the repeated charge that the impost, and anything like it, would "ruin South Carolina." Although they gave observers a preview of the tenor of debates over the tariff for decades to come, Lee and Butler would eventually lose their epic rhetorical battles as the Senate and House reconciled their bills by late June.[66] After almost a decade of debate, the United States finally had its impost.

However, Congress slowly reconsidered the wisdom of relying on merchants' virtue to help enforce the tariff. In May 1789 the Maryland delegation approached their state's impost collector, Otho Holland Williams, and asked him to write what would come to be known as the Collection Bill. Williams had been a general in the Continental Army and a confidant of George Washington before returning to Baltimore and taking up his post at the Baltimore custom house. Finding the state's customs laws to be vague and contradictory he took it upon himself "to get [the laws] revised." Most importantly, in a 1784 law, Williams centralized responsibility for the operation of each custom house to a single official for every port.[67] Williams used this 1784 Maryland law as the foundation for what became the lengthy federal Collection Act of 1789—"a most voluminous thing of more than 40 pages," sneered William Maclay derisively. The custom house was now to consist of three officers: a collector of customs, a naval officer, and a surveyor. The collector would make official entry of each vessel, examine the ship's papers to ensure an honest voyage, and be on the lookout for smuggled goods. The naval officer, who would answer to the collector, would calculate the duties. The surveyor was the lowest-ranking of the three and was chiefly in charge of searching the ship's cargo and guarding it while in port (see table 2).[68]

TABLE 2. Duties of Customs Personnel According to the Collection Act of 1789

Officer	Overview of duties
Secretary of the treasury	Although the secretary of the treasury enjoyed official control over the custom houses, most secretaries granted customs officers great administrative autonomy.
Collector of customs	These were the chief officers of the custom house, directly responsible for ensuring the implementation of federal tariff, licensing, and other policies. Inside the custom house, the collector's main duties were recording manifests and crew lists, estimating payment of duties, taking and holding bonds, and receiving and transmitting payment of duties.
Naval officers	These civilian officers were second in command. They often countersigned the collector's documentation. They also provided separate estimates and compiled independent data that could be compared to the collector's. They also corrected errors in daily paperwork.
Surveyors	These men were limited to larger ports. Collectors delegated most daily functions to surveyors in New York, Philadelphia, Boston, Charleston, and New Orleans, among other cities.
Inspectors	In larger ports surveyors delegated search and inspection duties to inspectors.
Weighers	In larger ports, these men reported to surveyors. Weighers recorded the weight of selected ship cargo and compared it to reported weights in the ship manifest.
Gaugers (also measurers)	In larger ports, these men reported to surveyors. Gaugers and measurers dealt primarily with liquid cargo, assuring that the volume of liquid cargo matched that listed in the ship manifest.
Auctioneers	Generally contract employees, auctioneers sold seized or forfeited commodities and transmitted the proceeds to the collector.
Carters	These were short-term employees who hauled cargo from inbound ships into the custom house, whenever necessary.

Source: 1 Statutes at Large 36, 37 (1789).

Williams's vision for how the custom houses should function closely followed British precedent. Collectors and naval officers were present in both systems. The American collectors absorbed the British office of the comptroller of customs, whose "only Duty" had been to collect fees and duties from sea captains. Perhaps the key difference was the importance of the surveyor in the American system. In the 1789 federal law, the surveyor patrolled the wharves, controlled a team that directly inspected vessels, and answered directly to the collector. In the British model, low-ranking "tidesmen" and "waiters" drew this duty, while "surveyors," also of lower rank, patrolled the coastline looking for smuggling vessels. In Williams's legislation the high command of the custom house—the collector, naval officer, and surveyor—directly supervised the daily affairs of the custom house.[69]

The federal customs laws of 1789 also mirrored the jurisdictional system that had arisen under the British navigation laws. The Collection Act superimposed a grid upon the young nation that made "legible" cities and other political units in terms of their economic value and importance to the nation. Each vector of the grid was its own jurisdiction with its own customs personnel.[70] Vessels carrying imported goods were permitted to enter the United States only at the congressionally designated "ports of entry." After the vessel had paid its customs duties, it could then proceed to minor ports, designated "ports of delivery," in order to sell imported goods. The grid, and the vision that undergirded it, were clearly British in origin. As historian Thomas Barrow explains, the idea of a jurisdictional "district" had first gained currency in the British Empire in the late seventeenth century. In this light, the first Congress embraced a broader imperial vision to "comprehend and lay claim to distant lands."[71]

As the United States reintroduced the British ports of entry, and added several new ones, Congress laid claim to a project of radiant, westward economic development that had burgeoned under British rule. The established mercantile metropolises—Boston, New York, Baltimore, and Charleston—had developed trade networks that extended beyond the Appalachians and encroached upon Spanish imperial holdings to the southwest. Yet the law also elevated a host of secondary ports, such as Salem, Sag Harbor, Perth Amboy, and Bermuda Hundred, to this same status.[72] Designation as a port of entry was a wager on these ports' future prosperity. As the republic grew, emerging cities would lobby for a place as a port of entry. This was an important divergence from the colonial experience, where Parliament had designated ports of entry based upon the self-serving advice of London merchant houses and the Board of Trade. Though American merchants and Treasury officials would wield similar influence over Congress, through petitions and memorials the people themselves would have a great deal of ability to place themselves on the customs grid.[73]

Congress also appropriated wholesale the customs bond—the inner connective tissue of the British imperial customs laws. Within the imperial customs system, the bond was an individual merchant's promise of obedience to the numerous aspects of the navigation system. It originated with the Navigation Act of 1660 but quickly became a staple of subsequent legislation. In the British Empire and the early United States, the customs bond was simply a promise to abide by the sovereign's rules of revenue and commerce. In this sense, it was a pledge of good behavior. On the other hand, and with bonds as promises for future payment of customs duties, it was a method of securing performance to fulfill a financial obligation. Above all, though, it was familiar. American merchants were well accustomed to posting bond at imperial custom houses for any manner of customs transactions: to pay duties at a later date, to visit only ports within the British Empire, to refrain from trading with the enemy, and to confirm the loss of official documents, to name a few instances.[74]

The compensation of customs officials was also an important difference between the British and American systems. Both used a "fee system" in which officials were compensated for each official act. As historian Nicholas Parrillo discusses, fees were incentives for officials to perform ably and conscientiously by aligning the execution of laws with the officer's self-interest. But the British had failed to define these fees, first relying on colonial assemblies for a fee schedule, and then on the vague standard of what was "customary" at each port. Predictably, by allowing the colonists to have a say in the matter, fees were a constant source of embarrassment and litigation for imperial customs officials in North America. By contrast, or perhaps in response to this situation, Congress established a uniform "table of fees" for customs officials. Officials in the major ports of Boston, Salem, New York, Philadelphia, Baltimore, Norfolk, and Charleston also received 1.5 percent of the total amount of customs revenue they collected. Congress evidently hoped that this "table of fees" would shield customs officials' purses from meddling by local communities.[75]

Administrative structure was a second major difference between the American and British systems. In the Collection Act, the collector of customs for each customs district reported directly to the secretary of the treasury, rather than to a regional surveyor of customs as under the British imperial system. This came as a surprise to some observers, such as Massachusetts Federalist Theodore Sedgewick, who had expected some equivalent of the surveyor to "superintend the conduct of the officers concerned in the immediate collection of the revenue."[76] There was more to this than met Sedgewick's eye. The colonial custom houses were overwhelmingly imperial creatures under the control of the Treasury and Board of Trade. But naval officers—the second in command—were appointed by, and generally political followers of, the governor of the colony. Colonists had proven adept at using this fragmented authority to pit the naval officers (and thus the governors) against imperial agents (and thus the Treasury). In the federal revenue system, however, the president appointed naval officers with congressional approval. Again, colonial waterfront dwellers taught the first Congress an important lesson about necessary improvements on the imperial customs system.

Legal procedures for customs violations were a third significant departure from British precedent. To be sure, Congress borrowed from British measures in designating most customs cases as in rem proceedings, or suits against vessels and seized goods, as opposed to in personam proceedings against owners or crew. The next step in a prosecution was also the same, as the collector of customs acted in a semipublic, semiprivate capacity and "informed" against the vessel by filing an "information" with the court. This made the customs officer the libelant. The owner of the libeled vessel or goods in question could file a claim, but if not, the items were forfeited to the government for sale, with the proceeds split between the Treasury for customs duties and the customs officer for his service as an informer. Where the two systems diverged was in the matter of jurisdiction. Parliament had long struggled with how to prosecute customs cases in front of hostile local juries until notoriously turning to Vice-Admiralty Courts in distant climes, much to the fury of colonists enraged over the loss of their constitutional right to be tried before their peers. On the other hand, the United States' customs system benefited from the existence of the lower federal courts. The Judiciary Act of 1789 apportioned a district court for every judicial district in the country, thus allowing prosecutions to remain local, but at once, national. Moreover, because Hamilton and Madison classified violations of customs laws as crimes against the federal treasury, subsequent proceedings were executed as criminal or debt cases under federal law, rather than under judge-made admiralty law. Merchants could no longer complain about being deprived of a trial by jury.[77]

This landscape of public law would constitute the foundation of the customs system for the next century. The United States had designed a customs system along British, imperial lines. What remained was to select people to operate this system, and then, finally, to bring it to life. The first of these tasks fell to President George Washington, and the second to his first secretary of the treasury, Alexander Hamilton.[78]

ALL THE PRESIDENT'S MEN

President Washington had to find 134 officers to fill positions in thirty-nine ports of entry. When Washington weighed appointments to the upper echelons of government, he prioritized finding men of reputation and distinction—"the first characters" of the Union. Finding personnel for the custom houses would be a bit more complicated.[79]

Interested parties inundated Washington with applications for positions in the ports, often with accompanying letters of support from men of influence or Washington's inner circle. From this mass of papers Washington tried to ferret out "Facts and testimonials" about the job seekers.[80] Washington left little information behind about how he managed to do this. Yet the first class of customs officials suggests a few basic standards, the most importance of which was competence. Competence was measured by the individual's experience collecting revenue or enforcing laws, the respect and deference paid to him in his community, or his support of the new Constitution.[81]

Applicants for custom-house jobs emphasized their expertise, community standing, and ideological commitment. Applicants wrote of their experiences to convey their sense of public duty and personal responsibility. Their applications suggest various understandings of the nature and character of the new nation's presidency, appealing to Washington's benevolence, militarism, political economy, and governance. The very novelty of the situation explains their different approaches. Washington, like other national leaders at this pivotal, formative moment, stood on "unstable ground with no path to safety."[82] Universally, these applications also featured support from politicians on the national scene with strong ties to George Washington, such as Richard Henry Lee, Charles Pinckney, James Bowdoin, Edmund Pendleton, and Thomas Jefferson.[83]

Of the 102 applicants who successfully attained office in this initial run, a dozen pulled at Washington's heartstrings and told stories of personal and familiar hardship. Most blamed the market or the war for their plight. Robert Ballard, who would gain a position in the Baltimore custom house, was unlucky enough to experience both the "sufferings of the unfortunate Soldier" and a scheme to "speculate to my distruction." Sharp Delany of Philadelphia cut a more elite jib than Ballard but nonetheless resorted to similar tactics. Washington knew Delany from the ranks of the Continental Army. He had lost his modest wealth in Congress's paper money and had "my property seized by the British" to boot. These "reasons of a private nature," he hoped, would convince Washington to appoint him collector of Philadelphia. In both instances, the applicants also emphasized their virtuous, public personae. They were good men in difficult times.[84]

Veterans appear to have believed that service in the great war entitled them to a government office. Many used language that aimed to make Washington recall his own military past. William Heth of Bermuda Hundred reminded Washington that his "pursuits and conduct in life are not unknown to you." Heth and many others could well have been addressing *General* Washington. After Washington resigned his command in December 1783, he became a living mythological hero who would forever be remembered in military dress.[85] As veterans invoked their military service, and raised the specter of General Washington, they were also suggesting that they knew how to follow orders. The preponderance of military men in the first class of customs officials suggests that Washington agreed. Despite a checkered battlefield record, Jeremiah Olney was considered a "distinguished war hero" by the time he accepted the collectorship of Providence, Rhode Island. Likewise, John Ross, of Burlington, New Jersey, had rapidly climbed the ranks of the New Jersey regiment from third captain in 1776 to lieutenant colonel by the end of the war. By the time of his appointment, Ross, too, was known for his "excellent service during the war." Almost every major custom house fell to the command of a high-ranking officer: Generals John Lamb in New York, Benjamin Lincoln in Boston, and Jedediah Huntington in New London; Captains Sharp Delany in Philadelphia and Isaac Holmes in Charleston. These men had already forged a bond of trust with Washington. Perhaps this trust would be a cure for the pathological withering of central governmental authority as it was stretched over long distances?[86]

For some, particularly high-ranking military officials, a second associational affiliation was important: membership in the Society of the Cincinnati. In the early 1780s, senior officers had created the Society to preserve the centralized might of the Continental Army in a civilian, associational form. The Society had a national structure with a federal secretariat, state associations, and local chapters.[87] Washington's selection of active Society members to serve as customs officials suggests that although charges of conspiracy are off the mark, the Society of the Cincinnati did ultimately influence the character of central government in the early United States. William Heth, Jeremiah Olney, Jedediah Huntington, Jeremiah Wadsworth, Otho Holland Williams, and Benjamin Lincoln were all noteworthy Society members who landed custom-house appointments. Alexander Hamilton was also active in the Society. In the aggregate, 37 of Washington's 178 customs appointees, or about 20 percent, were members of the Society.[88]

That so many members of the Society of the Cincinnati found their way into the custom houses suggests that Washington did pay a great deal of attention to political ideology. Most in the Cincinnati supported the new Constitution. But more broadly, they shared a vision of an orderly, republican society. William Ellery, who would receive the collectorship at Newport, Rhode Island, gave voice to this sentiment in an Independence Day toast some years later: "No tumults here will thrive, / While hoary veterans live / To guard the State; / Their swords, for public law / And order, they will draw, / Excite submissive awe / In Empire great." [89]

Applicants with a background in the state impost and revenue systems stood a good chance of getting a custom-house position. The language that these applicants and their recommenders used is telling, for they requested that these men "continue" in the office. George Abbott Hall, a South Carolinian "gentleman," requested that the president consider "continuing me in the Office of Collector of the port under the new Government which I have held for the State since the Revolution." In New Hampshire, Nathaniel Fosdick had been "naval officer for this Port . . . for some time past," and asked for a "continuation in the office under the new government." In Marblehead, Richard Harris hoped Washington would find no trouble "in reappointing me to the Office." In each of these instances, the applicants suggested an odd paradox: they wished to be "continued" in an office, although the office they actually sought was an entirely new creation of the new United States government. The paradox, though, is easily explained. Hall, Fosdick, and Harris all knew that they would be occupying a new, federal office, but they suspected that, in practice, their duties would be quite similar to what they had been under the state impost laws. The custom house might even be the very same building used by the state regime and quite possibly the British Empire.[90]

Washington chose to "continue" men in office because they had expertise in collecting revenue and implementing regulations in the world of Atlantic trade. The failure of the Articles of Confederation has quite possibly cloaked the degree to which this infrastructure of taxing and regulatory power was available to the founders in the first days of the new republic. In the 1780s, several states appointed officers to experiment with impost schemes. Disbanding or overlooking these networks of officialdom would have robbed Washington of one of the few advantages he had in establishing the new federal government. There was some measure of republican principle at play, too; as a candidate for a position in Savannah put it, he was "the choice of the people." This official, it turned out, had not been elected at all. Nevertheless, by "continuing" state impost officials at the federal custom houses Washington was deferring to the previous wisdom of the states (see table 3).[91]

There was also a more subtle reason to favor "continued" candidates. For the merchants who were to pay customs duties, and submit their goods and vessels for customs inspections, the experience of encountering the very same officer at the custom house who had manned the post for several years past would obscure the operations of the new central government behind established routine. To be sure, the Constitution of 1787 and the creation of the new United States was a radical, institutional break with the past. But "continuing" officers in the new federal custom houses had the effect of cloaking the central state in the mantle of the familiar. This was why, for instance, Washington was willing to appoint as rabid an anti-Federalist as John Lamb to the New York custom house, where Lamb had been collector for several years. Lamb was not only an anti-Federalist, but he was also a noted Clintonite and an equally noted opponent of Alexander Hamilton. But Lamb was a familiar figure in and around the custom house in lower Manhattan. Lamb, it seems, had conscientiously done his duty in ferreting out smuggled goods with a small crew of inspectors, cartmen, and measurers, including surveyor John Lasher, who would also be "continued." This institutional history, and New Yorkers' familiarity with John Lamb, bore more weight for George Washington than Lamb's politics.[92]

Policy allegiances, ideological commitment, displays of virtue, military backgrounds, and experience in revenue collection came together to form a "regime of notables," as scholars have recently put it. The men that Washington appointed were, in fact, "notable" in the sense of their accomplishments. Yet, Washington turned to these notables, not simply in deference to elite figures, but precisely because their authority was already woven into the everyday, routine, social fabric of American life.[93]

In the span of only a few months, George Washington and the first Congress had built the foundation of a national revenue system for the United States. This was a remarkable achievement, given the complexity of the issue and the incredible hostility to central governmental taxation just a

TABLE 3. Washington's "Continued" State Impost Officials as Federal Customs Officials, 1789

Port	Officer	Position sought
Savannah	John Berrien	Surveyor
Savannah	Benjamin Fishbourne	Naval officer (rejected)
Charleston	George Abbott Hall	Collector
Norfolk	William Lindsay	Collector
Norfolk	Daniel Bedinger	Surveyor
West Point (VA)	John Spotswood Moore	Surveyor
Tappahannock	Hudson Muse	Collector
Alexandria	Charles Lee	Collector
Alexandria	Richard M Scott	Surveyor
Annapolis	John Davidson	Collector
Georgetown (MD)	James W. C. Lingan	Collector
Upper Potomac	John C. Jones	Collector
Baltimore	Otho Holland Williams	Collector
Philadelphia	Frederick Phile	Naval officer
Philadelphia	Sharp Delany	Collector
Burlington (NJ)	John Ross	Collector
New York	John Lamb	Collector
New York	John Lasher	Surveyor
Boston	John Lovell	Naval officer
Charlestown	Thomas Melville	Surveyor
Falmouth (NH)	Nathaniel Fosdick	Collector
Barnstable	Joseph Otis	Collector

Source: Letterbook 22, Series 2, George Washington Papers, LOC.

few years before. Congress had divided the nation into customs districts, apportioned custom houses for the districts, and set down the basic regulations and procedures for collecting revenue and enforcing customs law. Washington nominated a corps of officers to fill the ranks. This was a political economic revolution that rivaled in importance the political revolution that produced it.

Importantly, though, before the new federal government could even consider circulating its authority throughout the nation, it first had to learn to command commerce. This was the lesson of empires and nation-states past.[94] Without central governmental control over the commercial marketplace, the federal government would be unable to collect the revenue that was necessary for it to act in all other spheres. It would also be unable to compete in the contests of empires and nations by regulating channels of trade. But these were not matters that could be solved in convention halls, partisan debates, or even appointments. Instead, they would be determined in practice, on the waterfront, in the far messier, overlapping worlds of commerce and governance.

CHAPTER THREE

Negotiating Authority in Federalist America, 1789–1800

By the summer of 1789 the time had come "to put the government in motion." In the preceding months, Congress had created a federal tariff and designated custom houses for ports throughout the nation. George Washington selected a small army of officeholders for these custom houses.¹ Now Washington turned to his able secretary of the treasury, Alexander Hamilton, to put the machinery of government into gear. Hamilton was an ideal choice. No one else had spent as much time pondering how the United States could build a central government, and no one else had argued as fervently in favor of the central government that emerged from the pages of the Constitution.²

Governing, of course, bore little resemblance to pamphlet wars or convention hall oratory. And at stake in Hamilton's performance were vital material and ideological matters. Revenue was paramount. Only by collecting customs duties could the Treasury pay debts and prove to its creditors that the United States was creditworthy. The young nation also needed to prove it was no pretender among a class of competitors who watched closely for weakness. Finally, the British fiscal-military model that Hamilton so passionately advocated for was also on the line. If the custom houses did not fulfill their promise, the consequences would be dire.³

Upon entering office in September 1789, Hamilton had little to build on. The books from the old Treasury Board were "constantly blank" or missing. No accounting system for tracking revenue, expenditures, and paperwork was to be found.⁴ The Treasury would also need to figure out how to communicate with the customs officials on the waterfront. On all of these fronts the Treasury would be surprisingly successful. By 1793 the custom houses were the federal government's sole reliable and significant stream of revenue. Within the Treasury, strict accounting procedures imposed order on the huge volume of commercial and fiscal data flowing from the custom houses to the Treasury. Organized correspondence connected the Treasury with the customs officials on the periphery. The quiet order and confidence that overtook the customs system and the Treasury in these early years are clear in Hamilton's masterworks, including the "Report on Public Credit" (1790) and the "Report on Manufactures" (1791). On the basis of this archive, Hamilton's contemporary admirers and critics, as well as several generations of scholars in the field of history, quite rightly identify the emergence of a "strong" central government.

Yet Hamilton's tidy accounting methods and his teeming political economic writings effaced a momentous contest at the custom houses. Almost as soon as the new customs laws went into effect, it became clear to customs officials—and eventually to Hamilton—that importing merchants and others who did business at the custom house expected to influence waterfront governance. This expectation had grown up in and around British imperial custom houses during the previous century, and neither revolution nor war nor a new constitution had displaced it. As they had for most of the eighteenth century to that point, American importing merchants and other commercial peoples swayed customs officials' everyday practices of governance on the waterfront—how they collected customs duties, how they interpreted and implemented federal laws—to favor their own commercial interests. Where, then, was the location of central governmental authority in the new republic? Who would determine the meaning and fabric of governmental authority?

As the negotiated authority between officeholders and customs officials that had loomed so large in the British Empire appeared once again under the new federal government, Hamilton was initially unnerved. After all, for all its success in using colonial commerce to expand its sphere of influence, the British Empire had never been much good at collecting revenue at the custom houses. So it was perhaps understandable that in the earliest days of the new federal government Hamilton spilled much ink emphasizing the rule of law, demanding uniform execution of laws, and disseminating his own instructions, to little avail. Yet the pressure that Hamilton exerted on customs officials paled in comparison to that applied by local importing merchants, who demanded that custom-house governance favor commerce, even at the cost of federal policies. In the first years of the new republic, the state itself was up for grabs.[5]

But something remarkable was happening: the revenue machine was working. The haunting initial questions about whether the federal government would be able to collect customs duties dissipated as multiple negotiations took shape involving merchants, customs officers, and the Treasury. Importing merchants paid customs duties but gained the ability to influence governance at the custom house. Customs officials transferred revenue to the Treasury but satisfied local merchants. And the Treasury accounted for the nation's precious revenue without alienating merchant capitalists.

By the time Hamilton abruptly resigned from Washington's cabinet in 1795, the federal government seemed to resemble two states rather than one. On the one hand, on the waterfront, government authority ebbed and flowed with the tides of commerce, and with the myriad negotiations that aligned customs law with local merchant communities. Hamilton was increasingly reluctant to enter this world. But he did not need to, because, as he discovered, a state was also to be built in words, numbers, and polemics, which would circulate in the public sphere at home and abroad. And he was in command of this state.

THE INVENTION OF NATIONAL SOVEREIGNTY

"Sir, The exigencies of Government require that I should without delay be informed of the amount of the Duties which have accrued in the several States, and the Monies which have been already received in payment of them, and the periods at which the remained will fall due." So read Secretary of the Treasury Alexander Hamilton's first "Circular," in September 1789, to his subordinate officers, the collectors of customs throughout the United States. His purpose in writing was to account for how much money the government had on hand, and how much it could count on having in the near future. This simple calculation was part of a basic act of accounting fundamental to modern states, according to historian Patricia Cline Cohen.[6] Surprisingly, however, Hamilton informed his collectors that "in this absolute precision is not expected, but a General Statement *accurate enough in the main to be relied on*." Accuracy was less important than "reliability" in Hamilton's calculations of the federal government's revenue.[7]

Between 1789 and 1794, Hamilton's Treasury developed accounting systems for revenue and commercial development to build confidence in the new federal government.[8] It was particularly important to generate confidence among the nation's creditors in the United States and Europe by showing the reliability of the nation's tax system. Hamilton hoped that these creditors, when faced with statistical evidence, would hold their public securities and, perhaps even more importantly, extend further credit to the United States. Then there was Congress. Hamilton hoped to convince Congress that his Treasury was not only capable of governing, but trustworthy enough to manage an even more ambitious agenda of statecraft. Orderly accounts were vital to creating political authority.[9]

Hamilton's first duty was to organize the Treasury in New York City. Legislation of September 2, 1789, made clear that the secretary of the treasury was "head of the department." Hamilton now filled subordinate offices with "numerical amateurs," a class of men without formal training in statistics, but with skill and interest in numeracy. His own assistant was to be the infamous William Duer, whose moral imperfections far outweighed both his considerable amateurism and his stunning numeracy. But Duer was the exception, and Hamilton chose wisely for the other key posts. Connecticut Federalist Oliver Wolcott Jr. would serve as auditor, and receive accounts and calculate debits and credits. Wolcott had distinguished himself as a state commissioner to settle wartime accounts with the federal government. Equally important was the register, the Treasury's de facto archivist of "receipts and expenditures" and all other papers. Here Hamilton turned to Joseph Nourse, who had served in a similar capacity under Morris's Treasury Board. Federalist Nicholas Eveleigh of South Carolina was named comptroller and would oversee customs officials' accounts of collected revenue and determine "final settlements" between officers and the Treasury.[10]

The Treasury was immediately flooded with paper. Most of this was official correspondences from the custom houses. Collectors dispatched weekly returns of the number of ships that passed through, the character of their commerce ("coastwise" or foreign), revenue collected, bills collected and paid, licenses distributed or revoked, and expenditures. At first, Hamilton prioritized "precise data" over the form of these accounts.[11] By the end of 1789, however, Hamilton devised "forms" and detailed instructions. "The public Service requires the strictest Care & punctuality in adhering to the forms now established, and in forwarding them regularly to this office," wrote Hamilton. "Care," in this context, meant that the accounts should contain all the requested information as well as supporting documentation, such as "Receipts." "Punctuality" meant that "the Returns required, may be certain of reaching me, with as little delay as possible." Forms, returns, accounts, care, and punctuality—these were the mechanisms and standards that Alexander Hamilton used to organize the federal government's fiscal affairs.[12]

The content of the forms merits mention. The "Impost Book" was "the principal ground of work of the whole business and some pains have been taken to make it as perfect as possible," explained Eveleigh. It was a large folio volume with columns for the date, arriving vessels, ports of origin, masters' names, goods, and duties owed. Collectors were ordered to attach a copy of each vessel's goods and duties paid "as vouchers to the Impost book" in case of future controversy.[13] The "Tonnage Book" ticked off each vessel and noted its status as a domestic or international trader. A "Drawback Book" held information on imported goods that were subsequently reexported to foreign markets and upon which merchants received bounties from the Treasury. Customs officials were also required to "keep a regular Journal and Ledger" with duties collected and custom-house expenditures. It was vital that these books appear as neat as possible. Thus there was little room anywhere on their pages for notes or calculations. For those operations, and anything that might disrupt the tidy operations of classification and calculation, officials were "to use a rough Blotter or Day Book."[14]

The Treasury Department wanted no part in wading through the sheer mass of data stored at the custom houses, so it issued succinct forms for officials to summarize their accounts. The collector was to compare his information on duties collected from all sources available at the custom house before translating the hulking Impost Book into a quarterly aggregate for the Treasury. The other forms became brief "abstracts," the most important of which were drawback bounties, employee pay, and accounts of bonds "taken and discharged."[15] In these forms there was no room for the personal. In fact, Hamilton required that officials convey revenue and trade information "separate from your letters, and unconnected with any other matter." The numbers had to speak for themselves. Even when there were no numbers. For Hamilton, even "if no business" had occurred, it was still "absolutely necessary" for customs officials to return a blank abstract. Without these forms, even the blank ones, he explained, "no reliance can be placed on statements of this office, relating to the business of the Custom House."[16]

The Treasury's autumn 1789 informational project mirrored English Treasury reforms of the seventeenth and early eighteenth century. As John Brewer writes, English tax officials collected a tangle of information that "was often organized in statistical, tabular or mathematical form: lists of ships entering and leaving ports; tables of prices; accounts, broken down by commodity and region, of tax returns; aggregates of military manpower and occupational data"—all for use by heads of state. Hamilton's was a more modest operation. It was precisely this smaller scale that gave Hamilton greater control over revenue information than his British counterparts had typically enjoyed. As late as 1780, Edmund Burke had thundered away at "traces of feudality" that hindered the central government from taking its due—or even knowing how much it was owed. "A beggarly account of empty boxes," he chided the government's audit power, channeling his inner bard, in comparing the Exchequer to the seedy apothecary that produced the western world's most famous tragedy. By 1791, as Hamilton's accounting systems fell into place, no such criticism could be leveled at the United States Treasury and custom houses.[17]

Armed with a remarkable "storehouse" of information spawned by these accounting practices, Hamilton set out on a campaign to persuade Congress and President Washington to follow his vision of fiscal-military political economy. Between 1789 and 1795 Hamilton "communicated" to Congress twenty-one documents teeming with calculations of "duties," "imports," "exports," and "value." These "reports" called for the immediate creation of new fiscal institutions—for instance, federal assumption of state debts, a national bank, monetization of national debt in interest-bearing bonds—that would give the young United States the political-economic spine of the English state that emerged around the time of the Glorious Revolution.[18] Hamilton's monopoly over the information coming from the custom houses also lent his grandiose proposals an unmatched authority.[19] In this regard, James Madison's use of congressional inquiries to harass Hamilton and embarrass the Treasury may have been counterproductive. Even on the defensive, Hamilton "published and published and published" no less than fifteen pamphlets—some by order of the House of Representatives—to take his campaign of persuasion directly to the people.[20]

Hamilton's persuasion campaign was also aimed abroad. For one thing, Hamilton's publications offered a far more sanguine view of the American future than the leading tract of the day, the Earl of Sheffield's patronizing *Observations on the Commerce of the United States*, which cast the United States as a bit player in a global economy centered on London. By contrast Hamilton offered an optimistic "projection" of American development. Pride was not the only thing at stake. The same foreign bankers on whom the United States depended for fiscal solvency believed "that it has become so absolutely indispensable to sovereigns to preserve their credit with money lenders." Hamilton's reports, and the visions built in and upon them, were material evidence of the United States' rambunctious legitimacy.[21]

Hamilton's accounting systems made it possible to produce knowledge about the United States' newly forged legitimacy. Citizens, creditors, and foreign powers alike could see, in Hamilton's reports, the United States government's successful exercise of sovereignty. The organization of this archive reflected precisely what its organizers wanted contemporaries and future generations to locate in its ledgers, accounts, and publications. Indeed, Hamilton's enemies would quickly fixate on the efficiency of the Treasury as evidence of the secretary's megalomania and antirepublican thirst for power. Since then, of course, Hamilton's reports have served as shorthand evidence of the Federalists' formidable central government. To be sure, Hamilton achieved a great deal in the fiscal reforms detailed in these reports. Yet the means of their production is itself an important story.[22]

But as Hamilton translated custom-house information into his eloquent reports, he propagated a fiction. Historians Stanley Elkins and Eric McKitrick have argued that Hamilton's arguments in his "Report on Public Credit" and other seminal works hinged on "a characteristic device" known as "projection," or "an ordering of facts and circumstances into patterns which present conditions have not as yet made actual but which future ones will." That is to say, Hamilton's reports made the young United States appear to be a new fiscal-military state on the up. In reality, however, Hamilton's writings masked a harshly different reality in which contingency and conflict seemed poised to subvert the new federal establishment.[23]

THE BONDS OF GOVERNANCE

As customs officials dutifully dispatched statistical abstracts to the Treasury in 1789, they found themselves in a bewildering, liminal position astride the state and the Atlantic market. The crux of the problem was not so different from the dilemma that faced judges in early America: heart or head? Reason suggested following the letter of the law. Human considerations suggested doing otherwise.[24] Above all, the merchants and men of the market who passed through the custom house and who inhabited the waterfront made it virtually impossible for customs officials to enforce laws as Congress and the Treasury had envisioned. Customs officials throughout the country would face a daily struggle to interpret and implement laws to satisfy the government or the local commercial communities in which they lived.

A big part of the problem was that the laws themselves provided little guidance. This was true even for Otho Holland Williams, the man who had written the Collection Act for Congress. He complained that "the dif-

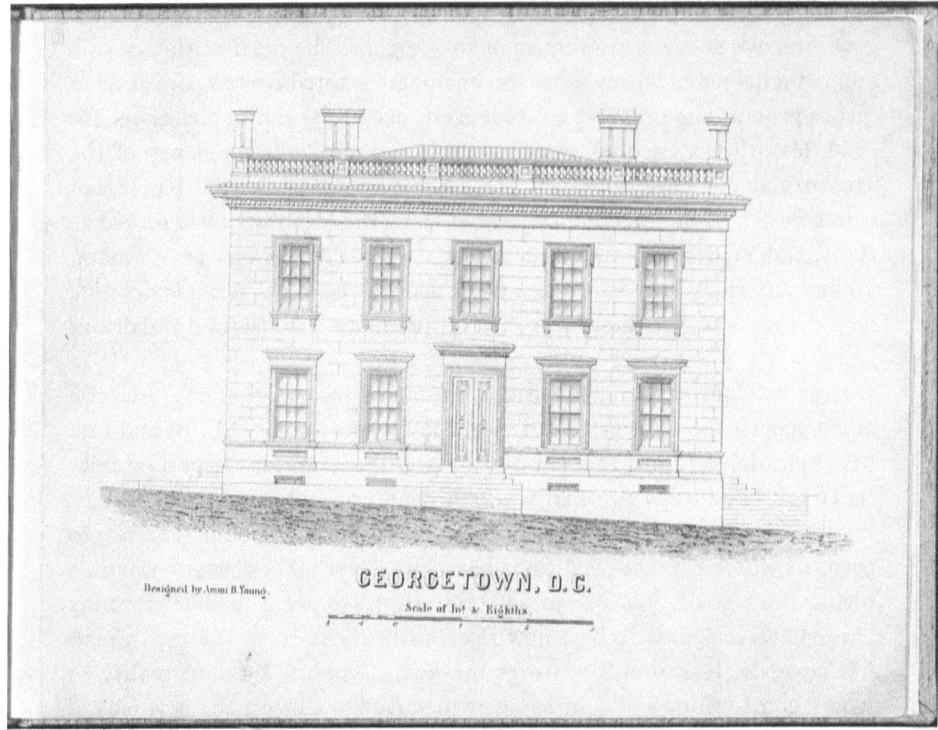

Fig. 6. The Georgetown custom house ([1856]). Ammi Burnham Young designed several custom houses, including the elegant one in Georgetown in the nation's capital. The United States Postal Service has occupied the first floor since construction was completed in 1858, but the Customs Service, which once used the basement and second floor, departed in 1867. Library of Congress, Prints and Photographs Division (LC-DIG-ppmsca-24848).

ficulties that have occurred in Execution of the laws respecting the Customs have been infinite and present themselves daily." The "difficulties" Williams identifies cut to the heart of the revenue system. A great number of Baltimore merchants had taken out bonds as a promise to pay customs duties at a later date. After that date arrived, and the bonds remained unpaid, the law directed Williams to file suit against each and every merchant with overdue bonds. Was Williams actually to file lawsuits against merchants who had missed payments on customs duty bonds? Or was he to use some discretion to decide whom and when to sue? Were officials to stick to the letter of the law and prohibit unlading of vessels until every cent owed in customs duties was calculated? Or should officials bend the law to help business keep moving? Were customs officials really required to inspect each and every parcel on a vessel as the law directed? Or perhaps there should be room to estimate duties to make things less burdensome for the merchants? For Williams and other officials, these questions had no clear answer in the statute book.[25]

Alexander Hamilton, however, initially believed it his responsibility to decide these questions. He used a communications device known as the "Circular Instruction" to disseminate instructions to all customs officials at once. This was a way to "produce a uniformity of practice." It also suited the gendered norms of administration in the eighteenth-century world. What historian Konstantin Dierks has shown regarding British administrative culture was much the same in the early United States: deference and compliments were key epistolary tools to communicate with superiors and peers, respectively. Hamilton rarely sounded imperious in these circulars. In fact, his strongest language was reserved for explaining "the true construction" of statutes.[26] The phrase "true construction" was legalese that a judge or justice might use to seize the preponderance of right. Although Hamilton expected customs officials to obey his circulars, he used the word "instructions" rather than "orders." He was sure to include gentlemanly phrases, too—"humble" and "honorable servant," for instance. After all, the men Hamilton addressed were distinguished figures, and Washington had chosen them precisely because of their status. For these men, harsh rebukes and orders would have been insults to their honor. The medium of the circular letter was doubly useful here because it encouraged a uniform rule to correct a problem without chastising a single officer. The dramaturgical displays of respect and esteem that were required to do business in the halls of Congress, and other domains of national politics, were similarly a prerequisite in the management of the Treasury.[27]

But the genteel overtones of Hamilton's circulars gave customs officials slack to diverge both from the letter of the law and from Hamilton's own instructions. It did not take long for Hamilton to notice that customs officials took ready advantage. On their own initiative, some customs officials changed the terms of customs duty bonds, much to the pleasure of the local merchants. In so doing, they manipulated the letter of a statute in which Congress tried to encourage cash payments for customs duties: merchants who paid their duties immediately, without taking out a bond promising future repayment, received a 10 percent discount. By generously interpreting what a "prompt" payment meant, these officials gave importing merchants discounts against the explicit terms of the law. "This," demurred Hamilton, "is not in my opinion, the true construction of the Act." He advised customs officials to cease the practice.[28]

With vague laws and official advice, customs officials tasked with interpreting and implementing the law were left very much on their own at the water's edge. There, local communities of merchants and other commercial peoples filled any void left by the distant federal government. The merchants who did business at the custom house, along with their attorneys and agents, made close study of Congress's revenue laws and the Treasury's published regulations. They quickly detected and sought to leverage the laws' loopholes. In Baltimore, Williams complained that poor drafting of the law regulating the Tonnage Act of 1789 gave no strict time frame in which merchants had to pay duties based on the volume and weight of their vessel. Ships that had the ability to "lay months in harbor" gave merchants the opportunity to evade payment. "In such case the Owners pay with reluctance, some will not pay *in ten Days*; others not at all without compulsion." Here Williams hit on a compound dilemma. With regard to "compulsion," "the law provides none." The Tonnage Act was devoid of any language allowing customs officials to demand duties from arriving vessels. Third, the law did not allow customs officials to hold a vessel in port. This meant that vessels were free to come and go as they pleased. "It depends upon the Interest, or Caprice of the Master whether he will comply with the law," concluded Williams. The merchants who owned the vessels and the masters who piloted the vessels thus had a great influence on the effectiveness of Congress's Tonnage Act.[29]

The commercial pressure customs officials faced becomes clear in the story of tariff revenue that went completely uncollected between August and September 1789. The letter of the law made duties payable as of August 1, but "the organization of the Custom Houses" became official on September 1. Hamilton ordered customs officials to collect the back duties. "It is incumbent upon the officers of the customs to claim them," he explained," and if disputed, to prosecute the claim to a legal determination." In Philadelphia, importing merchants denounced Hamilton's instructions both to Delany and to Federalist congressman Thomas Fitzimmons, himself a merchant and a future president of the Philadelphia Chamber of Commerce. Privately, Fitzsimmons observed that attempts to collect this not-inconsiderable sum left Collector of Customs Sharp Delany "much embarrassed." He also ominously warned Hamilton of "the difficulty that would arise" if the federal government pursued these debts to finality. In Connecticut, reported Collector Jeremiah Wadsworth, "the

Merchants of this State" had become "greatly agitated at the prospect of being obligded to pay the duties which arose before the office was opened." These "Merchants" had threatened Wadsworth with a flood of litigation. "There will be so many Actions brot & such disgust given," the old Federalist predicted, "that I fear the evil will be greater than ye good." Almost uniformly, the collectors of customs ignored Hamilton's instructions.[30]

Some customs officials made no secret of their advocacy on behalf of the merchants they were supposed to tax and regulate. "Some of the merchants are in opinion," wrote Boston's Benjamin Lincoln on December 9, 1789, that the customs laws should make "some allowance" in the calculation of duties on sugars of various consistency. "Ought we to do it?" asked Lincoln. This was hardly the only instance in which Lincoln would cite commercial interests in seeking what historian Frederick Dalzell describes as a "willingness to bend the law to meet the exegencies of legitimate commerce." In the summer of 1791, Lincoln attenuated a law concerning the inspection of imported, distilled spirits on the grounds that the law, as written, would "operate injuriously to the revenue & sour Many of our best merchants & friends to the Government." Lincoln had found a way to align the letter of federal law with the "opinion" of Boston merchants.[31]

But more often, the negotiations that occurred between importing merchants and customs officials were more subtle. In May 1791, Hamilton caught wind of a pattern of subversion in the practice of several custom houses regarding the inspection of imported goods. It appeared that "in some of the Custom Houses," officials calculated duties "by estimates formed upon the invoices, or the statements of the masters and owners of the vessels." In other words, customs officials took merchants and sea captains at their word about the veracity of their manifests and failed to actually inspect vessels. "This," responded Hamilton, "is not conformable to laws and may lead to practices very injurious to the revenue." Hamilton also sought to prove that this practice was not "necessary to the accommodation of the merchant." After all, a revision of the 1789 Collection Act allowed merchants to pay duties on goods only when those goods were unloaded at their port of destination. "At liberty to carry his goods from one district to another, paying the duties in the districts for which they are destined," the merchant would lose but little time during the inspection of those goods to be unloaded at any one port. Either way, however, customs officials simply could not blindly trust the word of merchants and sea captains. It was necessary to perform the "actual landing . . . measuring, weighing, and gauging in all cases wherein those operations are required by law."[32]

Customs officials were not passive automatons of merchant capital. For one thing, they used their discretion to buttress their own bottom lines. By 1790, customs officials in leading ports had corresponded about their often abysmal pay.[33] Several collectors interpreted the Enrollment Act of 1789 to provide themselves three separate fees of $0.60 for every arriving "inward cargo." Others pointed to the term "inward cargo" to justify a $0.60 fee on every single commodity that was on a manifest. Hamilton interpreted the law to provide a single payment of $0.60 per arriving vessel. By July 1792, however, as this contest over custom-house fees persisted, Hamilton relented. Although "my own view of the subject remains unchanged," he wrote, "each officer will them pursue that course which appears to him conformable to Law, to his own interest & safety, and to the good of the service." Hamilton's concession gestured to customs officials' formidable ability to look out for themselves amid the competing demands of commerce and government.[34]

Customs officials' instrumental approach to congressional statutes and Treasury instructions, whether it benefited them or the commercial community, was not a case of endemic corruption. Corruption had a very different meaning in revolutionary America than it would as the bureaucratic state expanded during the era of modern industrial capitalism. "Corruption," as J. G. A. Pocock has written of eighteenth-century political culture, referred to the power of "the executive" to lull the legislature into misconduct "by the offer of places and pensions, by retaining them to follow ministers and ministers' rivals, by persuading them to support measures . . . whereby the activities of administration grow beyond Parliament's control." In this theory of corruption, which would become a mainstay of revolutionary republicanism, "the remedy" was "to ensure that members of Parliament become in no way entangled in . . . the exercise of administration."[35] The governance that emerged on the docks in the first years of the new republic seemed more a republican antidote than corruption itself. After all, it was not the executive pushing the expansion of the state, but rather, society circumscribing the state from below.[36] It is surely not fanciful to imagine the custom-house crowd comparing their pliable new federal officials with the hated generation of His Majesty's officials who arrived in North America during the Revolution. Then colonists maintained that they objected not to customs laws themselves, but rather to the British Empire's unnecessarily coercive means of enforcing those laws. Such complaints would have sounded off key in the early 1790s.

Most likely, customs officials understood the structure of authority at the custom house as an expedient and desirable means of governance, rather than as a paean to revolutionary republicanism. Customs officials were, after all, drawn from the elite stratum of revolutionary leadership. Many of them contemplated often, and most seriously, what would become of their new republic. Otho Holland Williams had done more than any other person to piece together Congress's early revenue legislation. Benjamin Lincoln, even as he advocated for Boston's merchant community, often harangued Alexander Hamilton about matters of "very considerable importance to the revenue." Jeremiah Wadsworth proposed methods to "check the mischief" that might plague collection of customs duties. Joseph Whipple, the collector of comparatively sleepy Portsmouth, New Hampshire, would best capture this sentiment. Whipple promised to convey all that he could that would "promote the establishment of any Sy[s]tem beneficial to the pu[b]lic or that shall contribute to the permanency of a constitution of government in which the happiness of this extensive country depends." These officers understood the duties of their office as vital to "the permanency" of the new republic itself.[37]

Many customs officials also would have believed that long-distance merchants' elite social status entitled them to influence over the machinery of government. None other than Alexander Hamilton explained why the merchant occupied such an exalted position in high federalist ideology. As Hamilton wrote in *Federalist* 35, "mechanics and manufacturers" were likely to vote "merchants" into positions of power because "they know that the merchant is their natural patron and friend; and . . . their interests can be more effectually promoted by the merchant than by themselves." They also knew that "the influence and weight and superior acquirements of the merchants" opened political doors on the one hand, and facilitated a disinterested pursuit of the commonweal on the other hand that was simply not possible for those who worked for a living. "We must therefore consider merchants as the natural representatives of all these classes of the community," concluded Hamilton.[38]

Customs officials did not speak of merchants as Hamilton did, but many enjoyed close social ties to local merchant communities. In Charleston, George Abbott Hall was a slave importer turned aristocrat who classed himself among "the Merchants of Charles Town" and sought, with those merchants, "that Trade & Commerce would Flourish."[39] The family of Savannah collector John Habersham was synonymous with the cotton trade.[40] In Portsmouth, the same William Whipple who wrote of a desire to use his position in the custom house to cement "the permanency" of the new republic had been an overseas merchant and would be a close ally of Portsmouth merchant, privateersman, and insurance broker John Fabyan

Parrott. Whipple would eventually recommend Parrott for a custom-house post.[41] In Bath, Massachusetts (and later Maine), Collector William Webb had joined with leading merchants to press for a lighthouse that would render "the Maritime and Mercantile Interest . . . in a flourishing condition."[42] The collector of Sag Harbor, New York, was Henry Packer Dering, a former West Indies horse merchant in the 1780s before "returning to my native shores." As collector, Dering would continue to dabble in commerce. More importantly, however, Dering's home "became the center of social, political, and commercial activities, with captains, and whale hunters, farmers and layers congregating to discuss business and the news of the day." His home was also the custom house.[43]

The cozy relationship between custom houses and commerce did much to legitimize the new federal government. Customs officials' careful manipulation of the laws concerning the collection of customs duties best illustrates how governance spawned legitimacy. As discussed in the preceding chapter, the revenue laws relied on bonds, or promises to meet a behavioral or financial condition, backed by the threat of a monetary penalty. These penalties were significant. For instance, in the case of the bond required as a promise to deliver goods to customs districts as specified in a ship's manifest, merchants who could not meet their obligations faced prosecution for the amount of duty owed on the goods as well as $500 for "neglect." Inability to pay the customs duty bond when it came due meant, by law, immediate "prosecution . . . for the recovery of the money." Finally, under the logic of the revenue laws, when a merchant failed to meet the promise embodied in a bond, that merchant lost the trust of the central government. "No person whose bond for the payment of duties is . . . unsatisfied," stated the law, "shall be allowed a future credit for duties, until such bond shall be fully paid or discharged."[44] Hamilton was wise to the seriousness of placing a customs bond into prosecution. When the first "of the periods for the payment of Bonds taken for Duties" appeared on the horizon in late December 1789, Hamilton tried to steel the collectors against the inevitable local pressures that would intrude on their implementation of the law. The secretary demanded, "If the Bonds are not paid *as they fall due* they be immediately put in Suit." "On this point," he continued, "the *most exact punctuality* will be considered as *indispensable*." Hamilton knew that under the state revenue systems prior to 1789 "relaxations in this respect . . . obtained," but he considered "strict observance as essential, not only to the order of the finances, but even to the" vitality of the system of "procrastinated terms of payment of the Duties."[45]

Hamilton was right to suspect that customs officials would postpone prosecutions to protect local merchants. In Baltimore, during his tenure as naval officer in the 1780s, the venerable Otho Holland Williams had made a habit of allowing merchants to accumulate significant debts. Now, under the federal government, Williams seems to have persisted in this practice. As we have seen, he balked at prosecuting overdue customs bonds as early as the fall of 1789. Some years later his successor, Robert Purviance, "discovered unpaid and overdue bonds still on the books." In New York, Collectors John Lamb and Joshua Sands engaged in a similar pattern. Repeatedly, over the course of the 1790s, the Treasury warned the two that overdue bonds had gone unpaid. When David Gelston took office in 1802, he would demand of his predecessor Sands "an explanation" for having to inherit a "statement of bonds unpaid." A few years later, internal accounts of the New York custom house revealed "Bonds outstanding" at $3,555,623.21.[46]

The most infamous example of this lackadaisical approach to collecting bonds, however, was that of Charleston. Between 1789 and 1793, it seems, Collector Isaac Holmes had paid but little attention to the schedule of revenue bonds. By 1794, the Treasury observed that Holmes's custom house had about $260,000 in overdue bonds. Holmes came clean. He had reported revenue bonds "as cash on hand" and failed to even keep proper records of the bonds that had issued from the Charleston custom house. In February 1797, the amount of uncollected bonds totaled almost $580,000. Well into the nineteenth century, customs officials in Charleston would struggle to make Holmes's mess right. Moreover, at the Charleston custom house, this hesitation to police merchants' credit became surprisingly difficult to shake. In 1797, when Collector James Simons initiated suits against Robert Hazlehurst and five other merchants for overdue bonds, the merchants confidently relied on a pedantic defense: they claimed that their bonds were invalid because, "instead of an actual wax seal, on which an impression had been made, the 'pretended Bond' bore a 'printed or engraved Circle . . . with the printed Letters SEAL made by the printer.'" The federal circuit court sitting in Charleston rejected the flimsy defense, but Hazlehurst and the others, in arrears for close to $100,000, appealed to the United States Supreme Court. Here the cases died. Though the Supreme Court ordered a "Special Mandate" for each of the bond cases, "there is no mention of these mandates in the minutes of the circuit court . . . nor were there further proceedings in any of the six cases." Charleston merchants had little, if not nothing, to fear. And whether or not they liked it, Charleston customs officials had no alternative than to acknowledge the bargaining power and unaccountability of merchant credit and capital.[47]

Events in Philadelphia offer an instructive window on how, precisely, a customs official handled the matter of overdue bonds. Collector Sharp Delany initially found the pursuit of overdue bonds a "disagreeable necessity" but nonetheless enforced the law and put one bond in suit in December 1789. So "disagreeable" was this experience that Delany shrank from future prosecutions. By 1791, rumors circulated within the customs establishment "that Delany sometimes let customhouse debts slide."[48] This was not to say that Delany avoided prosecutions altogether. Rather, he seems to have followed a three-pronged strategy of discretionary prosecution. First, accounts of his prosecutions suggest that he only selectively pursued those bonds that he believed the merchant could make good on. Of the seventy-six bonds that Delany pursued in court between 1794 and 1799, only five remained unpaid in full. When a merchant could not pay, then Delany seems to have backed off. Delany's colleague in Bermuda Hundred, Virginia, William Heth, called this, collection *"in part."* Thus, the federal government would never see roughly $4,200 in uncollected bonds that had been prosecuted. This sum, it turns out, was lost forever. As was the far larger sum resulting from Delany's third strategy: the almost $2.8 million in overdue bonds that Delany never bothered to put into suit at all.[49]

What explains the sharp divergence between the Treasury Department's crisp, central accounting mechanisms and instructions and Delany's practices? And what did officials like Delany achieve in their use of discretion? In short, Treasury instructions and ledgers on the one hand, and customs officials like Delany on the other, occupied vastly different realms of governance. The orderly pages of the Treasury's central records, and the simplicity of its instructions, had meaning in the international language of national sovereignty and political economy. The customs official charged with giving life and reality to those laws, however, was a single officeholder in a crowd of commercial peoples. On the waterfront, this context and relationship gave central governmental laws a very different set of meanings.

In practice, Delany and other customs officials attenuated the letter of the stringent laws concerning customs bonds to protect their local commercial community and to preserve their own reputation and legitimacy. First, customs officials knew, sometimes from firsthand experience as merchants, that strict enforcement of the revenue laws interfered with the rhythms and institutions of Atlantic commerce, especially that of credit. Merchants hedged their risk by, in effect, insuring one another. The complexity of their investments often rendered it difficult to contemplate, from one moment to the next, their own wealth and prospects. Second, they funneled profits from one maritime "adventure" into another without a moment's pause. Moreover, it was quite common to commit expected returns from one enterprise to another. Regional and local demands added further complications. In the Chesapeake Bay region, for instance, planters' ability to market their tobacco in distant markets depended on, at least in terms of reputation, sound credit. Planters in the Chesapeake and beyond also used instruments of credit to purchase slaves.[50] Merchants, writes historian Jonathan Levy, "strained to foresee, control, and manipulate the contingent link between present and future." Access to and use of credit was central to their efforts. Herein lay the peril of prosecuting an overdue customs bond. Legal proceedings against the merchant could bring to a jarring halt the fluid motion of credit required within the commercial sphere. Worse yet, perhaps, the revocation of "future credit for duties" forced the merchant to pay precious cash to the state instead of being able to reinvest it in the market. Either scenario, in other words, could prove ruinous to the merchant.[51]

It was in this context that many customs officials quickly became advocates and shields for their commercial community. Boston collector Benjamin Lincoln, whom we have already observed speaking on behalf of the Boston importing merchants, implored the Treasury to allow more slack when it came to determining that a bond had become overdue. Often, he explained, "either from ignorance of captains . . . the loss of documents by accident, or from other causes," the documents required to "cancel" a custom-house bond "do not arrive in time" before a bond is due. "Something should be done for the relief of the merchant," he continued. "Even among our most attentive merchants," he explained, there would inevitably be instances when happenstance, and not any ill motive, delayed the prompt repayment of a duty bond. It was wrong that, in this instance, the merchant would "suffer a process." "This evil will be experienced by many of our most honorable merchants after every exertion in their power has been made." To the north of Boston, in the small port of Passamaquoddy in the United States-Canada borderlands, Collector of Customs Lewis Delesdernier "saw himself as a facilitator of trade," writes historian Joshua Smith. Customs officials understood the custom house, then, not simply as a central governmental institution to extract revenue from commerce, but as an institution to protect and stimulate commerce.[52]

Customs officials' discretion in the collection of bonds also made them the guardians of merchants' reputation. Prosecution and collection of debts usually triggered a chain of legal action on a regional, national, and sometimes international scale. Indeed, the Treasury explicitly instructed customs officials that "whenever any persons bond for duties shall be put in suit . . . you will transmit information to the Collectors of the Several Ports within the state . . . in order that further credit may be refused." Such measures may have been necessary to keep fellow officers up to speed, but the private marketplace was far more efficient when it came to matters of reputation. When, for instance, the Salem, Massachusetts, custom house finally prosecuted overdue bonds owed by a merchant house in Beverly, it became known that "creditors" sent as far south as Baltimore to get their due. Such an action trumpeted the merchants' demise, not only within the immediate vicinity of the custom house, but across the commercial landscape of the young nation. The official disposed to facilitating commerce was not likely to undertake legal proceedings that would surely damage the reputation of a local merchant.[53]

Moreover, in the republican worldview that circulated within early modern officialdom, the creditor who prosecuted for unpaid debt besmirched his own reputation. Yet custom-house credit was a comparatively static situation. The same merchants requested credit from the same official or officials on a fairly regular basis. Of the thirty-eight bonds issued by the Bermuda Hundred custom house in July 1792, for instance, ten went to repeat players. Unlike the private marketplace, where private latters meant that individuals considered demands in a buffer zone of time and space, the customs official operated face-to-face. He would most likely interact regularly with the merchant that he had prosecuted. This merchant, and those with whom he invested and socialized, thus held the customs official's reputation in their hands.[54]

Customs officials' lenient implementation of federal customs bonds undoubtedly benefited merchants and commercial interests. Perhaps more importantly, it was the very desire to align the law with the needs of commerce that motivated customs officials' decision making. The waterfront appeared to have imposed an authority—a logic of governance—that shaped how Congress's customs laws would work in practice. Was this a momentary aberration? The type of institutional permeability that is so often to be found in new, postcolonial institutions?

FEDERALISTS, NEGOTIATED AUTHORITY, AND EMPIRE

The Treasury would soon embrace customs officials' practice of negotiating authority with the merchants and commercial figures who did business at the custom house. In so doing, Hamilton and his successor, Oliver Wolcott Jr., sanctioned the distribution of a great deal of federal authority to the waterfront and placed it at the discretion of customs officials, who in turn would vest it with importing merchants in particular.

Hamilton came around only gradually. When his genteel circulars did not have the desired effect, Hamilton believed that the collectors of customs were deviating from the letter of the law because they were not sufficiently supervised. For this Hamilton blamed himself and his numerous responsibilities while "at the head of the Treasury." So in April 1790 he asked Congress to create a new group of customs supervisors to oversee customs officers in each state. These intermediary supervisors were required, explained Hamilton, because customs officials on the waterfront "receive a tint from the personal interest of individuals, and the local interest of districts." *Tint*. This was a remarkably precise way to describe what was happening at the custom houses as officials' good judgment and fealty to the law was colored by the interests and representations of local commerce. But the proposed class of supervisors would be located away from the ports and thus would be "free from the influence either of personal interests or local predilections." Of course, some twenty-five years before, the British Empire had contemplated a similar solution to a similar problem when it dispatched the American Board of Customs to rein in unreliable customs officials. Given this history, it is perhaps understandable that after nothing initially came of Hamilton's proposal, he never raised the matter again.[55]

Money rather than history best explains why Hamilton gradually embraced negotiated authority at the custom houses. The United States *was* collecting revenue from customs duties. That in itself was a remarkable break with the experience of the last several decades, to say nothing of American colonists' experience under the British Empire. Hamilton's books showed that customs duties totaled about $6.5 million between August 1, 1789, and December 31, 1791. The figure for 1792 alone was $3.9 million. And after appropriations—payments to federal employees, foreign treaties, interest and principal payments, lighthouses, private claims, and military payments—Hamilton's Treasury would record a surplus of $21,000 for 1792. Customs duties would only continue to increase: $4.25 million in 1793, $4.8 million in 1794, and $5.5 million in 1795, Hamilton's final year at the helm.[56] Even as federal officials faced immense pressure to align customs laws with local commercial interests, then, they were able to collect an impressive bundle of revenue. Or perhaps it was *because* customs officials had studiously negotiated authority with the importing merchants who passed through their custom houses that they were able to collect revenue on this scale?

It is impossible to say why exactly importing merchants in the 1790s willingly paid over duties to customs officials. Undoubtedly, some of those who made a living importing goods from the West Indies and Europe were swept up by the nationalist sentiments that were spreading across the young nation. In several cities, importing merchants made a show of proclaiming themselves "fair traders" while noting their disdain for smugglers. In Philadelphia, an "Association of a respectable part of the Merchants and Traders" came into existence "for the discouragement of Smuggling." Similar groups emerged in Alexandria and Portsmouth.[57] A related explanation might be that republicanism resolved American merchants' complaints about being taxed without representation. In the new republic, that is to say, American merchants and others were part of a polity that decided its own taxes.[58]

Yet when it comes to governance it is important not to overstate the importance of the American Revolution.[59] For over a century American merchants had interacted with custom houses and negotiated the terms upon which they would be taxed and regulated. The federal government emulated the British Empire in creating institutions and formulating a political economy. Hamilton's Treasury came to trust customs officials' discretion to align the national interest with local commercial expectations, just as Whitehall had in decades past.[60] In fact, Hamilton's handling of custom-house administration must be understood as a response to the difficult questions he had posed about central governance during the Constitutional Convention. In Constitution Hall he had argued that "distance has a physical effect upon mens minds," and that "execution of laws [was] feeble at a distance from government—particularly in the collection of revenue." By June 1792 he had reframed the issue. As he explained to the collectors of customs, "there is latitude to avoid a rigorous enforcing of the provision, & it is incumbent upon the Collector to make reasonable & due allowance, having regard to the usual course of business." There were "cases," Hamilton continued, "in which a provision, though not strictly *impracticable*, may be so inconvenient as to demand some degree of relaxation." Particularly with regard to "colateral precautions in Revenue Laws for the security of the Revenue, small deviations from literal strictness, may, with due circumspection, be admitted." *Latitude. Allowance. Relaxation. Deviations.* The problem had been the strength or weakness of the tax state. The solution was conforming the tax state to existing patterns of life and commerce.[61]

The customs system that came into view by the summer of 1792 bore a striking resemblance to its British imperial predecessor as it has existed from the Glorious Revolution until the American Revolution, with one major exception: the United States proved far better at collecting revenue. By October of that year, Hamilton had grown so confident in the ability of his customs collectors on the waterfront to interpret and implement customs laws to meet the approbation of local merchant communities that he took a fairly stunning step. "I have concluded to commit the immediate superintendence of the Collection of the duties," he wrote, "to the Comptroller of the Treasury." In the future, Hamilton required custom houses' accounting records—monies paid, bonds distributed, and currency figures—and little more.[62]

Hamilton did involve himself in custom-house affairs, however, when serious problems threatened local custom-house governance, most notably in the case of Jeremiah Olney, collector of customs in Providence, Rhode Island. As Frederick Dalzell has demonstrated in great detail, Olney was a slow study with regard to the pattern of commercial softening of federal customs laws. This was somewhat surprising because he was, after all, George Washington's ideal type of appointee to the civil list: a military man who had risen to the rank of general, a wealthy rentier aristocrat, and a Federalist through and through.[63] At least, the elite overseas merchants of Providence were surprised when Olney, "connected" as he was with "some" of them, proved fastidious in his refusal to cease his "vigorous and severe execution of the Revenue law." John Brown, Providence's leading merchant, wrote a remarkably candid assessment of Olney in 1793, not in private mercantile correspondence, but in a public petition for Olney's ouster. What had Olney done to provoke such calumny? Most importantly, he had "vigorously and strictly" implemented congressional laws about custom-house bonds. In 1791, and after consultation with Alexander Hamilton, Olney had followed the letter of the law in denying custom-house credit to a merchant named Welcome Arnold, whose previous bonds, to the tune of almost $2,000, were past due. "I cannot allow you any Credit for the Duties on the Cargo," explained Olney to Arnold's coconspirator Edward Dexter, "until his [Arnold's] Said Bonds shall have been Discharged." Refused "the usual Credit" by an officeholder, Arnold and Dexter used their authority as merchants in an important local commercial community to "Abide the Consiquence" and "seek My Remedy."

In the 1760s, Arnold and Dexter might have sparked a riot to articulate their position. In the 1790s, however, they believed rumor and social clout were adequate substitutes. As one observer noted, "The Merchants are all linked together[s] to push the custom House officers down (some small ones excepted). . . . They are determined if in their Power to get the Custom House under their Command." The importing merchants of Providence now pressed their case out of doors, in the court of public opinion. Thus appeared Brown's 1793 petition.[64]

The crux of this conflict at the Providence custom house was the competition between the power of officialdom and the authority of commercial peoples on the waterfront in the Federalist era. For Brown and the Providence merchants, Olney's literal interpretation of the revenue laws contradicted "the True Intent, & meaning of them." According to Brown, "It was the intention of the Legislature to afford every aid and accommodation to Commerce consistent with an exact, & punctual collection of the Revenue." This "aid and accommodation to Commerce" had, in fact, taken root "in other states, particularly in the principal towns & city." Olney's inflexibility was therefore "unexampled & unparalleled in other districts in the United States." In other words, according to the overseas merchants of Providence, the revenue laws were designed, first, to support Commerce and, second, to collect funds for the federal government.[65] Olney disagreed. His duty, and his power to execute his office pursuant to that duty, derived from a commission from the federal executive. "The good-will and Esteem of my fellow Citizens will always afford me real satisfaction when I can possess them in consequence of an upright, uniform, and impartial execution of the Duties of my Office," but "I disclaim them upon any other terms," he had written in August 1792. Whither, then, the legality of the custom house?[66]

Hamilton would intervene in the Providence debacle in the spring of 1793 with counsel to accede to the merchants' authority. "Some good men, who esteem you and think highly of your conduct," wrote the secretary, "have expressed to me an idea that it has been in some instances too punctilious, and not sufficiently accommodating." This, advised Hamilton, was an unwise and unproductive approach to governance. As Hamilton concluded, "The good will of the Merchants is very important in many sense, and if it can be secured without any improper sacrifice or introducing a looseness of practice, it is desirable to do so." How, though, was Olney to implement the laws in such a way as to secure "the good will of the Merchants" without "a looseness of practice"? Without "any improper sacrifice"?[67] Hamilton did not elaborate, most likely, because he did not know the answer. Hamilton could not speak for the overseas merchants of Providence. The United States Supreme Court ultimately found for Olney, allowing him "peculiar pleasure" but little more. *Olney v. Arnold* had far more to do with punishing the Rhode Island legislature for masquerading as a court of law than it did with validating Jeremiah Olney's practices of governance. Nor was it likely that the merchants of Providence would draft another petition providing specific recommendations to Olney. Rather, Olney would have to follow the example of customs officials throughout the country in devising, unevenly, and sometimes contradictorily, practices of governance that suited both commercial authority and the demands of central government.[68]

"Decision successfully exerted in one place will, it is presumable, be efficacious everywhere," wrote Alexander Hamilton in September 1792. It had been fourteen months since Congress had imposed an excise tax on "spirits distilled within the United States" and communities in western Pennsylvania had refused to comply.[69] Hamilton was ready to go to "war over the excise." "Not to subdue it," he wrote under the name of "Tully" in a Philadelphia newspaper, "were to tolerate it." So Hamilton volunteered himself "to go out upon the expedition against the insurgents" in western Pennsylvania.[70] A few months later, Hamilton found himself on the front, commanding militia forces "to suppress the combinations which exist in some of the western counties in Pennsylvania to the laws laying duties upon spirits." His aim was "to cause the laws to be executed." On November 15, Hamilton triumphantly wrote to President Washington of the capture of twenty ringleaders. They "are fit subjects for examples," he declared.[71]

Hamilton's military expedition to put down the Whiskey Rebellion was a testament to the fiscal solvency of the central government by 1794. Indeed, before he mounted the expedition, Hamilton drew $400,000 in funds, in the form of a loan, from the Bank of the United States to provide for "the large extra demand upon the Treasury, which has been occasioned by the expedition going on against the Western Insurgents." The revenue system that Hamilton had labored to manage, and which had hinged on the negotiation between sovereign power and local, commercially derived authority, had in effect made possible Hamilton's funding mechanism for this expedition. After all, Hamilton added to his request a reminder that the United States would soon owe $400,000 to the Bank of the United States "on account of a former loan." "This payment," Hamilton pledged, "will be then made accordingly." The Bank of the United States should not have had, and did not have, any doubts about the central government's fiscal health. It possessed the capacity to extract revenue from commerce, in the form of customs duties, to meet creditors' demands, and to secure further credit for military purposes. If the Constitution of 1787 created a fiscal-military state in theory, Hamilton's Treasury constructed one in practice.[72]

Why, then, did Hamilton so savor this expedition against an admittedly "inconsiderable part of a community"? And why was negotiated governance suitable for the commercial waterfront, while only submission to the letter of "constitutional laws" was required for the agricultural hinterlands of western Pennsylvania? How could Hamilton urge Jeremiah Olney to devise practices to secure "the good will of the merchants," while leading a military force against those tax resisters who "lead us from freedom to slavery," from "a GOVERNMENT OF LAWS" to "one of FORCE"?[73]

For one thing, the commercial pressure that shaped custom-house governance differed from resistance to the excise in scope and scale. Both were crowd actions. But the overseas merchants and others who secured deferential treatment at the custom house paid taxes to the federal government, so long as they essentially set the terms of customs officials' methods of tax collection and regulation. Perhaps remarkably, the establishment of the customs system occasioned no physical violence. The "insurgents" of western Pennsylvania refused to pay the excise and physically assaulted tax collectors. The different means of opposition related to the difference between customs duties and excise duties. Overseas merchants paid customs duties on imported goods and built the cost of these duties into the sales prices of commodities. Consumers of imported goods, in other words, ultimately paid customs duties. The frontier counties of western Pennsylvania, to say nothing of those in North Carolina and Kentucky, where farming communities offered serious resistance to the excise, had no comparable mechanism to distribute the weight of taxation. For these communities, whiskey was "the only cash crop" export that had to compete in foreign countries with local spirits. Passing along the excise tax in the cost of the exported whiskey would make it impossible to sell their product.[74]

More important than the scope and scale of these forms of resistance to the federal government's power, however, were their radically different meanings for the federal government's legitimacy. The whiskey rebels flouted power; commercial peoples negotiated it. Thus, Hamilton could parlay protests against the excise as nothing short of threats against the state itself. The merchants, captains, mariners, and others who operated in and around the custom house knew better than to do so from their long experience of attenuating the reach of central government. A more effective means of resisting unwanted encroachment on custom was the quiet yet inexorable pressure that influenced the custom house and in so doing reshaped the meaning of federal revenue law.

Of course, the entire matter ultimately came down to the relative positions of merchant capital and small, backwoods farmers in the political economy of high federalism. "Hamilton's policies encouraged consolidation, elite control of new investments, and subordination of small producers . . . to the new nation's commercial, financial, and speculative elites," writes a student of American political economy. Hamilton's entire career, argue Stanley Elkins and Eric McKitrick, was devoted to creating "a national economic context in which their [the merchants'] energies could function." Was there any better way to produce such a "release of energy" than to bind the merchant elite to the spine of national finance?[75]

PART III

Revenue and Crisis: Baltimore, 1808

James McCulloch was a good Republican. He had a mercantile background, but McCulloch became collector of customs for Baltimore in 1808 because he was influential Republican congressman Samuel Smith's man on the docks. According to the opposition press, so loyal was McCulloch to the administration that he approved of "tarring and feathering a citizen" who dared criticize Thomas Jefferson.[1] Whether or not McCulloch endorsed Republican mobbing, he never shied away from endorsing Jefferson's policies, even the embargo of 1808–9. McCulloch agreed that British depredations against American mariners and commerce had gone too far, and that Jefferson was right to put a halt to American overseas trade. He would also plead with the Treasury for more resources to make the embargo work.[2]

But the more time that McCulloch spent in the small, faded custom house on Gay and Lombard streets, the more his staunch Republicanism and his support of the embargo seemed to falter. Although Baltimore had become a commercial metropolis, McCulloch's custom house was crumbling, with its "very much worn out" weights and measures, a single "broke" thermometer to test imported spirits, and "very bent" tools for gauging goods in barrels.[3] The rule of law had also gone the way of the equipment. In the previous few years Baltimore customs officials became notorious for allowing merchants to pursue a shady commerce with black Haitian revolutionaries. Officials who tried to restrain this trade were shouted down with "insult" and obstructed with "every opposition." When customs officials did make the rare seizure of smuggled goods, merchants conspired against them. Attempts to prosecute prohibited trade ran into a commercial wall of silence as merchants bribed "Tavern Keepers" and other "witnesses of 25 or 30 Dollars per man as a reward for absenting themselves at the time of the trial." One official recalled that he "was threatened" by a merchant "with a suit for heavy damages" if he insisted on pursuing charges.[4]

The embargo exacerbated the conflict at the Baltimore custom house between Republican political economy and local merchants. The Treasury demanded strict enforcement of the embargo. But the city's merchants closed ranks against the law. McCulloch—and many other customs officials throughout the country—found a third way. To the Treasury McCulloch pledged that he was doing everything in his power to enforce the embargo. But on the waterfront McCulloch's men only nominally enforced the law. "The visiting officer comes along side asks for your papers casts his eye over there and leaves you with permission to pass," reported an informant. Slowly, thousands of barrels, and hundreds of thousands of dollars' worth of restricted goods departed Baltimore for foreign markets.[5]

As the volume of illicit commerce grew, Jefferson finally confronted McCulloch. How could so trusted an officer, who was appointed because of his political allegiance to the administration, turn out to be the weakest link in the enforcement of the embargo? McCulloch's explanation was stunning. When Secretary of the Treasury Albert Gallatin explained that custom-house officials were legally subordinate and required to follow customs laws, McCulloch did not disagree. "I fully understand the limitation intended to the Collectors discretion," he wrote. But McCulloch explained that he also answered to the merchants of Baltimore. "A Collector" was "generally connected with those around him by common if not by special ties," he explained, "and liable to bias from confidence in acquaintances accompanied with good will." In this contest, the "special ties" that connected McCulloch with the commercial men in and around the custom house were simply more powerful than administrative instructions from the Treasury. And so, a powerless White House simply watched as James McCulloch refused to change his ways. The embargo was no more in Baltimore.[6]

CHAPTER FOUR

Commerce or War?

The settlement forged between Alexander Hamilton's Treasury, customs officials, and local importing merchants made the federal government dependent on commerce for revenue and legitimacy. There was unmistakable promise to this arrangement. The fortunes of America's merchants boomed as the remaining economic difficulties of the 1780s gave way to sharp growth in imports and exports alike. As a result, and excepting a few bumps, customs revenue consistently grew between 1793 and 1807. By the time the Jefferson administration came to power, custom revenue reached eight figures, rising to an impressive $15.8 million in 1807.[1]

Yet not all was *doux* with American commerce. Most importantly, American riches were the direct result of the French Revolutionary and Napoleonic wars as war-torn Atlantic markets turned to the neutral United States as a source of trade and transportation. With reward came risk. American merchants who gouged wartime markets stood accused of violating embargoes, trafficking in contraband, and many other punishable offenses. Privateering, the practice of licensed wartime plundering of enemy vessels, only darkened the shadows that overlay these markets. As French and English privateers stalked American commerce in the Atlantic, they created greater uncertainty for American merchants. Privateers that visited stateside ports wreaked havoc, too, by smuggling prize goods into the United States and illegally augmenting their armaments with American aid. American merchants seeking to exploit market scarcities during the French Revolutionary and Napoleonic wars thus not only dealt in risk. They also imported into the United States violence and disorder.[2]

Customs officials, then, found themselves responsible for administering American neutrality policy. This meant that, for the first time, customs officials would have to look beyond the matter of revenue and pay serious attention to the behavior of American merchants. Congress directed customs officials to prevent Americans from trading with foreign privateers or navies to preserve the appearance of American neutrality. Most importantly, customs officials found themselves responsible for prosecuting commercial warfare by enforcing commercial restrictions. In times of acute diplomatic crises, the United States used these restrictions to prevent American merchants from trading with foreign countries in order to punish those countries for treating American commerce unfairly. These new regulatory demands strained the negotiated authority between merchants and customs officials that had prospered under the Federalists. How could customs officials suddenly reverse course and police rather than accommodate local merchants?

Among customs agents' most important but difficult regulatory tasks was the policing of firearms on merchant vessels. In the early modern Atlantic, vessels were often lightly armed to protect against pirates or other predators. But as American merchants waded into a maritime marketplace defined by European warfare, the status of armed merchant vessels came into question. Were armed American vessels that fired upon French or British ships participating in commerce or warfare? The boundaries between commerce and warfare had long vexed European political thought.[3] The Federalists, caught between a desire to enlarge commerce and a series of diplomatic crises, proved ambivalent on the question of armed merchant vessels. But the Republicans took a more aggressive approach. Between 1801 and 1807, American merchants flouted French prohibitions and embargoes to trade with black revolutionaries in Saint-Domingue and then Haiti. Sometimes these American adventurers shot their way past French authorities to do so. For some, the armed Haiti trade seemed a dangerous commercial pathway for the pathogen of black freedom to migrate to the slave South. But the more immediate problem was that this commerce threatened to jeopardize American neutrality.

For well over a decade after the outbreak of the French Revolutionary Wars, the federal government struggled to cope with American merchants who used armed vessels to do business with France, Britain, and their colonies.[4] Customs officials were simply unable to muster enough authority to enforce coercive legislation against the local merchant communities that had for so long helped anchor the legitimacy of the custom house. By 1807, Jefferson and his administration identified a problem. In order to sustain itself, the federal government would need to change the way governance worked at the custom house. Customs officials, whose discretion once aligned the interests of commerce and the nation, suddenly seemed suspect. And commerce, once a medium of federal governance, and the stuff of empire, had come to appear dangerous.

NEUTRALITY IN PRACTICE

"The duty and interest of the United States" required "conduct friendly and impartial towards the belligerent powers," declared President George Washington on April 22, 1793. With the Neutrality Proclamation, Washington pledged that the United States would not take sides in the sprawling conflict between revolutionary France and its opponents, especially Great Britain.[5] In early modern thought, neutral nations refrained from providing military aid to warring nations. But neutrality also had implications for commerce. To remain truly neutral, the United States would trade on equal terms with all European belligerents by forsaking "contraband," a notoriously vague category that covered goods capable of strengthening a foreign nation's military. And to ensure that the United States remained *truly* neutral, Washington promised to dispatch "instructions to those officers" to prosecute violators.[6]

On its face, neutrality seemed to benefit both American merchants and the federal government. As Europe sank its resources into war rather than trade it opened up vast opportunities for American commerce to make inroads into the maritime trade, freight, and labor markets. Neutrality made sense to Washington and the Federalists both geopolitically and economically. American merchants saw the same potential. This was why a "meeting of the merchants" in Boston enthusiastically cheered the Neutrality Proclamation. As a Philadelphia insurance agent put it, "As long as the war continues . . . this trade will yield great profits."[7] Indeed, the dramatic growth of commerce was an unmistakable feature of life in Federalist America. For one thing, American markets teemed with imported commodities from Europe and especially the West Indies. Importers brought tens of millions of pounds of coffee to the United States from the Swedish, Danish, Dutch, British, French, and Spanish West Indies between 1794 and 1798. Meanwhile, "farmers, merchant millers, and traders" in the Mid-Atlantic supplied massive amounts of flour for hungry European armies and colonists. American newspapers captured this commercial bustle in shipping and commercial news. More broadly, American commercial appetites sparked a cultural confrontation the likes of which paralleled the consumer politics of the American Revolution.[8]

The commercial boom that accompanied European warfare brought higher revenue for the federal government. Now, as revenues skyrocketed, Hamilton declared the federal government "prosperous beyond expectation." It was. Even though maritime war with France dented customs revenue in 1798 and 1799, the custom houses collected an average of about $6 million a year between 1793 and 1800.[9] Flush with funds, and perhaps more importantly, confident in the government's ability to collect revenue in the future, national leaders, Federalist and Republican alike, embarked upon nation-building activities. Nowhere was this more noticeable than in the Ohio country, where federal largesse funded military expeditions against the Northern Confederacy. On the lands they expropriated from Indians, General Anthony Wayne's forces built roads that themselves became conduits for federal funds to soldiers and, eventually, to Ohio merchants. The Treasury also began subsidizing western settlement by surveying, platting, and auctioning land in the national public domain. Though the new United States Postal Service generally paid its own costs, "the vast majority" of those who paid for its services were the merchants who were simultaneously benefiting from the commercial boom.[10]

The very same neutrality that made good sense in politics and political economy seemed altogether intractable on the waterfront, where customs officials had to choose which law actually fixed the terms of American neutrality. There was Washington's Neutrality Proclamation, but with it stood several treaties that the United States had negotiated with several of the warring parties. If customs officials adhered to the terms of those treaties, they would unquestionably give some advantages to one nation over another. Once such treaty was the Treaty of Amity and Commerce, which the United States had entered into with France in 1778. The treaty allowed both nations to inspect the other's vessels after visiting enemy ports, to haul prizes into each other's ports without scrutiny from customs officials, and to use each other's ports to restock after piracy, acts of God, or acts of war. The 1778 treaty also restricted France and the United States from allowing other nations' privateers to outfit and depart from French or American ports. How could American customs officials sanction the terms of the treaty without elevating French rights over, say, British rights?[11]

The infamous Genêt affair of 1793 and its fallout further reveal how diplomatic affairs helped complicate the meaning of neutrality for customs officials. French revolutionary emissary Edmond-Charles Genêt had come to the United States to create a bulwark for French naval efforts against Great Britain. Accordingly, Genêt instructed French consuls to replenish French privateers in American ports and to fit out a new crop of privateers. Perhaps most importantly, Genêt sought to man this new navy with sympathetic Americans. By midsummer 1793, the Boston customs establishment was at a loss as to how to deal with a French-owned privateer "cruising in the harbor" with American sailors on board. Could French citizens use American ports to fit out their privateers? asked United States Attorney Christopher Gore. Were Frenchmen who had lived in the United States for several years "to be considered Frenchmen or Americans"? The French government sowed further confusion by issuing overlapping and contradictory orders about the status of American shipping. By the summer of 1793 it was entirely unclear what goods American merchants were permitted to trade with France and its enemies.[12] Believing that the United States had invited France to press these advantages, Great Britain responded by unleashing its privateers against American merchants trading with the French. The French Revolutionary Wars had come to the water's edge.[13]

French and British attacks on American shipping put American merchants in a bind. War added value to transactions with war-torn markets. But pursuing that lucre put merchants' vessels and commodities in grave danger. For instance, the sensational French frigate *L'Embuscade*, which initially drew crowds on the East Coast as it hauled British vessels to port as prizes, had begun targeting American vessels by July 1793. In the papers, the shipping news had become a rumor mill for cataloguing sightings of French and British predators.[14] Tales abounded of Americans "much insulted and abused" by British and French privateers. In the case of the ship *Fanny*, a French privateer masqueraded as a pilot boat to lure an American vessel to its capture. But most damaging was the scale of Americans' loss of merchant capital. In Alexandria, Virginia, customs officials affirmed enormous commercial losses: for instance, the schooner *Hopewell*, seized nearby Cap-Français, Saint-Domingue, valued at $8,000; the schooner *Betsey*, condemned by a British prize court, worth $5,452; the ship *Sally*, waylaid by a privateer en route from Rotterdam to Alexandria, valued at $10,000.[15]

Yet American merchants seemed more than willing to brave the dangers of the militarized Atlantic market. Between 1790 and 1794, in fact, total American tonnage to the European West Indian holdings increased by about 21,000 tons, from 103,850 tons in 1790, to 124,245 in 1794.[16] American merchants' brazen assumption of risk should not be surprising. Since before the Glorious Revolution, American merchants doing business overseas had pursued commerce in the crosshairs of interimperial warfare, no matter its official legal status. This behavior, what with the elevation of the private purse over the commonweal at any cost, is difficult to distinguish from colonial merchants' cutthroat pursuit of lucre, in which historian Cathy D. Matson finds fractals of American liberalism.[17]

Congress would eventually attempt to more narrowly define American neutrality. The 1794 "Act in addition to the act for the punishment of certain crimes against the United States" criminalized American citizens' service on a foreign privateer, "fitting out" in American territory a privateer for foreign forces, and "augmenting the force" of any foreign privateer in American waters.[18] Responsibility for enforcing these provisions fell to the custom houses. Secretary of the Treasury Alexander Hamilton, who had long since given up his supervision of the custom houses' accounts and ledgers, now turned his attention to the regulation of commercial neutrality even as he trained his sights on the whiskey rebels. Shortly after passage of the 1794 law, Hamilton dispatched a circular to the collectors of customs demanding that they police "practices which are as contrary to good order as dangerous to the National Peace." "Much from your situation must depend on *your* vigilance," he continued. "I am sure the expectation will not be disappointed."[19]

As neutrality policy placed new regulatory demands on customs officials, it threatened to alter the negotiated authority that had sprung up between commercial communities, custom houses, and federal law, since 1789. Custom-house governance had hinged on a basic negotiation between customs officials bent on collecting revenue and local merchants seeking access to the profitable Atlantic market. As merchants consistently and reliably paid over customs duties to federal officials, they quietly pushed customs officials to interpret customs laws in ways that protected and benefited local commerce. But neutrality, with its emphasis on commercial regulation instead of revenue collection, appeared to pose a sharp challenge to this arrangement of authority. That challenge was evident to no less than Jeremiah Olney, who had enraged the merchants of Providence with his literal interpretation of customs laws in the early 1790s. Indeed, in the very same letter in which he plotted his defense against "the suits of Messrs. Arnold & Dexter," Olney pledged his "attentive observance" to Treasury instructions for preserving neutrality.[20]

Yet just as the government envisioned the custom house as an institution to regulate commerce, American merchants understood the custom house as an institution to protect commerce. Thus, while officers like Olney pledged fealty to the Neutrality Proclamation, they quietly brooked, and even enabled, shady trade with foreign privateers, rebellious European colonies, and even "the enemy." A most brazen example of this occurred in

Boston in 1796 as that port's merchants sought access to French and British markets. Both belligerents had informed Boston merchants that American vessels would need new institutional protections in order to safely fly under the American flag, such as France's insistence on American vessels bearing a *rôle d'équipage*, or special bill of lading, and England's insistence on American mariners bearing comprehensive proof of American citizenship. So Boston merchants requested that Collector Benjamin Lincoln create a new "certificate" that stated "the property was American" and noting that it was issued from the Boston custom house. Lincoln obliged the merchants' request, believing that the "certificate" would "serve the interest of our merchants" without "any possible injury to the United States." The Treasury was quick to point out that in empowering Boston's merchants, Lincoln's innovative certificate jeopardized the rest of the American merchant fleet that had no access to this new document.[21]

In New York and Philadelphia, merchants involved in overseas trade also convinced customs officials to generously attenuate defaults on customs duty bonds due to the loss of a vessel or goods to foreign privateers. Here the issue was the moral implications of seizure by a foreign privateer. Did seizure and condemnation of an American, ostensibly neutral vessel imply that the vessel was, in fact, violating neutrality? And if so, if the merchant had lost his vessel or goods because of his own illegal commerce, would not he still be obligated to pay off his custom-house bonds? Philadelphia attorney Alexander J. Dallas recalled that the northeastern "merchant's wits" had prevailed upon the "abracadabra of the law." Merchants in New York argued to customs officials that a "Proof of Loss Certificate" from a marine insurance company, attesting to the fact that a vessel had been wrongly seized and condemned by a foreign privateer, was proof enough for customs officials to cancel custom-house bonds. New York collector Joshua Sands was initially pensive. "The Question is whether the Certificate is sufficient to cancel all the bonds given," he penciled on a proof of loss certificate issued by the New York Insurance Company for the brig *Ohio* in 1798. In a memorandum on the matter, Sands concluded that the certificate was "proof" enough. By the time he saw the question attached to the bonds of the chip *Favourite* in 1801, Sands wrote: "It appears to me that the M[arine] Documents are a good warrant for cancel[ing] the Bonds. Where the underwriters are satisfied to pay the loss it is good evidence that matters are in general correct." This had become Treasury policy in 1799. As Comptroller John Steele explained, the proof of loss certificate was "an indispensable" piece of documentation for canceling a custom-house bond.[22]

A more precise sense of the negotiated nature of authority at the custom house came into relief during the Washington administration's general embargo on foreign shipping between March and June 1794. Congress approved the embargo to protect American vessels from British naval vessels and privateers in particular, which had ensnared several hundred American vessels overseas.[23] Congress and the Washington administration envisioned that customs officials would enforce the law by denying all vessels the necessary documents—"clearances"—to depart for "a foreign port or place." If customs officials encountered difficulties, Washington's cabinet opined, "it is advised unanimously, that the governors of the several States ought to be called upon to enforce the said embargo by the militia."[24] In one instance, a collector of customs did in fact place "a Detachment of Volunteer Artillery at the entrance of the Harbour with orders to prevent all Vessels . . . from departing." And there were occasional reports of American merchants sailing "in defiance of the embargo."[25] More common, however, were reports of waterfront crowds assisting customs officials in the enforcement of the embargo, especially against vessels flying foreign colors. In late March, "20 armed" New Yorkers took to "the custom-house boat" in successful pursuit of "two English vessels" that had fled the embargo. In Warren, Rhode Island, a few days later, "a number of patriotic inhabitants jumped on board of several boats" and caught up to a schooner with British papers that had violated the embargo. In Charleston, "a great number of volunteers . . . accompanied" the revenue cutter and militia forces in pursuit of the British *President*.[26] Meanwhile, people took to taverns and town halls to resolve in favor of the embargo. This included the merchant community. An anonymous Rhode Island "mercantile house," for instance, confirmed its support for the measure, "though we have vessels unemployed and cargoes in store . . . until government have security, that our property will not again be invaded." Residents of Newburyport, Massachusetts, agreed "the present Embargo ought to be continued as long as the public exigencies require it."[27]

Mercantile support for the Washington administration's 1794 embargo had as much to do with self-preservation as patriotism. As the Rhode Island firm had explained, the embargo made sense as a measure that would protect merchants' "property" from French and English wantonness at sea. American neutrality had opened new and lucrative opportunities for American commerce, then, but it also pushed American merchants into a market beset by unusually dangerous risks. In the institution of the custom house, merchants doing business with France and England seemed to find opportunities to lessen that risk by using their emerging influence over waterfront governance. But when those merchants took matters into their own hands, they would provoke serious questions about the propriety of such close relations between commerce and governance at the custom house.

OF ARMS AND MERCHANTMEN

When diplomatic treaties and administrative paper failed, American merchants turned to guns. In the Anglo-American maritime world during the age of sail, merchants routinely armed their vessels to act as privateers or merely as a means of self-defense in an Atlantic marketplace characterized by "zones of war, chaos, and brutality." This had surely been the case during the American War of Independence as approximately 1,700 American privateers, bearing roughly 15,000 guns, took to the Atlantic in search of prizes.[28] During the peace that followed, though, American merchants and sea captains only sporadically armed their vessels to protect against pirates. During the 1780s, in fact, Baltimore port officials observed only a few private vessels with arms. As European warfare again militarized the Atlantic, however, more American merchants and sea captains began to mount cannons on their commercial vessels. This practice would have momentous ramifications for the American state.[29]

Arming a merchant vessel was fairly simple, though by no means cheap. Merchants and sea captains obtained cannons or carronades from foundries, at vendue on the waterfront at home or abroad, and even from the United States Navy. Carpenters then set to work mounting the firearms, cutting "gunports" in the ship's outer walls, or bulwarks, and buttressing the bulwarks to support greater impacts. Ammunition and paraphernalia—shot, "cartridges, gun screws, rammers, and sponges"—brought the typical bill for arming to several thousand dollars.[30]

As the French Revolutionary Wars reached American shores, American merchants, shipowners, and sea captains again moved to arm their vessels. The experience of Portland, Maine, merchant and captain Edward Preble underscores the logic of armament. After a voyage to the French West Indies in 1797, Preble informed one newspaper editor that the region "still wears an alarming experience to the commerce of the *United States*." He regaled a second editor with tales of no less than twenty-seven American vessels that had suffered capture at the hands of French privateers. As for his own affairs, Preble's next adventure was to be a voyage of the newly built and purchased schooner *Phenix* to Havana. With an eye to protecting his new investment, Preble now sought to take no chances. "Having seen the activities of the Guadeloupe privateersmen on his last visit to the West Indies," Preble "took the precaution of arming the *Phenix*." In Charleston, District Judge Thomas Bee explained that in such dangerous times "all American Indiamen are armed, and it is necessary they should be so."[31]

Customs officials throughout the United States responded differently to the reappearance of private armed vessels. In Charleston in December 1794, an informant told Collector Isaac Holmes that the brig *Cygnet* "was arming in this Port." Holmes pledged that "she [the *Cygnet*] should not go out" of Charleston harbor. But Holmes found a middle ground between ignoring the *Cygnet*'s arming, and seizing the vessel: "Her Guns were taken out, her Port holes nailed up, and she permitted to clear." According to the same informant, by the following day, the *Cygnet* was again "completely Armed and manned." In Charleston, District Judge Thomas Bee believed that Holmes's method of disarmament was unlawful. "The laws of neutrality and nations in no instance," he argued, "interdict neutral vessels from going to sea armed and fitted for defensive war." In Portland, Maine, Edward Preble's armed *Phenix* "cleared through customs, Havana-bound, on 6 June 1797, without hindrance." In Philadelphia, a confused Collector Sharp Delany appealed to his superior, Secretary of the Treasury Oliver Wolcott Jr., for advice on how to treat these private armed vessels.[32]

The Treasury Department officially frowned on American merchants arming their vessels. As Secretary of the Treasury Wolcott explained to Philadelphia collector Delany in 1795, "The United States being also a neutral nation, the vessels of their citizens do not in most cases require to be armed." "The arming of such vessels," he continued, "therefore raises a presumption that it is done with . . . intent contrary to the prohibition of the Act of Congress" of June 5, 1794. That act made it illegal to arm a vessel in order "to cruise or commit hostilities upon the subjects, citizens or property of another foreign prince or state with whom the United States are at peace." Wolcott concluded, "No ship belonging to any citizen of the United States is to be permitted to be armed & to sail" unless an explicit "decision of the President . . . shall be made known." This was supposed to have been "settled long since & was supposed to have been so understood." For Wolcott, armed merchant vessels were more clearly instruments of war than participants in commerce.[33]

But the line between commerce and war was almost impossible to find. This much was clear from the Federalists' flailing attempts to define acceptable and illegal arming of British and French vessels in American ports. In 1793, Hamilton devised eight convoluted rules "Governing Belligerents" that began by broadly criminalizing "the original arming and equipping" of belligerent vessels "in the Ports of the UStates." Arming "Merchant vessels" belonging to citizens of the belligerents "is deemed lawful." But armaments "of a nature solely adapted to war are deemed unlawful." In October 1794, Wolcott attempted to clarify that "the arming and equipping of vessels . . . whether offensive or defensive, by any of the belligerent parties, is unlawful." This prohibition covered arms for "protection and defence" as much as those for "combat or offensive hostility." Hamilton would later patronizingly point out to Charleston collector Isaac Holmes the difference between armaments and other improvements to a vessel. "An oar is purely an instrument of navigation," but arms were different, and "defensive equipments was as much intended to be prohibited as offensive ones."[34] Ultimately the Supreme Court would come to the Treasury's aid with the augmentation of force doctrine, which defined illegal arming as any improvement on a vessel's offensive capability. Yet it would prove notoriously hard to measure whether armaments were augmentations, replacements, or even reductions of force.[35]

Restricting the behavior of American merchants would be even more difficult because by 1794 the Treasury had made peace with the reality that the merchants wielded great influence over custom-house governance. So Wolcott was quick to frame his instructions regarding the arming of vessels as advice rather than fiat. Wolcott explained, "It is not possible for me to do more than repeat the general principles which have been established; the application of them according to their true intent & meaning, is your duty, & that of the officers concerned." Thus, even after explaining the Treasury Department's official stance on the matter, Wolcott reassured Sharp Delany that Philadelphia customs officials would determine the fabric of governance at the Philadelphia custom house. The negotiations that took place between the Treasury, customs officials, and commercial peoples over the collection of the revenue was slowly taking place with matters of regulation. And just as they had with revenue collection, local customs officials would use their discretion to adapt commercial regulations to meet the expectations of local commerce. Recall Wolcott's counsel to William Heth, the collector of Bermuda Hundred, Virginia, in a dispute about revenue collection. As to *"practice"* at the custom house, "you ought to decide yourself," wrote Wolcott. "There are shades of difference in the execution of the Laws in different districts," he conceded, but "all agree that the officers do their *duty* properly." Heth was to "take some liberties" to "fulfill the intention" of revenue laws in a way that best fit his district. Sharp Delany was now to do the same for the regulation of armed vessels. Both men would then be doing their "duty."[36]

As the Treasury placed its trust in officeholders' discretion, customs officials found ways to accommodate merchants seeking to arm. The easiest method was to blindly accept promises from merchants or ships' crews that the vessel was, in fact, armed only for defensive purposes. In Charleston, for instance, two customs officials testified that they "expect candour" from ship captains about armaments and had no reason to believe otherwise. Another officer, identified only as "Weyman" in court documents, explained that he "had no business to give an opinion" about whether vessels were improperly armed. When faced with a specific instance of ignoring a vessel that was arming, this officer cited a technicality in the law that specified inspections only after vessels concluded taking on goods. What could he do if he received word about a vessel arming itself but that was only "half loaded"? Ultimately, though, he thought himself unqualified to decide when a vessel was arming itself, for "what could he know about the intention" of an individual? [37]

When French attacks on American commerce worsened, however, Wolcott reiterated the Treasury's prohibition on armed merchant vessels. Was it "lawful to arm the Merchant Vessels of the United States for their protection and defence, while engaged in regular commerce?" asked Wolcott in the spring of 1797. While vessels bound for Asian waters were permitted to arm to defend against "Pirates and Sea Rovers," vessels in "European or West India commerce" could not. In Atlantic waters, arming of merchant vessels betrayed "hostile intentions against some one of the belligerent Nations." Wolcott then directed "that the sailing of armed vessels" to Europe or the West Indies "be restrained until otherwise ordained by Congress." Even for Wolcott, who was no stranger to convoluted circulars, this language reached special levels of abstraction. Who would restrain these vessels? By what means? Should port officials expect Congress to intervene soon? Wolcott's inability to offer details undercut the Treasury's message, and there is little evidence that the circular influenced customs officials' positions toward arming. [38]

As the Treasury soured on armed merchant vessels, commercial communities rallied behind the practice. In fact, none other than Alexander Hamilton lambasted his protégé Wolcott for seeking to prevent merchant vessels from arming. The merchants were owed nothing less. As Hamilton saw it, "Passiveness in the Government and its inability to protect the Merchants requires . . . them to protect themselves." Other advocates for arming would soon be heard. In 1798, as news of French diplomatic indecencies during the XYZ affair stirred American anger, merchant communities in several major cities began soliciting funds through subscriptions to construct a privately funded, public navy. In Newburyport, Massachusetts, and led in part by Collector of Customs Dudley Tyng, merchants and others financed the construction of a twenty-gun warship in 1798. Philadelphians, including members of the Chamber of Commerce, the Bank of the United States, and the Insurance Company of North America, followed suit. Merchant John Brown, who had harangued Collector Jeremiah Olney into opening the doors of the Providence custom house to commercial influence, took on his own subscription ship. In Charleston, Secretary of the Navy Benjamin Stoddard turned to customs official James Simons to help convene a committee to produce another subscription. As Stoddard put it, "The public Interest will be best promoted, by putting the entire direction into the hands of intelligent Merchants of great respectability and character." Their "direction" would produce ten armed vessels.[39]

But the subscription ship movement was not enough. By January 1798, as a Federalist paper in Philadelphia put it, "The question whether our merchants shall arm their vessels for defence" appeared before Congress. A second Federalist screed some months later turned to a more fundamental authority for the right to arm vessels than mere necessity. Writing of "an *authority* to arm" the merchant's vessel, "a Citizen of the United States" argued "that right existed at Common Law" prior to any federal regulations by the Treasury Department. "It is one of those *unalienbale* rights for which the *Cambridge* Patriots so warmly contend," concluded the pseudonymous diatribe.[40] In Congress, legislation quickly materialized in February 1798, aiming to permit "any vessel of the United States" to be "equipped with guns . . . for necessary defense upon the high seas." This legislation would have lifted the Adams administration's prohibition on armed merchant vessels by directing the custom houses to clear any American vessel bearing arms, on condition of securing a bond that the vessel would not engage in any but defensive hostilities. After parliamentary measures scuttled the legislation, Adams took executive action. As Harrison Gray Otis explained, Adams revoked his "orders to Collectors" and "placed the right of arming upon the broad and original basis of the law of nature and nations." American merchants were now free to arm openly and as they pleased.[41]

The Adams administration's decision to permit the arming of merchant vessels was part of a naval strategy that relied on deputized maritime labor to compensate for the nation's slender navy. The centerpiece of this strategy was a privateering program during the Quasi-War with France between 1798 and 1800. Particularly in the nation's leading seaports, merchants and sea captains arrived in noticeable numbers at the custom house for the necessary paperwork to convert their vessels to carry "a light battery and a small crew" sufficient to deter French attacks.[42] Customs officials were to take bond from any vessel seeking to arm for "double the value of such vessel" on condition that it would refrain from any "unprovoked violence upon the high seas" against American allies. Customs officials were also to convey executive instructions for the regulation of the privateers. These instructions required privateers to enter at the custom house upon conclusion of their voyage to submit a journal of their voyage and, if lucky enough to have made a capture, to turn its prize over to the custom house in advance of prize proceedings at the closest federal court. Once the owner and captain of the privateer had agreed to these terms at the custom house, they received a letter of marque.[43]

As it sanctioned the arming of merchant and privateer vessels, Congress awoke to the very real fear that merchants and ship captains would use their arms to fight their way into French markets. So in June 1798, Congress prohibited trade with France for the duration of the war by requiring customs officials to secure a bond, equivalent to the value of the ship and its cargo, from merchant vessels trading to the West Indies. If the custom house detected commerce with France, or received intelligence thereof, the government would put the bond into collection.[44] But several custom houses interpreted this so narrowly as to enervate it. Wolcott then desperately "expressed to the Collecters . . . that *all Commerce with France and her dependencies, in every description of Vessells is prohibited.*" Again, customs officials in different districts found ways to allow this trade.[45] By January 1800, a dejected Wolcott conceded that American vessels had used St. Thomas and other locales in the West Indies to establish a de facto "direct trade between the United States & French ports." American vessels also engaged in the practice of collusive capture by meeting with French vessels through "preconcerted arrangements" and then claiming to have been seized at sea. Then there was the old "distress of weather" canard—claiming that inclement weather forced them to enter a French port for safety, wherein French government officials then "forced" them to exchange their goods with the French. The custom houses in the United States did little to interfere in these proceedings. Wolcott admitted that the customs officials' inaction was understandable, since "it is impossible to distinguish cases of real capture or distress, from those which are fictitious." Yet this subterfuge and others caused no small amount of consternation to a Federalist administration at war with a great European power.[46]

Throughout the 1790s, customs officials had allowed American merchants to arm their vessels in order to access an Atlantic marketplace awash in uncertainty and violence. Congressional and Treasury attempts to regulate this behavior repeatedly stalled because customs officers were unwilling to enforce restrictions, even in times of war. Perhaps the cost of revenue had grown too dear.[47]

THE REVOLUTION OF 1800?

By all accounts, the election of Thomas Jefferson to the presidency should have radically changed the course of federal governance. For one thing, his Republican vision of political economy and empire diverged sharply from that of the Federalists. Jefferson emphasized the westward expansion of the white, landed yeomanry, who worked their land, managed their families, and voluntarily assembled in a public sphere to communicate its politics.[48] This society required an active, interventionist state, then, dedicated "to the end of protecting liberty" by producing a society of free agents "in which ordinary people could develop their faculties in order to pursue their happiness." Financing this state would require revenue. For Jefferson, the custom houses would continue to play an important role in channeling Atlantic merchant capital to the end of westward expansion.[49]

Jefferson was also suspicious of the customs establishment on ideological and political grounds. While he acknowledged the need to regulate commerce in retaliation for European trade discrimination, his goal was to achieve a global commerce free of regulatory discrimination, instead of the permanent system envisioned by the Federalists.[50] Alexander Hamilton's relationship to the custom houses further raised Jefferson's hackles. For one thing, Federalists dominated the 944 customs appointments to 1801 and virtually monopolized the plum posts of collector, naval officer, and surveyor for each port.[51] Within the Washington administration, Jefferson had also witnessed Hamilton make direct and purportedly improper use of the custom houses.[52] Republicans accordingly criticized the customs establishment as bloated and corrupt. Albert Gallatin estimated that "the expenses of collection" of federal revenue cost taxpayers and custom-house patrons no less than $300,000 per year. Tench Coxe, the renowned Republican political economist who had worked in Hamilton's Treasury until he was unceremoniously removed by President John Adams, called for a wholesale removal of all "the incumbents." The Republican press complained about the "forms, obstructions, expenses, and abuses" heaped on the people by the customs establishment.[53] Jefferson and Gallatin would make a cause célèbre out of the case of William

Priestman, a Baltimore merchant who had several hundred watches seized on a technicality.[54]

Of course, for the Republicans, the rapacious customs establishment was but one part of a broader declension narrative of government under the Federalists. As he assumed the presidency, Jefferson offered an inherently restorative vision. "Let the general government be once reduced to foreign concerns only . . . our general government may be reduced to a very simple organization, & a very unexpensive: a few plain duties to be performed by a few servants," Jefferson wrote to Postmaster Gideon Granger in mid-August 1800. As an ideological matter, Jefferson sought executive power that would be used to truncate itself and guard against its future expansion. As historian Peter S. Onuf has written, "Doctrinaire republicans were prepared to see any distant central government, even one that was located in America, as 'foreign'" or, alternatively, as "vulnerable to penetration and capture" by corrupting influences like Hamiltonian federalism. By contracting the Federalists' disparate federal government, Jefferson safeguarded the republic from any future capture or abuse of power.[55]

Jefferson's boldest changes involved personnel. Here there was some red meat to throw to the hungry base. Of the 146 officials that Jefferson could remove, Jefferson gradually dismissed 50, 41 of whom were Federalists. He cleaned house of noted Federalists in Philadelphia, removing Sharp Delany—who had seized William Priestman's watches—and New York, replacing Joshua Sands. In Connecticut, which Jefferson "considered as the fortress" of federalism, the president replaced Elizur Goodrich with the seventy-year-old mayor of New Haven, Samuel Bishop, who Federalists complained could barely "write his name," lacked numeracy, and was "totally unacquainted with the Revenue Laws." Jefferson coolly explained to Federalist critics that the "will of the nation" had brought his party to power, and that he saw nothing wrong with this will having a "moderate" voice in the federal government.[56] But Jefferson and Gallatin were more careful in their appointments than has been appreciated. They solicited recommendations from leading Republicans and sought out intelligent and diligent officers, even when the right candidate was not a loyal partisan. The collectorship of New York went to importing merchant David Gelston, who was a Burrite and no particular friend to the administration, because Gelston's "credit is good" and "he is very highly respected by all parties and all honest Men, for his rigid & irreproachable probity." [57]

However, at the custom houses the revolution in federal governance that seemed poised to occur after the election of 1800 never came to pass.[58]

This was in part because the state that Jefferson inherited proved to be a far cry from the aggressive leviathan that had been portrayed in Republican thought. For one thing, the Federalists had not built the custom houses to whip votes. Rather, the Federalists hoped that their officeholders' paternal superiority and careful management of local commercial affairs would secure the political loyalty of the people. And in the more prosaic realms of revenue laws and commercial regulation, Jefferson and Gallatin discovered that Hamilton and Wolcott had presided over a remarkably ramshackle system.[59] Several collectors had not submitted records for years. In Great Egg Harbor in New Jersey, Daniel Benezet, brother of antislavery crusader Anthony Benezet, sent no accounts from 1790 to 1795. When Gallatin's Treasury discovered the oversight in 1802, the Great Egg customs records had disappeared. How could it be, thundered Republican congressman Joseph Clay of Pennsylvania, that the government took notice of this eleven years after his appointment, "seven years after his dismissal, five years after the death of his father, and four years after the final settlement . . . of his father's estate, and after his own death"?[60]

If the destructive spirit of party, and specifically Federalist Toryism, was not the driving force of federal governance in the early United States, then what was? As Jefferson and Gallatin confronted the difficulties of enforcing neutrality, they honed in on the remarkable power of local merchant communities to shape custom-house governance to their ends. As was the case with so much of American political culture in the early republic, the Haitian Revolution proved to be the turning point.

"FORCING A COMMERCE"

The Louisiana Purchase of 1803 furnished Jefferson with confidence that he could successfully channel the revenue gleaned from merchant capital toward the westward expansion of an agricultural empire of yeomanry. Jefferson and Gallatin found, as Washington, Hamilton, Adams, and Wolcott had before them, that the destructive war that enveloped Europe created an enormous, seemingly boundless amount of wealth for American merchants, and in turn, the federal government. On January 1, 1803, Gallatin estimated that the previous year's customs revenue exceeded $12 million, far outstripping previous years' tallies. The "large revenue on hand, together with the economies in expenditure" introduced by the Jefferson administration, "made it possible to consummate" the Louisiana Purchase "from the sale of the new stock and from funds on hand, without resorting to a temporary loan or even to new taxes." The Federalists stabilized customs revenue in pursuit of a commercial utopia. Jefferson appropriated their statecraft to add 838,000 square miles for western expansion.[61]

But customs regulation was a different story, especially the persistent problem of armed merchant vessels. In his November 8, 1804, annual message to Congress, Jefferson wrote, "Complaints have been received that persons residing within the United States have taken on themselves to arm merchant vessels and to force a commerce into certain ports and countries in defiance of the laws of those countries." The individuals responsible for "forcing a commerce" had undertaken "to wage private war, independently of the authority of their country." This behavior could not "be permitted in a well-ordered society." Ethics aside, to "force a commerce" was to provoke "other nations and to endanger the peace of our own." This was particularly true of France because the Convention of 1800 that had settled the Quasi-War prohibited American merchants from trading with France's enemies, and vice versa. With the stakes so high, Jefferson had no doubt that Congress "will adopt measures for restraining it effectually in future."[62]

Jefferson adopted this strong language against the arming of merchant vessels at Albert Gallatin's request. In the previous three years, the two men had been bedeviled by American merchants and sea captains who used the force of arms to fight their way into one market in particular: Saint-Domingue, soon to become Haiti in 1804. Americans had muscled their way through French blockades to trade with the black revolutionaries who had led a slave rebellion, emancipated themselves from the shackles of slavery, and achieved their independence from France. In so doing, however, these American merchants flouted French laws that restricted foreign commerce with the rebellious colony of Saint-Domingue. As the American merchants taunted French military administrators, they jeopardized the United States' relationship with France and threatened American neutrality—"the peace of our own." The crux of the problem, then, was how the Jefferson administration could "restrain" the armed Haiti trade. Its locale was the custom house. The Jefferson administration's losing struggle to regulate the armed Haiti trade would inform the United States and the world of the emerging contest between official administration and local commerce for control of the custom house.[63]

Americans had, of course, armed their vessels throughout the 1790s, both in contravention of and in accordance with federal laws and regulations. Congress's authorization for American armed merchantmen to harass French commerce during the Quasi-War had, in fact, lapsed. However,

John Adams's spring 1798 decree lifting all restrictions on private armed vessels had quietly remained in effect. Thus merchants and sea captains had no legal reason to disarm. Nor had the Atlantic become any less chaotic or dangerous after the suspension of the Quasi-War. In the span of a few years, Haitian revolutionaries expelled British forces and engaged invading French forces under General Victor Emmanuel LeClerc. Americans would thus contend with familiar foes in the form of British naval vessels and a French "armada hovering off the shores" of Haiti. The incorporation of the United States newest metropolis, New Orleans, after the Louisiana Purchase, also spread havoc from the Gulf of Mexico through the Leeward Islands as pirates and privateers—often in collusion with American merchants—stalked the gulf.[64]

Even in his earliest days as president, Jefferson likely knew that merchant vessels had retained their armaments. Gallatin would later explain to Senator Samuel Latham Mitchill of New York that Jefferson chose to ignore the issue in 1801. The problem was that Jefferson did not believe it his place—or any other president's place—to limit or regulate naval armament. Here Jefferson stood in stark contrast to his predecessor, John Adams. Jefferson simply did not think it the role of the executive "to permit or forbid, at his pleasure the arming of vessels." *At his pleasure.* Adams had sullied the presidency with his whimsical power grabs. For Jefferson, "so long as force was not used," or "used so rarely not to create alarm," the United States would not move "in a special manner against occasional acts of violence." That a handful of merchants and sea captains sporadically resorted to force was hardly a pretext for executive action.[65]

In addition to being squeamish about executive power, Jefferson was also loath to disrupt a long-established commercial pathway. As early as the 1780s, a New York merchant named Henry Packer Dering—whom Hamilton would make the collector of customs for Sag Harbor—observed markets in Saint-Domingue saturated with American competition. British discrimination against American commerce in the British West Indies pushed Americans to expand trade with French planters in Saint-Domingue in the early 1790s. As historian Alec Dun has shown, Saint-Domingue commerce occupied a steadily growing share of Philadelphia merchants' imports in the four years after ratification of the Constitution, culminating in approximately 15 percent of total imports by 1792.[66] This commerce continued to grow even during the Haitian Revolution. Leading merchant houses in New York, Philadelphia, and Baltimore delivered millions of tons of foodstuffs and "supplies" to French planters and colonial officials. Some even supplied vessels to ferry "French soldiers" to and from battle with the black revolutionaries.⁶⁷ With General Toussaint L'Ouverture's victory in 1796, American merchants transitioned to doing greater business with Saint-Domingue's black population. As a correspondent forecasted to New York merchant house Charles Rogers & Co., Toussaint's victory would undoubtedly "increase the wants and engage the speculators." During the Quasi-War, this commerce grew with the backing of the Adams administration but much to the chagrin of France. As historian Rayford Logan has explained, it seemed that Americans would do anything to reach Saint-Domingue, "by resorting to trickery at first and finally to force."⁶⁸

By 1801, the scope of American commerce with Saint-Domingue began to trouble France. For one thing, France refused to acknowledge the independence of Saint-Domingue even as Toussaint continued to accrue impressive gains. For the French, then, Americans were engaging in an illegal commerce with a criminal insurrection. What Americans traded was equally at issue for it was an open secret that New York, Baltimore, and Philadelphia shipped Toussaint military supplies in addition to food and provisions. The election of Thomas Jefferson offered some hope to the French. Jefferson's sympathies with the French were well known. As France planned a massive invasion of the island that would begin in early 1802, it approached Jefferson for aid. Perhaps a fellow republican could exert sufficient authority and influence on the merchants to sabotage Toussaint's supply lines?⁶⁹ Dispatches from Saint-Domingue, however, gave Jefferson reason to rebuff the French. United States Consul Tobias Lear, former aide-de-camp to George Washington, saw great potential in the young republic. "A new and important aera has commenced here," wrote Lear in mid-July 1801. Even in its war-torn state, "the Productions of this Island" were "immense" and "the consumption of our Articles great indeed." By this point it was clear that American vessels were finding their ways into Saint-Domingue ports en masse.⁷⁰

As it became clear that the Jefferson administration was unwilling to take measures against the Saint-Domingue trade, France took matters into its own hands. During their invasion of Saint-Domingue in February 1802, French forces had the authority to seize American "Vessels and Cargoes" if found in the waters of an insurrectionary colony. American merchants within Saint-Domingue faced only a slightly less draconian alternative as French military administrators forced them to enter into dramatically unfair bargains. On March 17, 1802, the French ambassador to the United States, Louis Pichon, informed Secretary of State James Madison that American commerce was banned from all ports in Saint-

Domingue other than the two under French occupation, Cap-Français and Port Republicain. All other voyages were subject to seizure and condemnation. Losses quickly mounted for American merchants and their insurers. In Baltimore alone, the five leading marine insurers posted total losses of close to $500,000 in late 1804.[71]

However meekly, the Jefferson administration publicly sided with France. Madison pledged that the United States would "respect" the French rule that "all foreign trade with the Island is limited to the two ports." Yet, it would be up to France to punish Americans who took it upon themselves to flout the regulations. The French declaration, explained Madison, "is understood as subjecting individual citizens to the penalties legally attached to prohibited commerce." The offending merchants were mere "individual citizens" committing criminal acts. The French were wise to Madison's coy language and demanded stronger action on the part of the Jefferson administration. Again, Madison walked a fine line between government policy and individual criminals. "The American government" pledged to respect French law, while "American merchants" flouted those laws on their own.[72]

The Jefferson administration's purposeful neglect of American armed merchant vessels all but gave unofficial license for them to pursue adventures to Haiti, and the French responded by unleashing their privateers and naval vessels on American shipping. For once, France and Great Britain would see eye to eye. By the summer of 1804, the British government observed that vessels had "armed in, and have sailed from, the different ports of the United States." Pichon, too, noted with distaste that disrepute had descended on American ports "from one end of the continent to the other." "American merchants," he explained, "publicly arm, in the ports of the United States." Both France and England wondered how the Jefferson administration could allow these vessels to arm without any "commission or authority whatever from the Government of the United States." The United States was not at war. Congress had not authorized custom houses to issue letters of marque to privateers. American merchants armed their vessels simply because they wished to do so.[73] None of this was denied in the United States. New York merchant George Barnewell openly conceded that he had indeed "armed for defence" two vessels bound for the West Indies and that "both these vessels were regularly cleared at the custom-house" in New York. From his lofty bench in Charleston, District Judge Thomas Bee added that "most of the vessels engaged in this trade went armed."[74]

United States custom houses were responsible for a second problem associated with the private armed vessels bound for Haiti. Most often, these vessels submitted papers to the custom house listing legally permitted destinations and then sailed to forbidden ports. Take, for instance, the Charleston brig *Nancy* with an armament of fourteen guns and a crew of forty. In August 1804, Charleston customs officials cleared the *Nancy* for a trip to the permitted French port of Port Republicain. It in fact sailed to the prohibited port of Port-au-Prince. In this way customs officials facilitated the voyage of an armed vessel to Haiti, while also providing sham paperwork intended to cover the voyage in legality. In this case, however, legal formalities mattered little. The British frigate *Desiree* stormed the vessel and pressed twelve of the crew. Undermanned and flailing, the *Nancy* now made an easy target for French vessels, and it was easily captured and condemned.[75]

By 1804, skirmishes between American merchant vessels—armed and unarmed—in the West Indies and French naval vessels and privateers had become commonplace. The brig *John*, for instance, had "entered the Cape [Français]" to trade legally with the French occupying forces but, "not finding a market," hovered nearby, raised the hackles of French forces, and then fell victim to French seizure. Merchants in Baltimore also reported the brigs *Dove* and *Swift Packet*, as well as the schooners *Peggy*, *John*, *Polly*, and *Joseph* to their insurers between February and December 1804. The Cap-Français firm Killen & Williams warned Baltimore marine insurance underwriters that the situation disallowed the possibility of an "accurate sketch of our Political Situation which is not yet organized."[76] Eventually, the risks of the waters around revolutionary Haiti became too much to bear for marine insurers in Baltimore. The McKim brothers of the influential Baltimore Insurance Company would revise their standard contractual interpretation to shield themselves from the liability of paying out policies for merchant vessels that sailed for permitted ports in French-controlled Saint-Domingue but that muscled their way into restricted ports. "The risk from Port to port in St. Domingo was not insured," explained Alexander McKim, because "if such a liberty could be taken, Insurers would find themselves on many risks they never contemplated."[77]

Finally, in the summer of 1804, the Jefferson administration explored strategies to clamp down on the armed Haiti trade. Philadelphia collector of customs John Peter Muhlenberg, a Jefferson loyalist of impeccable credentials—major general in the Revolutionary War, member of the Cincinnati, delegate to the Constitutional Convention, and former U.S. senator—conceived of the first approach. Because "vessels bound to Hispaniola were generally armed," Muhlenberg "thought it proper to require bonds and security from the owners that they shall not commit any acts of hostility against the subjects of powers at peace with the United States." In other words, merchants in the "Hispaniola" trade, or more generally the West Indies trade, could still arm their vessels so long as they pledged their word and a hefty bond to refrain from using their arms against French vessels.[78]

The Muhlenberg plan was a clever means of working within the negotiated authority at the Philadelphia custom house while appearing to take punitive action against merchants behaving badly.[79] For one thing, how exactly would Muhlenberg catch wind of American armed merchant vessels committing "acts of hostility" against the French? Presumably, Muhlenberg would have to search newspapers and mercantile gossip to discover a merchant's culpability. Even on a broader register, the plan fit neatly within the way authority had come to work at the custom houses. Bonds to ensure persons comported themselves according to the rules a bore striking resemblance to the aged and familiar common-law tool known as the "bond for good behavior." In fact, Secretary of the Treasury Albert Gallatin would use this formulation in discussing the Muhlenberg plan with Jefferson. As historian Joshua M. Stein has explained, colonial judges used bonds as a way to deter assaults, because a bond was more expensive than a "typical fine for those found guilty of assault." If an individual who had posted a bond for good behavior violated its terms by committing an assault, the judge placed the bond in collection. By the first decade of the nineteenth century, however, the bond for good behavior had come to appear to be a far lighter punishment than the judges' new favored practice for deterring assault: incarceration. Thus Muhlenberg's plan had the added benefit of appearing at once familiar, nominal, and harmless.[80]

Hopeful though they were that Muhlenberg's customs "bonds for good behavior" might quell French diplomatic protests, Jefferson and Gallatin worried about the program's legality. Muhlenberg, after all, had devised this new bond on his own accord, so, as Gallatin put it, it was "unauthorized by law." So Gallatin asked Muhlenberg to devise a test case, and Muhlenberg promised to keep an eye out for "any vessel [that] should by her arming give cause of suspicion that she might be employed in acts of hostility."[81] In August, Muhlenberg found his suspicious parties: Philip Nicklin and Robert Griffith, English émigrés whose commercial firm was among the Philadelphia's foremost. Nicklin and Griffith owned the *America*, "with twenty two nine pound Guns with Carriages complete," and sought to send it to the West Indies. They also had a well-known axe to grind against the French, who repeatedly attacked their vessels on the grounds of Nicklin and Griffith's English nationality.[82] Philadelphia customs officials' demand of a bond for good behavior surprised Nicklin and Griffith, who noted that the vessel had several times previously been "admitted to an Entry" at the Philadelphia custom house. They promptly refused to post the bond, leading to a hearing before District Judge Richard Peters. The Jefferson administration would probably have preferred another judge because Peters was a noted Federalist. But there was some reason for hope. Peters had received a very public rebuke from the Jay court a decade before for ordering the seizure of a French privateer in American waters. Chief Justice Jay had reminded Peters that a seizure could occur if and only if a vessel had armed itself in American waters in order to make war abroad with a nation at peace with the United States. Moreover, Peters's Federalist jurisprudence appeared to fit neatly with the administration's theory of the federal custom houses' power to use the common-law instrument of the bond for good behavior. In Worrall's Case (1798) Peters argued for requisite federal authority to punish any crime that augured "the subversion of any federal institution or at the corruption of its public officers." He would later confide that he "who believe in the *Common Law*" had "been willing to go farther to remedy the evils" of the "lamentably defective" federal criminal law.[83]

Judge Peters, however, proved unwilling to stretch the boundaries of federal law to encompass Muhlenberg's custom-house bond for good behavior. "This is a fine Theory," mocked Peters in a private letter to Timothy Pickering some years later. According to Peters's account, the district judge demanded that Philadelphia attorney Alexander J. Dallas "point out any Law to justify me," but that "Dallas knew better." Peters's specific problem was that bonds "to bind to good behavior and security of the peace" were "not intended to include ex-territorial cases." In short, the custom houses could not take bonds on the condition that merchants behave outside the United States. Customs officials could only govern commercial behavior within their legally defined jurisdiction. What was to be done, then, in the instance of a vessel that seemed to be arming "with intentions to commit hostilities, either defensive or offensive, against either of the belligerent powers"? Peters claimed that if faced with incontrovertible evidence of such behavior, he would issue writs against the owners, allowing the custom house to make a seizure.[84]

If the custom houses could not themselves develop legal means to regulate the armed Haiti trade, perhaps Congress could. Or so Jefferson and Gallatin hoped. This was how the 1804 annual message came to address the issue of armed merchant vessels. In addition to his choice words aimed at merchants who might "endanger the peace of our own," Jefferson exhorted Congress to "adopt measures for restraining it effectually in future." This rhetoric alone was crucial. As Jefferson explained to Thomas Paine, Napoleon "expressed satisfaction at that paragraph in my message to Congress on the subject of that commerce."[85]

Between November 1804 and March 1805, Congress considered legislation "to regulate the clearance of armed merchant vessels" from the custom houses. Jeffersonians in the House of Representatives, led by William Eustis and Joseph Clay, drafted the Muhlenberg plan of customs bonds for good behavior into a statute "to prevent the forced trade to St. Domingo," as Clay put it. In order to clear a custom house for a port in the West Indies, a merchant would have to post bond on the promise not to "make or commit any depredation, outrage, unlawful assault, or violence, against the vessels, citizens, subjects, or territory of any nation in amity with the United States." The bill met resistance from an unexpected quarter, however, in the person of John Eppes, Jefferson's son-in-law. Eppes simply did not trust the merchants involved in the Haiti trade. "What!" he exclaimed. "Shall it be permitted to every man, who can execute a bond, to *wield the arms of the nation*?" His distrust derived from the fact that sentiments other than patriotism and reverence for the public good motivated the merchant. By contrast, the merchant vessel "armed banditti" navigated on "whim, caprice, or a thirst of lucre"—principles in fact at odds with the rule of law. It was in this frame of reference that another congressman from Virginia, John G. Jackson, demanded that Congress carve out a new criminal jurisdiction, between the categories of "piracy or felony," for misdeeds performed by armed merchant vessels at sea.[86]

Meanwhile, northeastern Federalists, a few commercially oriented Republicans, and leading merchants sought to scuttle restrictions on arming merchant vessels. Senator William Plumer of New Hampshire declared that "Our merchants have traded to St. Domingo—Our government has never once intimated to them that the trade was unlawful—or that they ought not to arm their vessels in carrying it on." "On the contrary," continued Plumer, "our Merchants have at our Custom houses cleared out their vessels for that island, when they were known to be fully armed & manned." Louis Pichon would have agreed, however angrily, with Plumer's conclusions. "Not a single Collector has refused, or even hesitated, to give them a Clearance. Will our government now . . . expose our innocent merchants to ruin!"[87] The New York Chamber of Commerce, too, offered a memorial against the legislation. Of course, they had to arm their vessels in self-defense. Yet John Murray, president of the organization, offered a

Second Amendment rationale for arming. "The inhabitants of the United States have immemorially claimed the right of possessing arms for the defence of their houses, their lives, and property," argued Murray. No matter "at home," in "the bosom of the State, " or "upon the ocean," the American "may lawfully carry arms in self-defence." Knowing that unadulterated individualism may not have been the most timely sentiment, Murray also posited that the merchants were doing the work of government. Since "the commerce of the United States is too diversified and widely extended" for protection by naval "convoys," armed merchant vessels would do what the state could not.[88]

While commercial interests had been able to shape the practices of federal governance at the custom houses, their allies now intervened at a higher level. As historian Donald Hickey observes, Congress's resulting legislation regulating the armed Haiti trade was badly "watered down." The dilution was largely the work of Republican senator Samuel Smith of Maryland, who led a special committee to consider the legislation. Smith had made his considerable fortune as a merchant in the West Indies and other trades, and he remained a close ally of the Baltimore overseas merchants. Smith struck out most of the bill's most punitive measures. However, Smith, "Republican senators who were merchants themselves or closely connected with mercantile interests," and their temporary Federalist allies could not overcome a Republican majority loyal to Jefferson. The final version required merchants to post bond at the custom house that they would use their arms "merely for resistance and defence, in case of involuntary hostility."[89]

The 1805 law regulating the armed Haiti trade had little effect. Even allies of the Jefferson administration like Senator George Logan conceded that the legislation had been merely nominal. In fact, Logan believed that the armed trade had grown "to as great if not greater extent than formerly." The French concurred. Because of the failure of "neighboring neutral countries" to instill "measures which are in their power" against "the infamous cupidity" of the Haiti merchants, French general Louis Ferrand predicted a French naval onslaught on American vessels. For Ferrand, the whole situation could be blamed on the custom houses. Ferrand declared that "the officers of the customs, in several ports of the United States," were facilitating the armed Haiti trade. They custom houses also received the lion's share of blame for allowing merchants to arm in the first place.[90]

In at least one instance, the accusations against customs officials for undermining the 1805 armed Haiti trade law proved to be correct. In the summer of 1805, Philadelphia magnate Stephen Girard refused to take out a bond for his ship *Voltaire*, which had "4 pounders to be mounted as Signal Guns," bound for Havana. Philadelphia customs officials noted, "The owner binds himself to conform to the decision of the Treasury on the Question of what is to be considered Arming!" Girard's word would suffice. Undoubtedly, Girard's status allowed him to take this sort of action and employ this rationale, for there was no more powerful merchant in Philadelphia. Yet, the fact that customs officials felt no compunction about recording the transaction suggests that they expected others who would review the books to understand their own decision-making logic.[91]

The failure of the 1805 law was evident beyond the Philadelphia waterfront. Thomas Jefferson noted that continued tensions with France over the issue of "Santo Domingo" owed to "the conduct of our merchants." Meanwhile, William Johnson, associate justice of the Supreme Court, struck a grave chord in his lengthy circuit opinion upholding the United States' powers to punish merchants trading with black Haitians in violation of French law. "Every nation is bound to restrain its own citizens from the commission of offences against all other nations," began Johnson. Yet it was "impossible, in the present state of things for the most vigilant government to prevent those aggressions which a love of gain and spirit of adventure are hourly producing." American merchants who fought their way into Haitian-controlled ports were "waging an individual war." The lures of the Haiti market, it seemed, had again overawed the Treasury's administrative power.[92]

By late 1805, the persistence of the Haiti trade in the face of federal law implicated American merchants in an even greater scheme. Was it "sound policy" for Americans to nourish the free "black population of St. Domingo whilst we have a similar population in our Southern States," wondered George Logan. What if "an insurrection take place . . . in that part of the Union?" If the contagion of liberty did indeed spread from Haiti to the American South, commerce would no doubt bear the blame, for, as historian Peter Linebaugh has argued, sailing vessels were "the most important conduit of Pan-African communication before the appearance of the long-playing record." In this context the failure of the custom houses to meaningfully enforce the 1805 law threatened the nation's very fabric.[93]

Moved by racial fears and "the pressing remonstrances of France," Jefferson now moved for a second law to suppress the armed Haiti trade.[94] Since neither the merchants nor the custom houses could be trusted with a partial measure such as the bond for good behavior, Congress and the administration turned to an outright prohibition. In January 1806, Congress took up a measure to "*prohibit* the merchants of New York and other

Sea ports, from trading in the violent manner they have done with the revolted negroes of Hayti."[95] Some deemed the effort hopeless because the custom houses simply could not enforce any law restraining the Haiti trade. "No law," declared Representative Eppes, "can prevent the evasions of our merchants, if they are determined to trade with the inhabitants of that islands." Jacob Crowninshield, who had taken every which position on the 1805 law, now mocked the attempt to draft new legislation. "Pass what law you please," explained Crowninshield, for "you cannot stop the intercourse between the citizens of the United States and the inhabitants of St. Domingo."[96]

The February 1806 "Act to suspend the Commercial intercourse between the United States, and certain parts of the island of St. Domingo" suffered the same fate as its predecessor. As historian Donald Hickey explains, "The Haiti trade ban did not live up to the hopes and fears of contemporaries." American merchants and others still found ways to get to Haitian markets. This was not challenging. After all, American merchants had pursued this trade, under varying colors of legality, for several decades. As New York collector of customs David Gelston explained, it was a simple task for American vessels to secure a clearance for a nearby port, such as St. Thomas, and then "be employed to run to & from the Cape [Français]." Baltimore merchants added a clever twist to this practice by landing at St. Thomas, undertaking a sham sale of their vessels to "Danish Subjects and afterwards proceed to the Island of St. Domingo."[97] Other merchants used the uncertainty of war to their advantage. The owners of the vessel *Brutus*, for instance, sought a clearance for "the Island of Gonaive" off the northwest coast of Hispaniola, on the grounds that the French had recently taken control of the island. Gelston thought it fell under the 1806 prohibition. "Notwithstanding the respect due" to the merchants pressing their case, Gelston worried that the practice "appears to me so much like an evasion of the law." For Gelston, the question embodied in the *Brutus*'s proposed journey "appears to be of so much magnitude" as to determine the utility of the 1806 law. Thus he requested that the Treasury Department provide succor. He received no answer.[98]

The Treasury Department's pregnant silence on how, exactly, customs officials were to enforce the 1806 Haiti embargo betrayed the Jefferson administration's waning concern with and ability to police the armed Haiti trade. Senator George Logan conceded privately that in drafting the law, "it was not his intention to prohibit the trade," but rather solely "to please the French, which he said this bill would do—& not injure our own traders."[99] This was a remarkably cynical interpretation of several years' worth of efforts to rein in a commerce that had, at different times, augured racial apocalypse and world war. Indeed, the federal government had for several years tried to police a commerce that promised to jeopardize the national interest. Repeatedly, the custom houses had proven unable to strike a balance between local commercial pressure and official policy. Commerce that had so recently been celebrated had come to appear dangerous. Governance that had once bestowed revenue and legitimacy now seemed untrustworthy.[100]

On July 12, 1804, Alexander Hamilton died. Just a day before he had made his ill-fated journey to the dueling ground at Weehawken, New Jersey, and was wounded by Aaron Burr. Just a few months later, Thomas Jefferson's annual message would accuse American merchants involved in the armed Haiti trade of endangering the national good. It would be the first of many moments when the ghost of Alexander Hamilton would seem to haunt the Republicans. It was Hamilton, after all, who had counseled customs officials to more loosely interpret statutes and Treasury instructions in ways that would secure the "good will of the Merchants." It was Hamilton, too, who established the powerful precedent that the central government would not involve itself in the daily affairs of the custom houses. And finally, it was on Hamilton's watch that commercial peoples and federal officials negotiated sharp limits on the custom houses' ability to coerce merchants and others involved in the import trades. For the better part of the Federalist era, it had been unnecessary to test those negotiated limits. As a result of the vicissitudes of the Napoleonic Wars, however, the Jefferson administration was compelled to do so in the first decade of the nineteenth century.[101]

Historians are fond of telling the story of the early American republic through the intellectual conflict between Hamilton and Jefferson. They are unquestionably convenient proxies—with Hamilton standing for commerce, strong government, and Federalism, and Jefferson for agrarianism, statelessness, and Republicanism. Yet, what occurred on the waterfront, in the custom houses, and in the Treasury Department between 1801 and 1807, and especially in the context of the Haitian Revolution, illustrates that central government and governance were no less vexing under Jefferson than they had been under Washington and Adams. Indeed, the "Revolution of 1800" did not displace the practices that had taken root and flowered at the custom houses at the behest of the Federalists. This Republican government was stuck with Federalist governance.[102]

CHAPTER FIVE

Jefferson's Embargo and the Era of Commercial Restrictions, 1807–1815

Through the problem of armed merchant vessels during the Haitian Revolution the Jefferson administration began to see that all was not well at the custom houses. Although revenue was continuing to flow into the Treasury, regulations on commerce were increasingly difficult to enforce. Customs officials proved either unwilling or unable to effectively curb a commerce that posed unmistakable danger to the nation's well-being. This struggle would grow dramatically in the next few years as Jefferson and Madison tried to use custom houses to "peaceably coerce" France and England, through embargoes and related commercial restrictions, to treat American commerce fairly. At stake was America's standing in the world. Despite great pressure from the Treasury, customs officials continued to favor local commerce over federal law. Soon the United States would have no choice but to declare war against Great Britain.

Throughout the United States, from the Great Lakes to the southeastern borderlands, from Charleston to Boston, from Baltimore to New Orleans, import and export merchants and merchant sailors pressured customs officers to soften or abandon the federal government's commercial restrictions. Where innuendo did not suffice, waterfront peoples emerged and gathered in intimidating or riotous crowds. These crowds monitored official behavior, invaded custom houses, meted out beatings, and stole seized goods until customs officials gave in. The commercial crowd's influence in local courtrooms proved equally useful. Stubbornly zealous officers faced lawsuits before unsympathetic juries and the prospect of financial ruin. But most customs officials knew better.

The extent of the problem of governance at the custom houses was a great surprise to Thomas Jefferson, James Madison, and Albert Gallatin, among others in the nation's capital. They had not been so naïve as to forget the events of the Haiti trade. Yet they believed that the nationalist fervor occasioned by French and British depredations on American commerce would temporarily subdue the waterfront spirit of gain and adventure. Moreover, in the embargo's temporary restriction of American commerce abroad, they saw the potential to liberate American trade from foreign meddling.[1]

The Republicans were wrong on both counts. Their sense of national citizenship simply did not exist among the commercial people of the early United States, or if it did exist, it was insufficient to overcome established norms of governance. The bigger problem lay with customs officials, however, and their seemingly unshakable deference to the commercial world that surrounded the custom house.

THE LEGAL ARCHITECTURE OF COMMERCIAL RESTRICTIONS

Between 1806 and 1815, Congress, with the approval of Presidents Jefferson and Madison, enacted twenty-four laws that restricted American commerce with the rest of the world. Each restriction had its own immediate precipitant. But they all had two things in common. First, the commercial restrictions presupposed that strategically limiting American commerce with foreign markets would push European powers into treating American vessels and sailors more fairly. Second, the custom houses were responsible for enforcing them.[2] To no small extent, then, the laws and their enforcement would dictate the American diplomatic position during the Napoleonic Wars. They would also test the nation's republican bona fides. Were American merchants capable of sacrificing their bottom line for the greater good? Could Jefferson and Madison muster authority enough to subordinate merchant capital to the commonweal?

The diplomatic and commercial crises that precipitated Republican commercial restrictions had been brewing for some time. French privateers had been a nuisance since 1793. British policy toward American commerce and maritime laborers would prove even more important. First, the 1805 *Essex* decision by the British admiralty prohibited indirect trade between enemy countries or colonies. Under what would come to be known as the doctrine of continuous voyage, it did not matter that a vessel carrying goods from one enemy jurisdiction to another broke up its voyage in a neutral port. This doctrine was poised to shatter the United States' reexport trade, which had boomed since the outbreak of European hostilities in 1793. A second policy concerning maritime commerce, the so-called

Rule of 1756, allowed privateers and the Royal Navy to seize neutral ships participating in wartime commerce that would have been restricted during peacetime. The only way to avoid triggering either rule was by "a bona fide importation into the United States," according to historian Bradford Perkins.[3] American merchant vessels found themselves boarded repeatedly by the British navy. Proceedings in the British admiralty were swift and punitive. The demonstrable tilt of the playing field against American carrying merchants fueled commercial communities' scorn toward Great Britain. "Such a set of villains as the Court of Admiralty is never before existed," growled one American merchant.[4]

The British policy of naval impressment furnished a second direct cause of American commercial restrictions. Great Britain had long employed the press gang to fill out the decks of the Royal Navy. After the outbreak of the conflict with the French in the 1790s, British officials suspected that thousands of the Crown's subjects had migrated to the more favorable maritime labor market in the United States. British cruisers trawled the North Atlantic for potential conscripts, and crews were prone to seize mariners on the slightest possibility of British citizenship. By 1806, one estimate claimed 2,273 American citizens had been impressed. Congress tried to protect American sailors with official documentation of their identity and consular networks to advocate for the impressed.[5] But the consuls performed unevenly, and protections afforded by identification documents were paper thin. Impressments both disrupted the United States maritime labor market and reminded the world of the inchoate nature of United States citizenship.[6]

The Jeffersonians turned to commercial restrictions to save the young nation's already fragile sense of honor.[7] The basic concept of the restrictions assumed the existence of a muscular federal power to regulate commerce. Though the Constitution explicitly granted the federal government the power to regulate interstate and international commerce, Congress and the Washington, Adams, and Jefferson administrations had asserted the commerce power chiefly through customs regulations reminiscent of the British navigation laws—licensing vessels for interstate or international trade, for instance. Instead, commercial restrictions policed access to and participation in the market. The 1806 "Act to prohibit the importation of certain goods," or Non-Importation Act, declared "it shall not be lawful to import into the United States" entire classes of commercial goods, to wit, "all articles of which leather," "silk," "hemp or flax," or "tin or brass is the material of chief value." It also enumerated narrower categories such as "woollen cloths whose invoice prices shall exceed five shillings sterling per square yard," "window glass," "paper of every description," "nails and spikes," "and pictures and prints," to name a few. Though motivated by very different causes, the law "to prohibit the importation of Slaves into any port or place within . . . the United States" made the federal government responsible for policing labor, perhaps the most valuable commodity of all. It took effect on March 2, 1807, just as the Jefferson administration was beginning to make use of commercial restrictions. It criminalized at the federal level an entire species of commerce in human flesh. Importantly, in one iteration of these restrictions, prohibited goods were poisoned fruit. Thus, even after contraband may have breached the maritime border, customs officials were empowered to search conveyances "of any kind whatsoever, and to stop any person travelling on foot" for goods "which shall have been introduced into the United States in any manner contrary to law." The federal government had forayed into the world of market regulation—which was traditionally the purview of localities—to determine what goods the people could import, export, buy, and sell.[8]

The most significant of these commercial restrictions were the Non-Importation Acts of 1806 and 1808, the Embargo Acts of 1807, 1808, 1809, and 1813, the Non-Intercourse Act of 1809, and "Macon's Bill Number 10" of 1810. The nonimportation laws aimed chiefly to curb British imports. Jefferson's embargo was actually a set of statutes aimed at halting American exports to Europe, but especially Great Britain. The December 1807 bill was but a scant few paragraphs, and it would require substantial revisions over three separate bills the following year. The 1809 embargo law, discussed at length below, overhauled the entire restriction system with more stringent administrative requirements and exacting penalties. With the demise of Jefferson's embargo, Congress enacted the Non-Intercourse Act of 1809. This law banned American exports to Great Britain and France, as well as imports from Great Britain and France. The "war" embargo of 1812 kept American vessels from becoming trapped in Europe at the outbreak of hostilities.[9]

Republican commercial restrictions relied on customs officials for enforcement. Each statute provided the authority and duties of customs officials, some in more detail than others. The 1806 and 1809 Non-Importation Acts gave customs officials in each port the power to seize illegally imported goods as well as "to enter any ship or vessel, dwelling-house, store, building or other place" suspected of concealing contraband. A supplementary embargo law of January 9, 1809, allowed unlading of goods only after acquiring a "permit" from the collector. Even the 1812 statute that authorized privateers, thereby legalizing the plunder of commercial vessels belonging to the enemy, likewise granted a supervisory role to the "collector or other chief officer of the customs."[10]

Customs bonds were the chief enforcement provisions in these commercial restrictions, as had been the case with their predecessors aimed at the Haiti trade. The 1808 embargo made the "collector of the district" responsible for securing bonds "in a sum of double the value of the vessel and cargo" to hold the merchant to the promise that the vessel was en route to a domestic port. This provision was soon thereafter extended to all vessels "licensed for the coasting trade." In practice, this meant that, during the duration of the embargo, each vessel departing one port for another had to take out a bond of considerable value on the promise to remain and trade within national borders.

The president gained expanded powers to administer and implement the commercial restrictions. Under the 1808 embargo the president was "to give such instructions to the officers of the revenue . . . as shall appear best adapted for carrying the same into effect." An 1814 law directed the president to authorize customs officers to grant permissions to out-of-state vessels returning home. The president, in other words, could allow exceptions to the commercial restrictions. He could also unilaterally end the embargo. According to a brief, one-paragraph law of April 1808, the president could "during the recess of Congress . . . suspend, in whole or in part, the act laying an embargo on all ships and vessels." Finally, the president could convene a *posse comitatus* to enforce a restriction on trading with the enemy enacted during the War of 1812, including the use of the army and navy "co-operating with the officers of the customs."[11]

The new emphasis on central governmental control of the custom house was at odds with the reality of localized waterfront governance that had emerged since the early 1790s. Above all, the laws promised to thrust the federal government into public life and to reorient the federal government's authority from the waterfront to the nation's capital. Though Congress had enacted several commercial restrictions since 1789, none were as far reaching as the embargo of 1808–9. Nor did any of the Federalists' commercial restrictions spark anything near the conflict generated by the Republicans' measures. This was because the Federalists had been content to allow the local, commercially friendly, negotiated authority at the custom houses to mediate their commercial restrictions. The Jefferson and Madison administrations were not.[12]

What made possible the Republicans' new vision of federal authority? The commercial restrictions themselves reflected a view that the federal government's powers to regulate economic behavior were analogous to those of France, Spain, and Great Britain. Commerce was the arena of European power politics, and the United States now vied to become a player. More specifically, European states had long used embargoes as a means of preparing for and fighting wars. As Philadelphia lawyer William Lewis put it in 1808, "Embargoes have been so frequently laid, and from such early periods," that the laws surrounding them "might naturally be supposed to have been long since settled." And, by 1806, the French and British used dueling embargoes to try to squeeze the economic life out of one another. Jefferson, it seems, pushed for commercial restrictions to take advantage of ostensible British weakness in the face of Napoleon's Continental System, which walled off the British Isles from the trade of continental Europe.[13]

To a lesser extent, the Republican commercial restrictions embodied a critique of Atlantic commerce. Jefferson had long offered Americans a vision of a yeoman agricultural republic as an alternative to the Federalist commercial society. In this context, the drawbacks of a commercial society were difficult to ignore. For men of letters such as Charles Brockden Brown and Hugh Henry Brackenridge, the commercial marketplace's capture of the United States exposed a weakness of American character—greed—that could only be tamed by a new ethic of self-control. Republican political economist Thomas Cooper attacked the merchant community's seeming stranglehold on the nation's political economy. "I have great objection to the interest of the whole nation being sacrificed, our citizens and our property wasted by wars and taxes . . . to serve a few bold mercantile speculators," wrote Cooper in *Political Arithmetic*. The Republican-dominated House Committee on Commerce and Manufactures defended the embargo with the same logic. "The love of domination, and the cupidity of commercial monopoly," were to blame for "this extraordinary crisis." These sentiments alone did not make the embargo inevitable. But Republicans had carved out an ideological and intellectual space of critique against commerce itself that would allow Jefferson, among others, to conceive of policing commerce for the broader national good. Commercial restrictions asked merchants to limit their profits for the sake of the nation.[14]

The promise of American manufacturing also helped Republicans rationalize commercial restrictions. Production itself, and manufacturing in particular, were emerging discursive fields in political economy and the public imagination in the early American republic. As historians Lawrence Peskin and Drew McCoy explain, the Jeffersonians saw in American manufacturing the prospect of national self-sufficiency. As Americans substituted domestic, household productions for restricted European luxury items, they would lay the material foundations for a permanent prosperity wholly disconnected from the dangerous waters of the European Atlantic. Here was a specific context where long memories of homespun and other domestic manufactures, once the ideological materiel of revolution, again rang true. Notably, though, the Republicans also saw the opportunity to use the state, and specifically the military, to stimulate domestic industry. Tench Coxe would use his perch as purveyor of public supplies of the United States to stimulate domestic manufacturing by procuring materials for military use. Albert Gallatin requested that customs officials provide detailed reports about "the state of manufactures" in each customs district. The secretary of the treasury must have been heartened to hear from the collector of Providence, Rhode Island, in November 1809, that "the Embargo I have heard mentioned" pushed "many, to place their dormant capital into manufacturing." However haltingly, and to some extent unsuccessfully, the central government had begun to make legible a domestic manufacturing sector.[15]

Finally, Presidents Jefferson and Madison believed that an ascendant sensibility of American economic nationalism would legitimize these interventions of central government into the economic marketplace. Jefferson had nurtured this nationalism in the early years of his presidency. As one Jeffersonian acolyte put it in 1808, foreign strife was a "strike to the feelings of every true American & arouse the spirit of 76." The "spirit of 76" was more than verbiage, for both the commercial restrictions and revolutionary "consumer boycotts" hinged on the idea that restricting consumption of imported goods safeguarded virtue and independence. And of course the enemy had not changed.[16] Jefferson believed that the nationalist outcry after the British navy's H.M.S. *Leopard* fired on and boarded the U.S.S. *Chesapeake* in November 1807 in search of four deserters would spark American national pride to support retaliatory measures. Moreover, even when support waned and ultimately disappeared for commercial restrictions, this economic nationalism would continue to dominate the public sphere in these years. Most importantly, it undergirded the familiar phrase "free trade and sailor's rights," which would be the rallying cry for the War of 1812.[17]

The Republican commercial restrictions between 1806 and 1815 clearly enunciated a new vision of the role of the federal government in American life. It was to be more central, to begin with, what with the emphasis on executive authority and Treasury control of the custom houses. Yet it also built upon the rising tide of popular nationalism and promised to extend the reach of the state to obscure venues of American public life.

ECONOMIES—MORAL AND POLITICAL

The Republican commercial restrictions failed. They did not, as the framers of the embargo intended, teach Great Britain a lesson about the value of American commerce or the sovereignty of American subjects. They did not materially weaken British fortunes in the Napoleonic Wars. Nor did the embargo do much to spur manufacturing in the long term. Rather, the chief effect of the embargo was to shut down the United States' valuable overseas commerce, and with it the main supply of government revenue. Customs revenue had soared under Jefferson as Americans had swooped in to take advantage of opportunities created by war in Europe. The year before the embargo, the custom houses had collected $16.3 million. In 1808, Gallatin reached into the federal surplus, which had previously been dedicated to paying down the national debt, to supplement revenue numbers depressed by the embargo. The real cost was to come the following year, in 1809, when customs revenue was only $7.7 million, the lowest tally in a decade. The year 1809 also saw the Jefferson and Madison administrations incur a deficit of about $2.5 million, which would require "draconian cuts in military spending" notwithstanding the dull but increasingly noticeable drumbeat of war.[18]

The embargo also shattered the fragile alignment between overseas merchants and the federal government that had emerged through the custom houses since 1789. Most merchants were furious. The Tontine Coffee House, the switchboard of commercial opinion in New York, pulsed with rage. In the nation's capital, a leading merchant predicted the "law will be very unpopular." A group of "Merchants & Traders of Philadelphia," though willing to bear "the common pressure, which the commerce of the country feels from the law," found the burdens imposed by the embargo "uncommon and peculiar." Savannah merchant Charles Machin explained that "the oppressive Embargo" forced him, and presumably others, to pursue their trade "in violation of the existing Laws."[19] A Federalist rag summarized the mood on the Boston waterfront as the embargo descended on January 1, 1808. Surly merchants were already "stalking through the streets." A cryptic reference to merchant mariners suggested darker days to come. "Hundreds of poor but industrious men, even on the second day of the Embargo, standing without any employment," would crowd the waterfront, desperate for "some means of earning a day's support for their family." "WILL THEY BE SUPPORTABLE?" If so, who would bear the cost of employing this mass of disaffected mariners? If not, could this measure "be borne with dignity and patience"? In Baltimore the embargo had "oc-

Fig. 7. The New York custom house (ca. 1845). The New York custom house on Wall Street is portrayed here as viewed from Broad Street. Here the hustle and bustle outside the custom house, in the form of haggling merchants, peddlers, and slaves and horse-drawn carriages in motion stands in stark contrast to the orderliness of the entrance to the building. Library of Congress, Prints and Photographs Division (LC-USZ62-1067).

casioned disorder among the people it particularly affects & confined them here when idleness & intemperance had begun to work." Shortly after the onset of the embargo in New York City, "the sailors . . . rose in a mob (of 500)" at the behest of "British influence" and "tories" intent to "set the minds of the people against the Embargo." So assembled, this "mob" "presented a petition" and then "went on peaceably." The perceived threat was covered by only the flimsiest of veils.[20] Merchants without adventures, sailors without employ—both would congregate on the waterfront. "Then each to his post, / And see who will do most, / To knock out the blocks of Embargo," explained a poem in New Hampshire. "If not remov'd shortly will make a MOB RAGE," announced an Alexandria, Virginia, newspaper. This crowd was poised to emerge out of doors.[21]

Though it is impossible to say with any certainty, in all likelihood only a small fraction of American merchants smuggled on a large scale. Many ships went nowhere during the embargo. "Embargo. Embargo. O grab me. Damn it," was the preface to marine insurance agent William Thomas's list of thirty-two ships, twenty-four brigs, and eight schooners marooned in Portsmouth, New Hampshire. Yet a large amount of smuggling undoubtedly took place. According to economic historian Jeffrey Frankel, merchants from the United States managed to land £1.7 million worth of goods in Great Britain between 1808 and 1809, including 12,228,397 pounds of cotton from the southern states. Prices of American goods in Great Britain would, in fact, increase, but hardly enough to teach Great Britain a lesson, or warn it off its confrontational position toward American commerce.[22]

Illicit commerce prospered during the embargo because most customs officials allowed it to do so. For all the innovative statecraft, republican ideology, and economic nationalism embodied by the commercial restrictions, the laws nonetheless hinged on the same means of governance that had for decades past carefully negotiated authority between commerce and the state at the custom house: officeholders' discretion. The Non-Importation Act of 1806 gave officers of the customs "the power and authority to seize goods"; the Embargo Act of 1807 authorized the president to distribute "instructions to the officers of the revenue . . . as shall appear best adapted for carrying the same into full effect" but, in a scant two paragraphs, left it to customs officials to devise means of enforcement; the supplemental embargo legislation of January 1809 demanded that customs officials distribute permits to vessels thought presumably trustworthy enough to obey the law's requirements; the Non-Intercourse Act of 1809 directed customs officials to make seizures in acts "contrary to the intent and meaning of this act." Customs officials decided when and where to seize, how to enforce, and whom to trust. They would use the discretion implicit in these laws, together with a zone of discretion they had developed over the years, to turn the Embargo Act against itself.[23]

Sabotage of the embargo began even before the law took effect. The letter of the law made the embargo active on January 1, 1808. Things were different in practice. In New Orleans, Collector William Brown—soon to become known as a larcenous scoundrel for stealing from the custom house safe—informed local merchants that the embargo would not take effect until he had in his hands a physical "copy of the law." In the meantime, it was business as usual on the New Orleans waterfront. Only on February 8, 1808, after "official advice of the Embargo reached New Orleans," did any enforcement begin. Other customs officials gave Brown's tactic legal cover. In Baltimore, officials would only prosecute embargo violators from New Orleans if the violation postdated "at what time the supplementary Embargo Act was received at N. Orleans."[24] Baltimore collector James McCulloh also scurried about the docks warning merchant vessels to depart for foreign ports before a copy of the law arrived. Even after the mails finally brought "the advice of the Embargo" to the Baltimore custom house, McCulloh frenetically pushed a vessel out of port toward Barbados. Only thereafter did the embargo take effect in Baltimore.[25]

Once a copy of the law arrived at a custom house, customs officials found other means to blunt the impact of the law. Some officials in Virginia, Delaware, New Jersey, North Carolina, and Maryland simply threw their hands up in surrender because of a lack of manpower. Others pointed to unfilled offices in several districts to justify a lack of prosecutions. Albert Gallatin agreed, and worried that under these conditions "the Embargo will certainly be evaded."[26] Elsewhere, however, officials made but little effort to enforce the law. In Providence, Collector William Ellery admitted awareness "that there are plans forming in contravention of the Embargo Laws," but conceded "the great difficulty is to prevent their execution." Baltimore, again, furnishes the best evidence, as Collector James McCulloh's meager attempts at enforcement meant that local merchants were "violating it at their pleasure." Customs officials literally looked the other way.[27]

While some officials ignored smuggling occurring under their noses, others more actively used discretion to help smugglers on their way. The embargo prohibited trade from the United States to foreign countries but permitted trade within the United States. Since 1789, merchant vessels held either foreign registers to trade abroad or domestic licenses to trade at home. In the early days of the embargo, the entire United States merchant fleet sought to exchange foreign for domestic licenses. "The likely intent to evade the embargo was obvious," concludes legal scholar Jerry L. Mashaw. Yet customs officials distributed the new licenses without hesitation. After all, it was up to them to decide which merchants could be trusted. As the embargo neared its third month, Jefferson came to realize that the custom houses had cloaked these vessels with legitimacy. "There is no source from whence our commerce derives so much vexation," wrote the president, "as from forged papers & fraudulent voyages."[28]

There were also customs officials who intervened more directly for the interests of their commercial friends. Customs officials in Vienna, Maryland, and Georgetown, District of Columbia, simply released vessels suspected of smuggling. Philadelphia was also a prized destination.[29]

Washington, D.C., merchant John Teackle channeled a considerable volume of trade to Philadelphia merchant Charles Nicoll Bancker because of the uniquely hospitable climate at the Philadelphia custom house. In 1807, merchant and officeholder John Shee replaced as collector John Peter Muhlenberg, who had been the architect of the regulations against the armed Saint-Domingue trade in 1804. Shee, as historian F. P. Prucha puts it, "was a shadowy figure" about whom little is known.[30] Shadowy, but also shady. As Teackle saw it, Shee, who had "lately taken over part situations of your Collector," was an easy mark for getting goods through to England. An inspector named "Ashmead" was also suspected of permitting vessels to land imported goods. The morally questionable behavior at the Philadelphia custom house did not fail to make an impression on republican printer and politico William Duane. The "Custom House is proverbially a den of disorganization and has been constantly one of the most fatal means" to "friends of public policy," thundered Duane. Teackle and Bancker also had a similar arrangement in Baltimore where their contact, Charles Farrow, quietly put out the word that his wheels of enforcement were in need of grease. Farrow was said to be "as accommodating a man, perhaps as any you know." He was quick with advice about "the ways & means of doing the business" in order to evade the embargo. "A clearance may be obtained," wrote Teackle, "for a vessel with a foreign certificate or a vessel of our sort," and the vessel "may be cleared at a trifles expence."[31]

Custom-house bonds were another area where customs officials proved helpful to the merchant community. In Philadelphia, customs man John Steele devised an unofficial policy of voiding the interest payments on customs duty bonds because it was "more favourable to the merchant."[32] There was also a great deal of play with the customs bonds that vessels took out as a promise to abide by the terms of the embargo. These bonds would be refunded when the ship returned and upon the collector's satisfaction that no illegal, foreign trading had occurred. Routinely, customs officials accepted even the most outlandish explanations to justify canceling these custom-house bonds. Often, they exploited a statutory loophole that allowed customs officials to excuse visits to foreign ports if "proof shall be produced" of a "loss by sea, or other unavoidable accident." Merchants regaled customs officials with tales of biblical storms, epic disasters, and naval abductions. Vessels whose voyages should have taken a few weeks returned after a few months but failed to raise many eyebrows. By December 1808, Jefferson acknowledged "that the fabrication of proofs of leaky ships, stress of weather, cargoes sold under duress, are a regular part of the system of infractions of the embargo." Against the system of Republican commercial restrictions, merchants involved in smuggling had devised a "system" of their own.[33]

Customs officials also abused their legal discretion to issue special licenses for vessels to pass through international waters. One type of these "permissions" allowed vessels to recover goods abroad that were purchased before the embargo took effect on January 1, 1808. The other, which proved the more troublesome, covered vessels en route to New Orleans. In the spring of 1808, Baltimore collector James McCulloh and Philadelphia collector John Shee, whose custom houses were perhaps the friendliest to commerce during the embargo, lobbied the Jefferson administration to allow "regular trading vessels to N. Orleans which act like packets & belong to persons of whom there is no suspicion" to "be permitted generally to go & take cargoes" as they pleased. Most importantly, it was McCulloh, Shee, and the other collectors of customs who would judge the character of merchants and decide whether they were "persons of whom there is no suspicion." Given New Orleans's location on the Gulf of Mexico, the discretion enjoyed by McCulloh, Shee, and the others provided legal cover for merchant vessels to trade with European West Indian colonies.[34]

It was impossible to ignore the illicit trade that passed through and around the custom houses. As always, the Baltimore custom house was responsible for the most scandalous incident. By the summer of 1808, Baltimore flour flooded New England en route to British merchant vessels in the Maine-Canada borderlands and ultimately to the British West Indies.[35] Often smugglers had good paper for a voyage to Nantucket but veered sharply north. As historian Joshua Smith demonstrates, New Brunswick colonial officials enticed American smugglers to deposit their flour in Passamaquoddy Bay by permitting goods without valid American customs documents. The collector of customs in Passamaquoddy, Lewis Frederick Delesdernier, who had become known for his "encouragement of illicit border trade," attempted at several junctures to police this massive shadow market, to no avail. After August 1808, Delesdernier ceased pursuing prosecutions against flour smugglers. A contraband political economy that began on the Baltimore waterfront now extended, unchecked, through New England and Canada to the West Indies.[36]

THE PROBLEM OF DISCRETION

A few customs officials did try to conscientiously enforce the commercial restrictions. New York saw thirty-three prosecutions between March 1808 and 1809. Even as smugglers spread the word about the ease of smuggling in Philadelphia, officials still made sixty-three seizures in 1808. A single federal court in Boston heard 150 cases against embargo violators. But the devil was in the details. In New York, where United States Attorney Nathan Sanford enjoyed the highest conviction rate, only twenty-two merchants "paid" for their crime. The rest were "acquitted by the court," were "said not to pay costs," or were simply "given up." In Boston, Judge Davis condemned twenty-six vessels and acquitted twenty-four between 1808 and 1809. Boston juries were less generous, tallying fifty-three acquittals to only twelve convictions. The record in Philadelphia was stunning: fifty-seven of the sixty-three appeals against customs forfeitures resulted in refunded fines, discontinued suits, or both. No one knows what happened to the other six cases. Philadelphia officials were also known to reclassify embargo violations as minor transgressions, such as failing to possess a license to sail on rivers.[37]

The Jefferson administration struggled to make sense of customs agents' behavior. Political party and affiliation seemed to be a good start. The enforcement record in New England and the Great Lakes furnished evidence that Republicans seemed more reliable than Federalists. To Gallatin, it made sense that officers who supported Jefferson's agenda would treat it more respectfully than those in the ranks of a particularly cantankerous "opposition." So Jefferson appointed avowed Republican allies to replace Federalists at custom houses in New Bedford, Sacketts Harbor, and Oswego.[38] As 1808 wore on, Jefferson decided that all appointments to the revenue cutters, which patrolled the waters in search of smugglers, would be decided on applicants' "satisfactory evidence of his politics." "The federalists are so generally disposed to defeat the embargo," he added, "that no new trusts for the execution of it shall be confided to them." "Every federal collector" now faced "suspicion" for allowing "their party passions to slacken their vigilance in the execution of the laws."[39]

But the facts did not add up in Jefferson's correlation of political party and enforcement. Philadelphia and Baltimore were stocked with Republican customs appointees but were hubs of illicit commerce. In New Haven, party leader Abraham Bishop gave not a whit when smugglers took over his custom house. Then there was the fact that the two most zealous collectors in terms of embargo prosecutions were a Federalist and a Burrite—Benjamin Lincoln in Boston, and David Gelston in New York.[40] These ostensibly confusing observations suggest important facts about politics and political economy in the age of Jefferson. First, it was not just the Federalists who were friends to commerce. For all the bluster in Republican circles between the mid-1790s and the War of 1812 about the corrosive role of commerce in American society, a good many in the Republican coalition were strong advocates of commercial development. This was true at the level of national politics, as seen in the likes of John Swanwick, Samuel Smith, Jacob Crowninshield, and other procommercial Republicans who would tussle with the Jefferson administration over commercial restrictions. It was equally true at the custom houses. The difference between the influence of commerce on these two venues, however, was that the political checks on commercial influence that suffused the nation's capital—arbitrage, arm twisting, and electioneering—were nowhere to be found in the custom house. On the waterfront, commercial ties often proved to be a more powerful influence than Republican principles. Party sentiment and political communication may well have mobilized voters, won elections, and enacted policies, but they had a far less decisive effect on governance at the custom houses.[41]

Eventually Jefferson and Gallatin came to understand that close ties between customs officials and local commerce were the chief obstacle to enforcing the embargo. Their first attempt to counteract this arrangement of authority was in an April 1808 law to supplement the Embargo Act. It limited customs officials' discretion and required that they follow Jefferson's instructions. The eleventh section was the most important: "That the collector of customs be, and they are hereby respectively authorized to detain any vessel ostensibly bound with a cargo to some other port of the United States, whenever in their opinions the intention is to violate or evade any of the provisions of the acts laying an embargo, until the decision of the President of the United States be had thereupon."[42] Customs officers were to detain any vessel "ostensibly bound" to a legitimate destination but *possibly* up to no good. Decisions as to guilt or innocence, however, were now beyond the pay grade of the collector of customs. Rather, they would be made by "the President of the United States."

Jefferson rejoiced at the enactment of the supplemental legislation. "Finally," he wrote to Gallatin on May 6, 1808, Congress had awarded the administration "the power of Detention as the Panacea, and I am clear we ought to use it freely." It was not just the ability to detain vessels that impressed Jefferson, however. Speaking of the flourishing illicit market in flour "ostensibly bound" for Nantucket and other New England ports, but actually en route to foreign markets, Jefferson believed "we should say boldly" that the trade was de facto suspicious. What made the flour trade "too suspicious to be permitted" was a simple economic test: where a city or region had no consumer demand for the commodity in question, the trade would not be allowed. So in deciding whether or not to issue a clearance to a vessel, customs officials would first determine the degree of "want of these" goods on board the vessel "at particular places" listed as destinations. This test of consumer demand was intended to supplant any competing rationale for customs officials in their decision making about departing vessels. And just to be sure that Gallatin and customs officials understood his position, Jefferson hypothesized a scenario where a manifest provoked some doubt about the "true intentions" of the vessel's crew. "Consider me as voting for detention," wrote Jefferson, "being satisfied that individuals ought to yield their private concerns to this great public object."[43]

On May 6, 1808, the same day that Jefferson celebrated the "panacea" of the "power of detention," Gallatin dispatched a circular to the collectors of customs that attempted "to eliminate the discretion" that remained with the them to administer the embargo laws. As Gallatin wrote, "[Jefferson] recommends therefore, that every shipment" of flour and other suspect commodities "for a place where they cannot be wanted for consumption, should be detained." Gallatin provided specifics on this market-based test: "[Jefferson] perceives no necessity at present for the transportation of flour and similar articles from one port on the waters of the Chesapeake . . . to another port on the waters of the same bay; or from any port whatever to ports in the Chesapeake, Delaware or Hudson, or to other places which export such articles," continued Gallatin. The circular made collectors of customs judges of the legitimacy of commercial adventures based upon the demand for commodities at the vessel's destination. However, by prohibiting entirely commerce "from any port whatever to ports in the Chesapeake, Delaware or Hudson, or to other places which export such articles," Gallatin hoped to rob collectors of the ability to use their discretion for the benefit of commerce, and against the state.[44]

But worms would bring the Jefferson administration's efforts to a sudden halt. These were not just any worms, but the fearsome teredo worm, *Teredo navalis*, or "shipworm," which inhabited many American ports. This small, slender bivalve was infamous as a "marine wood borer" that destroyed wooden hulls. Cotton merchants Adam Gilchrist and J. Sanford Barker's vessel the *Resource* was sitting idle in Charleston harbor packed with cotton when they became gripped with fear that it would "be totally destroyed by worms." They commissioned a trip to Baltimore to deliver about 600 bales of cotton. To ensure that the vessel could be "navigated with safety," Gilchrist and Barker claimed they needed to add some weight to it, so they added about 200 barrels of rice. The shippers did not worry about raising the suspicion of Charleston customs officials because "the same was shipped by permit from the custom house" just "two weeks since." But Collector Simon Theus, a former merchant and cashier of the State Bank, refused Gilchrist and Barker's application for a clearance. Theus admitted to Gilchrist and Barker that he "has no suspicion, that the clearance demanded is to cover . . . or to infringe or evade the existing laws." But Theus claimed he was "bound to refuse such clearance under the directions of the executive of the United States, which he conceives he is bound to obey."[45]

Much to Theus's delight, Gilchrist and Barker took their case to federal court. This had been Theus's goal all along. In claiming that he had no reason to be suspicious of the *Resource*, but that he was bound to obey the instructions of the president to detain the vessel nonetheless, Theus attempted to paint as irrational the supplementary embargo legislation that had usurped his discretion in matters of enforcement. In his own affidavit to the federal circuit court sitting in Charleston, Theus admitted that "he submits the question to the court upon the cause" because he was "unwilling, on the one hand, to injure individuals; and, on the other, equally so, to commit a breach of his duty." He could not shirk his duty, but he could not rob "individuals" of their pursuit of commercial wealth. So either the court would "injure individuals" of its own accord by upholding Theus's decision not to issue a clearance, or else it would rebuke the government's rationale for restricting commerce by compelling Theus to release the *Resource*.[46]

Had they known of the events in Charleston, Jefferson and Gallatin would likely have been bullish. The case would be heard in the United States Circuit Court before federal district judge Thomas Bee, and associate justice of the United States Supreme Court—riding circuit in Charleston—William Johnson. Bee was a learned, cautious judge who had written some of the most foundational maritime decisions since the founding of the republic. Among these decisions was *United States v. The Hawke* (1794), in which Bee pointedly defended the federal government's power to police domestic trade on the high seas through the use of licenses. "The laws would be nugatory," and the damages to the nation's interest myriad, he opined, if courts allowed individuals to plead exceptional circumstances.[47] Even greater faith was to be placed in Johnson, whom Jefferson had nominated to the Supreme Court in 1804. Gallatin and Jefferson had selected Johnson because of both his indisputably strong Republican credentials and his renown as a lawyer. The administration seemed poised for victory.[48]

Instead, Justice Johnson's opinion in *Gilchrist v. Collector of Charleston* crippled the embargo. Johnson was not entirely skeptical of Jefferson's market approach to issuing clearances. It made sense to the justice that if a commodity was not locally available, then it was a legitimate commerce that fetched the commodity to the place of scarcity or want, and vice versa. Likewise it was suspicious for a "port that usually exports" a commodity to receive imports of the same commodity. But when applied to the case of Adam Gilchrist and J. Sanford Barker, Johnson wondered why these rules justified detaining the *Resource*, which had been laden with Carolina cotton and rice, en route to Baltimore. What could possibly be suspicious about shipping Carolina cash crops to Baltimore?[49]

But the bigger issue in *Gilchrist* was governance. In short, Johnson argued that the administration could not demand that customs officials do its bidding. The April 1808 embargo legislation specifically left "the granting of clearances . . . absolutely to the discretion of the collector." As Johnson understood the statute, it was thus up to the collector to decide, based on whatever information he saw fit to employ, to clear or detain a vessel. The statute also barred interference by the central government. Gallatin's instructions were merely "the language of recommendation, not of command; at the utmost the collector could only plead the influence of advice, and not the authority of the treasury." This was a remarkably accurate description of how custom-house governance had worked since Alexander Hamilton's first days as secretary of the treasury. With the embargo, however, the Jeffersonians attempted a new, increasingly centrally determined means of governance. It was firmly rejected in *Gilchrist* by Justice Johnson.[50]

So damaging was the *Gilchrist* decision to the embargo that the Jefferson administration resorted to a desperate response. On July 15, 1808, Attorney General Caesar Rodney published a letter that excoriated Johnson's decision as undue interference in the executive branch's ability to govern. If the courts could "direct the use to be made" of executive authority, "it would seem that under the name of a judicial power, an executive function is necessarily assumed, and that part of the constitution defeated," which entrusted "executive function" to the president. *Gilchrist* left "all the executive officers," once thought "subordinate to the president at least," now at the whim of "the judiciary and contrary to . . . the executive."[51] Justice Johnson did not take kindly to the administration's public airing of grievances. His rejoinder hewed closely to the legal matters at hand, especially the problem of customs officials' discretion. The April 1808 statute vested customs officials with discretion and "the instructions of the executive deprived him of that discretion," wrote Johnson. Not only did the Jefferson administration run afoul of the law, but it jeopardized sound principles of republican governance. The collector of customs was not "a mere ministerial officer," who acted "at command, under superior authority." Instead, the collector's "functions are among the most important exercised by any officer of the United States, and call for the frequent exercise of his own will, judgment and discretion." Each customs official "must frame his conduct." "The officer," he concluded, "is himself the paramount judge and arbiter of his own actions." Johnson's extremely public rebuttal to Rodney left no mistake about the fact that the location of power and authority of waterfront governance remained in 1808 at the waterfront, and in the custom houses.[52]

The administration made a last-ditch attempt to salvage its authority in enforcing the embargo. Jefferson had Gallatin issue instructions to the custom houses to ensure that the "decisions by the Collector might also be as uniform as possible," and that a set of "general & equal rules throughout the state" would lead to "some outlines for the government of the discretion of the Collectors." Johnson, however, had essentially made it impossible for the White House to regulate the collectors' "discretion." There would be no uniformity in the enforcement of the embargo now. "In the hands of an hundred collectors," wrote Jefferson, "all sorts of characters, connections & principles" would dictate custom-house practices.[53]

The ramifications of the *Gilchrist* decision were most manifest in Baltimore, where, by the fall of 1808, Collector James McCulloch discarded even the pretense of enforcing the embargo. But Justice Johnson had tied the administration's hands. "Shall we write to McCulloch to be more strict," asked Albert Gallatin of President Jefferson, "or shall we answer that the restrictions . . . not being legal but only recommendatory, each collector must exercise his discretion?" The administration did not have the power to do more than request that McCulloch "be more strict" or concede the matter entirely to "his discretion." Jefferson opted for the former.[54] If Gallatin could not force McCulloch to "be more strict," he would shame him into doing so. In two letters to the collector of Baltimore, Gallatin aimed to attack McCulloch's honor and reputation. It was clear that "greater indulgence has taken place" in Baltimore than elsewhere, began Gallatin. This had excited "jealousy and complaints" among "the ports in the vicinity" of Baltimore. In order to ensure "that no charge of partiality in respect to ports or persons should arise," Gallatin hoped McCulloch would embrace "new caution & rigor." In other words, McCulloch and the Baltimore custom house were already well known to their neighbors. A second letter suggested that McCulloh's malfeasance had sunk his star in the administration. His actions had run afoul of "the intention of the

President" and thus betrayed the trust of the president. "Great confidence has been, and is placed in your zeal and judgment" as collector of customs. The only way to preserve what was left of his reputation in the president's eyes was "a greater degree of strictness than you had heretofore thought sufficient."[55]

McCulloch responded with a defense of "Collectors discretion." This was a topic he had discussed with Gallatin before, for in a discussion that almost exactly coincided with the unfolding of the *Gilchrist* case, McCulloch boldly asserted his right to pass "judgm't on the nature & sufficiency of the evidence" against purported embargo violators. Without this discretion, "we might at once stop all coast'g commerce." Now McCulloch offered his own understanding of how customs officials should determine their duty and execute their trust. McCulloch explained, "A Collector is connected with those around him by common if not by special ties." This admittedly left him "liable to bias from confidence in acquaintances accompanied with good will and hardly free from prejudices against some other." This was simply how things worked. Customs officials like James McCulloch interpreted and implemented the law through a frame of reference derived from his connections "with those around him." He had mentioned something of this sort to Gallatin a few months prior. "By standing with our fellow men we learn their situation," he explained. "I perceive many things important in judging of them, that may be overlooked from a higher situation." McCulloch's "special ties" with his "fellow men" in and around the custom house trumped the political will of even the president of the United States.[56]

BETWEEN FACTS, NORMS, AND FORCE

While most customs officials succumbed to the vociferous sentiments against commercial restrictions on the waterfront, a few persisted in trying to enforce the law. In so doing, they ran headlong into a phalanx of merchants, sailors, and other waterfront denizen who were determined to hinder if not sink the embargo and subsequent nonintercourse laws. These stories are important to consider because they occurred in public. The men who were determined to defeat the embargo used formal and informal institutions that were pillars of early American life: law and violence. Local and state courts proved useful venues to harass overzealous customs officials. Crowd actions were the most powerful method of indicating the limits of government authority. Two legalities—both rooted in aging but formidable commercial and political custom—allowed commercial peoples to organize from below, to circumscribe the Jefferson administration's reconstitution of federal power from above.

The law was a particularly diverse tool for merchants, sailors, and their allies to hinder customs enforcement. Just as during the gathering of the American Revolution, they benefited from friendly juries who acquitted those accused of violating or seeking to violate commercial restrictions. But the trend was most apparent in Massachusetts, where "juries generally did not convict alleged Embargo violators." In fact, in 1808, federal juries in Massachusetts convicted none at all in nineteen cases. Legal scholar Douglas Lamar Jones suggests that this may have been due to the fact that these juries consisted of coastal Massachusetts residents who were friendly in spirit to the alleged embargo violators. This was precisely what had occurred in Rhode Island. As Newport collector William Ellery recalled, a jury of local merchants hastily acquitted a known smuggler on a contrived technicality. Indeed, once the Massachusetts District Court diversified its jury pool, they convicted twelve parties in forty-six cases.[57] Sympathy for the merchants extended well beyond juries. New Orleans and Baltimore courts were notorious for overtly protecting contraband trade. Rhode Island District Judge David Leonard Barnes refused to allow prosecutions for violations of customs bonds associated with the 1809 Non-Importation Act on the grounds that the bonds themselves "are waste paper, or entirely useless."[58] In New Hampshire and New York the bench and bar conspired to prevent prosecutions. In New York and environs, a customs official noted, "I almost daily find that our witnesses are dying, other leaving the city, very little doubt of their being bought off."[59]

The ordeal of New York collector of customs David Gelston reveals the potency of systematic judicial opposition to the embargo. Toward the end of the embargo, in March 1809, Gelston discovered that his counterpart in Perth Amboy, New Jersey, had offered up "facilities . . . for illegal exportation" and that New York merchants were beginning to find their way across the harbor. Gelston halted all vessels en route to Perth Amboy. He also dispatched New York customs officials to seize a known smuggling vessel, the *Courtney Norton*. The owners of the *Courtney Norton* resorted to legal threats: unless the ship "be delivered up immediately," they would sue Gelston for wrongly seizing the vessel.[60] Since the days of the British Empire, customs officials were personally liable in instances where they improperly seized a vessel or goods belonging to a private party. Common-law actions of trespass targeted customs officials' justifications for seizures. Actions of trover were brought to recover personal goods, or the value thereof, that were wrongly in the possession of a customs official. Either action could land a collector of customs in debt to the tune of thousands. This was what had befallen a customs official in Oswego, New York, who insisted that he was simply doing his duty in enforcing the embargo in a legal appeal that was rejected by the New York Supreme Court. Customs officials in Vermont were prosecuted and jailed "for having searched a home wherein they had good reason to suspect goods illegally imported to have been concealed." The Massachusetts Supreme Court likewise sustained a trover verdict against Salem collector Joseph Otis. In such cases, the customs official had no recourse other than filing a private bill for indemnification before Congress.[61] Given this history and context, the *Courtney Norton*'s threat was far from idle.

Gelston quickly found himself facing a perfect storm. The United States District Court for the Southern District of New York acquitted the *Courtney Norton* on the grounds that Gelston lacked "reasonable cause for the seizure." While Gelston demanded that United States Attorney Nathan Sanford appeal to the United States Supreme Court, the owners of the *Courtney Norton* delivered on their threat to sue him for trespass in New Jersey. Gelston asked the New Jersey Supreme Court to intervene and stop the suit because a federal court had already ruled on the matter. This should have been "a complete bar to all further proceedings," he informed New Jersey District Attorney William McIlvaine. During a private, pretrial meeting with New Jersey Supreme Court Justice William Sanford Pennington he previewed his argument that the case should "be removed to the Circuit Court of the United States." The New Jersey high court rejected Gelston's claim.[62] A Bergen County court subsequently found no merit in Gelston's jurisdictional argument, nor in his claim that he "had no personal agency in the seizure" of the *Courtney Norton* because other customs officials had actually detained the vessel. Gelston's appeal to the New Jersey Supreme Court was equally fruitless.[63]

Meanwhile, New York District Judge Brockholst Livingston further punished Gelston for attempting to enforce the embargo. Livingston and Gelston had once been allies in the New York Republican Party. But as a justice on the New York Supreme Court, Livingston repeatedly found Gelston liable in suits against him for seizures of vessels and goods. "Probable cause," he wrote in *Imlay v. Sands* (1804), "will not shield the defendant." A year later, in *Seaman v. Patten*, Livingston opined that as customs officials performed their duties, "they act at their peril." In *Woodham v. Gelston* (1806), Livingston upheld monetary damages to a merchant that stemmed from a seizure at the New York custom house.[64] As a federal district judge in 1810, Livingston overturned Gelston's seizure of the *Isabella* for violating the embargo two years before. Livingston lambasted Gelston's investigation as "superficial" before revealing how clearly his sentiments lay with the merchants, and against the custom house. "It must ever be the disposition of a court, if a leaning in any case be justifiable, to lean against the forfeiture," he wrote. "No man should be stripped of a very valuable property, perhaps of his all—be disenfranchised, and consigned to public ignominy and reproach, unless it be very clear that such high penalties have been annexed by law to the act which he has committed," he wrote in September 1810, in overturning Gelston's seizure of the *Enterprise* for an embargo infraction. Finally, that same month in the *William Gray* case, Livingston looked back at the embargo, by now adjudged to have been a failure, with remorse that perhaps "a firm adherence to its letter" would have better allowed its enforcement. "But it is too late for speculations of this kind," concluded Livingston, as he reversed yet another of David Gelston's seizures.[65]

Violence toward customs officials was equally instrumental. In the Maine-Canada borderlands—the channel for Baltimore and Mid-Atlantic smuggled goods to reach British markets—Collector of Customs Lewis Delesdernier witnessed his son, Lewis Jr., an inspector at the Passamaquoddy custom house, suffer a vicious beating at the hands of Aaron Olmsted, a local who had dabbled in illicit trade. Previously, too, "the mob had threatened to burn his house." Delesdernier "found it impossible to execute the law." Violence signaled the "collapse of Delesdernier's authority," according to historian Joshua Smith. As Delesdernier and the custom house shrank in fear, smugglers became more brazen and violent. Smith recounts the voyage of the schooner *Peggy*, under the control of a smuggler named John McMaster, to retake a large volume of seized flour. Armed with "muskets, blunderbusses, and cutlasses," the crew murdered a warehouse guard before liberating McMaster's goods. The situation was little different in nearby Bar Harbor, Maine, when in mid-1809 Collector Melatiah Jordan's custom house was overrun by "a number of boats from the Islands assisted by some of the people." "People in this Quarter I am sorry to say are inimical to our just and equitable laws," concluded Jordan. In the infamous *Black Snake* affair in 1808, lumber smugglers from Quebec murdered several customs officials.[66]

In New Haven, a "burning affray" served to remind customs officials that the commercial community would not brook enforcement of the embargo. In early March 1809, the United States revenue cutter detailed to ensnare smuggling vessels apprehended and detained the sloop *Hope*. As the revenue cutter crew unloaded contraband into the custom house's "public store," they were "much insulted" by a vigilant crowd. On March 8, locals launched two attacks "upon four men, who were guarding the prize by the wharf." The second attack drove the customs men to sea. The crowd plundered the custom house's warehouse, including "furniture & cabin windows." That night, "between 2 & 3 in the morning the Sloop was on fire & in the morning was burnt to the water's edge." There was some token effort at prosecuting the offender, but Collector Abraham Bishop was wise to hang back. Bishop summarized the sentiment in town: "*Nobody* burnt the vessel & *nobody* can tell who were the rioters."[67]

By late 1811, smuggler violence had effectively rendered useless United States custom houses on the Canadian border. The collector of customs in Oswego, New York, explained that local critics of commercial restrictions had now become active abettors of smugglers. "Many of our people on our northern frontier are determined to oppose the Revenue officers in detecting smugglers," he explained. Champlain, Vermont, collector Peter Sailly knew the same to be true. His small troop had been jailed, fired upon, and mobbed. Federal commercial restrictions "agitated or infuriated the populace to an extreme degree."[68] The situation was most dire in Sacketts Harbor, New York, where Collector Nathaniel Massey waged a courageous but hopeless war against several gangs of smugglers plying their trade at the opening of the St. Lawrence River into Lake Ontario. In November 1811, Massey decisively lost. First, "in the dead of night" the smugglers invaded the home of John Hays and banished him and his wife from the area with death threats. With Hays gone, the gang made its move. "By night" members emerged into town "armed with guns and bayonets," roaming the streets and waterfront. Most likely, the mere presence of this armed force swayed customs officials to look the other way as the robust illicit commerce swept through Sacketts Harbor. Just to be sure, though, the gang issued "such threats" as were needed. "No officer dares serves a warrant on them," concluded Massey, who no doubt referred to himself.[69]

The sad demise of Providence, Rhode Island, collector of customs Jeremiah Olney reveals just how difficult it was for even the most upstanding customs officer to enforce the Republican commercial restrictions. Back in the 1790s, John Brown, Welcome Arnold, and other leading overseas merchants had schooled Olney in the necessity of bending customs law to favor the mercantile interests of Rhode Island. Hamilton had memorably advised Olney that his enforcement of the laws had "been in some instances too punctilious, and not sufficiently accommodating." To acquire "the good will of the Merchants," Olney would change his ways.[70] Indeed, throughout 1808, Olney had rarely run afoul of the commercial community's vehement distaste for the embargo. In early 1809, however, smugglers attempted such brazen, public violations of the embargo that Olney and his men at the custom house were forced to seize goods. On the morning of January 23, 1809, "a large body of rioters, from two to three hundred," pillaged the custom house and "forcibly took possession" of a seized vessel. Olney appealed to Republican governor James Fenner but was informed that the state "would not turn out his militia company in support of the Embargo laws." Meanwhile, Olney learned "that a person of good standing in society" had confided that "the life of a Collector, after I had quit the office, would not be safe if he attempted to enforce the Fatal Embargo Act." So Olney retired from public service. In his final letter to the Treasury Department, he fretted about his own safety, but also that of the country. So long as the embargo was the law, "in my candid opinion . . . it will shake the empire to its centre, and deluge this once happy land in Blood."[71]

The violence that ended the career of Jeremiah Olney made a lasting impression on William Ellery, his friend and colleague in nearby Newport. "I recollected the days of the Stamp Act and occurrences of the Revolution," he wrote in February 1809. "The determined spirit of 1764" seemed once again to have descended upon the Rhode Island waterfront. That is to say, though the United States was entering its third decade of existence, the problem of governance that helped break down the British Empire now seemed poised again to "shake the empire to its centre" in Washington, D.C., as Olney had put it. Customs officials like Olney, Ellery, Massey, and Gelston had for several years kept a fragile peace at the custom house between federal law and political economy on the one hand, and local commercial peoples on the other. With the embargo, the peace seemed broken and irreparable. "The powers given [customs officers] by your Laws are not little," Ellery explained, but "how brief" was "their authority."[72]

THE WAR OF 1812 AND THE ECLIPSE OF IMPERIAL GOVERNANCE

The ineffectiveness of commercial restrictions was abundantly clear by the late summer of 1808. The continued impossibility of enforcing the Jefferson and Madison administrations' commercial restrictions all but forced the United States to begin the War of 1812.[73]

The War of 1812 marked the apogee of the imperial-style governance that had structured the relationship between customs officials and merchant communities since the days of the British Empire. The Madison administration's ill-fated attempts to use customs regulations during the war suggested the persistence of an arrangement of power in which local commercial interests shaped governance at the custom house. That is, even in the face of wartime nationalism, customs officials were unwilling and unable to prevent American merchants from smuggling and trading with the enemy hovering off the coast.

Madison initially hoped that the march toward war would shame American merchants into obeying commercial restrictions against trade with England. In late 1811, Madison warned that war would transform smuggling from a merely "odious" practice to a treasonous one. Smuggling "attaints its utmost guilt" during wartime as it "blends" the "pursuit of ignominious gain" with "a treacherous subserviency in the transgressors to a foreign policy, adverse to that of their own country."[74] Madison had some reason for optimism, for the demise of diplomacy with Great Britain seemed to rekindle nationalistic and patriotic fires throughout the United States, save for New England. This surge had begun in 1807 during the infamous U.S.S. *Chesapeake* incident that Jefferson believed would turn American merchants' opinions in favor of the Embargo Act. A similar incident occurred in 1811 when the U.S.S. *President*, which was dispatched to prevent further British impressments of American sailors, exchanged fire with the H.M.S. *Little Belt* off the coast near Norfolk, Virginia. Newspapers, elections, and public discussions were filled with anger about Britain's besmirching of American honor and with a sensibility that the time had come to abandon feckless commercial restrictions for a more muscular foreign policy.[75]

Ironically, though, it was a commercial restriction that all but announced the war. On April 4, 1812, Congress enacted a ninety-day embargo on foreign trade. The law closely resembled commercial restrictions of the previous years but added an interesting new penalty: violators would "never thereafter be allowed a credit for duties on any goods" at the custom houses.[76] By this time it had become wholly predictable what fate awaited customs officials who did attempt to enforce the wartime commercial restrictions. Historian Donald Hickey explains that New Orleans customs officials complained that they had no capacity to stand up to the wave of illicit commerce that swept through that city's waterfront. Up the river in Mobile, Collector Addin Lewis complained of constant "strong threats of violence" before finally coming to fear being felled by the "Dagger of the assassin." In upstate New York, customs officials seeking to prosecute smugglers could not find a court willing to do so. The Maine-Vermont-Canada borderlands that had been the cradle of a steady illicit trade witnessed increasingly creative ways of skirting commercial restrictions but still fell back on the tried-and-true methods of rioting and effigy burning.[77]

As most customs officials chose not to scrutinize illicit commerce some clear patterns came into view. The most obvious branch of this trade was in the shipment of Mid-Atlantic flour to Canada. The port of Passamaquoddy, Maine, which had distinguished itself several times already for attracting smugglers, again became a focal point. New York collector David Gelston explained that it was all too easy for a vessel laden with flour to make its way through the porous maritime border separating Passamaquoddy from Canada. He cited the case of the *Maria Theresa*, which was supposed to be bound for Cadiz before the wartime embargo went into effect. Two days later the ship's owners turned in the vessel's "register," which licensed it to trade internationally, and obtained "coasting papers" allowing it to trade domestically. The *Maria Theresa* was now bound for Eastport, Maine. Gelston was all but certain that the vessel would make its way through Passamaquoddy to Canada. There was nothing Gelston could do about it, though, because he had no "authority in the law which would justify me in refusing a clearance or detaining the ship," he explained to Albert Gallatin. Gelston's colleague in Boston, Henry A. S. Dearborn, took a more desperate view of the situation. "For God's sake do something," he implored customs officials in Passamaquoddy.[78]

Gelston's hunch was right as a great deal of illicit American trade would find its way through Canada to the Iberian Peninsula. This commerce derived from the British "license trade," in which the British navy issued licenses for enemy vessels to trade in British ports. The license trade was an outlet for those merchants with stores teeming with domestic agriculture that would otherwise go to waste. What seemed like good business sense to some was a high political crime to others. To obtain a license, the American merchant had to pledge that he was "well inclined toward the British interest." The license then stated that the bearer was free "to proceed without unnecessary obstruction or detention in her voyage." Nonetheless, the license trade would thrive because of ambivalence in Washington, D.C. Congress and the Madison administration were well aware of the British license policy and, in the July 1812 Enemy Trade Act, specifically prohibited American merchants from using the licenses to trade with British ports. But according to historian Donald Hickey, Republicans sympathetic to the plight of American farmers specifically did not prohibit the license trade to "non-British ports." This distinction was meaningless for the British. An American vessel with a license was empowered to find the best market for its goods, whether or not it was under British control.[79]

The Enemy Trade Act, though, failed to consider the question of American merchants doing business in neutral ports with British subjects. And within days of the law's passage, customs and Treasury officials, as well as merchants invested in foreign trade, identified this gaping loophole. Most of the interest came from those merchants involved in the Iberian trade, where British merchants purchased a large volume of American flour. The market had emerged in 1811 when American merchants ran roughshod over the Non-Importation Act. In the second half of that year, 284 of 759 vessels entering Lisbon harbor, or about 37 percent, were American vessels with grain and other goods.[80] A year later the Iberian market was especially lucrative because American grain would directly feed British forces under the Duke of Wellington that had been penned into western Portugal and the Mediterranean coast of Spain by Napoleon's armies. One estimate had 80,000 barrels of flour, 57,000 bushels of wheat, and 50,000 bushels of corn finding their way to the Iberian market. As Admiral Sir David Milne explained from Lisbon, there were "provisions plenty, but principally from America." "If it was not for the supplies from America," he concluded, "the army here could not be maintained."[81]

Customs officials who were certain that American goods would end up in enemy hands were powerless to interfere. New York collector David Gelston, for instance, knew for a fact that a Charleston vessel laden with cotton and timber was "unquestionably bound to England" after stopping first at Antwerp. Almost rhetorically, he asked the secretary of the treasury, "Ought not the ship & cargo to be detained under the existing circumstances?" In Baltimore, where news of the bustling American trade with the British was almost impossible not to notice, angry war hawks would try to take matters into their own hands. On July 7, 1812, Collector James McCulloh "regularly cleared at the Custom House" the schooner *Josepha* bound for the Iberian market. An armed mob immediately forced it back to port. McCulloh then put the *Josepha* under what he seemed to suggest was a protective detention, but he later revealed his pleasure at doing something to stop "trading with enemies." Albert Gallatin responded with uncharacteristic anger toward McCulloch's initiative: "The question is not what the law in yr opinion ought to be, but what it is." McCulloh had no authority to restrain the *Josepha*.[82]

The problem of trading with the enemy worsened considerably in the spring of 1813 when Great Britain blockaded the American coast. In theory, it was not difficult for small, mobile American ships that had the proper papers to trade domestically to venture beyond to the British line and back again to port. This was precisely what occurred, especially from the Long Island Sound through New England.[83] Collector Thomas Coles of Providence identified this pathway as the taproot of an "extensive" trade "between our citizens and vessels of war of the enemy." Congress flailed about in search of another round of commercial restrictions to prohibit the license trade but to no end. So Madison turned to the armed forces for an alternate plan. In July 1813, the secretary of the navy—who was also filling in for Albert Gallatin at the Treasury Department—issued a general order to the navy to stop any vessel "apparently intending to proceed towards the enemy's vessels." The navy would do what the custom houses, the "regulation of the revenue laws," and "the penalty of the law" could not.[84]

The military embargo of 1813 brought maritime commerce to a halt within the United States. In Baltimore, things were so quiet that William Jones fired the crew and staff of the custom house's revenue cutter. In Philadelphia, flour merchants such as Levi Hollingsworth, who had once depended on the license trade, grew desperate to find "some outlet to the towns of New England," with little success. Philadelphia's own markets were of even less help, as Hollingsworth observed, "It would seem as if the inhabitance of our city had declined eating."[85] Those merchants who tried to find a way through the naval embargo were surprised to discover that the navy would not interpret the law in their favor as customs officials had for several decades before. Alexandria's William Barnewell, for example, was twice prevented from shipping flour to Cadiz by the U.S.S. *Adams* on suspicion that his *Baltic Trader* would furnish "the Enemy" with "succor & intelligence," to say nothing of flour. Barnewell eventually sued the *Adams* and its Captain Morris, but not before abandoning about 5,000 barrels of flour and taking a loss of $40,000.[86]

But the federal government had cut off its nose to spite its face. In seeking to halt the comings and goings of virtually all merchant vessels, it had found a way to prevent a great deal of illicit trade with the enemy. Dependent as the federal government was on customs revenue, this decline in commerce starved the Treasury of revenue. Fearing this eventuality, Albert Gallatin had firmly rejected James McCulloh's interpretation of Iberian trade restrictions as disallowing commerce with British merchants in Cadiz and Lisbon: American vessels would return to the United States chock-full of dutiable imported goods. This tactic and an increase in customs duties brought the federal government $8.9 million in 1812 and $13.225 million in 1813. Things got dire in the following two years with only $5.99 million and $7.28 million in customs revenue.[87]

Gallatin had long since understood that a war with a European power would choke off maritime commerce and decimate customs revenue. As early as 1807, he had produced a blueprint of wartime finance that relied on loans. But even within this system, customs revenue played the same crucial role that Robert Morris and Alexander Hamilton had determined during the 1780s: it would be used to service the interest on government loans on the one hand, while instilling government creditors with confidence of the government's creditworthiness. In this way, even in the loan-financing scheme, customs revenue was vital. By 1814, however, the lack of customs revenue meant that the federal government had to borrow to pay the interest on other borrowed funds.[88]

From the founding of the new republic until the War of 1812, the federal government had prioritized revenue collection while allowing customs officials on the waterfront to enforce commercial regulations and restrictions as they saw fit. The federal government's inability to enforce commercial restrictions, however, put the United States in a geopolitical bind and pushed the nation into war. During the war, customs revenue declined, and government debt skyrocketed. By the end of 1814 the federal government "teetered on the brink of bankruptcy." The customs system was hardly the only institution of political authority that suffered through the shock of the war. Military and militia units were racked with disillusionment. New England Federalists talked openly of secession at the Hartford Convention. The White House and Treasury were set ablaze. Complete collapse seemed inevitable.[89]

The custom house had become a problem for Republican leaders by the end of the War of 1812. Commercial regulations and restrictions were unenforceable because customs officials refused to abandon their entrenched deference to local merchants and commerce. Worse yet, during the War of 1812, the revenue spigot that had seemed so formidable since the third year of Federalist rule sputtered badly. As these events unfolded, a few prominent Republicans began to question how governance worked at the custom house. It seemed that customs officials had too much latitude to interpret and enforce laws, and that they used that latitude too often to the benefit of those who had business at the custom house. But solutions were not forthcoming as the Jefferson and Madison administrations recycled aging legal and administrative solutions to no avail.

There was no question that the crux of the problem was the seemingly intractable independence of customs officials. In the wake of the disastrous *Gilchrist* decision in May 1808 an anonymous correspondent pondered whether "the orders to the officers of the Customs will be best executed if they are positive without allowing them any discretion." Jefferson would later ask of his secretary of the treasury, "Would it not be well" if "the discretion of the Collector expressly subjected to instructions from hence?"[90] This idea of tightening the administrative control over customs officials' decision making at the custom house was a leitmotif of the final Embargo Enforcement Act in January 1809, which demanded that officials obey "instructions" from the president. The same language would find its way into the Embargo Act of 1813. By ensuring that the collectors "are *bound* to obey," summarized the New York *Columbian*, the law "prevents collectors from exercising the powers given in this act" contrary to "instructions from the president."[91] While these measures reflected anxiety about the legal status of the collector of customs, they did little to address the overall problem. After all, for decades now customs officials had often pledged to execute the law and obey the Treasury, only to find it necessary to chart a different path in practice. The whole point was that the gap between the letter of the law and the reality of the waterfront had become very real. Mere additions to the statute books would be of little use.

So how could the Republicans ensure that customs officials would not fall back on their discretion, as they had for so long? In answer to this question Gallatin resuscitated an old idea. In 1811, Gallatin proposed a new class of Treasury officials "who should . . . visit all the custom houses, examine the books, the manner of ascertaining duties, and generally the conduct of the collectors." Of course, Gallatin was not the first to call for greater "supervision" of custom houses. Great Britain had dispatched the surveyors general of the customs to the colonies. Before the negotiated authority between commercial peoples, customs officials, and federal policy had coalesced in the early 1790s, Alexander Hamilton had recommended that Congress institute precisely the same supervisory mechanism now called for by Gallatin. None of these endeavors succeeded. The fate of the surveyors of customs was the stuff of folklore even before the War of Independence began. Congress ignored Hamilton's proposal in 1791, and it did the same to Gallatin's in 1811.[92]

By 1815, then, the problems posed by the custom house generated only the same old solutions. Something needed to be done. After three terms of Republican rule in the White House, not even wartime necessity could displace the "special ties" between local commercial communities and customs officials, as James McCulloh put it, that continued to trump the federal government's relationship with its agents. This arrangement of power that had enabled empires past now seemed poised to enfeeble the republic.

PART IV

Reform: Boston, 1817

On Custom-House Street, between the commercial bustle of India and Broad streets, stood the custom house, its stately facade crowned by "an eagle and mercantile emblems." Seven years before, the federal government had relocated the custom house from State Street, once known as King Street, where it had been the backdrop of the Boston Massacre. The new locale was well chosen. "It is the opinion of the Merchants and others who have been consulted," reported Collector H. A. S. Dearborn, "that no site . . . would accommodate the merchants better." The custom house's location was convenient because of its proximity to "the three large wharves, at which nine tenths of the vessels lie which are concerned in foreign trade." It had also "drawn around it most of the business of the Town." In fact, "the largest amount of Duties are paid by Merchants immediately within its vicinity."[1]

While the custom house itself had been liberated from a past defined by smuggling, local influence, and crowd actions, Dearborn knew that the fabric of governance at the custom house had not. Indeed, after the War of 1812, Dearborn found that the custom house's reputation as a friendly venue for commercial interests was a constant source of consternation among his superiors. Dearborn himself was under a new, intense scrutiny to make sure that federal customs regulations and revenue laws were being dutifully and faithfully enforced. Dearborn did what he could to stand in front of Boston's commercial community. "I find the merchants are fair and honest in their transactions at the Custom House" because of their "pride of character and a respect for the laws of their country," he explained. "In Europe," by contrast, merchants were considered "sharpers and knaves" who concocted elaborate "schemes" to evade oppressive tax burdens and "the vigilance of the customs." But American merchants differed "from those of any nation" because of their respected status in society. "They are interwoven with our legislatures, governors, civil, military and naval officers" and always proved willing to serve "the National government" in "stations of distinction and responsibility." In short, for Dearborn the interest of the merchant and the interest of the government were one and the same.[2]

Congress and the Treasury Department were unconvinced. For over a decade following the conclusion of the War of 1812, the Boston custom house was swimming in inquiries about revenue collection, customs enforcement, and the rule of law. Why were customs officials miscalculating duties? Dearborn insisted he knew of no systematic "attempts to defraud the revenue in this District." Were customs officials ignoring attempts to pass off cheap knockoffs as high-end fabric? Distinguishing between types of cloth required "a certain delicate tact," replied Dearborn, "which long practice in a factory alone can give," and which he believed his men possessed. Were customs officials looking the other way at rampant smuggling? "A vast amount of little articles" were ignored, Dearborn conceded, but these were mere "trifles." Were customs officials allowing merchants to lie about the quantity and quality of goods they were importing? It was a possibility, Dearborn allowed. Were customs officials too deferential to the merchants who did business at the custom house? Dearborn did not think so—his men strived for "impartiality." Each response seemed to raise another question. The days of Republican office holding and the Treasury Department's salutary neglect were a distant memory. On a routine basis Dearborn would need to prove he could be trusted to do the work of the government without succumbing to outside commercial agitators.[3]

As closely watched as the Boston custom house had suddenly become, Dearborn suspected that something dramatic was taking place. "Hitherto, the liberal policy of the government has encouraged individual enterprise, and enabled every industrious and honest citizen to enter the lucrative field of commerce," Dearborn explained in 1825. The merchant's ability "to meet those governmental exactions without embarrassment" at the custom house was the cause of "the successful and rapid increase of our commerce and navigation." The United States merchants "have in truth been let alone," he continued. "I doubt the propriety of removing any of the present facilities of transacting business, or creating any new embarrassments to the adventurous career of those citizens concerned in commerce and navigation," he explained. Revenue laws and regulations seemed poised to become punitive. Suffice it to say that Dearborn was not alone in his appraisal of the changing fabric of governance at the Boston custom house. Having checked with "some of our most intelligent merchants," Dearborn learned that "severally they have expressed strong doubts of making the change contemplated."[4]

CHAPTER SIX

Dismantling Discretion, 1816–1828

In 1817, President James Monroe toured the eastern United States. The spectacle of his visits to cities and small towns—greeting citizens, delivering speeches, inspecting federal military installations, all to the tune of "drums a-beating, fifes a-playing"—brought the grammar of nationhood into the everyday to an extent unseen since the posthumous immortalization of George Washington. "It has had a wonderful effect," explained Boston collector of customs Henry A. S. Dearborn, as Monroe had "broken down party spirit and harmonized the whole people." Monroe sought to unify a nation that had been fractured by the tumult of the Napoleonic Wars. In New England, where a significant political movement had contemplated separating from the United States over the War of 1812, this cultural work took on the added importance of absolving "past sins." "Union already existed but was always in a state of becoming," writes historian David Waldstreicher. For Monroe, the goal of the tour was to secure "a nation, unmixed and complete."[1]

With nation building came the related project of state building. One of the stated goals of Monroe's tour was to review the federal establishment—naval yards, army formations, and of course, the custom houses. It was difficult for the public not to see the review as a prelude to reform. A New York newspaper, for example, called for investigations of officeholders who "have vexed and oppressed the people, &c." In fact, during Monroe's presidency and for the next few decades, American politics would be consumed with competing visions of a new and increasingly modern American state. States and municipalities developed police forces and regulatory institutions that reshaped the contours of everyday life. American legal discourse was preoccupied with the question of the role of government in the economy and society.[2] At the federal level, Americans became exceedingly comfortable with the standing army and its use to expropriate and murder Indians in the West and Southwest, while abolitionists and slaveholders grew fixated on the radical possibilities of federal power. The rise of mass political parties also brought with it a new concept of personnel and party patronage that would push federal bureaus toward bureaucracy.[3]

The custom houses had an important role to play in these visions of a new American state. For one thing, the underlying logic of the customs system was in flux. In the model of the fiscal-military revolution the custom houses were to extract revenue from Atlantic merchant capital and impose some semblance of regulatory order on the revolutionary Atlantic market. With the end of the age of revolution, however, an emerging system of Atlantic states consolidated the Atlantic market around manufacturing centers in London. To maximize American standing in this system, the custom houses were to be reconceived as redistributive, police, and political institutions. Henry Clay and his allies would propose their "American System" of protective tariffs to stimulate American industry and to distribute federal funds to states to invest in infrastructure. Even Clay's opponents saw customs revenue as key to important national goals such as debt extinction and westward expansion. As the geographic boundaries of the United States moved ever westward, jurists and politicians looked to the custom houses to do their part in upholding the rule of law and incorporating new communities into the national fabric. And the custom houses—especially in larger ports—what with their numerous offices, seemed the perfect laboratory for experimenting with political patronage.[4]

Yet as Congress and successive presidential administrations tried to implement these ambitious revenue, regulatory, and administrative reforms, they came up against the reality of custom-house governance, which had taken root in the 1790s and become reified in the next decade and a half. In short, customs officials proved unable and sometimes unwilling to meet Washington's new revenue and regulatory demands. The crux of the problem was customs officers' use of their discretion to bend federal laws in favor of local commerce and merchants and at the expense of federal policy. First, during the Panic of 1819, which shook American capitalism to its core, customs officials were caught red-handed indulging a decades-old practice of only selectively collecting custom duties owed to the Treasury. Money that the federal government believed was its own did not actually exist. Second, amid debates about the American System, ascendant protectionists called for strict and uniform discrimination against foreign goods, but this was impossible as long as customs officers continued to defer to local merchants. Finally, the old ways of commercial deference at the custom house posed an inherent obstacle to a personnel system that relied on political patronage. The custom houses could not serve two masters. As long as local merchants wielded such influence over officeholders, political bosses could not.

The specter of this moral and legal crisis emerged during Monroe's tour as the president visited waterfronts where only a few years before federal custom houses had been cowed into submission by merchants' pressure, intimidation, and violence. Monroe dined with an aging William Ellery, who had witnessed in the resistance to the embargo the spirit of the American Revolution. He toured New Haven with Collector Abraham Bishop, who had stood aside as a mob invaded the custom house in 1809. No doubt some in his Providence audience who had mobbed the old Federalist Jeremiah Olney into retirement blushed when Monroe spoke about the ease of "administering" the federal government, while hoping that the people's "just confidence in the stability of our government may continue to increase."[5]

Before the federal government could build itself anew, then, it would first have to dismantle the norms that had ruled at the custom houses since colonial times. During investigations into revenue collection, inspections, and smuggling, this effort centered on eliminating as much as possible customs officers' discretion to interpret and implement the law. Curtailing discretion was the only way to uproot the cozy relationship between officers and merchants that had become so prevalent within the custom houses. During the 1820s, Congress and the Treasury invaded the confines of the custom house and began to usurp the influence once almost exclusively enjoyed by local commerce. The process of reconstituting the custom house in American law and politics was messy and was only the first stage of a decades-long transformation. But by the time Andrew Jackson left the White House, the governing practices American customs officers had borrowed from their imperial predecessors, which necessitated negotiating with local merchants and commerce, were quickly becoming relics of a bygone age.

ATLANTIC CAPITALISM, OLD AND NEW

The custom-house mob became scarce after the War of 1812. Local importing merchants who paid customs duties and experienced customs regulations continued to pressure officers to interpret laws to the benefit of commerce. But the local pressure on the custom house was a far cry from the structural, overwhelming force that had so profoundly influenced custom-house governance in decades past.

The sudden disappearance of the custom-house mob was due in part to the shifting plate tectonics of Atlantic capitalism. The epoch of warfare between the Seven Years' War and the Napoleonic Wars had created lucrative shadow markets that American merchants, urged on by the United States' neutrality policy, pursued with abandon. Merchants had relied on the mob, or even the threat of the mob, to ensure that customs officers allowed them access to these opportunities. But when the fighting stopped, what would become of this commerce and the tactics of riot, lawsuits, and intimidation that it had visited on the custom houses? In speculating on European strife since 1793, American overseas merchants had seized what historian Michelle Craig McDonald has called "the chance of the moment."[6] But that moment was now over. Peace in Europe and the West Indies instantaneously displaced the shadowy liminal markets that had facilitated the lucrative if illicit commerce—smuggling, collusive captures, and trading with the enemy—that demanded accommodation in the United States. The new Atlantic commercial order that soon emerged had been stripped to a great extent of the gray zones—wartime scarcity, embargoes, blockades, privateering, and trading with the enemy—that had provided American merchants with opportunity and wealth. The custom-house mob, the merchants' prized tool of persuasion for maintaining access to the gray zone of the revolutionary Atlantic market, disappeared along with that old commercial world.[7]

The restoration of peace in Europe sparked a metropolitan centralization of Atlantic capitalism. No longer able to exploit the margins of the European Atlantic system, American commerce fell into orbit within an Atlantic political economy rooted in London's dominant financial and manufacturing markets.[8] It was true that the geographical expansion of the United States introduced new ports, such as Amelia Island and Galveston, with booming illicit commerce in slaves and other goods. But these were noteworthy because they were exceptions.[9] More generally, transatlantic commerce, which had once been widely dispersed throughout the country's ports, became consolidated into a few leading commercial centers—namely, Boston, New York, Philadelphia, Baltimore, and Charleston. Each city swallowed shares of commerce that had once reached smaller ports within their sphere of influence. This had already occurred in the South—excepting North Carolina—because of the standardization of staple crop exports, such as tobacco and cotton. In the Mid-Atlantic and Northeast, smaller ports of entry would begin a slow rust that would be immortalized in Hawthorne's introduction to the *Scarlet Letter*. Salem, "once a bustling wharf," was "now burdened with decayed wooden warehouses" with "few or no symptoms of commercial life."[10]

The Madison and Monroe administrations tried to adapt the nation's political economy to these shifting market conditions. The custom houses, which had served as the United States' institutional means of "peaceably coercing" the European belligerents, would now be understood through the prism of the tariff. Alongside slavery, the tariff was the single biggest issue in the political life of the early American republic.[11] Though regions and economic interest groups had vied for leverage over the calculation of customs duties since the founding of the republic, the stakes of the contest were greater in the years following the War of 1812 because the tariff became understood as a tool for economic development. Accordingly, groups other than urban importing merchants began to take an interest in the goings-on at the custom houses. Protectionism was particularly important in this regard. Beginning in 1815, when President James Madison proposed a tariff that would discriminate against foreign imports and stimulate American manufacturing, interest groups saw the tariff as means to the end of remaking the United States economy to their own advantage. Though opposed to protectionism in general, southern cotton planters, too, would pay close attention to customs policing of smuggling, since cheap English cloth in American markets would depress the price of their cotton.[12]

The ascendance of Andrew Jackson in 1828 did not amount to a signal change in the nation's political economic design. Jackson would continue to seek to extract tax revenue from merchant capital for use by the federal government. He was fortunate to win the presidency during a boom time for customs revenue. To the end of the War of 1812, the highest amount of customs revenue in a single year had been $16.3 million in 1808. The next two decades saw enormous customs hauls—$36.3 million in 1816, $20.1 million in 1825, $28.5 million in 1832, for instance.[13] It was in the uses of those funds that Jackson parted ways with the preceding administrations. He was, to some extent, a protectionist. As a senator, Jackson had voted in favor of a fairly protectionist tariff in 1824, and he would reiterate his support for it on the campaign trail. But Jackson recoiled at the idea of spending the subsequent revenue for "internal improvements." Instead, while not hesitating to use federal funds to stimulate Indian removal and westward expansion, he would devote the federal government to the goal that "the public debt [be] paid off." Here, too, Jackson benefited from the actions of his predecessors, for the Republicans had reduced the

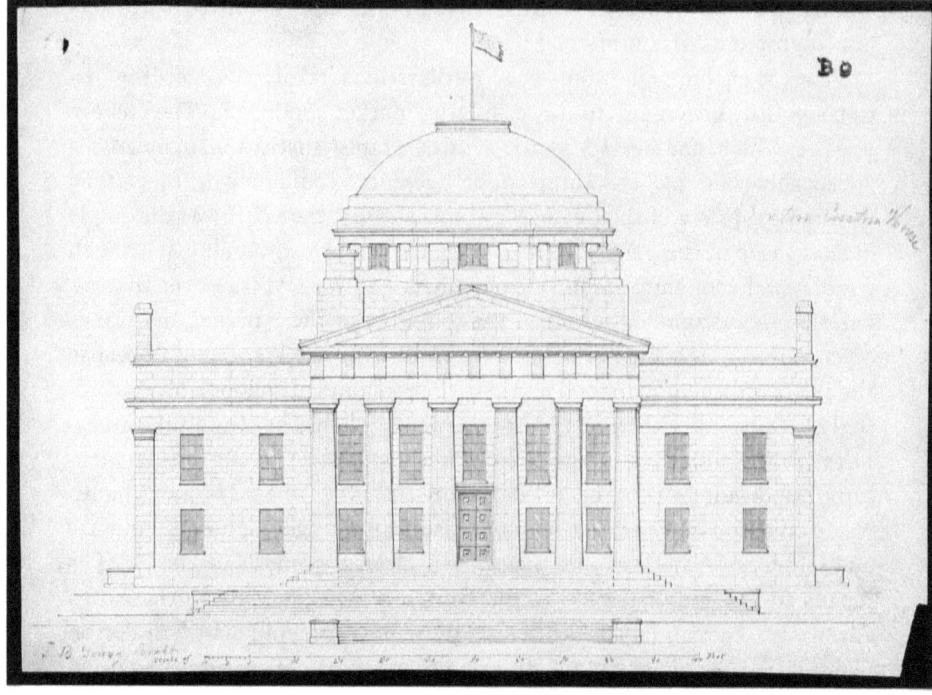

Fig. 8. Sketch of the Boston custom house (1837). Ammi Burnham Young's sketch for a majestic, Greek-revival custom house in Boston came to fruition in 1849. The new structure on India Street abutting Central and Long Wharves, which housed the Customs Service until 1986, replaced a small warehouse on Custom-House Street. Library of Congress, Prints and Photographs Division (LC-DIG-ppmsca-31774).

nation's debt from $123 million at the start of the Monroe administration to $83.8 million at the start of John Quincy Adams's only term to $48.6 million when Jackson entered the White House. By the time Jackson left office, the national debt stood at $338,000.[14]

Western expansion was a second important use of federal resources in the period following the War of 1812. Though the Jefferson administration had overseen land sales in the old Northwest and the Madison administration had created the General Land Office in 1811, the system truly came into its own around 1819. Western migrants followed the Ohio, Mississippi, Cumberland, and Tennessee rivers toward land that was slowly being purged of indigenous inhabitants by white settlers with the support of state governments and the United States military. By 1833, the federal government operated forty-eight land offices that supervised the clearing, surveying, and sales of parcels of land at modest prices to settlers and speculators alike. In addition to stimulating continued westward migration and providing the foundation for the drastic growth of plantation slavery and the "cotton kingdom," these land sales also came to constitute a significant stream of federal revenue, although it would fall well short of revenue from customs duties.[15] As the lucre of the western economy grew, fueled largely by the dramatic expansion of plantation slavery, an emerging Pacific market also came into view on the strength of the fur trade, trans-Pacific commerce, and rapid white migration to the region. As historian Kornel Chang argues, the federal government's repeated claims of territorial sovereignty in the Pacific Northwest unleashed a legion of "white settlers" as "shock troops" that expropriated indigenous peoples and began integrating the Pacific market into the main currents of American capitalism.[16]

Between 1816 and 1836, customs officers would struggle to adjust to the changing economic conditions of the world around them. For three decades after the founding of the new republic, these agents had survived by negotiating authority with both the merchants who visited them and the Treasury Department in the nation's capital. But those tactics were increasingly disapproved of by Congress, the Treasury, and the courts. In fact, as scandal after scandal enveloped the custom houses, policymakers and jurists came to question how the custom house had come to function in this way. What they discovered was a moral crisis, which, if unchecked, was poised to drown the federal government in lost revenue and smuggled goods.

THE PANIC OF 1819 AND THE BONDS OF NATIONHOOD

The first scandal that visited the custom houses after the War of 1812 occurred around the time of the Panic of 1819. It turned out that customs officers had lost a lot of the federal government's money. In particular, officers had chosen to ignore a great many overdue customs bonds. These officers made this choice because it was an important tool with which to negotiate authority among the merchants in their community. But in Washington, D.C., this choice and the logic that undergirded it quickly became a major national scandal. And as Congress and the Treasury investigated the matter further, it seemed that the one and only way to prevent the problem in the future was to take away customs officers' discretion over duty bonds. By the 1820s, customs officials, doing the bidding of the Treasury Department, would be forced to take an unwaveringly strict position on enforcing collection of duties. Soon thereafter, the prosecution of overdue duties would be removed entirely from the purview of the custom house.

Since 1789 the customs duty bond had been the central instrument of the American fiscal system. Instead of paying customs duties at once, customs law gave merchants the option of taking out a customs duty bond, backed by two sureties, on the promise to pay duties in a fixed period of time, between two months to over a year. In the span of a single month in 1792, for instance, Bermuda Hundred, Virginia, collector of customs William Heth issued thirty-seven customs duty bonds to be paid in 1793. These bonds served large merchants and small alike. For New York merchant and insurance magnate Archibald Gracie, the bonds facilitated a trade that most likely brought British manufactured goods to Virginia, and then New York, after sales of Virginia tobacco and other agricultural goods in London and Liverpool. The mutilated entry for the smallest bond issued, for $56.36, obscures the name of the importing merchant, but Collector Heth thought the matter negligible enough that he failed to record the names of the sureties. Merchants preferred duty bonds because they allowed them to put off the payment of duties for several months, thereby saving their cash on hand for further trades.[17]

Between 1789 and 1815, customs officials freely distributed customs duty bonds to merchants. Though customs law demanded that custom houses suspend a merchant's credit if the merchant fell into arrears on bond payments, few customs officials followed through on this threat. To recall why this was so, it is worthwhile to briefly revisit the ordeal of Jeremiah Olney. In 1791, Olney had refused to issue a customs duty bond to Welcome Arnold because the Providence merchant had failed to deliver on a previous bond payment. Olney sued Arnold as the law directed, but sparked a movement "to push the Custom House officers down." As the situation in Providence worsened, Alexander Hamilton counseled Olney to use his discretion to decide when to sue for overdue bonds. Olney quickly learned his lesson. Just a few years later the merchant John Brown, who had led the charge for Olney's ouster, asked and received a favor from the collector of customs to "hold the bond" that had gone overdue until a "check is passed to you."[18]

Before the War of 1812, most customs officials hesitated to prosecute overdue customs duty bonds. According to Hamilton's figures, by the end of 1791, the custom houses had collected the impressive sum of $6,494,225. But overdue and uncollected bonds totaled almost $2 million: Baltimore merchants owed $142,235; Charleston merchants owed $172,625; Boston merchants owed $175,651; and New York merchants owed $423,700.[19]

Charleston collector Isaac Holmes was the most egregious case because he both failed to prosecute and lied about the amount of revenue he was able to recoup. In fact, Holmes sanitized his reports by recourse to a trick that would endear him to the most nefarious corporate accountants of modern times: he counted outstanding bonds as cash-on-hand. While Holmes bought himself time, however, the problem only got worse. By 1796 the Charleston custom house held $500,000 worth of overdue and unaccountable bonds. By this time, however, even Treasury officials joined Charleston customs officials in abandoning prosecution for the overdue bonds. In 1797, and again in 1799, the Treasury sanctioned Charleston collector James Simons in further forestalling prosecution against the delinquents.[20]

Elsewhere, too, customs officials were turning a blind eye to overdue customs bonds. Between 1800 and 1812 Baltimore officials sued for only fourteen overdue bonds. In 1807, new appointments to the Baltimore custom house were surprised to find that their predecessors had "discontinued"

Fig. 9. Charleston, South Carolina, custom house ([ca. 1850–57]). The stately Charleston, South Carolina, custom house, is here depicted by C. C. Kuchel in the 1850s. Library of Congress, Prints and Photographs Division (LC-DIG-pga-01103).

prosecutions for a number of overdue bonds "by whose order or directions I cannot learn." Collector Gabriel Christie undertook a review of the customs bond records, only to find that previous collectors had nowhere maintained a list of overdue bonds. Perhaps the worst situation was to be found in Alabama. By 1811 Collector Addin Lewis admitted that "not one" duty bond taken at Mobile since it became part of the union had been collected.[21]

Why had so many duty bonds gone uncollected? For one thing, even with the millions lost in uncollected bonds and interest, the custom houses were collecting more than enough funds for the federal government's key nation-building activities: funding the debt, compensating the military, expanding western land offices, and subsidizing a national communications network. Between 1789 and 1816, customs revenue constituted 86 percent of total federal revenue. Before the era of commercial restrictions, this customs revenue left the federal government on sound fiscal footing.[22] Yet this also had something to do with the political culture of the first decades of the early republic. Debt collection for customhouse bonds disturbed the negotiated authority between commercial communities and the custom house. Mass litigation against merchants would have alienated the milieu of merchant capitalists expected to provide federal revenue and thus besmirched customs officials', to say nothing of the Treasury Department's, honor.[23]

Both the national purse and the national mood appeared quite differently after the War of 1812. The war cost about $158 million. The Jefferson and Madison administrations had slashed the national debt from $83 million to $45 million between 1801 and 1812. But the war ramped up the debt to $127 million. "Our Treasury is nearly exhausted," reported former Secretary of the Treasury and present Secretary of the Navy William Jones. The consequences of fiscal default were potentially dire, for without revenue, Jones worried about the fate of the federal government itself. "It is folly to talk of a vigorous administration without means," he wrote, in a tone reminiscent of the *Federalist*.[24]

The unenviable task of righting the wrongs of national finances in the period of the War of 1812 fell to Philadelphia Republican and renowned attorney Alexander J. Dallas. The Dallas plan built on Hamilton and Gallatin's precedents: customs duties would supply revenue, and a national bank would manage the debt.[25] But Dallas was far more aggressive. To secure chartering of the Bank of the United States in 1816, after Congress had allowed it to lapse just years before, took an enormous effort. Behind the scenes, too, Dallas ferociously lobbied state banks to resume specie payments in order to address the lingering inflation from the war. As for revenue, Dallas had a weaker hand. The return of peace jump-started commerce and produced upward of $25 million in revenue from duties in 1815—a startling sum given the "entire failure of the customs" during the war. Dallas nonetheless demanded a sharp increase in both customs and excise duties. And perhaps to remind Congress of the comparatively unobtrusive character of customs duties, the Treasury had investigated taxing individual income and property. The final tariff that passed Congress in 1816 raised rates as high as 45 percent on iron bars but generally fell short of Dallas's recommendations by 2 to 3 percent, according to calculations by political economist Mathew Carey.[26]

With the call for new revenues came a push to make sure customs officers properly collected old revenues. In April 1816, Congressman Benjamin Huger of South Carolina penned a report on the problem of "unsettled balances" owed to the United States, which, if remedied, might provide the general government with fiscal succor. Huger was bewildered by his own findings. In parsing statutes, circulars, and ledgers, Huger had descended "into a labyrinth, the intricacies of which increased at every step." Within the "labyrinth" lived a multitude of problems, "especially among the collectors," that demanded nothing short of a "general revisal" of customs law. With the ink barely dry on the Huger report, the House directed the comptroller of the Treasury, Joseph Anderson, to "dispose of" all "unsettled balances."[27]

Beginning in 1816, Comptroller Anderson and the Treasury took a new invasive approach to customs duty bonds. Whereas previous Comptrollers Gabriel Duval and Richard Rush had paid little attention to duty bonds, Anderson now declared that his "rules" on bonds were a final "decision" that was binding on officials. If the Treasury decided a case was actionable, customs officials would be bound to prosecute the delinquent merchant.[28] There were some immediate results. In Boston, Collector H. A. S. Dearborn began prosecuting merchants like Thomas and Ralph Haskins, not only for defaulting on customs duty bonds, but for having assigned themselves as sureties for other merchants in default. "We are imprisoned," pleaded the prostrate brothers Haskins, as they pledged to pay their debts by selling their homes.[29] Collector Archibald S. Bullock of Savannah was sure to check for instructions from the Treasury in cases of overdue bonds. His hands were tied when it came to indulgences on customs bonds, Bullock would reply when faced with merchants' complaints.[30]

But the problem of overdue bonds would only continue to grow. In 1818, Joseph Anderson found $1,125,870.21 in overdue duty bonds. Worse yet, it seemed that much of the money could never be recovered.[31] Jeremiah Clark, once collector of York, Maine, owed $31,552.27, but "he has absconded." The estate of John Lamb, who had been collector of New York in the Federalist years, owed $24,032.72. Lamb's colleague Sharp Delany of Philadelphia had suffered an adverse judgment for almost $45,000, but the district attorney, though "repeatedly urged to have the property of principal and sureties sold," had not done so. Then there was Isaac Holmes of Charleston, whose bungling of duty bonds had caught the attention of the Wolcott Treasury in the late 1790s. Holmes's surety had paid $30,000, but over $156,000 remained adrift. This "residue is lost," believed Anderson. Finally, "Dead and insolvent" Richard Wall of Savannah owed $351,709.16 in uncollected bonds.[32]

The Panic of 1819 made overdue customs bonds a topic of national consternation. The panic began when Europe markets decreased imports of American agricultural staples, such as grain. The Dallas and Crawford Treasury also funneled too much customs and other federal revenue to the retirement of the national debt that was held by foreigners, so that the government was spending its funds abroad, rather than within the United States. The resulting drain of wealth to foreign creditors, coupled with a longer-term drain of specie that had begun during the War of 1812, felled confidence in currency and banks. "The United States economy was headed for disaster," concludes economic historian Clyde Haulman, and that disaster struck in early 1819.[33] At the custom houses, the panic meant that merchants found themselves without cash to pay duty bonds that were coming due. Customs officials, already facing pressure from Washington, were unwilling to extend the terms of the bonds. Customs officials would either prosecute defaulting merchants en masse or concede the loss of millions of dollars in government revenue.[34]

As the Panic of 1819 brought the problem of overdue bonds into full view, it provoked a moral critique of customs officials' behavior. Why did customs officers grant bonds to merchants who could not pay? This was the question at the heart of three dozen inquiries into the customs bond issue between 1816 and 1830. It reverberated across virtually every page of a massive abstract of overdue bonds that appeared in the early days of the panic. Philadelphia collector John Steele listed eighty-seven bonds from the 1790s of which he "kn[e]w nothing," but "consider[ed] the claims hopeless." Dozens of bonds from the first decade of the nineteenth century were either "hopeless" or "very doubtful" in terms of prospects for recovery. Worse yet, since 1815, the Philadelphia custom house listed ninety-one bonds that were either entirely lost or doubtful.[35] Baltimore collector James McCulloch explained away the vast difference between "our weekly returns" and the present investigation by noting that many overdue bonds had laid "in the hands" of the United States attorney without prosecution, or "in our hands" at the direction of the Treasury Department. Whatever the reason, over $330,000 remained outstanding.[36]

Secretary Crawford stood to answer for the missing revenue by 1820. It was true that most of those "indebted to the government" were "importers of foreign merchandise." With this class Crawford knew of only one deterrent: "The refusal of credit at the custom house, as long as a revenue bond shall remain due, if rigidly enforced, will ensure sufficient punctuality." *If rigidly enforced.* That, of course, was the key to the matter. In ascertaining why customs officials had let so many bonds go uncollected for so long, and why so many customs officials had failed to freeze merchants' "credit at the custom house," Crawford now came to suspect that long tenure in office wore down collectors' probity. Though he did not elaborate, the point itself evokes Baltimore collector James McCulloch's cryptic description of the "special ties" that came to exist between local commercial peoples and customs officials during the embargo years. Yet Crawford believed that heightened supervision by the federal government could disrupt these connections, so in 1822 he put the Treasury to work compiling and tracking "a register . . . of all the bonds then existing, as well as . . . those subsequently taken" throughout the country. The Treasury pursued other measures on the waterfront. For Crawford, only a constant reshuffling of officeholders would obviate the problem of "special ties." "The periodical appointment of all officers employed in the collection of the revenue," he explained, "will probably ensure a more vigilant execution of the duties required of them, than would otherwise be secured."[37] Crawford's proposal of "periodical appointment," or rotation, in fact anticipated what is often described as a Jacksonian innovation of American statecraft, not as a means of extending the patronage and concomitant reach of the Republican Party, but rather as an instrument for preserving the custom house from the corrosive influence of the local and the commercial. On May 15, 1820, Congress enacted legislation that made possible an organized system of rotations by limiting "for the term of four years" every major federal office, including, of course, "collectors of customs."[38]

Congress was already turning its attention to the more drastic reform of abolishing the customs duty bond. According to a December 1819 report, cash payment of duties would ensure that money supposed to have been inside the nation's coffers was actually there. This was the only way to guarantee that the United States would honestly address "a deficit in the revenue of five million dollars," plus "five millions more" to cover the claims of the 1819 Adams-Onis Treaty and "ten millions of dollars" "to occupy the Floridas." There was a more pressing moral imperative, too, to discard the credit system. The 1819 report, authored by protectionist Republican David Tremble of Kentucky argued that duty bonds were incentives to encourage imports that simultaneously "discourage[d] manufactures." Trimble's resolution went nowhere, however, as Samuel Smith of Maryland, who had made his fortunes in the very system Trimble proposed to abolish, explained that the resolution "would be laying the axe to the root of the whole system of revenue."[39] Throughout the 1820s, however, the question of abolishing duty bonds would persist as Congress routinely inquired of the Treasury how much of the nation's revenue had disappeared into thin air.[40]

Congressional inquiries into overdue duty bonds continued. In response to an 1824 House inquiry, the Treasury Department found $2.9 million in overdue bonds that had been counted as collected revenue by customs officials. Of this sum, $1.575 million "is stated to be lost." Of $758,000 of the remainder, "recovery is doubtful." Only $613,000 was "supposed to be recoverable," but this sum was not guaranteed. The biggest losers, as suspected previously, were the nation's great seaports: New York ($461,327.14), Philadelphia ($419,010.74), Boston ($108,102.31), and Charleston ($97,909.60). What was striking about the 1824 report, however, was that significant losses had been incurred throughout the customs system. St. Mary's, Georgia, had long been a shady site of smuggling and related activities, but now it became known that customs officials had lost $26,020.23 in bonds since 1789. The generally insignificant port of Washington, North Carolina, owed $15,881. Wiscasset, Maine, tallied $12,014.12 in losses.[41]

Congressional and Treasury scrutiny of overdue customs bonds pushed customs officials to sharply increase the number of prosecutions against delinquent merchants. James McCulloh, once the standard-bearer of negotiating authority with the merchants in and around the custom house, initiated 332 prosecutions for delinquent bonds between 1816 and 1825: 36 suits in 1816, 85 in 1818, 79 in 1819, and 65 in 1825.[42] The Philadelphia custom house had prosecuted an average of eight overdue bonds per year between 1800 and 1810. In 1818 and 1819, Philadelphia officials initiated 187 proceedings for overdue bonds. Though numbers would fluctuate wildly in the 1820s, the rise in prosecutions is unmistakable: 60 in 1822; 38 in 1824; 145 in 1825.[43]

Philadelphia customs officials' 145 prosecutions of overdue duty bonds in 1825 coincided with Congress's most invasive investigation into the crisis of unpaid bonds. A resolution in the House of February 5, 1825, singled out the Philadelphia custom house for an extended inquiry into lapsed bonds since 1815. Even a cursory scan of the resulting list of the approximately 450 unpaid bonds revealed the reason why so many bonds had gone uncollected. In August 1818, for instance, a merchant named "R. Waln, jun." took out several duty bonds with merchant "R.W. Wells" as his surety. Meanwhile, "R.W. Wells" took out several bonds with "R. Waln, jun." as his surety. The failure of Wells's enterprise meant the government would not be able to collect from him as a surety for Waln, and vice versa. And so it was for the great mass of the unpaid bonds in Philadelphia. Collector John Steele defended his practice of allowing merchants to serve as sureties for one another by claiming that the merchants had long been trustworthy. "Acting from the best knowledge we possessed, and information acquired respecting the parties, they were deemed satisfactory at the time they were taken," he explained. It was the panic that had ruined everything—"a protracted season of embarrassment" that touched "many persons in business." Accordingly, "the means of judging in those cases were rendered less certain, as it became more difficult, I may say almost impracticable, if not impossible, to acquire any correct knowledge of the true circumstances of men, which it became their interest, pending their embarrassment, cautiously to conceal." In a previous time, Steele believed it was simple for a customs man to estimate a merchant's trustworthiness and creditworthiness. Of those whose duty bonds had lapsed, Steele "formerly" had "no ground of distrust." The cadence of commerce had overrun customs officials' ability to understand who was trustworthy and who was not.[44]

As customs officials seemed to lose the ability to deem merchants trustworthy, the federal government seemed to lose its trust in customs officials. United States Attorney Charles Ingersoll confirmed that the entire "credit system" of custom-house bonds was "a system of mere trust and conjecture, subject to much abuse and injury." "All the precautions and vigilance, that may be exercised, by the most judicious and upright administration of the customs," he concluded, "cannot guard against incompetent sureties and fraudulent impositions." Indeed, customs personnel took precautions and used vigilance—they embodied "judicious and upright administration of the customs"—but no official, no matter his virtue and abilities, could have prevented the frauds and failures that lay at the heart of economic panic. So intertwined were customs officials with men and proceedings of the commercial marketplace that even the most upstanding official was unable to differentiate between a good and a risky bet.[45]

Despite the vast attention Congress lavished on the customs duty bond problem in the 1820s, neither President Monroe nor John Quincy Adams offered a solution. Rather, it was President Andrew Jackson who prioritized the issue from the beginning of his administration. Less than a month after inauguration, Jackson personally directed Secretary of the Treasury Samuel D. Ingham to issue a "circular, to all the Collectors," with this message: "That they use *great vigilance & care*, that in every case, the payment of import duties be *well secured by solvent endorsers*." Moreover, from that moment onward, collectors would not be permitted to collect fees on any transaction for bonds that became "lost to the government." In early June, a Treasury circular demanded that customs officials organize "a Bond Account with each extensive Importer; that you may be able, at a glance, to see the amount of his debts." A ledger, rather than an officeholder's discretion, would determine if a merchant could be trusted.[46]

Jackson's initial measures would stop the bleeding, but more structural reforms were needed. Jackson's first message to Congress in 1829 upped the ante by faulting the "remissness in the agents charged with its collection" that accounted for "the large amount of public money which appears to be outstanding." He demanded that Congress undertake "prompt adoption of judicious measures for the collection of such as may be made available." Specifically, Jackson would call for a new federal office, under supervision of the United States attorney general to coordinate suits for the collection of unpaid bonds immediately as they fell delinquent. Through this new central governmental institution, Jackson hoped to deprive customs officials of the slack that they had used since the Federalist years for obscuring bonds to protect local commerce and merchants. Jackson's proposal moved the location of authority to handle lapsed bonds to a higher and more central governmental aerie.

Jackson's proposed reorganization of customs duty bond supervision came to fruition—though in a slightly different format than he had desired—in 1830 as Congress created the position of the solicitor of the Treasury. Immediately, supervision of customs bonds shifted out of the purview of customs officers to the offices of United States attorneys, who answered to the solicitor of the Treasury. As soon as a custom house issued a bond, that bond was sent to the United States attorney, who compiled a list of the bonds. The change was apparent in Mobile, where Collector George W. Owen forwarded each and every customs bond, like the bond he wrote out for merchant Swanton Whitmore in September 1830 to District Attorney John Elliot. In the past, Elliot's office had waited up to five years and repeatedly requested payments of any kind before putting a bond in suit. Now, though, if a bond went past due, Elliot and his fellow district attorneys had standing instructions from the solicitor of the Treasury to institute a suit in "all cases."[47] In Bath, Maine, that same year, the new procedure caused "a little bustle," as it was learned that Boston customs officials were "handing over the bonds for collection." When the Bath custom house did so, it caught merchant Peter Green off guard. "When I asked you for the accommodation of $100 and delay the payment of the above named bonds," he wrote with shock and surprise to Collector William King, "I understood you to say, 'the arrangements could be made.'" Instead, the bonds had been placed in prosecution through a process in which King had only the slightest involvement. "It seems to me somewhat extraordinary that an indulgence frequently extended to myself and others should be refused now," complained Green.[48]

Attorney General Benjamin F. Butler explained the new policy a few years later. "The Solicitor of the Treasury may grant indulgences upon custom-house bonds, in the form of instructions to district attorneys who shall have received them for prosecution," wrote Butler. On the other hand, the collectors of customs had no authority whatever to involve themselves in the matter of the bonds. In light of the experience of the previous decade, Butler interpreted the operative statute (which dated back to 1799) as intending "to take away all discretion from the collector, and to compel him . . . instantly to deliver such bond to the district attorney." "No indulgence can be granted by the collector, on his own motion, after a bond shall have become due."[49]

About a decade before Benjamin Butler declared it necessary "to take away all discretion from the collector" regarding customs duty bonds, the House contemplated but ultimately tabled abolition of the credit system. Samuel Smith's warning—that the House "would be laying the axe to the root of the whole system of revenue"—seems to have dissuaded his colleagues from this radical measure. Jackson and Butler's method was a way of preserving the credit system and "the whole system of revenue."[50] It solved, at least for the time being, the problem of local, commercial influence over the collection of customs duty bonds by cutting customs officials out of the process as much as possible.

THE HUNT FOR "FRAUDS ON THE REVENUE"

As the scandal around duty bonds unfolded, Congress and the Treasury Department detected a second area in which it seemed customs officials had once again been lulled into complacency by their close ties with local commercial communities. This was the basic question of how customs officials were calculating the duties merchants owed on imported goods. Once again it would come to appear that customs officials' lapses in judgment cost the nation a great deal of revenue. Nationalism and protectionism would also come to play an important part in reforming the way the custom houses calculated duties. The hunt was on for "frauds on the revenue" at the custom houses between 1816 and 1828.

Congress and the Treasury were led to believe that things were not as they seemed at the custom houses after the War of 1812. Several key officials believed something nefarious was afoot. Henry A. S. Dearborn, the collector in Boston, believed that an entire class of *"white-washed* vessels" that were "made to evade the Embargoes and non-intercourse law, and the laws prohibiting a trade with the Enemy during the war," now roamed the United States' East Coast in attempts to cheat the customs. Dearborn was particularly concerned about merchants peddling fraudulent manifests in order to evade or minimize their liability under the tariff. Dearborn had detected and thwarted one such attempt—to import glass decanters as a lesser brand of "glass"—in December 1815. He seized a second batch of goods bearing a false invoice as having entered the country through Lake Memphramogg, on Vermont's border with Canada. On February 10, 1816, he lobbied Secretary of the Treasury Dallas to demand that Congress pursue "some act being passed to prevent and punish such acts."[51]

Secretary of the Treasury Alexander Dallas aired Dearborn's concerns in his annual report on the Treasury a few days later. The system of collecting duties on imports had depended since the founding "more upon the integrity of the commercial community than upon the rigor of the laws, or an expensive vigilance at the custom-house." But the War of 1812 "kindled" a "spirit of illicit commerce" that now threatened "the security of the revenue." Dallas offered thirteen proposals to Congress, six of which concerned fraudulent manifests or invoices. Customs officials were no longer to trust the word of merchants. "In all cases" they were to "send merchandise imported to the public stores for examination; and that they shall be there compared with the invoice, identified as to the kind and quality . . . weight and measure, and estimated as to the value." This was more far-reaching than it seemed, for Dallas wanted Congress to require that customs officials open and compare each and every imported parcel against a ship's invoice.[52]

Dallas's proposals to guard against falsified invoices would have upended a method of waterfront arbitration that had been law since the Federalist era. When an invoice seemed incorrect, the Collection Act of 1799 directed a seizure of goods before the collector selected "one merchant" to inspect the goods and determine the duties.[53] In a structural sense this protected merchants from repeated jury trials. And in practice the system greatly favored the merchant. Routinely, importing merchants with suspect invoices paid less than it seemed the law prescribed. The merchant princes of Rhode Island had gamed the system. Slave trader and importing merchant extraordinaire James DeWolf employed as a clerk the collector of Bristol, Charles Collins. When Collins had to appraise for value DeWolf's hemp, which had arrived on the ship *Winnifred* in 1810, he called on none other than John Brown, DeWolf's equal in nearby Providence. DeWolf, needless to say, did well by the appraisal. In Providence, the appraisal process had for a time descended into a drunken farce. Collector Thomas Coles suspected that rum invoiced as French in origin was, in fact, British. He lined up appraiser after appraiser who happily sipped the rum—likely some of Jamaica's finest—but who pledged it "was not British." "While it is very generally supposed by all classes of people that a great proportion of rum imported is British," explained Coles, "none can be found in this quarter who will publicly pronounce it in their opinion to be so." In Baltimore, too, "the principal officers of the customs as well as the natural merchants" selected for appraisal duty agreed as a principle that British sugar was not British sugar.[54]

When Congress failed to take action about the problem of false invoices, Treasury Secretary William Crawford dispatched his own policy to the custom houses. The plan was basically what Dallas had proposed in 1816. Boston collector Dearborn, who had first raised alarms about fraudulent invoices, would lead the experiment in expanding the investigation of imported goods. A minor calamity ensued. Beginning in May 1817, whenever Dearborn encountered a potentially fictitious invoice, he convened a group of three or four merchants—all expert in the specific commodities at hand—to investigate. But for the following five months he found no evidence of "any thing wrong."[55] Then the merchants began to complain loudly about the "vexatious and very troublesome business" that now plagued custom-house transactions. Dearborn suggested that the Treasury leave it up to the discretion of customs officials to seize and investigate goods only "where we have actual cause to suspect collusion." Seeing no way out of this bind between angering merchants and permitting illicit trade through false invoices, Crawford again put his trust in the collector's discretion. At least for the time being, Crawford would leave it to the collectors of customs to decide when it was necessary to subject packets of imported goods to heightened scrutiny.[56]

As Crawford struggled with the problem of false invoices, Congress finally took notice. Senator Nathan Sanford of New York focused public attention on the problem of calculating "ad valorem" duties, or duties determined by the value of imported goods. Since 1789, customs officials had calculated ad valorem duties not by market price in the United States, but rather by the "cost in the foreign country from which it came." And how did customs officials know this information? It was simple—they took the word of the "owner, consignee, or agent" who made out the invoice. But just because the merchant "swears that they are true," was it actually so? What about the liars and cheats who packed "into one parcel" all types of different goods and mischaracterized it on the invoice? What about the Englishman with an axe to grind against the United States who let his animus influence the "invoices which accompany the goods to this country"?[57] For Sanford, customs officials were also a big part of the problem. It was true they had the power to investigate when they "suspect fraud." "He may exercise it or not, at pleasure," explained Sanford. By and large, "the power is, in fact, not often exercised," he concluded. Even when a customs official tried to pursue a false invoice, contended Sanford, the odds were against him because most respectable merchants were "often unwilling to engage in these odious investigations." This was a global system of fraud protected by customs officials' unwillingness to use the investigative powers at their discretion. Sanford believed that all of this cost the United States $5 million a year.[58]

The wave of protectionist sentiment that swept across the United States in these years also played a part in publicizing the problem of false invoices. After the War of 1812, a legitimate pro-tariff movement grew out of the burgeoning northern industrial sector, buttressed by the polemics of Matthew Carey and Hezekiah Niles. For protectionists, the tariff was the fundamental tool to stimulate American manufacturing, by raising duties on imported manufactures to prohibitively high levels.[59] But the tariff would work only if it was properly enforced. Could customs officials actually do so? The question invited further scrutiny of the operations of the custom house while also shining an accusatory light on the foreign interests that were manipulating American revenue laws. For hardened protectionists, postwar nationalism and persisting anti-British sentiment magnified the importance of tariff enforcement. Customs officials themselves fell prey to the mania, none more so than Henry A. S. Dearborn, who was fond of blaming any and all enforcement problems at the Boston custom house on "foreign merchants."[60]

The Appraisement Act of 1818 was Congress's answer to the problem of fictitious invoices. It satisfied nationalist critics by singling out foreign merchants for special oaths and heightened inspections. But it transformed governance at the custom houses. Customs officials were now required to inspect at least one package from each invoice, and at least one out of every fifty packages. No longer would customs officials trust the local "respectable" merchant to assist in these inspections. Rather, the 1818 law appointed two U.S. appraisers at a salary of $1,500 a year for Boston, Philadelphia, Baltimore, Charleston, and New York. When a suspicious invoice was encountered, the U.S. appraiser would produce an estimate of duties, while the merchant was to select a "respectable resident merchant" to do the same. Any merchant who refused to serve as an appraiser faced a $50 fine. The law also created strong financial incentives for customs officials to find fault with an invoice. If the appraisers found an invoice to have undervalued goods by more than 25 percent, the importer faced the enormous penalty of 50 percent of the total value of the goods. Customs officials who oversaw this proceeding to fruition received half of this fine.[61]

Just a month after the Appraisement Act became law, the new machinery of valuation and calculation at the custom house groaned into operation. The first appraisers, drawn from the ranks of middling merchants, quickly realized the enormity of their task.[62] In Boston, Dearborn ordered Appraisers Isaac Waters and William Little to "transcribe" the Appraisement Act "into the book of instructions" that they were to carry with them, and "refer to," at all times. Whether or not they memorized the law, the appraisers quickly complained that it took "7 to 8 hours per day" in "constant attendance" simply to discharge "the ordinary duties of our office." In busy seasons, the appraisers arrived "early in the morning and we seldom leave it till night." Merchants, too, would complain about the weeklong delays that attended the removal of packages "to the Store" for appraisement. Eventually, the Boston appraisers received permission from the Treasury to hire two laborers who were "constantly employed in opening and repacking goods for appraisement," as well as a "store keeper" who supervised the coming and going of upward of 4,000 packages.[63]

The Appraisement Act also materially reconstituted the landscape of customs regulation in major cities. The thousands of packages that were to be opened, inspected, calculated, repackaged, stored, and returned to importers required space, and space was at a dire premium at the aging custom houses of the early republic. By October 1818, Savannah collector A. S. Bullock faced "much embarrassment in carrying into operation" the Appraisement Act due to "the wont of public ware houses in which to deposit merchandise intended for appraisement." Bullock had pleaded with "private establishments"—most likely warehouses owned by the city's leading merchants—but these were "scattered about" Savannah and "without the control of the collector." Appraisers "waste their time" at these warehouses because goods are buried under "private property" belonging to the warehouse owners or, even worse, "cannot be found" at all. Bullock had already received word that the Treasury was constructing new "public stores" in the following year, but pleaded with Secretary Crawford for a more immediate solution: renting a warehouse near the custom house. Fragmentary records from the New York custom house suggest the rapid expansion of these warehousing facilities: to Staten Island ("Richmond") in 1819, new "Wall Street" and "Greenwich" locations in 1822, "21 Broad Street" in 1828, "109 Washington Street" and "17 Nassau Street" in 1841, and finally, "270 Water Street" and "230 Cherry Street" in 1844.[64]

As the business of the office of the U.S. appraiser rapidly increased, so, too, did the appraisers' stature. In Boston, Appraisers Waters and Little would demand pay increases "equal to the Naval Officer or Surveyor at least" because "our duties are certainly more arduous, require much more personal supervision, and we may say without vanity, talents of as high attainments." The appraisers' inflated sense of worth sparked turf wars within the custom house. Waters and Little grew frustrated with Collector Dearborn after "several interviews" over the issue of how exactly to calculate the value of invoices. Dearborn's deputy would privately delight at an 1821 district court hearing in which the judge upbraided and "order'd the appraisers to review their work." Three years later, the appraisers went directly to the secretary of the treasury to declare that the collector had "no . . . authority and no control over our opinions," and that their official commission vested them "with the high and responsible office of arbitration between the Government and the Importers." "We cannot surrender any part of it," continued Waters and Little, before concluding, "We are the judges both of the law and facts on all cases of appraisement." From the beginning, New York collector David Gelston went out of his way to avoid referring cases to the meticulous, and perhaps nettlesome, appraisers, until a scolding note from William Crawford to the collector "who has the power, and who will exercise it, or state to the party the reason why he does not do it."[65]

Frayed relations between appraisers and collectors of customs boiled down to the simple fact that the appraisers had taken charge of one of the custom house's central functions: the calculation of customs duties. In fact, as the appraisers came to see themselves as uniquely qualified experts on the matter, they took the extraordinary step of attempting to harmonize their practices on a national scale. Not more than six months after the Appraisement Act received James Monroe's signature, New York appraisers Lawrence and Pratt approached Boston's Waters with precisely such a proposal. "We fully accord with you," wrote Waters, and speaking for his colleague Little, "that an interchange of opinion with each other in the principle Ports relating to our office duties, is highly desirable." About a year later, Waters and Little struck up a correspondence with Philadelphia appraisers Samuel Ross and Thomas Stewart to exchange ideas for "uniformity of proceeding in respect to the detection of frauds which must always be our first desire." When a merchant complained of inequitable practice in Boston as compared to New York, Waters and Little, "exceeding anxious of establishing a uniformity of rates of duty between your District + Ours," wrote to their colleagues and enclosed a sample of "the article" in question. The appraisers took it upon themselves to harmonize practice from one district to another, rather than following local norms and awaiting, if it ever arrived, intervention by the central government.[66]

The appraisers' harsh treatment of importing merchants also robbed collectors of customs of their old arsenal of diplomacy and suasion. Waters and Little, for instance, did not hesitate to scrutinize "the entries of many of our respectable merchants," many of whom Collector Dearborn relied upon for intelligence and legitimacy. "The Merchants here have considered our scrutiny too rigid," noted Waters, before reiterating his "duty to enforce rigidly the provisions of the appraisement law." By the mid-1820s Dearborn turned against the Appraisement Act because it was "very vexatious to the merchants." "Knowing how troublesome and onerous the merchants consider it," Dearborn hoped "to have it repealed."[67] Instead the federal judiciary moved to strengthen the appraisal system. In *Tappan v. United States* in 1822, Joseph Story, associate justice of the United States Supreme Court, issued a circuit opinion that prevented collectors of customs from altering appraisers' calculations. "What practical use would it be to require such formal appraisements," asked Story, if "they could always be revised and overturned at the will of the importer?" Story's language was fairly damning: the collector interfered in appraisements at the behest of the "importer." On the contrary, the appraisers appear to be "perfectly impartial" and "free of all improper bias." "They may truly [be] said to be legislative referees," he concluded.[68]

In 1826, the Supreme Court upheld Story's circuit opinion and further limited collectors of customs' ability to participate in the valuation process. For many years, collectors and appraisers had disagreed as to how to calculate duties. Collectors used the "true value" of goods or the purchase price paid by the importer abroad. Appraisers used "actual cost," or the general market value at the location where the importer acquired the goods abroad. The court sided with the appraisers. In so doing, it also sought to make the appraisal process more transparent. If importers disagreed with an appraisal, it would be up to a jury to decide whether the appraisers correctly determined the "actual cost" of goods. Any suit against a custom-house appraisement would force the collector, under oath, "directly to criminate some of the importers; in other words accusing them of perjury, and this too when they may be innocent or guilty, for his suspicions may be groundless, however, apparently well founded." Not only did the appraisement law force Dearborn to assume a punitive posture toward merchants, but he would now have to do so in public.[69]

If the *Tappan* court had narrowed the collector's purview and discretion in appraisement cases, the Tariff of 1828 obliterated it altogether. Appraisement was now "mandatory" on all ad valorem goods and on a great many goods with specific values. An 1830 law that sought to clarify procedure when goods did not match invoices, according to Secretary Samuel Ingham, "leaves no discretion with the Collector."[70] Since 1818, the collector's "suspicion" had been necessary to launch the appraisal process, but no more. Dearborn would no longer have to worry about his place among the importing merchants of Boston. But this provision in the Tariff of 1828 revealed that, since 1816, to say nothing of 1789, the position of the collector of customs had devolved dramatically. The creation of the position of the solicitor of the Treasury had all but removed customs officials from the handling of customs duty bonds. The appraisement system now minimized the collector's and other customs officials' roles in the inspection of goods and calculation of duties. The collectors had once been trusted because of their ability to negotiate authority with commercial waterfront communities. By 1828, that relationship had come to appear as a liability.

CENTRIPETAL FORCES

During the 1820s, the logic of daily practice at the custom houses had drifted away from the systemic deference to local commercial norms that had dictated everyday governance since the first days of the new republic. By the time Andrew Jackson took office, however, customs officials found themselves viewing the meaning and function of the custom house through a new lens: that of politics. Indeed, as Congress, the judiciary, and the Treasury forcibly intervened to separate the custom house and the federal state from the forces of the marketplace, a revolution in political organization would reconstitute the custom houses as vital outposts of party influence.

Of course, the custom house had always borne some measure of importance to political parties. Alexander Hamilton used the custom houses to stovepipe political intelligence to his office to undermine his rival Thomas Jefferson during the days of the Gênet affair. Jefferson himself tried, without much success, to use the Revolution of 1800 to induce customs officials to follow his instructions, rather than embedded commercial norms. Monroe's review of his civil corps in 1817 subjected the civil list to the authority of both the president, and the leader of the Republican Party. Moreover, every president from Washington to Monroe decided appointments to the customs, to some extent at least, based on a potential candidate's political allegiance to the administration's agenda. What occurred between 1817 and 1828, however, was a qualitative revolution in the custom house's role in American politics. The custom house, which had for several decades kept the peace between local commercial peoples and the federal state's political economy, now served to align local party branches with national party leadership.

The system of rotating officeholders every four years, pioneered by William Crawford, and eventually mastered by Andrew Jackson, was crucial to the reconstitution of the custom house as a chiefly political institution. Ideologically speaking, rotation allowed as many citizens as possible to participate in the machinery of government, thereby ensuring that the government remained an accurate reflection of the people's will and the people themselves.[71] Yet as an instrument of political organizing, rotation played a crucial role in the formation of the second-party system. On the one hand, rotation, along with actuarial realities, would remove from office a class of aging officers who had held office for lengthy tenures—indeed sometimes for decades. David Gelston of New York retired in 1821 at age seventy-seven after two decades in the collector's office. None of his successors would even come close to matching his length of tenure. H. A. S Dearborn in Boston hung on until 1829 when he was turned out of office by Andrew Jackson. John Steele, who had been collector in Philadelphia since 1807, died in office in 1827. Of the old guard, only Baltimore collector James McCulloch, Annapolis collector John Randall, and Salem collector James Miller would continue through the Jackson administration. By the end of the Jackson administration, by contrast, it became commonplace to expect the wholesale dismissal of customs employees at a particular port.[72]

On the other hand, rotation allowed the incoming or incumbent administration to fill the custom house with political allies. Jackson believed that his predecessor's officeholders had "stained our National Character," and it was high time "to wash it out." Samuel Swartwout, who would be Jackson's choice for the collector of the Port of New York, agreed as to the necessity of a thorough stable-cleaning. "The power & patronage of the Executive is so great, that none but a *pure* patriot can make head against the thousand corrupt sources of power which he can bring to bear directly upon the people," wrote Swartwout with reference to Jackson.[73] So Swartwout composed a list of fifty-two employees—inspectors, weighers, and gaugers—who were to be removed. A second list of new appointments to the now-vacant positions began the task of designating officeholders who would guard the people from the "corrupt sources of power" that had once pervaded the federal government. It was not all ideological warfare. Party-based appointments were crucial for transforming the rag-tag Democratic alliance of the 1820s into a well-oiled electoral machine. In particular, a savvy appointment could align the White House's wishes with those of the state leadership.[74]

The New Orleans custom house in the age of Jackson best illustrates how party politics displaced an older brand of governance that had been friendly to commerce. There, Collector Martin Gordon "ruled the custom house with an iron grip" by appointing loyal subordinates willing to do virtually anything he asked in order to keep their positions. As one informant ventured, *"His will is law."* A band of brave merchants believed Gordon "substituted his will for law." A countinghouse employee named Carl Kohn marveled at the "obnoxious" Gordon and his "most ridiculous interpretation of the laws" to punish those perceived as anti-Jackson. "It is really a sham," confided Kohn, "that one man should thus make his will a law, subject . . . people continuously to petty vexations . . . with impunity." Only some of Gordon's victims were actually opposed to Jackson, while others were simply guilty by suspicion. Most "get over their grievances in silence, and are afraid to show any antipathy to the man, lest he might subject them to new ones." Gordon was by no means opposed to merchants and commerce as much as he was determined to ensure that custom-house governance served the Democratic Party. Politics had evicted commerce from the calculus of governance at the New Orleans custom house. [75]

In at least one case, Jackson chose a collector to disrupt locals' influence over custom-house administration. That collector was Samuel Swartwout in New York. Swartwout was a down-on-his-luck speculator whose appointment infuriated the city's merchant community. C. C. Cambreleng explained that Swartwout was from elsewhere and had spent the last decade "engaged in large and unfortunate speculations." This hardly qualified Swartwout to take charge of the nation's leading port. John Jacob Astor took umbrage at the mere suggestion that he was a supporter of Swartwout.[76] The commercial community had good reason to worry. From the start, Swartwout was convinced that New York harbor was shot through with smuggling from neighboring states and cities. "Manly, prompt, and vigorous suppression" of illicit trade became the official policy under Swartwout's watch. He appointed a "confidential agent" named Robert Lawrence to keep an eye on smuggling. No vessel was above suspicion, not even those of the United States Postal Service. It did not take long for "several of our merchants," "gentlemen of wealth and integrity," to complain to the Treasury Department for the "single indulgence" that Swartwout slacken his unnecessarily strict inspections, especially if it meant the prompt arrival of the mails. Meanwhile, Swartwout appointed more nightwatchmen and demanded stricter enforcement. "They have prevented much smuggling," Swartwout wrote of his nightwatchmen, before conceding that "several have died from exposure."[77]

Swartwout also became convinced that there were rotten apples inside the New York custom house. In the figure of Henry Levely, a lowly measurer of coal and other goods, Swartwout struck gold. Typically, when Levely completed his measurements of imported goods he had three days to submit his findings to the collector's office. Some merchants, seeking to make a deal in the interim while they waited for goods to clear customs, asked Levely and other measurers and gaugers for a "private return" or certificate attesting to the quantity and quality of the imported goods. Levely was hardly the first to supply this service. The practice, he explained, had "become a law among them particularly as it was for extra services rendered for the accommodation of Merchants." For their labors on behalf of the merchants, the customs employees received a small sum—"sixty two and a half cents for every thousand bushels" of coal in Levely's case. Swartwout agreed that the practice had reigned at the custom house since the days of "General Hamilton and Colonel Burr," who had officially determined "there was no impropriety in it." But he chafed at the idea that customs officers could moonlight for merchants for a fee. Secretary of the Treasury William Duane would agree, and in a stinging rebuke to Levely, he explained that "no man can faithfully serve two masters, of opposite interests," and that "public agents should have but one paymaster." Where Levely saw the need to accommodate the merchants, Duane and Swartwout believed customs officials and merchants represented "opposite interests." Jackson's plan to reconstitute governance at the New York custom house seemed well on its way.[78]

For a few years, Swartwout's aggressive treatment of the New York merchants seemed to suggest that collectors of customs with the proper reformist disposition could successfully wage battle against old patterns of deference to commerce. Perhaps customs officials could be trusted after all? Swartwout's departure to England in 1838 with $1 million in embezzled custom-house funds quickly did away with any such sentiment. It is difficult to overstate the shock that Swartwout's defalcation caused in the Treasury and within Congress. Special committees spilled ink on almost 800 pages seeking answers in the immediate aftermath of the revelations. By the following spring, congressional anxiety about future Swartwouts resulted in a law that "all money paid to any collector of the customs" be immediately placed under the credit of the secretary of the treasury, no matter whether the funds were in litigation, or any other mitigating circumstance. Swartwout, once chosen in part to limit the influence of the market on the custom house, seemed to prove more decisively than any previous event that the customs officials could no longer be trusted near the government's revenue. "There probably cannot, in human relations, be brought to bear upon human frailty and cupidity stronger temptations to err from duty and rectitude, than spring from the possession and control . . . by individual office-holders, of large and extraordinary masses of Government money," argued a House committee investigating Swartwout's larceny.[79]

As Congress searched for answers to the Swartwout affair it became convinced that inadequate supervision of the custom houses was to blame. Simply put, customs officials like Swartwout continued to wield too much discretion. If Swartwout was allowed to be a "lawgiver" it stood to reason "why any collector" would not do the same.[80] Swartwout had flouted the opinions of Treasury officials and others because "the collector is permitted to execute the law only as he understands it," complained the House investigators. With "the submission of the higher to the subordinate officers" of the custom house, the entire idea of government had been turned on its head. Both Secretary of the Treasury Levi Woodbury and the House Committee on Commerce had stumbled upon the same problem a few years earlier when investigating a possible reorganization of the Treasury. "Officers at the different ports" had "a great diversity of opinion" about "the powers confided to them by law." There was "a great want of uniformity" in bookkeeping. There even appeared to be "a great difference in the rates of duty paid at different ports." Woodbury demanded a new "Commissioner of the Customs" while the House committee suggested a new "bureau" to ensure customs "will be less likely to be negligent of their duty." The Tariff of 1842 finally settled the matter. It was "the duty of all collectors and other officers of the customs to execute and carry into effect all instructions of the Secretary of the Treasury relative to the execution of the revenue laws." If customs officials disagreed with the Treasury's construction of laws, "the decision of the Secretary of the Treasury shall be conclusive and binding."[81]

The practices of custom-house governance that had taken root during the times of the British Empire and structured the rise of the new federal government began to crumble between the end of the War of 1812 and through the presidency of Andrew Jackson. Customs officials had once been depended upon to use their discretion to align the letter of federal revenue and customs law to fit the expectations of the local merchant communities that paid customs duties and experienced commercial restrictions. But in these years, that very discretion had come under fire. Discretion, it seemed, had lost the republic millions in revenue in the duty bond scandal that surrounded the Panic of 1819. Discretion, too, seemed to have abetted frauds on the revenue through falsified invoices. Through investigations, executive regulations, laws, and political appointments, different parts of the federal government tried to strip away the layers of customs officials' discretion that seemed so troublesome. Above all, it suddenly seemed vital to segregate customs officials' practices of governance from the influence of the men of commerce who did business at the custom house.

The attempt to build a wall between the state and the marketplace in American politics was just beginning. Between 1833 and 1866, the Treasury Department began compiling thick tomes entitled *Letters Received Relating to Charges Against Customs Officers*. Boston official Adams Bailey and New Orleans collector J. W. Breedlove—Martin Gordon's successor—were said to be pawns of the banks, a wholly unsavory occupation for any good Jacksonian Democrat. Henry Benton, deputy collector of Genesee, was in league with smugglers, and John Daugh of Teche, with counterfeiters. In Jacksonville, Collector James Dell was said to have pretended to hire two temporary inspectors while in fact employing "his slaves from the field" and pocketing their wages. Gabriel Floyd of Apalachicola was thought to be "the passive instrument in the hands of the 'Florida, or Apalachicola Company,'" the area's most powerful commercial conglomerate. John McNiel, surveyor in Boston, was believed to be in the pocket of the city's sugar importers—a fact perhaps underscored by a memorial in his favor by "Sugar Merchants of Boston." B. I. Harrison, surveyor in Louisville, Kentucky, as well as Alphonso Mason, surveyor in Gloucester,

Massachusetts, were known to be grafters. In almost all of these cases, the Treasury Department would investigate only to find nothing untoward had occurred.[82]

If the Treasury's investigations are to be believed, it did not take much for customs officials to be tarred as corrupt. In one way or another, the accused were said to have put their office into play in the market. On the one hand, the charges point to a wholesale change in the meaning of corruption, which had once been about the misuse of office against the commonweal, but which now referred to a specific crime of profiting from public office. On the other hand, the emergence of the crime of corruption was a sign of how much federal governance had changed since the summer of 1789. Then it had been necessary for customs officials to court merchants and commerce by aligning revenue laws and customs regulations with local commercial norms and expectations. As the federal government had collected customs revenue, however, local commercial influence gained outsized stature at the custom house. The legal and political assault on customs officials' discretion was the strongest indication that the old means of custom-house governance were no longer suitable for a changing world. At the custom house, the old commercial bonds of imperial governance had been undone. It was not entirely clear what lay ahead. Bureaucratic modernity was a long ways off. The nation-state was still yet to come into its own. But the necessity of segregating the inner workings of the state from the operations of the marketplace had become clear. And there would be no turning back.

Epilogue: Charleston, 1832

Large crowds denouncing the tyranny of central taxation. Subscription lists for nonconsumption agreements. Sartorial politics. Officers "on guard" for "the safety of our community." Such was the raucous milieu around the Charleston custom house during the American Revolution and also some seventy years later during the Jacksonian era (see fig. 10).[1] There the similarities ended. In the mid-eighteenth century merchants such as Henry Laurens had demanded "all possible indulgence" by imperial customs officials. Charleston customs officials were to balance their official duties and local obligations by being "kind to the subject & strictly just to his Master."[2] During the Nullification Crisis in the 1820s and 1830s, there were no such demands for kindness or "indulgence" from federal customs officials. The "Nullies" objected, not only to the presence of the custom house, nor only to its function, but to the entire federal state that had emerged through the enforcement of revenue and commercial laws. "The surrender of our custom houses, was the one fatal error committed by our fathers in forming the Constitution," explained Robert Barnwell Rhett. Now it was time to retake them.[3]

A dual anxiety lay at the heart of the nullification movement. Above all, it had come to appear all but inevitable to South Carolina's planter-class oligarchy that the federal government would move to regulate slavery. According to Robert Barnwell Rhett, Congress might "at any moment, deprive us" of "all the property we possess" and "transfer it northward."[4] But this fear could only exist because of a more foundational anxiety. That is to say, planters' fears about a federal intrusion into the business of slavery presupposed the existence of a federal government capable of doing so. The nullification movement was as much a protest against the emergence

Fig. 10. Charleston, South Carolina, custom house (1860). *Harper's* depicts a large palmetto tree, the state tree of South Carolina, in front of the custom house to emphasize the conflict between the state and the federal government. During the nullification movement in 1832, the Charleston custom house again became the scene of rollicking protests against central governmental taxation and regulation. When South Carolina did finally secede from the Union in 1860, it took control of the facility. Library of Congress, Prints and Photographs Division (LC-USZ62-129745).

of a new, potentially muscular federal government as it was about a national debate about the status of slavery in the Union.

The rise of the nullification movement coincided with the transformation of the federal government. The War of 1812 marked the turning point where South Carolina's political class, including Vice President and Senator John C. Calhoun, became fervently anti-tariff. Likewise after the war the federal government narrowed customs officials' discretion and dismantled the negotiated governance between officeholders and merchants that had for decades ruled the custom houses. At the Charleston custom house, South Carolina's Nullifiers rebelled against a purportedly overbearing federal government at precisely the moment when the federal government began to gather its authority, once dispersed to the waterfront.

The symbolism of the Jackson administration's response to the Nullification Crisis—assembling the military to protect the nation's fiscal capacity—is as poignant as it is obvious.[5] But also important were the administrative instructions from the nation's capital to the small force of beleaguered customs officials in the Charleston custom house within the Old Exchange.[6] Secretary of the Treasury Louis McLane demanded "unshrinking firmness and fidelity in the discharge of your duties" from Collector J. R. Pringle. Unlike the suggestive instructions of the 1790s, these instructions were to be considered ironclad. McLane specifically prohibited Pringle from using discretion for "taking any important or unusual step." Pringle was instead always to "apply to the Department for further instructions" for the duration of the crisis.[7]

The Treasury also directed Pringle to take advantage of the federal government's increasingly centralized regulation of customs duty bonds to ensure that the custom house continued to function. As Secretary McLane explained, when a vessel made entry at the custom house, customs officials were to issue customs bonds for duties owed to the federal government. But since the Panic of 1819 and the crisis over money lost to the federal government in unpaid customs bonds, customs collectors like Pringle were only to issue bonds to those with the capacity to pay them back. He was to steadfastly refuse bonds to those who "have formed a determination not to pay the Bonds or to comply with his obligation." If the Nullifiers could not enter their vessels, they could not nullify the law. The duty bond, which had been the vehicle for reforming custom-house governance, had again come in handy.[8]

Perhaps the most telling aspect of the Jackson administration's response to the Nullification Crisis, however, lay in orders for Pringle to move the custom house from the Exchange in downtown Charleston to Fort Moultrie and Castle Pinckney in Charleston harbor.[9] Some seventy years before, Congress and the Washington administration had been careful to situate federal custom houses in venues familiar and friendly to local merchants. They selected officeholders who were prominent, respected members of local communities to legitimate federal authority. Now, in 1833, Andrew Jackson hardly hesitated before literally uprooting the custom house from its mercantile roots. The merchants of Charleston did not skip a beat. Although Governor James Hamilton made public promises to rescue a shipment of seized sugar from the custom house, the revenue laws went on without much interruption.[10]

Indeed, the revenue laws had to go on without interruption, for they were a foundation of a federal government and an American state that had emerged from the shadows of the Revolution and through the tumult of the early republic. This federal government would persist through the long nineteenth century, growing dramatically during the Civil War and then retrenching after Reconstruction. Yet the spine of this state remained intact until the advent of the income tax and the New Deal era's administrative revolution.[11]

Thus about thirty years after the uproar in Charleston, the Lincoln administration studied the Nullification Crisis as the South again contemplated secession.[12] Abraham Lincoln finally took military action against the Confederacy to resolve the conflict of slavery and freedom that divided the nation. But it was of no small significance that the legal justification of the war was that "the laws of the United States for the collection of the revenue cannot be effectually executed."[13]

ABBREVIATIONS

AHR	*American Historical Review*
Annals/Annals of Congress	United States Congress, *The Debates and Proceedings in the Congress of the United States: with an Appendix Containing Important State Papers and Public Documents, and All the Laws of a Public Nature/ with a Copious Index; Compiled from Authentic Materials* (Washington, D.C.: Gales and Seaton, 1834–56)
Archives I	National Archives, Washington, DC
Archives II	National Archives, College Park, MD
ASP	United States Congress, *American State Papers: Documents, Legislative and Executive, of the Congress of the United States, Commerce and Navigation* (Washington, DC: Gales & Seaton, 1832–61)
DHSCUS	Maeva Marcus, ed., *Documentary History of the Supreme Court of the United States, 1789–1800* (New York: Columbia University Press, 1985–)
HSP	Historical Society of Pennsylvania, Philadelphia, PA
JAH	*Journal of American History*
JEH	*Journal of Economic History*
JER	*Journal of the Early Republic*
LOC	Manuscript Reading Room, Library of Congress, Washington, DC
MHS	Massachusetts Historical Society, Boston, MA
NARA-Atlanta	National Archives and Records Administration, Morrow, GA

NARA-Boston	National Archives and Records Administration Regional Branch, Waltham, MA
NARA-College Park	National Archives, College Park, MD
NARA-NY	National Archives and Records Administration Regional Branch, New York
NARA-Phila	National Archives and Records Administration Regional Branch, Philadelphia
NHHS	New Hampshire Historical Society, Concord, NH
NYHS	New-York Historical Society, New York, NY
PAH	Harold D. Syrett, ed., *The Papers of Alexander Hamilton* (New York: Columbia University Press, 1961–87)
PAJ	Sam B. Smith and Harriet Chappell Owsley, eds., *The Papers of Andrew Jackson* (Knoxville: University of Tennessee Press, 1980–)
PTJ	Barbara Oberg et al., eds., *The Papers of Thomas Jefferson* (Princeton, NJ: Princeton University Press, 1950–2014)
PHL	Philip M. Hamer, ed., *The Papers of Henry Laurens* (Columbia: University of South Carolina Press, 1968–2003)
PRM	E. James Ferguson et al., eds., *The Papers of Robert Morris, 1781–1784* (Pittsburgh, PA: University of Pittsburgh Press, 1973–99)
RIHS	Rhode Island Historical Society, Providence, RI
WMQ	*William and Mary Quarterly*

NOTES

INTRODUCTION

1. Alexander Hamilton, "First Report on the Further Provision Necessary for Establishing Public Credit," December 13, 1790, in *The Papers of Alexander Hamilton*, ed. Harold D. Syrett (New York: Columbia University Press, 1961–87), 7:232–36 (hereafter cited as *PAH*); U.S. Constitution, art. I, sec. 8, cl. 1. On the difference between direct and indirect taxes, see John Phillip Reid, *Constitutional History of the American Revolution: The Power to Tax* (Madison: University of Wisconsin Press, 1986), 33–43.

2. Hamilton, "First Report," 7:232. It was a truism of early modern political economy that excessively high customs duties depressed commerce and encouraged smuggling. See, for instance, Adam Smith, *An Inquiry into the Nature and Causes of the Wealth of Nations*, ed. Edwin Canaan (London, 1776; repr., Chicago: University of Chicago Press, 1976), 2:412.

3. The best treatment of the customs service in the early republic is Frederick Arthur Baldwin Dalzell, "Taxation with Representation: Federal Revenue in the Early Republic," (PhD diss., Harvard University, 1993). Dalzell concludes that customs officials "accommodated" merchants in order to secure revenue. See also Dalzell, "Prudence and the Golden Egg: Establishing the Federal Government in Providence, Rhode Island," *New England Quarterly* 65, no. 3 (September 1992): 355–88; Joshua Mitchell Smith, *Borderland Smuggling: Patriots, Loyalists, and Illicit Trade in the Northeast, 1783–1820* (Gainesville: University of Florida Press, 2006); Laurence F. Schmeckebier, *The Customs Service: Its History, Activities, and Organization* (Baltimore: Johns Hopkins University Press, 1924); Carl E. Prince and Mollie Keller, *The U.S. Customs Service: A Bicentennial History* (Washington, DC: U.S. Customs Service, 1989); Don Whitehead, *Borderguard: The Story of the United States Customs Service* (New York: McGraw-Hill, 1963); James Pitkin et al., *Three Centuries of Custom Houses* (Washington, DC: National Society of the Colonial Dames of America, 1972).

4. Scholars who have focused on other regions and empires have looked to tariffs and customs administration to understand statecraft. See, for example, John Brewer, *Sinews of Power: War, Money, and the English State, 1688–1783* (Cambridge, MA: Harvard University Press, 1988); Hans ven de Ven, *Breaking with the Past: The Maritime Customs Service and the Global Origins of Modernity in China* (New York: Columbia

University Press, 2014); Philip Thai, "Smuggling, State-Building, and Political Economy in Coastal China, 1927–1949" (PhD diss., Stanford University, 2013); Victor Treadwell, "The Irish Customs Administration in the Sixteenth Century," *Irish Historical Studies* 20, no. 80 (1977): 384–417; Stuart Jenks and Justyna Wubs-Mrozewicz, eds., *The Hanse in Medieval and Early Modern Europe* (Leiden: Brill, 2012).

5. On political economy and its centrality to politics and society in the early modern world, see Steve Pincus, "Rethinking Mercantilism: Political Economy, the British Empire, and the Atlantic World in the Seventeenth and Eighteenth Centuries," *WMQ* 69, no. 1 (2012): 3–34; John C. Robertson, "The Enlightenment above National Context: Political Economy in Eighteenth-Century Scotland and Naples," *Historical Journal*, 40, no. 3 (1997): 672–75.

6. Charles Davenant, *An Essay Upon Ways and Means* (1695), in *The Political and Commercial Works Of that Celebrated Writer Charles Davenant, LL.D.* (1695–1712; Farnborough, Eng.: Gregg Press, 1967), 1:136. Smith, *Wealth of Nations*, 1:394. On the origins of the fiscal-military state, see Brewer, *Sinews of Power*; Steven Pincus, *1688* (New Haven, CT: Yale University Press, 2011), esp. 305–436; Christopher Storrs, ed., *The Fiscal-Military State in Eighteenth-Century Europe: Essays in Honour of P. G. M. Dickson* (Burlington, VT: Ashgate, 2009); Margaret Levi, *Of Rule and Revenue* (Berkeley: University of California Press, 1989); Charles Tilly, *Of Coercion, Capital, and European States, A.D. 990–1992* (New York: Cambridge University Press, 1995); Patrick K. O'Brien and Philip A. Hunt, "England, 1485–1815," in *The Rise of the Fiscal State in Europe, 1200–1815* (New York: Clarendon Press, 1999), 53–100.

7. Max M. Edling, *A Revolution in Favor of Government: Origins of the U.S. Constitution and the Making of the American State* (New York: Oxford University Press, 2003), 209–10; Robin L. Einhorn, *American Taxation, American Slavery* (Chicago: University of Chicago Press, 2006), 155; Romain D. Huret, *American Tax Resisters* (Cambridge, MA: Harvard University Press, 2014), 3.

8. Eve Tavor Bannet, *Empire of Letters: Letter Manuals and Transatlantic Correspondence, 1688–1820* (New York: Cambridge University Press, 2005), 236. So vast is this archive that I have had to omit a great many narratives about crucial aspects of custom-house governance, none more so than the interaction between customs officers, slaves, and slaveholders. Several secondary works touch on this literature, however; the best of these is Craig B. Hollander, "Against a Sea of Troubles: Slave Trade Suppressionism during the Early Republic" (PhD diss., Johns Hopkins University, 2013). See also Jenny Martinez, *The Slave Trade and the Origins of International Human Rights Law* (New York: Oxford University Press, 2012); Ernest Obadele-Starks, *Freebooters and Smugglers: The Foreign Slave Trade in the United States after 1808* (Fayetteville: University of Arkansas Press, 2007); James A. McMillen, *The Final Victims: Foreign Slave Trade to North America, 1783–1810* (Columbia: University of South Carolina Press, 2004).

9. The location and cubic footage of customs documents can be found at http://www.archives.gov/research/guide-fed-records/index-numeric/001-to-100.html#RG036.

10. See, for instance, Daniel Bluestone, "Civic and Aesthetic Reserve: Ammi Burnham Young's 1850 Federal Customhouse Designs," *Winterthur Portfolio* 25, no. 2/3 (1990): 131–56; Dan McCall, "The Design of Hawthorne's 'Custom-House,'" *Nineteenth-*

Century Fiction 21, no. 4 (1967): 349–58; Stanton Garner, "Herman Melville and the Customs Service," in *Melville's Evermoving Dawn: Centennial Essays*, ed. John Bryant and Robert Milder (Kent, OH: Kent State University Press, 1997), 276–95.

11. For studies that emphasize the strength of the early American state, see Max M. Edling, *A Hercules in the Cradle: War, Money, and the American State, 1783–1867* (Chicago: University of Chicago Press, 2013); Edling, *Revolution in Favor of Government*; Richard R. John, *Spreading the News: The American Postal System from Franklin to Morse* (Cambridge, MA: Harvard University Press, 1995); John, "Governmental Institutions as Agents of Change," *Studies in American Political Development* 11, no. 2 (1997): 347–80; William J. Novak, *The People's Welfare: Law & Regulation in Nineteenth-Century America* (Chapel Hill: University of North Carolina Press, 1996); Brian Balogh, *A Government Out of Sight: The Mystery of National Authority in Nineteenth-Century America* (New York: Cambridge University Press, 2009).

12. See, for example, George Washington to Alexander Hamilton, September 20, 1790, *PAH*, 7:61–62; George Washington to Alexander Hamilton, November 4, 1790, ibid., 7:140–41. See also Leonard White, *The Federalists: A Study in Administrative History, 1789–1801* (New York: The Free Press, 1948), 317–18. Generally on the production of this type of authority, see Pierre Bourdieu, *The Logic of Practice*, ed. Richard Nice (Stanford, CA: Stanford University Press, 1990), 128–29.

13. See Sven Beckert, *Empire of Cotton: A Global History* (New York: Knopf, 2014), xvi; Eliga Gould, "Zones of Law, Zones of Violence: The Legal Geography of the British Atlantic, circa 1772," *WMQ*, 3rd ser., 60, no. 3 (2003): 470–510; Christopher Magra, *The Fisherman's Cause: Atlantic Commerce and Maritime Dimensions of the American Revolution* (New York: Cambridge University Press, 2009); Denver Brunsman, *The Evil Necessity: British Naval Impressment in the Eighteenth-Century Atlantic World* (Charlottesville: University of Virginia Press, 2013); Richard Pares, *War and Trade in the West Indies, 1739–1763* (New York: Taylor & Francis, 1963).

14. "Commercial peoples" is borrowed from Paul Cheney, *Revolutionary Commerce: Globalization and the French Monarchy* (Cambridge, MA: Harvard University Press, 2010), 100.

15. Peter S. Onuf and Cathy D. Matson, *A Union of Interests: Political and Economic Thought in Revolutionary America* (Lawrence: University Press of Kansas, 1990); T. H. Breen, *The Marketplace of Revolution: How Consumer Politics Shaped American Independence* (New York: Oxford University Press, 2004). On the power of commerce in shaping culture and society, see Albert O. Hirschman, "Rival Interpretations of Market Society: Civilizing, Destructive, or Feeble?," *Journal of Economic Literature*, 20, no. 4 (1982): 1463–84; Hirschman, *The Passions and the Interests: Political Arguments for Capitalism before Its Triumph* (Princeton, NJ: Princeton University Press, 1977); Cheney, *Revolutionary Commerce*; Istvan Hont, *Jealousy of Trade: International Competition and the Nation-State in Historical Perspective* (Cambridge, MA: Harvard University Press, 2005). The following works explore dimensions of merchant capitalism: Hannah Atlee Farber, "Underwritten States: Marine Insurance and the Making of Bodies Politic in America, 1622–1815" (PhD diss., University of California, Berkeley, 2014); Thomas M. Doerflinger, *A Vigorous Spirit of Enterprise: Merchants and Economic Development in Revolutionary Philadelphia* (Chapel Hill: University of

North Carolina Press, 1986); Andrew M. Schocket, *Founding Corporate Power in Early National Philadelphia* (Dekalb: Northern Illinois University Press, 2007); Cathy D. Matson, *Merchants & Empire: Trading in Colonial New York* (Cambridge, MA: Harvard University Press, 1998); James Fichter, *So Great a Proffit: How the East Indies Trade Transformed Anglo-American Capitalism* (Cambridge, MA: Harvard University Press, 2010); Dael Norwood, "Trading in Liberty: The Politics of the American China Trade, c. 1784–1862" (PhD diss., Princeton University, 2012).

16. In early America, informal power structures and formal authority together constituted a pluralist legal order. See Christopher L. Tomlins and Bruce H. Mann, eds., *The Many Legalities of Early America* (Chapel Hill: University of North Carolina Press, 2001); Hendrik Hartog, "Pigs and Positivism," *Wisconsin Law Review* 4 (1985): 899–935; Kathleen Wilson, "Rethinking the Colonial State: Family, Gender, and Governmentality in Eighteenth-Century British Frontiers," *AHR* 116, no. 5 (2011): 1294–1322.

17. Many merchant communities were also important to party formation. See James H. Broussard, *Southern Federalists, 1800–1816* (Baton Rouge: Louisiana State University Press, 1978); William Nisbet Chambers, *The First Party System: Federalists and Republicans* (New York: Wiley, 1992); Shaw Livermore Jr., *The Twilight of Federalism: The Disintegration of the Federalist Party, 1815–1830* (New York: Gordian Press, 1962).

18. Pauline S. Maier, *From Resistance to Revolution: Colonial Radicals and the Development of American Opposition to Britain, 1765–1776* (1972; New York: W.W. Norton, 1991), 6–9, 9 n. 7. According to Maier (9 n. 7), "These customs uprisings should be distinguished from the organized opposition to Britain that emerged in 1765" because "customs incidents were above all local in character and, at least before the Townshend Revenue Act, devoid of explicit ideological justifications."

19. On American ambivalence regarding the market as a source of both opportunity and anxiety, see, for example, Brian Phillips Murphy, *Building the Empire State: Political Economy in the Early Republic* (Philadelphia: University of Pennsylvania Press, 2015); Schocket, *Founding Corporate Power*; John Lauritz Larson, *The Market Revolution in America: Liberty, Ambition, and the Eclipse of the Common Good* (New York: Cambridge University Press, 2009); Onuf and Matson, *Union of Interests*.

Notably, several federal statutes criminalized conflicts of interest, but only rarely did this type of malfeasance make headlines. See, for instance, William Lee to Fulwar Skipwith, April 2, 1805, Causten-Pickett Papers, Box 8, Folder L-Q, LOC. On the law governing conflicts of interest, see Jerry L. Mashaw, *Creating the Administrative Constitution: The Lost One Hundred Years of American Administrative Law* (New Haven, CT: Yale University Press, 2012), 58–64. On the distinction between gift giving and corruption, see Natalie Zemon Davis, *The Gift in Sixteenth-Century France* (Madison: University of Wisconsin Press, 2000), 85–99.

"Regulatory capture," wherein the special interests overtake and control the government agency, is far too vague a term to make sense of the complicated power relations that ruled at the custom house. See Daniel Carpenter and David A. Moss, introduction to *Preventing Regulatory Capture: Special Interest Influence and How to Limit It*, ed. Daniel Carpenter and David A. Moss (New York: Cambridge University Press, 2014), 1–22. Like "capture," "corruption" is a popular way to make sense of governmental agents who consistently veer away from the letter of the law. But as Richard White argues, corruption "is not always the same; it has a history." Richard White, "Information, Markets, and Corruption: Transcontinental Railroads in the Gilded Age," *JAH* 90, no. 1 (June 2003): 19.

20. It is no coincidence that the rise of modern administrative law coincided with the emergence of industrial capitalism. Theorists and modern administrators have long been deeply concerned with configuring appropriate boundaries between the state and the marketplace. See, generally, Max Weber, "Bureaucracy," in *From Max Weber: Essays in Sociology*, ed. Hans Gerth and C. W. Mills (New York: Oxford University Press, 1946), 196–262; Susan Rose-Ackerman, *Corruption: A Study in Political Economy* (New York: Academic Press, 1978).

21. On the constitutive role of commerce in the British Empire, see, for example, David Hancock, *Citizens of the World: London Merchants and the Integration of the British Atlantic Community* (New York: Cambridge University Press, 1995); Nancy F. Koehn, *The Power of Commerce: Economy and Governance in the First British Empire* (Ithaca, NY: Cornell University Press, 1994); Robert Brenner, *Merchants and Revolution: Commercial Change, Political Conflict, and London's Overseas Traders, 1550–1653* (New York: Verso, 2003).

22. The role of negotiated authority in imperial governance is explained by Jack P. Greene, "Transatlantic Colonization and the Redefinition of Empire in the Early Modern Era: The British-American Experience," in *Negotiating Empires: Centers and Peripheries in the Americas, 1500–1820*, ed. Christine Daniels and Michael V. Kennedy (New York: Routledge, 2002), 267–82; Elizabeth Mancke, "Negotiating an Empire: Britain and Its Oversea Peripheries, c. 1550–1780," ibid., 32–74; Jack P. Greene, *Negotiated Authorities: Essays in Colonial Political and Constitutional History* (Charlottesville: University Press of Virginia, 1994).

23. Sarah Kinkel, "The King's Pirates? Naval Enforcement of Imperial Authority, 1740–46," *WMQ* 71, no. 1 (Jan. 2014): 3–34; John W. Tyler, *Smugglers and Patriots: Boston Merchants and the Advent of the American Revolution* (Boston: Northeastern University Press, 1986); Matson, *Merchants & Empire*; Thomas W. Truxes, *Defying Empire: Trading with the Enemy in Colonial New York* (New Haven, CT: Yale University Press, 2008). Leading studies of British customs enforcement are Thomas C. Barrow, *Trade and Empire: The British Customs Service in Colonial America, 1660–1775* (Cambridge, MA: Harvard University Press, 1967); Elizabeth Evelynola Hoon, *Organization of the English Customs System, 1696–1786* (1938; New York: A.M. Kelley, 1968); William J. Ashworth, *Customs and Excise: Trade, Production, and Consumption in England, 1640–1845* (New York: Oxford University Press, 2003); Dora Mae Clark, *The Rise of the British Treasury: Colonial Administration in the Eighteenth Century* (New Haven, CT: Yale University Press, 1960).

24. Abigail Swingen, *Competing Visions of Empire: Labor, Slavery, and the Origins of the British Atlantic Empire* (New Haven, CT: Yale University Press, 2015); Nuala Zahedieh, "Making Mercantilism Work: London Merchants and Atlantic Trade in the Seventeenth Century," *Transactions of the Royal Historical Society* 9 (1999): 143–58; Zahedieh, "Trade, Plunder, and Economic Development in Early English Jamaica," *Economic History Review* 39, no. 2 (1986): 205–22; Zahedieh, "The Merchants of Port Royal, Jamaica, and the Spanish Contraband Trade, 1655–1692," *WMQ* 43, no. 4 (1986): 570–93.

25. For contests over the location of central governmental authority beyond the Atlantic, see Bethel Saler, *The Settler's Empire: Colonialism and State Formation in America's Old Southwest* (Philadelphia: University of Pennsylvania Press, 2015); Anne F. Hyde, *Empires, Nations, and Families: A History of the North American West, 1800–1860* (Lincoln: University of Nebraska Press, 2011); Catherine Cangany, *Frontier Seaport: Detroit's Transformation into an Atlantic Entrepôt* (Chicago: University of Chicago Press, 2014); Walter Johnson, *River of Dark Dreams: Slavery and Empire in the Cotton Kingdom* (Cambridge, MA: Belknap Press of Harvard University Press, 2013).

26. The imperial dimensions of governance in the early republic are the subject of Saler, *Settler's Empire*; Edling, *Revolution in Favor of Government*; Peter S. Onuf and Eliga H. Gould, eds., *Empire and Nation: The American Revolution in the Atlantic World* (Baltimore: Johns Hopkins University Press, 2005); Eliga Gould, *Among the Powers of the Earth: The American Revolution and the Making of a New World Empire* (Cambridge, MA: Harvard University Press, 2012); Daniel Hulsebosch, *Constituting Empire: New York and the Transformation of Constitutionalism in the Atlantic World, 1664–1830* (Chapel Hill: University of North Carolina Press, 2005); Jack P. Greene, "Colonial History and National History: Reflections on a Continuing Problem," *WMQ* 64, no. 2 (Apr. 2007): 235–50.

27. On the influence of foreign empires over the early American republic, see, for example, Ira Katznelson and Martin Shefter, eds., *Shaped by War and Trade: International Influences on American Political Development* (Princeton, NJ: Princeton University Press, 2002); Edling, *Revolution in Favor of Government*; Gould, *Among the Powers of the Earth*; Peter J. Kastor, *The Nation's Crucible: The Louisiana Purchase and the Creation of America* (New Haven, CT: Yale University Press, 2004); Eric Hinderaker and Peter C. Mancall, *At the Edge of Empire: The Backcountry in British North America* (Baltimore: Johns Hopkins University Press, 2003); James E. Lewis, *The American Union and the Problem of Neighborhood: The United States and the Collapse of the Spanish Empire, 1783–1829* (Chapel Hill: University of North Carolina Press, 1999); Kevin Arlyck, "Plaintiffs v. Privateers: Litigation and Foreign Affairs in the Federal Courts, 1816–1822," *Law and History Review* 30, no. 1 (Feb. 2012): 254–78.

28. Mashaw, *Creating the Administrative Constitution*, 56–59.

29. See Karen Orren, "Officers' Rights: Toward a Unified Field Theory of American Constitutional Development," *Law & Society Review* 34, no. 4 (2000): 873–909; Keith Wrightson, "Two Concepts of Order: Justices, Constables, and Jurymen in Seventeenth-Century England," in *An Ungovernable People: The English and Their Law in the Seventeenth and Eighteenth Centuries*, ed. John Brewer and John Styles (New Brunswick, NJ: Rutgers University Press, 1980), 21–46.

30. On the difficulty of finding evidence of merchants contemplating smuggling and other acts, see Oliver M. Dickerson, *Navigation Acts and the American Revolution* (Philadelphia: University of Pennsylvania Press, 1951), 128–29.

31. On the demise of the idea of a stateless American past, see John, "Governmental Institutions as Agents of Change"; and William J. Novak, "The Myth of the Weak American State," *AHR* 113, no. 3 (2008): 752–72. Stephen Skowronek is generally credited with introducing the idea of an ambivalent early American state that was not much felt but that nonetheless "fought wars, expropriated Indians, secured new territo-

ries, carried on relations with other states, and aided economic development." Stephen Skowronek, *Building a New American State: The Expansion of National Administrative Capacities, 1877–1920* (New York: Cambridge University Press, 1982), 19, 24, 27, 26. On the misunderstood legacy of *Building a New American State*, see Daniel P. Carpenter, "The Multiple and Material Legacies of Stephen Skowronek," *Social Science History* 27, no. 3 (2003): 465–74. For a small sampling of the literature on local, municipal, and state power in the early republic, see William J. Novak, *The People's Welfare: Law & Regulation in Nineteenth-Century America* (Chapel Hill: University of North Carolina Press, 1996); Hendrik Hartog, *Public Property and Private Power: The Corporation of the City of New York in American Law, 1730–1870* (Ithaca, NY: Cornell University Press, 1983); Laura F. Edwards, *The People and Their Peace: Legal Culture and the Transformation of Inequality in the Post-Revolutionary South* (Chapel Hill: University of North Carolina Press, 2009).

32. Edling, *Revolution in Favor of Government*; Gould, *Among the Powers of the Earth*; David Armitage, *The Declaration of Independence: A Global History* (Cambridge, MA: Harvard University Press, 2007).

33. For leading studies of early federal government and federal policy, see John, *Spreading the News*; Robin Einhorn, *American Taxation, American Slavery* (Chicago: University of Chicago Press, 2007); Edling, *Revolution in Favor of Government*; Balogh, *Government Out of Sight*; William H. Bergmann, *The American National State and the Early West* (New York: Cambridge University Press, 2012); Laura Jensen, *Patriots, Settlers, and the Origins of American Social Policy* (New York: Cambridge University Press, 2003); Mark R. Wilson, *The Business of Civil War: Military Mobilization and the State, 1861–1865* (Baltimore: Johns Hopkins University Press, 2006); Adam Rothman, *Slave Country: American Expansion and the Origins of the Deep South* (Cambridge, MA: Harvard University Press, 2005); Brian Schoen, *The Fragile Fabric of Union: Cotton, Federal Politics, and the Global Origins of the Civil War* (Baltimore: Johns Hopkins University Press, 2009); Sean Patrick Adams, *Old Dominion, Industrial Commonwealth: Coal, Politics, and Economy in Antebellum America* (Baltimore: Johns Hopkins University Press, 2004); B. Zorina Khan, *The Democratization of Invention: Patents and Copyrights in American Economic Development, 1790–1920* (New York: Cambridge University Press, 2005); Stefan Heuman, "The Tutelary Empire: State- and Nation-Building in the 19th Century United States" (PhD diss., University of Pennsylvania, 2010); Andrew John Beardsley Fagal, "The Political Economy of War in the Early American Republic, 1774–1821" (PhD diss., Binghamton University, 2013). Leonard White's early twentieth-century project of documenting administrative history in the early republic is also significant. See Richard John, "In Retrospect: Leonard D. White and the Invention of American Administrative History," *Reviews in American History* 24, no. 2 (1996): 344–60.

34. On the politics and memory of the history of the federal government, see Jill Lepore, *The Whites of Their Eyes: The Tea Party's Revolution and the Battle over American History* (Princeton, NJ: Princeton University Press, 2010); Danielle S. Allen, *Our Declaration: A Reading of the Declaration of Independence in Defense of Equality* (New York: W.W. Norton, 2014); Akhil Reed Amar, *The Bill of Rights: Creation and Reconstruction* (New Haven, CT: Yale University Press, 1998).

PHILADELPHIA, 1769

1. John Swift to Commissioners of the Board of Customs, October 13, 1769, Vol. 10, Port of Philadelphia Custom House Records, 1704–1789, HSP (hereafter cited as Philadelphia Customs Records).

2. Ibid. Edmund S. Morgan and Helen M. Morgan discuss a similar dynamic that unfolded in Rhode Island, as Collector of Customs John Robinson's "only crime" in the eyes of locals "was enforcing the Laws of Trade." Edmund S. Morgan and Helen M. Morgan, *The Stamp Act Crisis: Prologue to Revolution* (1953; Chapel Hill: University of North Carolina Press, 1962), 41.

3. Clark, *Rise of the British Treasury*, 135. On the role of West Indies commerce in Philadelphia's economy, see Marc Egnal, "The Changing Structure of Philadelphia's Trade with the British West Indies, 1750–1775," *Pennsylvania Magazine of History and Biography* 99, no. 2 (1975): 156–79; Michelle Craig McDonald, "The Chance of the Moment: Coffee and the New West Indies Commodities Trade," *WMQ*, 3rd ser., 62, no. 3 (2005): 441–72; Arthur L. Jensen, *The Maritime Commerce of Colonial Philadelphia* (Madison: State Historical Society of Wisconsin for the Dept. of History, University of Wisconsin, 1963), 107–12; Cathy Matson, "Accounting for War and Revolution: Philadelphia Merchants and Commercial Risk, 1774–1811," in *The Self-Perception of Early Modern Capitalists*, ed. Margaret C. Jacob and Catherine Secretan (New York: Palgrave, 2008), 183–204; Linda Kerrigan Salvucci, "Development and Decline: The Port of Philadelphia and Spanish Imperial Markets, 1783–1823" (PhD diss., Princeton University, 1985).

4. Thomas Willing Balch, "The First 'Assembly Account'—Philadelphia, 1748," *Proceedings of the American Philosophical Society* 41, no. 170 (Apr. 1902): 261–62; Alfred S. Martin, "The King's Customs: Philadelphia, 1763–1774," *WMQ*, 3rd ser., vol. 5, no. 2 (Apr. 1948): 201–16.

5. Jensen, *Maritime Commerce of Colonial Philadelphia*, 136–37.

6. Greene, *Negotiated Authorities*, 11.

7. Swift to Commissioners of the Board of Customs, October 13, 1769.

8. John Swift to Commissioners of Customs, December 20, 1770, Vol. 11, Philadelphia Customs Papers.

CHAPTER 1

1. John Adams, argument in *Rex v. Weems* (1770), in *The Legal Papers of John Adams*, ed. L. Kinvin Wroth and Hiller B. Zobel (Cambridge, MA: Belknap Press of Harvard University Press, 1965), 266; John Agresto, "Art and Historical Truth: The Boston Massacre," *Journal of Communication* 29, no. 4 (1979): 170–74; Marcus Rediker, "The Revenge of Crispus Attucks; or, the Atlantic Challenge to American Labor History," *Labor: Studies in Working-Class History of the Americas* 1, no. 4 (2004): 35–45.

2. On colonial mobs, see Maier, *From Resistance to Revolution*. The link between customs enforcement and revolutionary mobilization is made by Oliver M. Dickerson, *The Navigation Acts and the American Revolution* (Chicago: Octagon Books, 1974); Barrow, *Trade and Empire*; Bernhard Knollenberg, *Origin of the American Revolution* (1961; Indianapolis: Liberty Fund, 2002); Breen, *Marketplace of the Revolution*, 217–331.

3. Henry Hulton, "Some Account of the Proceedings of the People of New England," Andre De Coppet Collection, Bd MS No. 1, Princeton University Libraries, 56.

4. See Benjamin Irvin, "Tar, Feathers, and the Enemies of American Liberties, 1768–1776," *New England Quarterly* 76, no. 2 (2003): 197–238.

5. Lauren A. Benton, *A Search for Sovereignty: Law and Geography in European Empires, 1400–1900* (New York: Cambridge University Press, 2009), 290. E. P. Thompson, "Moral Economy of the English Crowd in the Eighteenth Century," *Past and Present* 50 (1971): 78–79.

6. P. J. Marshall, *The Making and Unmaking of Empires: Britain, India, and America c. 1750–1783* (New York: Oxford University Press, 2005), 4. On imperial governance in these years, see Hulsebosch, *Constituting Empire*; James A. Henretta, *"Salutary Neglect": Colonial Administration under the Duke of Newcastle* (Princeton, NJ: Princeton University Press, 1972).

7. After the Seven Years' War the British Empire searched for new modes of centralized "rule" in the colonies. Marshall, *Making and Unmaking of Empires*, 5.

8. A parallel military and political tale is uncovered by Andrew Jackson O'Shaughnessy, *The Men Who Lost America: British Leadership, the American Revolution, and the Fate of Empire* (New Haven, CT: Yale University Press, 2013), 5.

9. Brewer, *Sinews of Power*, xvii. P. K. O'Brien, "The Political Economy of British Taxation, 1660–1815," *Economic History Review* 41, no. 1 (1988): 1–32.

10. Brewer, *Sinews of Power*, 54, 95–99. Brewer illustrates that excise taxes provided the lion's share of revenue in these years. On the emergence of the tax state, see Charles Tilly, *Coercion, Capital, and European States, AD 990–1990* (New York: Oxford University Press); Einhorn, *American Taxation, American Slavery*.

11. The farmers of the customs had been centralized in 1604 with the establishment of a Great Farm, and expanded in 1632 with the establishment of the Petty Farms. In 1671 Charles II absorbed into the state the aged network of private revenue collectors known as the farmers of the customs, which dated back to the fourteenth century. These private collectors were most often merchants of some note who collected the king's revenue and took for their services a slice from the king's treasure. The new customs establishment retained the basic structure of the old "Great Farm." Edgar Kiser and Joshua Kane, "Revolution and State Structure: The Bureaucratization of Tax Administration in Early Modern England and France," *American Journal of Sociology* 107, no. 1 (July 2001), 192, 197.

12. Michael J. Braddick, *The Nerves of the State: Taxation and the Financing of the English State, 1558–1714* (New York: Manchester University Press, 1996), 49–67; Hoon, *Organization of the English Customs System*, 128; Ashworth, *Customs and Excise*, 133–37.

13. Peter Linebaugh, *The London Hanged: Crime and Civil Society in the Eighteenth Century* (New York: Verso, 2003), 159; Neil McKendrick, "The Consumer Revolution in Eighteenth-Century England," in *The Birth of a Consumer Society: The Commercialization of Eighteenth-Century England*, ed. Neil McKendrick, John Brewer, and J. H. Plumb (London: Europa, 1982), 9–33.

14. Barrow, *Trade and Empire*, 8–9. There were also several important commercial regulations. The 1660 law mandated that predominantly English crews in only English

vessels carried all colonial produce to English ports (and only English ports). The Staple Act of 1663 required that all foreign merchandise imported to the English colonies first arrive in England. And finally the 1673 law required vessels carrying enumerated goods from the colonies to England to post bond or prepay duties to ensure that they would not deviate from their lawfully stated port of call in England.

15. Ashworth, *Customs and Excise*, 139–64. In theory, customs officials followed the same procedures in the colonies. See John Tabor Kempe, "Custom House," in *Opinions and Notes*, Box 16, Folder 10, John Tabor Kempe Papers, NYHS.

16. Brewer, *Sinews of Power*, 96–97.

17. W. Wood to Portsmouth Customhouse, February 20, 1747, in *Portsmouth Customs Letter Books, 1748–1750*, ed. G. Hampson and J. G. Rule (Hampshire, Eng.: Hampshire County Council, 1994), 4; Exeter Letterbook, Entries for July 11 and 15, 1690; January 4, 1692, reprinted in G. Graham Dixon, "Notes on the Records of the Custom House, London," *English Historical Review* 34, no. 133 (Jan. 1919): 72.

18. Pincus, *1688*, 6–10.

19. Ibid., 6–7. Ultimately, "Britishness" and state-oriented religious institutions provided a cultural foundation for this new state, according to Linda Colley, *Britons: Forging the Nation, 1707–1837* (New Haven, CT: Yale University Press, 2005), and Brent S. Sirota, *The Christian Monitors: The Church of England and the Age of Benevolence, 1680–1730* (New Haven, CT: Yale University Press, 2014).

20. Thompson, "Moral Economy of the English Crowd," 79.

21. Ashworth, *Customs and Excise*, 165–183.

22. Patrick Colquhoun, *A Treatise on the Police of the Metropolis* (London: H. Fey, 1796), vii, 55; Linebaugh, *London Hanged*, 161. Scholars have debated the ideological significance of this smuggling economy. See Paul Monod, "Dangerous Merchandise: Smuggling, Jacobitism, and Commercial Culture in Southeast England, 1690–1760," *Journal of British Studies* 30, no. 2 (April 1991): 150–82.

23. Cal Winslow, "The Sussex Smugglers," in Douglas Hay, Peter Linebaugh, and E. P. Thompson, et al., *Albion's Fatal Tree: Crime and Society in Eighteenth-Century England* (New York: Pantheon Books, 1975), 136–39.

24. Paul Monod, *Jacobitism and the English People, 1688–1788* (New York: Cambridge University Press, 1989), 7, 114–16, 125, 346.

25. B. R. Leftwich, "The Later History and Administration of the Customs Revenue in England (1671–1814)," *Transactions of the Royal Historical Society* 13 (1930): 194; Hoh-cheung Mui and Lorna H. Mui, "Smuggling and the British Tea Trade before 1784," *AHR* 84, no. 1 (1968): 73.

26. Most outports had about ten officers, along with a small vessel manned by approximately seven officers. Leftwich, "Later History," 193.

27. Leftwich, "Later History," 197.

28. Ibid., 195; Hoon, *Organization of the English Customs*, 192.

29. The term "provincializing" is borrowed from Hulsebosch, *Constituting Empire*.

30. Pincus, *1688*, 6. On the intellectual underpinnings of this maritime, commercial notion of empire, see David Armitage, *The Ideological Origins of the British Empire* (New York: Cambridge University Press, 2000). For a detailed discussion of the logistics of overseas commercial expansion, see Robert Brenner, *Merchants and*

Revolution: Commercial Change, Political Conflict, and London's Overseas Traders, 1550–1653 (New York: Verso, 2003).

31. John J. McCusker and Russell R. Menard, *The Economy of British America, 1607–1789* (Chapel Hill: University of North Carolina Press, 1985); Cathy D. Matson, ed., *The Economy of Early America: Historical Perspectives & New Directions* (University Park: Pennsylvania State University Press, 2007); Stanley L. Engerman and Robert E. Gallman, ed., *The Cambridge Economic History of the United States*, vol. 1, *The Colonial Era* (New York: Cambridge University Press, 1996).

32. Nuala Zahedieh, "Overseas Expansion and Trade in the Seventeenth Century," in *The Oxford History of the British Empire: The Origins of Empire*, ed. Nicholas Canny (1998; New York: Cambridge University Press, 2005), 405–6; Zahedieh, *The Capital and the Colonies: London and the Atlantic Economy, 1660–1770* (New York: Cambridge University Press), 36–38; Dickerson, *Navigation Acts and the American Revolution*, 7–30.

33. Ian Kenneth Steele, *Politics of Colonial Policy: The Board of Trade in Colonial Administration, 1696–1720* (New York: Clarendon Press of Oxford University Press, 1968), 3–8; Steele, "Metropolitan Administration of the Colonies, 1696–1775," in *The Blackwell Encyclopedia of the American Revolution* (Cambridge: Basil Blackwell, 1991), 8–16.

34. Grant of the Office of Surveyor & Auditor, n.d., Journal of William Blathwayt, Treasury 64, vols. 88–90, Public Record Office, Transcript, LOC, 1; Clark, *Rise of the British Treasury*, 61; Charles M. Andrews, *The Colonial Period of American History: England's Commercial and Colonial Policy* (New Haven, CT: Yale University Press, 1938), 187–91.

35. Alison Games, *The Web of Empire: English Cosmopolitans in an Age of Expansion, 1560–1660* (New York: Oxford University Press, 2008), 148. Although by 1696 the small island of England had fifty customs outports, the sprawling colonies in 1760 had only forty-one custom houses to police commerce from present-day Maine to Georgia. Hoon, *Organization of the English Customs*, 168–69; Barrow, *Trade and Empire*, 262–64.

36. Pitkin et al., *Three Centuries of Custom Houses*, 3, 13, 17, 36, 147; Edward H. Hart, *Almost a Hero: Andrew Elliot, the King's Moneyman in New York, 1764–1776 . . .* (Unionville, NY: Royal Fireworks Press, 2005), 7; Commissioners of Customs to Charles Stewart, November 27, 1765, Vol. 4, Philadelphia Customs Records, HSP. See the description of the Bristol custom house in John Latimer, *The Annals of Bristol in the Eighteenth Century* (London: for the Author, 1893), 82; and Henry Bell's custom house at Lynn in P. H. Ditchfield, *Vanishing England* (New York: E.P. Dutton, 1910), 38.

37. Hulsebosch, *Constituting Empire*, 45, and on difficulties of revenue collection, 48; Zahedieh, *Capital and the Colonies*, 38–39.

38. Barrow, *Trade and Empire*, 24; Stephen Saunders Webb, *1776: The End of American Independence* (Syracuse, NY: Syracuse University Press, 1995), 153; Andrews, *Colonial Period of American History*, 208.

39. Michael Garibaldi Hall, *Edward Randolph and the American Colonies, 1676–1703* (Chapel Hill: University of North Carolina Press, 1960), 4, 57, and generally on this episode, 55–57. Randolph secured a victory on December 29, 1682, when a jury

convicted a shipmaster named Kotch for illegally importing "divers European Goods" prohibited by the Navigation Act of 1660. Edward Randolph, Report, 1682, LOC.

40. Edward Randolph et al., "Account of Proceedings of the New Government," June 1, 1686; Edward Randolph to William Sancroft, Archbishop of Canterbury, August 2, 1686, in *Edward Randolph: Including His Letters and Official Papers*, ed. Robert Noxon Toppan (Boston, 1899; New York: Burt Franklin, 1967), 4:81; Hall, *Edward Randolph*, 111–28.

41. Pincus, *1688*, 6.

42. Hall, *Edward Randolph*, 149, 152–53. Council of Trade to King, September 10, 1696, Colonial Office, Class 5, Reel 1, vol. 1–4, LOC; Hulsebosch, *Constituting Empire*, 84; Andrews, *Colonial Period of American History*, 198–201.

43. Christopher L. Tomlins and Bruce Mann, eds., *The Many Legalities of Early America* (Chapel Hill: University of North Carolina Press, 2001). On the fate of royal authority in the colonies, see Brendan McConville, *The King's Three Faces: The Rise and Fall of Royal America, 1688–1776* (Chapel Hill: University of North Carolina Press, 2006); Eric Nelson, *The Royalist Revolution: Monarchy and the American Founding* (Cambridge, MA: Harvard University Press, 2014).

44. Edward Randolph, "A Narrative of My Survey in Tour of his Maj'ys Colonys & provinces on the Continent of America," May 9, 1698, Richard Peters Papers, Vol. 1, HSP.

45. Barrow, *Trade and Empire*, 68; Randolph, "Narrative of My Survey," May 18, 1698, May 19, 1698; Hall, *Edward Randolph*, 192–98. Smuggling and piracy had blossomed in New York harbor under the guidance of Customs Collector William Dwyer, according to Matson, *Merchants & Empire*, 63.

46. Randolph, "Loss of Revenue from Tobacco, &c.," November 5, 1700, in Toppan, *Edward Randolph*, 5:230, 232, 233. Randolph also heaped blame on the "mall administrat[io]n of the Governors in the Severall Properties on the Continent of America and Islands Adjacent," n.d., 1701, in *Randolph Letters*, 5:268–73. He had lodged similar complaints some years earlier, as seen in Edward Randolph to Commissioners of Customs, November 10, 1696, Colonial Office, Class 5, Reel 1, Vol. 1–4, LOC; Konstantin Dierks, *In My Power: Letter Writing and Communications in Early America* (Philadelphia: University of Pennsylvania Press, 2009), 16–17.

47. Barrow, *Trade and Empire*, 69; William Byrd, "Representation of Mr. Byrd Concerning Proprietary Governments Anno 1799 [I.E. 1699]," in *An Essay Upon the Government of the English Plantations on the Continent of America*, ed. Louis B. Wright (1701; New York: Arno Press, 1972); Steele, *Politics of Colonial Policy*, 85–108.

48. Peter Linebaugh and Marcus Rediker, *The Many-Headed Hydra: Sailors, Slaves, Commoners, and the Hidden History of the Revolutionary Atlantic* (Boston: Beacon Press, 2000), 144; Benton, *Search for Sovereignty*, 290. See also Wim Klooster, *Illicit Riches: Dutch Trade in the Caribbean, 1648–1795* (New York: Brill Academic, 1998); Klooster, "Inter-Imperial Smuggling in the Americas, 1600–1800," in *Soundings in Atlantic History: Latent Structures and Intellectual Currents, 1500–1830*, ed. Bernard Bailyn and Patricia L. Denault (Cambridge, MA: Harvard University Press, 2009), 141–80; Pares, *War and Trade in the West Indies*, 1–28.

49. Gould, "Zones of Law," 474.

50. Claudia Schnurmann, "Atlantic Trade and American Identities: The Correla-

tions of Supranational Commerce, Political Opposition, and Colonial Regionalism," in *The Atlantic Economy during the Seventeenth and Eighteenth Centuries: Organization, Operation, Practice, and Personnel*, ed. Peter A. Coclanis (Columbia: University of South Carolina Press, 2005), 186; Matson, *Merchants & Empire*, 6; Pares, *War and Trade in the West Indies*, 396–97; Truxes, *Defying Empire*.

51. Clark, *Rise of the British* Treasury, 45; Jacob M. Price, "Who Cared about the Colonies? The Impact of the Thirteen Colonies on British Society and Politics, circa 1714–1775," in *Strangers within the Realm: Cultural Margins of the First British Empire* (Chapel Hill: University of North Carolina Press, 1991), 395–436.

52. Henretta, "Salutary Neglect," 142.

53. Steele, *Politics of Colonial Policy*, 85–108.

54. Henretta, "Salutary Neglect," 24–25, 267. Cadwallader Colden to Peter Collison, n.d. [spring 1740], in *The Letters and Papers of Cadwallader Colden* (New York: New York Historical Society, 1918), 3:210.

55. Frank Moya Pons, *History of the Caribbean: Plantations, Trade, and War in the Atlantic World* (Princeton, NJ: Markus Weiner Publishers, 2007), 97–98, 101, 112, 115; Ruth Bourne, *Queen Anne's Navy in the West Indies* (New Haven, CT: Yale University Press, 1939), 144, 168–69, 195; Matson, *Merchants & Empire*, 124–25; Albert B. Southwick, "The Molasses Act—Source of Precedents," *WMQ* 8, no. 3 (1951): 390.

56. "Reasons Against Prohibiting Trade & Commerce with Spain the West Indies," n.d [March 18, 1702 or 1703]; Board of Trade to Earl of Nottingham, January 28, 1703, Colonial Office, Class 5, Reel 1, Vol. 1–4, LOC. See also Matson, *Merchants & Empire*, 124–25.

57. "Objections may be made," the board warned the Earl of Nottingham, "that requiring and Exacting such Bonds is not warranted by Law." North American colonists would also likely object that the bond policy "is a Burden upon Trade." Board of Trade to Earl of Nottingham, January 28, 1703, Colonial Office, Class 5, Reel 1, Vol. 1–4, LOC. See also Matson, *Merchants & Empire*, 124–25.

58. Board of Trade to Queen, January 10, 1705, Colonial Office, Class 5, Reel 1, Vol. 1–4, LOC; "An Act for the Better Regulation of Charter Proprietary Governments in America, and for the Encouragement of the Trade of this Kingdome and of Her Majesty's Plantations," Colonial Office, Class 5, Reel 1, Vol. 1–4, LOC.

59. Steele, *Board of Trade*, 157–58; Klooster, "Inter-Imperial Smuggling in the Americas," 165.

60. Caleb Heathcote to Board of Trade, January 28, 1715; September 7, 1719, reprinted in Dixon Ryan Fox, *Caleb Heathcote: Gentleman Colonist* (New York: Charles Scribner's Sons, 1926), 181, 184, 187–88. Formal, legally constituted institutions, even courts of law, "possessed extremely modest abilities to compel obedience," observes William M. Offut Jr., "The Limits of Authority: Courts, Ethnicity, and Gender in the Middle Colonies, 1670–1710," in Tomlins and Mann, *Many Legalities of Early America*, 357.

61. Edward Northey, Untitled, June 3, 1715, Opinions of Counsel in Customs Cases, 1708–1717, #8832, British Museum, Additional Manuscripts, Transcript, LOC (hereafter cited as British Museum Transcript); Northey, "Plantation Officers May Sue Their Offenders," April 10, 1718, Opinions of Counsel in Customs Cases, 1717–1724, #8833, ibid.

62. Northey, "Plantation Officers May Sue Their Offenders."

63. Thomas Pengelly, "Deputy Secretarys Fees in the Courts of Maryland...," February 28, 1722, Opinions of Counsel in Customs Cases, 1717–1724, #8833, British Museum Transcript, LOC. See also 1714–1722, Maurice Birchfield's Account of Fees, Early State Records Online, Maryland State Archives, (www.msa.md.gov/megafile/msa/speccol/sc4800/sc4872/003175/html/); R. J. Rockefeller, *Their Magistrates and Officials: Executive Government in Colonial Maryland, 1715–1775* (New York: Rowman and Littlefield, 2010), 175–76.

64. The Molasses Act of 1733, quoted in Southwick, "The Molasses Act," 394. On the interest-group politics behind the Molasses Act, see Richard B. Sheridan, "The Molasses Act and the Market Strategy of the British Sugar Planters," *Journal of Economic History* 17, no. 1 (1957): 62–72; Dickerson, *Navigation Acts and the American Revolution*, 82–87.

65. Barrow, *Trade and Empire*, 136; Clark, *Rise of the British Treasury*, 62.

66. Peter Randolph to William Peters, Collector of the Port of Philadelphia, July 20, 1750, Vol. 1; John Swift to Henry Hulton, March 21, 1770, Vol. 10, Philadelphia Customs Records; Alfred Simpson Martin, *The Port of Philadelphia, 1763–1776: A Biography* (Spokane: printed by author, 2001), 110–11. "Hhd" was the abbreviation for "hogshead."

67. Serena R. Zabin, *Dangerous Economies: Status and Commerce in Imperial New York* (Philadelphia: University of Pennsylvania Press, 2011); George Arthur Wood, *William Shirley, Governor of Massachusetts, 1741–1756: A History* (New York: Columbia University Press, 1920), 1:392; Cadwallader Colden to Lords of Trade[?], n.d. [ca. 1740], in *Letters and Papers of Cadwallader Colden*, 4:224–25.

68. The British Empire took a more stringent position against piracy, according to Nikolas Fryman, "Pirates and Smugglers: Political Economy in the Red Atlantic," in *Mercantilism Reimagined: Political Economy in Early Modern Britain and Its Empire*, ed. Philip J. Stern and Carl Wennerlind (New York: Oxford University Press, 2014), 218–39.

69. Henretta, "Salutary Neglect," 92; Hulsebosch, *Constituting Empire*, 82–87.

70. Lauren Benton, *Law and Colonial Cultures: Legal Regimes in World History, 1400–1900* (New York: Cambridge University Press, 2002), 2.

71. Games, *Web of Empire*, 165; Hulsebosch, *Constituting Empire*, 121. See also Arthur M. Schlesinger, *Colonial Merchants and the American Revolution, 1763–1776* (New York: F. Ungar, 1957), 44; Heather Mary Alice Welland,"Interest Politics and the Shaping of the British Empire, ca. 1720–1791" (PhD diss., University of Chicago, 2011), 40.

72. The problem of empire occupied British politics more broadly, too, according to Jack P. Greene, *Evaluating Empire and Confronting Colonialism in Eighteenth-Century Britain* (New York: Cambridge University Press, 2013).

73. Matson, *Merchants & Empire*, 270–71: Doerflinger, *Vigorous Spirit of Enterprise*; Brooke Hunter, "Wheat, War, and the American Economy during the Age of Revolution," *WMQ* 62, no. 3 (2005): 505–25; Michael Duffy, *Soldiers, Sugar, and Seapower: The British Expeditions to the West Indies and the War against Revolutionary France* (Oxford: Clarendon Press, 1987).

74. See, for instance, James Clifford to Jonathan and Thomas Tipping, December 24, 1759; Clifford to Jonas Maynard, December 26, 1759; Clifford to Isaac Cox, December 9, 1760; Vol. 27, Clifford Correspondence, MSS484A, Pemberton Family Papers, HSP; Pares, *War and Trade in the West Indies*, 403–18.

75. Pitt, Circular to Governors, August 23, 1760, 5:330; Thomas Clifford to Jacob Gould et al., February 8, 1760, Vol. 27, Pemberton Family Papers.

76. Pitt, Circular to Governors, August 23, 1760, 5:330.

77. Commissioners of Customs to John Temple, November 3, 1763, Vol. 2, Philadelphia Customs Records (emphasis added).

78. Alexander Colden to Cadwallader Colden, May 8, 1756; July 12, 1757, in *Letters and Papers of Cadwallader Colden*, 5:73, 157; Meeting of Charleston Merchants with Daniel Moore, May 26, 27, 1767, in *The Papers of Henry Laurens*, ed. George C. Rogers Jr. (Charleston: South Carolina Historical Society, 1976), 4:260 (editor's note).

79. These bonds are scattered in the pages of the Philadelphia Customs Records, Vols. 1 and 2, HSP.

80. "Note of Recognizances Taken by Mr. Justice Horsmanden of Persons Accused of Illegal Correspondence with His Majesty's Enemies and Filed July Term 1762," Box 1, Folder 2, Kempe Papers; Hulsebosch, *Constituting Empire*, 120–21. For prosecutions, see *Alexander Colden qui tam v. Brigantine Elizabeth*, n.d., 1761, Box 9, Folder 8; and *Alexander Colden qui tam v. 24 Hogsheads . . . Sugar*, April 1762, Kempe Papers, NYHS. The difficulties faced by imperial customs officials in North Carolina are detailed in Don Higginbotham, introduction to *The Papers of James Iredell* (Raleigh, NC: Division of Archives and History, Department of Cultural Resources, 1976), lv; Carl V. Ubbelohde, *The Vice-Admiralty Courts and the American Revolution* (Chapel Hill: University of North Carolina Press, 1960), 33.

81. John Swift to Unknown [mutil.], December 1762; John Swift to Charles Pettit, January 11, 1763, Philadelphia Customs Records, Vol. 2, HSP; Thomas Clifford to John Rockett, September 11, 1760, Vol. 27, Clifford Correspondence, MSS 484A, Pemberton Family Papers, HSP.

82. Matson, *Merchants & Empire*, 272; Swift to John Hatton, September 19, 1763, Philadelphia Customs Records, Vol. 2, HSP. In August 1759, the Board of Trade issued a report outlining the problems with the colonial customs establishment. Truxes, *Defying Empire*, 175.

83. Neil R. Stout, *The Royal Navy in America, 1760–1765: A Study of Enforcement of British Colonial Policy in the Era of the American Revolution* (Annapolis: Naval Institute Press, 1973), 9, 41–50; John Tabor Kempe and William Smith Jr., November 7, 1763, "Opinion of the Attorney and Solicitor-General, Kemp and Smith, at New York, on the distribution of forfeitures, under the acts of trade," in *Opinions of Eminent Lawyers on Various Points of English Jurisprudence . . .* , ed. George Chalmers (Burlington, VT: C. Goodrich and Company, 1858), 578; Ubbelohde, *Vice-Admiralty Courts*, 39, 41; Christopher P. Magra, *The Fishermen's Cause: Atlantic Commerce and Maritime Dimensions of the American Revolution* (New York: Cambridge University Press, 2009), 99–126.

84. Henry Laurens to Clay & Habersham, October 26, 1767, in Rogers, *Papers of Henry Laurens*, 4:377.

85. Alexander Colden to Cadwallader Colden, July 12, 1757, 157 (emphasis in original); John Tabor Kempe to Cadwallader Colden, September 29, 1760, Box 15, Folder 1, Letters Sent, Kempe Papers, NYHS.

86. George Spencer to John Tabor Kempe, October 27, 1760, Box 14, Folder 6, Kempe

Papers, NYHS; Ubbelohde, *Vice-Admiralty Courts*, 34; Hulsebosch, *Constituting Empire*, 121.

87. George Spencer to Charles Stewart, August 3, 1765, Philadelphia Customs Records, Vol. 3, HSP; Truxes, *Defying Empire*, 12; Spencer to Commissioners of Customs, March 27, 1765, Philadelphia Customs Records, Vol. 3, HSP.

88. Truxes, *Defying Empire*, 12, 15, 186; Spencer to Commissioners of Customs, March 27, 1765.

89. Commissioners of Customs to Charles Stewart, August 9, 1765, Philadelphia Customs Records, Vol. 3, HSP.

90. Allen S. Johnson, *A Prologue to Revolution: The Political Career of George Grenville (1712-1770)* (Lanham, MD: University Press of America, 1997), 165; see also Stout, *Royal Navy in America*, 25–33; Smith, *Wealth of Nations*, 2:411. Henry McCulloh estimated annual customs revenue as follows: New York, £600; Connecticut, £100–£250; Maryland, £100–£300; southern Virginia, £450–£550; northern Virginia, £200–£400; North Carolina, £660; Charleston, £600. Georgia, Port Royal, Whyniah, New Hampshire, Nova Scotia, and Rhode Island produced negligible revenue. Henry McCulloh, "Remarks with respect to the Collectors of the Customs in North America," n.d. [December 12, 1763], in *Jenkinson Papers, 1760-1766*, ed. Ninetta S. Jucker (London: Macmillan & Co., 1949), 1:229–30.

91. Commissioners of the Customs to the Treasury, July 21, 1763, quoted in Thomas Barrow, "Background to the Grenville Program, 1757-1763," *WMQ* 22, no. 1 (1965): 94.

92. Fred Anderson, *Crucible of War: The Seven Years' War and the Fate of Empire in British North America, 1754-1766* (New York: A.A. Knopf, 2000), 574. On the specific "provisions immediately related to the customs service," see Barrow, *Trade and Empire*, 182–84.

93. Barrow, *Trade and Empire*, 177. "Hovering" was a common tactic off the English coast as well, according to Henry Atton and Henry Hurst Holland, *The King's Customs* (New York: A.M. Kelley, 1967), 198; Ubbelohde, *Vice-Admiralty Courts*, 44–57; Andrews, *Colonial Period of American History*, 222–71.

94. Thomas Whately, *The Regulations Lately Made Concerning the Colonies, and the Taxes Imposed Upon Them, considered* (London: J. Wilkie, 1765), 44, 56, 58, 79, 88, 100; Morgan and Morgan, *Stamp Act Crisis*, 23 n. 6. For the staggering rise of the public debt, see B. R. Mitchell with Phyllis Deane, *Abstract of British Historical Statistics* (New York: Cambridge University Press, 1962), 402.

95. Hulton, "Account," 40, 42; Barrow, *Trade and Empire*, 171–74. On imperial officials' sense of the pressures from both above and below, see Hulsebosch, *Constituting Empire*, 71–144; and Hart, *Almost a Hero*, 13–17.

96. Breen, *Marketplace of the Revolution*, 217.

97. Benjamin Franklin to John Hughes, August 9, 1765, John Hughes Papers, MS 302, HSP; Thomas Clifford to Harper & Hartshorne, October 28, 1765, Vol. 27, Clifford Correspondence, MSS 484A, Pemberton Family Papers, HSP.

98. William Gage to W. Conway, September 23, 1765, Bancroft Transcript, Stamp Act Collection, LOC; John Hatton to Charles Stewart, November 15, 1765, Vol. 4, Philadelphia Customs Records; Barrow, *Trade and Empire*, 245–46.

99. *Newport Mercury*, October 21, 1765, excerpted in Morgan and Morgan, *Stamp Act Crisis*, 157 (emphasis added).

100. Morgan and Morgan, *Stamp Act Crisis*, 143; Stout, *Royal Navy in America*, 92.

101. Richard Penn to Thomas Penn, February 12, 1766, Vol. 10, Official Correspondence, #485A, Penn Manuscripts, HSP; John Swift to Benjamin Chew, November 2, 1765; Andrew Eliot and Lambert Moore to Charles Stewart, October 20, 1765, and November 27, 1765; Vol. 4, Philadelphia Customs Records, HSP. See also Hart, *Almost a Hero*, 50.

102. Hulton, "Account," 21, 24-25.

103. Hulton, "Account," 26; Dora Mae Clark, "The American Board of Customs, 1767-1783," *AHR* 45, no. 4 (1940): 780; James Tilghman to Thomas Penn, October 29, 1774, Vol. 11, Official Correspondence, #485A, Penn Manuscripts, HSP; Hart, *Almost a Hero*, 40-61. There is more evidence of a movement to Anglicize the colonial customs service, such as a requirement that new customs officials attend training at the London custom house before departing for the New World; and a positive restriction on colonial assemblies' powers to tamper with customs officials' pay. Barrow, *Trade and Empire*, 187, 189.

104. Memorial of the Commissioners of Customs in America, February 12, 1768, reprinted in Thomas Bradshaw to W. Phelps, May 7, 1768, Bancroft Transcript; Barrow, *Trade and Empire*, 230-31; Alfred S. Martin, "The King's Customs: Philadelphia, 1763-1774," *WMQ* 5, no. 2 (1948): 206-11.

105. Swift to Board of Customs, February 5, 1771, Vol. 11, Philadelphia Customs Records.

106. Morgan and Morgan, *Stamp Act Crisis*, 312; Hulton, "Account," 168-70; Stout, *Royal Navy in America*, 114-20; Barrow, *Trade and Empire*, 227-28.

107. Philadelphia Custom House Cashbook, 1762-1772, Vol. 2; Swift to Board of Customs, March 27, 1770, Vol. 10, Philadelphia Customs Records; John Tabor Kempe to Cadwallader Colden, September 18, 1766, Box 15, Folder 1, Letters Sent, Kempe Papers, NYHS.

108. Thomas Moshett to John Swift, January 28, 1772, Vol. 12; Swift to Board of Customs, October 13, 1769, Vol. 10, Philadelphia Customs Records; Diary of James Allen, May 25, 1772, HSP.

109. Hulsebosch, *Constituting Empire*, 84.

110. Board of Customs to Swift, October 7, 1771, Vol. 11, Philadelphia Customs Records; Reid, *Constitutional History of the American Revolution*, 197-98; Swift to Board of Customs, May 5, 1769, Vol. 10, Philadelphia Customs Records; Swift to Board of Customs, November 30, 1771, Vol. 12, Philadelphia Customs Records; Barrow, *Trade and Empire*, 203; Dickerson, *Navigation Acts and the American Revolution*, 250-51. Notably, Solicitor General William de Grey confirmed the dubious constitutional grounds of issuing writs of assistance in the colonies; William de Grey, Opinion of October 17, 1766, Law Officers' Opinions, 1763-1783, Treasury 64, Vol. 188, Public Record Office, Transcript, LOC.

111. Martin, "King's Customs," 216; Stout, *Royal Navy in America*, 143.

112. Swift to Board of Customs, August 23, 1769, Vol. 10; Swift to Board of Customs, December 20, 1770, Vol. 11, Philadelphia Customs Records. See also Richard

Beale and John Nicoll to Commissioners of the Customs, April 22, 1768, Boston Office Letters, 1765-1775, Papers of the American Slave Trade, Part 1, Reel 12.

113. Ruma Chopra, *Unnatural Rebellion: Loyalists in New York during the Revolution* (Charlottesville: University of Virginia Press, 2011), 35. Colonial takeovers of imperial custom houses are described in Colden to Lord Dartmouth, May 3, 1775, in *The Colden Letter Books* (New York: New-York Historical Society, 1877-78), 10:402. Thomas Clifford to Thomas Frank, June 23, 1774, Vol. 29, Clifford Correspondence, MSS 484A, Pemberton Family Papers, HSP.

114. Reid, *Constitutional History of the American Revolution*, 33-52; Morgan and Morgan, *Stamp Act Crisis*, 41-90; Greene, *Constitutional Origins of the American Revolution*.

115. Breen, *Marketplace of Revolution*, 24, 291. See also Joseph S. Tiedemann, *Reluctant Revolutionaries: New York City and the Road to Independence, 1763-1776* (Ithaca, NY: Cornell University Press, 1997), 185-97; Dierks, *In My Power*, 137.

116. Thomas Clifford to Lancelot Cowpur, February 28, 1769, Vol. 28, Clifford Correspondence, MSS 484A, Pemberton Family Papers, HSP.

117. Breen, *Marketplace of the Revolution*, 236; Charles M. Andrews, *The Boston Merchants and the Non-Importation Movement* (New York: John Wilson and Son, 1917), 161, 166, 201; Schlesinger, *Colonial Merchants and the American Revolution*, 475-503.

118. Breen, *Marketplace of the Revolution*, 257, 262; Handbill to the Pilots of Delaware, October 13, 1773, Philadelphia Tea Shipment Papers, 1769-1773, #1027, HSP.

119. Breen, *Marketplace of the Revolution*, 227, 234. James and Drinker to Benjamin Booth, October 8, 1774, James and Drinker Letterbooks, 1756-1786, Henry Drinker Business Papers, Mss 176, HSP.

BERMUDA HUNDRED, 1795

1. For Heth's involvement with the Cincinnati, see William Heth to Henry Knox, November 17, 1784, Reel 2, Society of the Cincinnati Papers, LOC. Heth's military background is described in Harry M. Ward, *For Virginia and for Independence: Twenty-Eight Revolutionary War Soldiers from the Old Dominion* (Jefferson, NC: McFarland & Company, 2011), 58-60.

2. Edmund Randolph to George Washington, February 12, 1789, George Washington Papers, Series 7, LOC. On the gentry's sense of obligation to serve in public office, see Robert H. Tillson Jr., *Accommodating Revolutions: Virginia's Northern Neck in an Era of Transformations, 1760-1810* (Charlottesville: University of Virginia Press, 2010), 274-75.

3. William Heth to Oliver Wolcott Jr., June 10, 1795; December 10, 1795, Reel 2, Oliver Wolcott Jr. Papers, The Connecticut Historical Society, Hartford, Connecticut (hereafter cited as Wolcott Papers).

4. William Heth to Oliver Wolcott Jr., June 10, 1795; December 10, 1795, Reel 2, Wolcott Papers.

5. Abstract of Payments made to Inspectors, Gaugers, Weighers, Measurers and Other Contin[illeg.], October 1-December 31, 1792, United States, Bureau of Customs, Accounts, 1791-1793 [Bermuda Hundred and City Point, Virginia], Mss 4 UN 3763d, Vir-

ginia Historical Society, Richmond, VA (hereafter cited as Bermuda Hundred Customs Accounts). In only one instance did Heth officially reprimand a subordinate for claiming a day's work where none seemed to have occurred. The disallowed payment is dated October 19, under the account of Charles Eppes Fees, December 31, 1792.

6. Osborne's New Hampshire *Spy*, May 8, 1790, 15.

7. Wolcott to Heth, November 24, 1797, Reel 2, Wolcott Papers.

CHAPTER 2

1. American historians have spent a great deal of time illustrating the many and often competing strands of republicanism in late eighteenth-century America. For a summary of this literature, Daniel T. Rodgers, "Republicanism: The Career of a Concept," *JAH* 79, no. 1 (1992): 11–38; James T. Kloppenberg, "The Virtues of Liberalism: Christianity, Republicanism, and Ethics in Early American Political Discourse," *JAH* 74, no. 1 (1987): 9–33; Robert E. Shalhope, "Republicanism and Early American Historiography," *WMQ* 39, no. 2 (1982): 334–56. Key works in this tradition are Bernard Bailyn, *Ideological Origins of the American Revolution* (1992; Cambridge, MA: Harvard University Press, 1967); Gordon S. Wood, *Creation of the American Republic, 1776–1787* (Chapel Hill: University of North Carolina Press, 1969); Wood, *The Radicalism of the American Revolution* (New York: Vintage Books, 1991); Maier, *From Resistance to Revolution*; Henry F. May, *The Enlightenment in America* (New York: Oxford University Press, 1976).

2. Edling, (*Hercules in the Cradle*, 20) sagely describes this achievement as an organizational revolution in terms of the ordering of political authority and political economy in the United States. See also Richard B. Morris, foreword to Merrill Jensen, *The New Nation: A History of the United States during the Confederation, 1781–1789* (1950; Boston: Northeastern University Press, 1981), vii; Jensen, ibid., 44–53; Richard Vernier, "The Fortunes of Orthodoxy: The Political Economy of Public Debt in England and America during the 1780s," in *Articulating America: Fashioning a National Political Culture in Early America*, ed. Rebecca Starr (New York: Madison House, 2000), 93–131. For the underlying historiographic controversies that informed these naming conventions, see Richard B. Morris, "The Confederation Period and the American Historian," *WMQ*, 3rd ser., vol. 13, no. 2 (Apr. 1956), 139–56.

3. Bailyn, *Ideological Origins*, vii.

4. United States Congress, *The Public Statutes at Large of the United States of America, from the Organization of the Government in 1789, to March 3, 1845*, ed. Richard Peters (Boston: Little and Brown, 1845), 1:24 (hereafter cited in the following form: 1 *Statutes at Large* 24 [1789]).

5. George Washington to Samuel Vaughan, March 21, 1789, in *The Papers of George Washington, Presidential Series*, ed. Dorothy Twohig (Charlottesville: University Press of Virginia, 1987), 1:429–30.

6. Thaddeus Burr to Jeremiah Wadsworth, June 5, 1778, Folder 1, Wadsworth-Putney Family Papers, LOC; Richard Peters, Board of War, to George Washington, May 10, 1779, in *The Papers of George Washington*, ed. Theodore Crackel (Charlottesville: University Press of Virginia, 2010), 20:409–11.

7. E. Wayne Carp, *To Starve the Army at Pleasure: Continental Army Administration and American Political Culture, 1775–1783* (Chapel Hill: University of North Carolina Press, 1984), 181. See also Nathanael Greene to George Washington, April 1, 1779, in Crackel, *Papers of George Washington*, 20:149.

8. Lieutenant Colonel John Brooks to Alexander Hamilton, July 4, 1779, *PAH*, 2:91; William Gordon to Alexander Hamilton, August 25, 1779, *PAH*, 2:142.

9. Joanne B. Freeman, *Affairs of Honor: National Politics in the New Republic* (New Haven, CT: Nota Bene, 2001), 69. Hamilton fumed at the possibility that Washington's reputation would suffer as a consequence of the Gordon affair. See Hamilton to Gordon, September 5, 1779, *PAH*, 2:153–56.

10. Jerrilyn Marston, *King and Congress: The Transfer of Political Legitimacy, 1774–1776* (Princeton, NJ: Princeton University Press, 1987), 67. In fact, the United States' experiment with central governmental institutions began in 1776 with the Declaration of Independence. The Declaration began with discussions of individual equality but ended with a forthright assessment of the state. The United States, "as Free and Independent States, they have full Power to levy War, conclude Peace, contract Alliances, establish Commerce, and to do all the other Acts and Things which Independent States may of right do." The United States would exercise its own "powers of states" so as to become a member of "an international community of independent sovereign states," as David Armitage has explained. Armitage, *Declaration of Independence*, 30; Pauline Maier, *American Scripture: Making the Declaration of Independence* (New York: Vintage, 1998), 142.

11. Roger H. Brown, *Redeeming the Republic: Federalists, Taxation, and the Origin of the Constitution* (Baltimore: Johns Hopkins University Press, 1993), 19; E. James Ferguson, *The Power of the Purse: A History of American Public Finance, 1776–1790* (Chapel Hill: University of North Carolina Press, 1961), xv; Ben Baack, "Forging a Nation State: The Continental Congress and the Financing of the War of American Independence," *Economic History Review* 54, no. 4 (Nov. 2001): 639–56.

12. Thomas Paine, *A Letter Addressed to the Abbe Raynal, On the Affairs of North-America. In Which the Mistakes in the Abbe's Account of the Revolution of America Are Corrected and Cleared Up* (Philadelphia, C. Dilly, 1782), 25; Ferguson, *Power of the Purse*, 26, 32, 46; Michael Hillegas to James & Robert Purviance, November 10, 1778, Michael Hillegas Letterbook, Mss 287, HSP; Charles C. Calomiris, "Institutional Failure, Monetary Scarcity, and the Depreciation of the Continental," *Journal of Economic History* 48, no. 1 (Mar. 1988): 56. See also Benjamin H. Irvin, *Clothed in the Robes of Sovereignty: The Continental Congress and the People Out of Doors* (New York: Oxford University Press, 2011), 79, and more broadly, 75–96.

13. William Short to Alexander Hamilton, December 18, 1790, William Harris Crawford Papers, Duke University Library; James C. Riley, "Foreign Credit and Fiscal Stability: Dutch Investment in the United States, 1781–1794," *JAH* 65, no. 3 (1978): 658; Brown, *Redeeming the Republic*, 19.

14. Alexander Hamilton to Unknown, n.d. [December 1779–March, 1780], *PAH*, 2:240, 237–38 n. A, 238–39. Political economist Pelatiah Webster also contemplated reform along similar lines. Edling, *Hercules in the Cradle*, 27–31.

15. Hamilton to Unknown, 240, 237–38 n. A, 238–39.

16. Hamilton to Unknown, 245, 247, 244. On the significance of the Bank of England, see P. G. M. Dickson, *The Financial Revolution in England: A Study in the Development of Public Credit, 1688–1756* (New York: St. Martin's Press, 1967).

17. Hamish Scott, "The Fiscal-Military State and International Rivalry during the Long Eighteenth Century," in Storrs, *Fiscal-Military State in Eighteenth-Century Europe*, 24, 29; Gary W. Cox, "War, Moral Hazard, and Ministerial Responsibility: England after the Glorious Revolution," *Journal of Economic History* 71, no. 1 (2011): 133–61.

18. Hamilton to Unknown, 142, 145.

19. Hamilton to Duane, September 3, 1780, 401, 402; Lawrence S. Kaplan, *Alexander Hamilton: Ambivalent Anglophile* (New York: Rowman & Littlefield, 2002), 41–43.

20. Hamilton to Duane, September 3, 1780, 402, 404.

21. Hamilton to Duane, September 3, 1780, 404, 405.

22. Alexander Hamilton to Robert Morris, April 30, 1781, *PAH*, 2:604–35; Hamilton, *Continentalist* IV, August 30, 1781, *PAH*, 2:669–71; and for the other entries of July 12, 19, and August 9, 1781, *PAH*, 2:649–53, 654–57, 660–65.

23. Christopher Storrs, "Introduction: The Fiscal-Military State in the 'Long' Eighteenth-Century," in Storrs, *Fiscal-Military State in Eighteenth-Century Europe*, 4; Pelatiah Webster, "A Dissertation on the Nature, Authority, and Uses of the Office of a Financier-General, or Superintendant of the Finances," January 24, 1781, in *Political Essays on the Nature and Operation of Money, Public Finances and Other Subjects* (1791; New York: Burt Franklin, 1969), 168, 170. See also Henry Barrett Learned, "Origin of the Title Superintendent of Finance," *AHR* 10, no. 3 (1905): 565–73.

24. Jan Glete, *War and the State in Early Modern Europe: Spain, the Dutch Republic, and Sweden as Fiscal-Military States, 1500–1660* (New York: Routledge, 2002), 23; Robert D. Harris, *Necker: Reform Statesman of the Ancien Regime* (Berkeley: University of California Press, 1979); J. F. Bosher, *French Finances 1770–1795: From Business to Bureaucracy* (New York: Cambridge University Press, 1970).

25. Robert Morris to Samuel Huntington, May 14, 1781, in *The Papers of Robert Morris, 1781–1784*, ed. E. James Ferguson et al. (Pittsburgh, PA: University of Pittsburgh Press, 1973–99), 1:63–64 (hereafter cited as *PRM*).

26. On the growth of customs collection in early modern Europe, see Richard Bonney, ed., *The Rise of the Fiscal State in Europe, c. 1200–1815* (New York: Oxford University Press, 1999); Patrick K. O'Brien and Peter F. Mathias, "Taxation in Britain and France, 1715–1810: A Comparison of the Social and Economic Incidence of Taxes Collected for the Central Governments," *Journal of European Economic History* 5, no. 3 (1976): 601–50; Glete, *War and the State in Early Modern Europe*, 11–15.

27. South Carolina, for instance, targeted imported alcohol with a significant duty. Massachusetts annually renewed its impost between 1692 and 1774. New York, too, relied heavily on import duties from 1734 until the outbreak of the War of Independence. Because the impost was so familiar a mode of taxation in the colonies, the Continental Congress began to contemplate a national impost beginning in 1778. Brown, *Redeeming the Republic*, 23; William Hill, "Colonial Tariffs," *Quarterly Journal of Economics* 7, no. 1 (Oct. 1892): 94, 95, 97; Einhorn, *American Taxation, American Slavery*, 133.

28. Einhorn, *American Taxation, American Slavery*, 133. There were two other significant benefits. Historian Robin Einhorn rightly argues that only the impost made it

possible to discuss taxation "without talking about slavery," since "slavery was a huge institution in the American political economy." There would be no discussions about what might count as taxable property; who constituted a taxable person; what institutions might receive higher or lower tax rates (Einhorn, 120).

29. *Journals of the Continental Congress*, November 8 1780, 18:1033; Morris to Pierre Landais, January 16, 1782, *PRM*, 4:54; Morris to Samuel Holden Parsons, February 1, 1782, *PRM*, 4:146–47; Thomas Paine to Morris, November 20, 1782, *PRM*, 7:86–88; Brown, *Redeeming the Republic*, 22–31; H. James Henderson, *Party Politics in the Continental Congress* (New York: McGraw-Hill Company, 197), 268–80, 319–20, 390.

30. Brown, *Redeeming the Republic*, 23–24; Einhorn, *American Taxation, American Slavery*, 119.

31. Tone Sundt Urstad, *Sir Robert Walpole's Poets: The Use of Literature as Pro-Government Propaganda, 1721–1742* (Newark, DE: University of Delaware Press, 1999), 109; Jacob Soll, *The Information Master: Jean-Baptiste Colbert's Secret State Intelligence System* (Ann Arbor: University of Michigan Press, 2009), 127.

32. Bailyn, *Ideological Origins*, 4–5. Robert Morris, Diary, September 18, 1781, *PRM*, 2:290; RM, Memorandum on Thomas Paine, February [n.d.], 1782, *PRM*, 4:327–28; Henry Laurens to Thomas Bee, December 11, 1781, Papers of Thomas Bee, LOC. See Craig Nelson, *Thomas Paine: Enlightenment, Revolution, and the Birth of Modern Nations* (New York: Penguin, 2007), 146–80; Eric Foner, *Tom Paine and Revolutionary America* (New York: Oxford University Press, 1976), xix, 192.

33. Frank Greene Bates, "Rhode Island and the Impost of 1781," in *Annual Report of the American Historical Association for the Year 1894* (Washington, DC: Government Printing Office, 1895), 353; Drew R. McCoy, "The Virginia Port Bill of 1784," *Virginia Magazine of History and Biography* 83, no. 3 (1975): 292, and generally, 288–303; J. Kent McGaughy, *Richard Henry Lee: A Portrait of an American Revolutionary* (New York: Rowman & Littlefield, 2004), 167; Samuel Osgood to John Lowell, January 6, 1783, Samuel Osgood Papers, LOC. On New York's impost, see Cathy Matson, "Liberty, Jealousy, and Union: The New York Economy in the 1780s," in *New York in the Age of the Constitution, 1775–1800*, ed. Paul Gilje and William Pencak (Rutherford, NJ: Fairleigh-Dickinson Press, 1992), 118.

34. October 30, 1781, in United States Continental Congress, *Journals of the Continental Congress, 1774–1789* (Washington, DC: Government Printing Office, 1904–37), 21:1087–88; Keith L. Dougherty, *Collective Action under the Articles of Confederation* (New York: Cambridge University Press, 2001), 1, 6; Brown, *Redeeming the Republic*, 11–17; Ferguson, *Power of the Purse*, 32–47; Donald R. Stabile, *The Origins of American Public Finance: Debates over Money, Debt, and Taxes in the Constitutional Era, 1776–1836* (Westport, CT: Greenwood Press, 1998), 23–33, 41–59, 71–81.

35. Brown, *Redeeming the Republic*, 14; Dougherty, *Collective Action*, 66; Woody S. Holton, *Unruly Americans and the Origins of the Constitution* (New York: Hill and Wang, 2007), 65 and generally, 65–82.

36. Hamilton to Morris, June 17, 1782; Hamilton to Comfort Sands, June 12, 1782, Reel 1, Papers of Alexander Hamilton, LOC; Hamilton to Morris, July 22, 1782, *PRM*, 6:7–9; Alexander Hamilton to RM, August 31, 1782, *PRM*, 6:290.

37. Hamilton to Morris, August 13, 1782; Morris to Hamilton, August 28, 1782; *PAH*, 3:136, 154.

38. Continental Congress, Remarks on the Redemption of Continental Currency, November 26, 1782, *PAH*, 3:199–200. See also related motions between 1782 and 1783, *PAH*, 3:202, 206–7, 213–23; 3:229, 245–47, 248, 265, 285.

39. Hamilton to George Washington, April 8, 1783, *PAH*, 3:318. Continental Congress, Unsubmitted Resolution Calling for a Convention to Amend the Articles of Confederation, n.d. [July 1783], *PAH*, 3:420–26, esp. 423; Henderson, *Party Politics*, 318–49, 320, 357.

40. Forrest McDonald, *Alexander Hamilton: A Biography* (New York: Norton, 1982), 93–94; Allan Nevins, *The American States during and after the Revolution* (New York: A.M. Kelley, 1969), 290.

41. Jack N. Rakove, *Original Meanings: Politics and Ideas in the Making of the Constitution* (New York: A.A. Knopf, 1996), 60.

42. Max Farrand, ed., *The Records of the Federal Convention of 1787* (New Haven, CT: Yale University Press, 1911), 1:284, 285 (hereafter cited as *Farrand's Records*). Though there was no federal law at the time, states used the Confederation as an "umpire" to mediate disputes. "Federal" prize courts also operated in these years, although their decrees were rarely honored. See Peter S. Onuf, *The Origins of the Federal Republic: Jurisdictional Controversies in the United States, 1775–1787* (Philadelphia: University of Pennsylvania Press, 1983); Henry J. Bourguignon, *The First Federal Court: The Federal Appellate Prize Court of the American Revolution, 1775–1787* (Philadelphia: American Philosophical Society, 1977). Leonard L. Richards, *Shays's Rebellion: The American Revolution's Final Battle* (Philadelphia: University of Pennsylvania Press, 2003).

43. *Farrand's Records*, 1:305.

44. The problem of "double setts of officers" also translated to the classical republican fear of "imperium in imperio." See Hartog, *Public Property and Private Power*; Hulsebosch, *Constituting Empire*, 71–144; Rakove, *Original Meanings*, 194.

45. Distance stretched the bonds that held society together and thereby threatened the "good order" that was "the soul of republicanism." On the problem of distance, see Jane Kamensky, *The Exchange Artist: A Tale of High-Flying Speculation and America's First Banking Collapse* (New York: Viking, 2008), 52.

46. Hamilton, "Number VI," 108.

47. Hamilton, "Number XXX," *Federalist*, 212, 216; Brewer, *Sinews of Power*, 118. See Max M. Edling and Mark D. Kaplanoff, "Alexander Hamilton's Fiscal Reform: Transforming the Structure of Taxation in the Early Republic," *WMQ* 61, no. 4 (2004): 713–44.

48. Hamilton, "Number XXXVI" and "Number XII," *Federalist*, 237, 138; Einhorn, *American Taxation, American Slavery*, 111–99.

49. Hamilton, "Number XXI," *Federalist*, 176; Hamilton, "Number XXV," *Federalist*, 231. Adam Smith makes the same point in the *Wealth of Nations*: "An injudicious tax offers a great temptation to smuggling." Smith, *Wealth of Nations*, 4:351.

50. Hamilton, "Number XII," 136. Hamilton's history was extremely selective. In

fact, high excise taxes were a main source of political discontent in eighteenth-century England. See Ashworth, *Customs and Excise*, 66–93.

51. Hamilton, "Number XVII," *Federalist*, 158. See Balogh, *Government Out of Sight*; Gautham Rao, "Out of Sight, but on the Horizon: The Secret Life of the American Nation-State," *Common-Place* 10, no. 1.5 (2009), www.common-place.org/interim/reviews/rao.shtml; Edling, *Hercules in the Cradle*, 68.

52. Einhorn, *American Taxation, American Slavery*, 149; Edling, *Hercules in the Cradle*, 49; Charlene Bangs Bickford and Kenneth R. Bowling, eds., *The First Federal Congress, 1789–1791* (Lanham, MD: Madison House, 1989), 29; 1 *Annals* 107 (April 9, 1789).

53. 1 *Annals* 108–9 (April 9, 1789).

54. Edling, *Hercules in the Cradle*, 70–74. Several state delegations demanded protection for their major industries, while South Carolinians threatened that already-disaffected upcountry farmers would take to arms if the impost did not "operate equally" on the states. There were other, equally divisive issues as well, such as the question of commercial discrimination, and the desirability of a "drawback" system of subsidies for reexporting goods to Europe. Thomas Tudor Tucker, 1 *Annals* 113 (April 9, 1789); William L. Smith, 1 *Annals* 167 (April 16, 1789). The best summary of this debate is Jacob E. Cooke, *Tench Coxe and the Early Republic* (Chapel Hill: University of North Carolina Press, 1978), 134–38.

55. James Madison, Elias Boudinot, 1 *Annals* 132 (April 14, 1789); Jeremiah Wadsworth, 1 *Annals* 203 (April 24, 1789).

56. M. E. Kelley, "Tariff Acts under the Confederation," *Quarterly Journal of Economics* 2, no. 4 (July 1888): 473; William Frank Zornow, "Tariff Policies in South Carolina, 1775–1789," *South Carolina Historical Magazine* 56, no. 1 (1955): 31–44; Zornow, "The Tariff Policies of Virginia, 1775–1789," *Virginia Magazine of History and Biography* 62, no. 3 (1954): 306–19; Zornow, "Georgia Tariff Policies, 1775 to 1789," *Georgia Historical Quarterly* 38, no. 1 (1954): 1–10; Lemuel Molovinsky, "Taxation and Continuity in Pennsylvania during the American Revolution," *Pennsylvania Magazine of History and Biography* 104, no. 3 (1908): 365–78; Maurice H. Robinson, "A History of Taxation in New Hampshire," *Publications of the American Economic Association* 3, no. 3 (1902): 135; Robert A. Becker, *Revolution, Reform, and the Politics of American Taxation* (Baton Rouge: Louisiana State University Press, 1980).

57. James Madison, 1 *Annals* 134 (April 14, 1789); Edling, *Hercules in the Cradle*, 56–57; H. James Henderson, "Taxation and Political Culture: Massachusetts and Virginia, 1760–1800," *WMQ* 47, no. 1 (1990): 106 n. 18; Thomas Melville, Fees Received at the Naval Office Port of Boston from June 1 1788 to June 1 1789, Reel X, Lemuel Shaw Papers, MHS.

58. John Ross to George Washington, June 25, 1789, Letterbook 22, Series 2, George Washington Papers, LOC; Kenneth R. Bowling and Helen E. Velt, eds., *Diary of William Maclay and Other Notes on Senate Debates* (Baltimore: Johns Hopkins University Press, 1988), 50.

59. "An Act respecting the Commerce of this state, to prevent frauds in the customs, and to direct the duty of naval officers, and to regulate the conduct of masters and mariners of merchant vessels," in *Laws of Maryland . . .* , ed. Alexander Contee Hanson (Annapolis: Frederick Green, 1785), n.p.; McCoy, "Virginia Port Bill of 1784,"

298; "An act for better securing the revenue arising from customs" (October, 1785), in *The Statutes at Large . . . of Virginia*, ed. William Waller Hening (1823; Charlottesville: University Press of Virginia, 1969), 12:46–47.

60. *Phile Qui Tam v. The Ship Anna*, 1 U.S. (1 Dall.) 197 at 205–6 (1787); Robert Morris, Diary entries for September 16 and September 17, 1782, *PRM*, 6:381, 384; Frederick Phile to George Washington, March 7, 1789, Letterbook 22, Series 2, George Washington Papers, LOC.

61. Case Papers of the Court of Admiralty of the State of New York, 1784–1788, RG 21, M948, Archives I; Julius Goebel Jr., ed., *The Law Practice of Alexander Hamilton: Documents and Commentary* (New York: Columbia University Press, 1969), 2:831–41. For evidence of small-scale prosecutions under Massachusetts' impost, see Fees Received by Thomas Melville, n.d. 1789, Reel 2, Folder 1, Lemuel Shaw Papers, MHS.

62. Speech of Fisher Ames, 1 *Annals* 311 (May 9, 1789). For a description of Ames's position during this debate, see Winfred E. A. Bernhard, *Fisher Ames: Federalist and Statesman, 1758–1808* (Chapel Hill: University of North Carolina Press, 1965), 83–84. Generally on the role of smuggling during the American Revolution, see Tyler, *Smugglers and Patriots*.

63. Thomas Tudor Tucker, 1 *Annals* 304 (May 8, 1789). See also speech of Jackson, 1 *Annals* 326 (May 9, 1789).

64. Speech of Fisher Ames, 1 *Annals* 312 (May 9, 1789). Ames, though, would become an ardent defender of the customs revenue system. Herbert E. Sloan, *Principle and Interest: Thomas Jefferson and the Problem of Debt* (New York: Oxford University Press, 1995), 136.

65. Speeches of Fisher Ames, James Madison, and Roger Sherman, 1 *Annals* 312, 315, 317 (May 9, 1789). For a similar sentiment to Sherman's, see speech of Thomas Fitzsimons, 1 *Annals* 320 (May 18, 1789).

66. Bowling and Velt, *Diary of William Maclay*, 57, 65, 72. Lee had delivered a similar performance some years earlier while debating the supposedly oppressive nature of the Navigation Acts. Dickerson, *Navigation Acts and the American Revolution*, 121.

67. Otho Holland Williams to George Washington, May 12, 1789, Papers of George Washington, Series 7; A. C. Hanson, *Laws of Maryland, Made Since M, DCC, LXIII . . .* (Annapolis: Frederick Green, 1787), 428–37. One major problem with the old impost laws that Williams encountered was that shipowners required a permit from the governor to register their vessels, but the law did not explain how to obtain a permit. On the problem of issuing registers, see Hanson, 261. According to William Maclay, the House had begun a similar law in May 1789, but voted it down once it became known that "Mr. Williams of Baltimore is making One, of his own motion." Bowling and Velt, *Diary of William Maclay*, 47.

68. Bowling and Velt, *Diary of William Maclay*, 50; Maryland Historical Records Survey Project, *Calendar of the General Otho Holland Williams Papers in the Maryland Historical Society* (Baltimore: Maryland Historical Records Survey Project, 1940), 172, 175.

69. 1 *Statutes At Large* 145 at 154–55 (1789); Barrow, *Trade and Empire*, 10–18, 77–78.

70. James C. Scott, *Seeing Like a State: How Certain Schemes to Improve the Human Condition Have Failed* (New Haven, CT: Yale University Press, 1998), 2.

71. 1 *Statutes at Large* 145; Barrow, *Trade and Empire*, 18; Christian J. Koot, "The Merchant, the Map, and Empire," *WMQ*, 3rd ser., vol. 67, no. 4 (Oct. 2010), 604, 641; Bruckner, *The Geographic Revolution in Early America: Maps, Literacy, and National Identity* (Chapel Hill: University of North Carolina Press, 2006), 120. See also Kariann Akemi Yokota, *Unbecoming British: How Revolutionary America Became a Postcolonial Nation* (New York: Oxford University Press, 2011), 119–61.

72. Notably, the law prohibited vessels arriving from beyond the Cape of Good Hope, or in other words, vessels involved in the East Asia trade, from these minor ports of entry. 1 *Statutes at Large* 24 at 35. The cultural and economic problem of the China trade has been studied in great detail by Norwood, "Trading in Liberty."

73. See, for instance, Memorial of Sundry Merchants of St. Louis, in the State of Missouri, praying that St. Louis may be Made a Port of Entry, December 35, 1825, *United States Serial Set* 125, sessional volume 1, S.doc.9.

74. Navigation Act of 1660, 12 Charles II, c. 18, p. 1. Philadelphia Customs Records, Vol. 1, HSP, has a large sampling of these bonds. Between February and October 1761, thirty-nine were to prevent "frauds" in overseas commerce; four to account for missing manifests or shipping papers.

75. 1 *Statutes At Large* 29 at 45; Barrow, *Trade and Empire*, 178–79, 189–90; Nicholas R. Parrillo, *Against the Profit Motive: The Salary Revolution in American Government, 1780–1940* (New Haven, CT: Yale University Press, 2013), 59, 221–54.

76. Theodore Sedgewick to Benjamin Lincoln, August 1, 1789, Reel 9, Benjamin Lincoln Papers, MHS (hereafter, Lincoln Papers).

77. 1 *Statutes At Large* 145 at 176–77; Knollenberg, *Origin of the American Revolution*, 168–69; L. Kinvin Wroth, "The Massachusetts Vice Admiralty Court and the Federal Admiralty Jurisdiction," *American Journal of Legal History* 6 (1962): 268. The Judiciary Act is 1 *Statutes At Large* 73–93 (1789).

78. The persistence of this statutory foundation is evident in the Customs Service's more recent enforcement struggles. See Andrew Wender Cohen, *Contraband: Smuggling and the Birth of the American Century* (New York: Norton, 2015).

79. Stanley M. Elkins and Eric McKitrick, *The Age of Federalism* (New York: Oxford University Press, 1993), 49. In speaking of the need for "first characters," Washington referred to the judiciary. White, *Federalists*, 259; Washington to James Madison, September 23, 1789, in Twohig, *Papers of George Washington*, 4:67–68; Carl Russell Fish, *The Civil Service and the Patronage* (Cambridge, MA: Harvard University Press, 1904), 9 n. 2. Yet there is no evidence that Washington used this same measure for the appointment of subordinate employees in the customs. Importantly, though, Washington did not appoint party hacks, either. Carl Prince has argued that Washington relied chiefly on partisan affiliation to fill out the ranks. But Prince's own statistics seem to undercut his argument about Washington's overwhelming political consideration in appointing customs personnel. According to his study, of the 295 customs officials for whom data is available for the period between 1789 and 1801, 178, or about 60.6 percent were known Federalists. Carl E. Prince, *The Federalists and the Origins of the U.S. Civil Service* (New York: New York University Press, 1977), esp. 2–4, 275 table 1.

80. George Washington to James Kelso, May 21, 1789, Letterbook 22, Series 2, George Washington Papers, LOC.

81. Elkins and McKitrick, *Age of Federalism*, 55. Although there was no specification that only men could serve as customs officers, I have not found any evidence of women soliciting office or being considered for the office.

82. Freeman, *Affairs of Honor*, 9. These official applications thus were relevant to personal communications during the mid-eighteenth century, when men describing their place in market activities emphasized "family duty and personal responsibility." Dierks, *In My Power*, 166.

83. These recommendation letters were typically brief and to the point, although some bore significant flourishes. William Moultrie, the South Carolinian general and Federalist, described an applicant for the Charleston collectorship as a "Gentleman," most likely to indicate the degree to which he fit within the notoriously socially hierarchical city. In other instances, applicants included legislative resolutions honoring their service to city and country as proof of their public worthiness. William Moultrie to George Washington, March 12, 1789; Extract from the Journal of the Virginia House of Delegates, November 25, 1788, in William Heth to George Washington, April 23, 1789, Letterbook 22, Series 2, George Washington Papers, LOC.

84. John Ballard to George Washington, January 1, 1789; John Muir to George Washington, Sharp Delany to George Washington, April 20, 1789; Letterbook 22, Series 2, George Washington Papers, LOC. See, more generally, Heath J. Bowen, "Your Obedient Servant: Government Clerks, Officeseeking, and the Politics of Patronage in Antebellum Washington City" (PhD diss., Michigan State University, 2011).

85. Irvin, *Clothed in Robes of Sovereignty*, 280.

86. Dalzell, "Prudence and the Golden Egg," 359; H. H. Waters, *The New-England Genealogical Register* (Boston: New England Historical and Genealogical Society, 1896), L:426.

87. Republican critics had worried that the Cincinnati might be the fountainhead of a secretive, standing military power over society. George Washington, Draft Circular to the State Society of the Cincinnati, n.d. [1784], Reel 1, Society of the Cincinnati Papers, LOC; Markus Hunermorder, *The Society of the Cincinnati: Conspiracy and Distrust in Early America* (New York: Berghahn Books, 2006), 44. Generally, see Sarah J. Purcell, *Sealed with Blood: War, Sacrifice, and Memory in Revolutionary America* (Philadelphia: University of Pennsylvania Press, 2002), 86–90.

88. See entry of the Secret Journal of the Cincinnati, May 4, 1784, for mentions of Olney, Huntington, Heth, and Williams; Wadsworth was a signatory to Delegates of the State Societies of the Cincinnati to President George Washington, May 4, 1790, Society of the Cincinnati Journals, Reel 1, Society of the Cincinnati Papers, LOC. Heth's activity is clear in William Heth to Henry Knox, November 17, 1784, Reel 2, ibid. On Hamilton, see Hamilton et al., Circular Letter to the New York Society of the Cincinnati, November 1, 1786, Reel 3, ibid. Prince, *Federalists*, 276 table 2.

89. William Ellery, "Ode," July 4, 1801, Papers of the American Slave Trade, Frame 512, Reel 13.

90. For other "continued" candidates, see Anon. to George Washington, n.d., 1789; Richard Henry Lee to George Washington, July 27, 1789; Robert Peters, Brooke Brall, Bernard O'Neill, et al. to George Washington, May 12, 1789; James Lovell to George Washington, n.d., 1789; Samuel Otis to George Washington, March 12, 1789; Frederick

Phile to George Washington, March 7, 1789, Letterbook 22, Series 2, George Washington Papers, LOC.

91. Benjamin Fishbourn to George Washington, May 18, 1789, Letterbook 22, Series 2, George Washington Papers, LOC. After Congress rejected Fishbourn's nomination for reasons unknown, Washington explained that he nominated the Georgian because he "must have enjoyed . . . the confidence of the Council to have been appointed Collector of the Port of Savannah." George Washington, 1789, quoted in Elkins and McKitrick, *Age of Federalism*, 54. See also Gaillard Hunt, "Office-Seeking during Washington's Administration," *AHR* 1, no. 2 (1896): 271–72.

92. Lamb's performance as collector is detailed in Case Papers of the Court of Admiralty of the State of New York, 1784–1788, RG 21, M948, Archives I.

93. On the idea of the "regime of notables," see Jerry L. Mashaw, "Recovering American Administrative Law: Federalist Foundations, 1789–1801," *Yale Law Journal* 115 (2006): 1319; Martin Shefter, "Party, Bureaucracy, and Political Change in the United States," in *Political Parties: Development and Decay*, ed. L. Maisel and Joseph Cooper (Beverly Hills: Sage Press, 1978), 211. On Lincoln's notable quality, see David B. Mattern, *Benjamin Lincoln and the American Revolution* (Columbia: University of South Carolina Press, 1995), 212–13.

94. See Sophus A. Reinert, *Translating Empire: Emulation and the Origins of Political Economy* (Cambridge, MA: Harvard University Press, 2008); Cheney, *Revolutionary Commerce*; Hont, *Jealousy of Trade*.

CHAPTER 3

1. Joseph Jones to George Washington, April 21, 1789, George Washington Papers, Series 7.

2. Appointment as secretary of the treasury, September 11, 1789, *PAH*, 26:481; J. Willard Hurst, "Alexander Hamilton, Law Maker," *Columbia Law Review* 78 (April 1978): 486.

3. Report on Manufactures, December 5, 1791, *PAH*, 10:256; Gould, *Among the Powers of the Earth*; Benjamin Lincoln to Alexander Hamilton, February 16, 1790, Reel 4, Hamilton Papers, LOC.

4. Alexander Hamilton to Arthur Lee, Walter Livingston, and Samuel Osgood, September 14, 1789, *PAH*, 5:372. On the Board of Treasury's lax record-keeping, see Samuel Osgood and Arthur Lee to Nathaniel Gilman, August 24, 1786, Box 2, Continental Congress Collection, LOC; and Report of the Board of Treasury, March 14, 1787, Reports of the Board of Treasury, 1785–1787, Vol. 3, LOC; Report of the Board of Treasury, March 15, 1787, Reports of the Board of Treasury, 1785–1787, Vol. 3, LOC.

5. Elkins and McKitrick, *Age of Federalism*, 50.

6. Alexander Hamilton, Circular to Collectors of Customs, September 14, 1789, RG 56, M735, Circular Letters of the Secretary of the Treasury, 1789–1878, Reel 2, National Archives-College Park (hereafter, Treasury Circulars); Patricia Cline Cohen, "Statistics and the State: Changing Social Thought and the Emergence of a Quantitative Mentality in America, 1790 to 1820," *WMQ*, 3rd ser., vol. 38, no. 1 (Jan. 1981): 44. See also Ian Hacking, *The Taming of Chance* (New York: Cambridge University Press, 1990), 16.

7. Alexander Hamilton, Circular to Collectors of Customs, September 14, 1789, Treasury Circulars, Reel 2.

8. See Catherine M. Desbarats, "France in North America: The Net Burden of Empire during the First Half of the Eighteenth Century," *French History* 11, no. 1 (1997): 5.

9. Max M. Edling, "'So immense a power in the affairs of war': Alexander Hamilton and the Restoration of Public Credit," *WMQ* 64, no. 2 (Apr. 2007): 287–326.

10. "An Act to Establish the Treasury Department,' 1 *Statutes at Large* 65 (1789) at 65–67. George Gibbs, ed., *Memoirs of the Administrations of Washington and John Adams Edited from the Papers of Oliver Wolcott Secretary of the Treasury* (1846; New York: Burt Franklin, 1947), 1:15–16. For sources on these appointments, see Robert F. Jones, "Wiliam Duer and the Business of Government in the Era of the American Revolution," *WMQ* 32, no. 3 (1975): 393–416; Richard D. White Jr., "A Tale of Two Bureaucrats: Joseph Nourse, Oliver Wolcott, Jr., and the Forerunners of American Public Administration," *Administration & Society* 40, no. 4 (2008): 384–93, 390; Clarence L. Ver Steeg, *Robert Morris: Revolutionary Financier* (Philadelphia: University of Pennsylvania Press, 1954), 80; Oscar P. Fitzgerald, *In Search of Joseph Nourse, 1754–1801: America's First Civil Servant* (Washington, DC: Dumbarton House, 1994); Leonard Dupee White, "Public Administration under the Federalists," *Boston University Law Review* 24 (1944): 158.

11. Alexander Hamilton to Gouvernor Morris, December 6, 1788, Reel 4, Hamilton Papers, LOC; Alexander Hamilton, Circular to Collectors of Customs, September 14, 1789; Sharp Delany to Alexander Hamilton, November 2, 1789, in Sharp Delaney, *Facsimile of a Letter Book of Colonel Sharp Delaney* (Washington, DC: Department of the Treasury, 1987), 16.

12. Alexander Hamilton, Circular to Collectors of Customs, December 1, 1789, Treasury Circulars, Reel 2.

13. Nicholas Eveleigh, Comptroller's Circular to Collectors of Customs, December 1, 1789, Treasury Circulars, Reel 2.

14. Ibid.

15. Ibid; Robert Mayo, *A Synopsis of the Commercial and Revenue System of the United States* (Washington, DC: J. & G.S. Gideon, 1847), 253.

16. Alexander Hamilton, Circular to Collectors of Customs, September 23, 1789, Treasury Circulars, Reel 2.

17. Brewer, *Sinews of Power*, 222. Edmund Burke, "A Plan for the Better Security of the Independence of Parliament, and the Economical Reformation of the Civil and Other Establishments," in *Works of the Right Honourable Edmund Burke* (London: Bell & Daldy, 1972), 2:72. See William Shakespeare, *Romeo and Juliet*, act 5, scene 1, line 45, in *The Complete Works of William Shakespeare* (Hertfordshire, UK: Wordsworth Editions, 1996), 274. Richard Bonney ("Revenues," in *Economic Systems and State Finance*, ed. Bonney [Oxford: Clarendon Press, 1995], 445) places the Burke speech in the context of failed attempts at "Treasury unification." On Hamilton's mimetic instincts at this moment, see Ron Chernow, *Alexander Hamilton* (New York: Penguin Press, 2004), 295–96.

18. *American State Papers: Documents, Legislative and Executive, of the Congress of the United States, Commerce and Navigation* (Washington, DC: Gales & Seaton,

1832–61), 1:v (hereafter, *ASP-C&N*); White, "Tale of Two Bureaucrats," 391; Circular to Collector of Customs, January 2, 1792, Treasury Circulars, Reel 2.

19. On the relationship between possession of statistical information and authority, see Joan W. Scott, *Gender and the Politics of History* (New York: Columbia University Press, 1999), 115; Christopher Grasso, *A Speaking Aristocracy: Transforming Public Discourse in Eighteenth-Century Connecticut* (Chapel Hill: University of North Carolina Press, 1999), 392.

20. Hacking, *Taming of Chance*, 32. A sampling of Hamilton's publications: *United States Department of the Treasury, Estimate of the Expenditure for the Civil List of the United States, for the year 1789* (New York: Thomas Greenleaf, 1789); *Report of the Secretary of the Treasury to the House of Representatives, relative to a provision for the support of the Public Credit of the United States . . .* (New York: Francis Childs and John Swaine, 1790); *Estimate of the Expenditure of the Civil List of the United States . . . for the year 1792* (New York: Francis Childs and John Swaine, 1791[?]); *The Argument of the Secretary of the Treasury upon the Constitutionality of a National Bank* (Philadelphia: s.n., 1791); *The Treasurer of the United States' Accounts of Payments and Receipts of Public Monies, from 1st October, 1790, to 30th June, 1791* (Philadelphia: Childs and Swaine, 1791); *Report of the Secretary on the Subject of the Public Debt* (Philadelphia: Childs and Swaine, 1792); *The Secretary of the Treasury, to whom were referred by the House of Representatives the several petitions . . . praying the renewal of certain certificates . . . respectfully makes the following report thereupon* (Philadelphia: Childs and Swaine, 1792); *Treasury of the United States, February 28th, 1792: Sir, My specie account, ending the 31st December, 1791* (Philadelphia: Childs and Swaine, 1792); *The Treasurer of the United States, accounts and payments and receipts of public monies . . . to the 30th of September, 1792* (Philadelphia: Childs and Swaine, 1793); *Accounts of the Treasurer of the United States, of payments and receipts of public monies* (Philadelphia: F. Childs, 1794); *Statements in Relation to the foreign and domestic debt . . .* (New York: s.n., 1794); *Report of the Secretary of the Treasury, for the improvement and better management of the revenues of the United States . . .* (Philadelphia: Francis Childs, 1795); *Report of the Secretary of the Treasury . . . containing a plan for the further support of public credit* (Philadelphia: John Fenno, 1795).

21. John E. Crowley, *Privileges of Independence: Neomercantilism and the American Revolution* (Baltimore: Johns Hopkins University Press, 1993), 81–83; Elkins and McKitrick, *Age of Federalism*, 69. William Short to Alexander Hamilton, December 18, 1790, William Harris Crawford Papers, Duke University Library.

22. Ann Laura Stoler, *Against the Archival Grain: Epistemic Anxieties and Colonial Common Sense* (Princeton, NJ: Princeton University Press, 2009), 3; Oz Frankel, *States of Inquiry: Social Investigations and Print Culture in Nineteenth-Century Britain and the United States* (Baltimore: Johns Hopkins University Press, 2006), 2, and more broadly, 75–103. Doron Ben-Atar, "Alexander Hamilton's Alternative: Technology Piracy and the Report on Manufactures," *WMQ*, 3rd ser., vol. 52, no. 3 (July 1995): 389–414; Jacob E. Cooke, "Tench Coxe, Alexander Hamilton, and the Encouragement of American Manufactures," *WMQ*, 3rd ser., vol. 32, no. 3 (1975): 369–92.

23. Elkins and McKitrick, *Age of Federalism*, 115.

24. Peter Karsten, *Heart versus Head: Judge-Made Law in Nineteenth-Century America* (Chapel Hill: University of North Carolina Press, 1997).

25. Otho Holland Williams to Alexander Hamilton, October 23, 1789, *PAH*, 5:459. See also Dalzell, "Taxation with Representation."

26. Alexander Hamilton, Circular to Collectors of Customs, December 23, 1789, Treasury Circulars, Reel 2; Circular to Collectors of Customs, October 6, 1789, Treasury Circulars, Reel 2.

27. Freeman, *Affairs of Honor*, 11–61.

28. Alexander Hamilton, Circular to Collectors of Customs, October 6, 1789, Treasury Circulars, Reel 2; 1 *Statutes at Large* 42 (1789).

29. Williams to Hamilton, *PAH*, 5:462–63. The law regulating practice for the Tonnage Act stated, "That all the duties imposed by law on the tonnage of any ship or vessel, shall be paid to the collector, within ten days after entry made, and before such ship or vessel at the time of entry, shall be lodged in the office of the collector, and there remain until such clearance." 1 *Statutes at Large* 29 at 43 (1789).

30. Hamilton, Circular to Collectors of Customs, October 31, 1789, Treasury Circulars, Reel 2; Delany to Hamilton, September 19, 1789, *PAH*, 5:378; Thomas Fitzsimons to Alexander Hamilton, November 18 1789, Hamilton Papers, Reel 4; Jeremiah Wadsworth to Alexander Hamilton, December 17, 1789, *PAH*, 6:15–16.

31. Benjamin Lincoln to Alexander Hamilton, December 9, 1789, *PAH*, 6:13; Benjamin Lincoln to Alexander Hamilton, July 13, 1791, *PAH*, 8:548–49; Dalzell, "Taxation with Representation," 180.

32. Hamilton, Circular to Collectors of Customs, May 13, 1791, Treasury Circulars, Reel 2.

33. Sharp Delany to John Lamb, February 6, 1790, Facsimile of a Letter Book, 16–19; Otho Holland Williams to Benjamin Lincoln, February 21, 1790, Calendar, 204.

34. Hamilton, Circular to Collectors of Customs, Treasury Circulars, Reel 2; Circular to Collectors of Customs, July 22, 1792, Treasury Circulars, Reel 2.

35. J. G. A. Pocock, "Machiavelli, Harrington, and English Political Ideologies in the Eighteenth Century," *WMQ*, 3rd ser., vol. 22, no. 4 (Oct. 1965): 565–66. See also J. G. A. Pocock, *The Machiavellian Moment: Florentine Political Thought and the Atlantic Republican Tradition* (Princeton, NJ: Princeton University Press, 1975), 406–22; Bailyn, *Ideological Origins*, 48; Mary Lindemann, "Dirty Politics or 'Harmonie'? Defining Corruption in Early Modern Amsterdam and Hamburg," *Journal of Social History* 45, no. 3 (2012): 582–604.

36. Richard White, "Information, Markets, and Corruption: The Transcontinental Railroad in the Gilded Age," *JAH* 90, no. 1 (2001): 19–21; Richard R. John, *Network Nation: Inventing American Telecommunications* (Cambridge, MA: Harvard University Press, 2010), 254.

37. Benjamin Lincoln to Alexander Hamilton, May 25, 1791, Benjamin Lincoln Papers, Reel 9; Jeremiah Wadsworth to Alexander Hamilton, *PAH*, 5:422–23; Joseph Whipple to Alexander Hamilton, December 17, 1789, *PAH*, 6:19–21. See also William Ellery to Benjamin Huntington, February 21, 1790, William Ellery Papers, Box 1, Folder 1790–1794, Mss 407, RIHS.

38. Hamilton, *Federalist* 35, 233–34.

39. "The Humble Address of the Merchants of Charles Town," March 22, 1760, in *The Papers of Henry Laurens* (Columbia: South Carolina Historical Society, by the University of South Carolina Press, 1972), 3:30–31; Margaret Middleton Rivers Eastman, *Remembering Old Charleston: A Peek behind Parlor Doors* (Charleston, SC: The History Press, 2008), 37–42.

40. Brian D. Schoen, *The Fragile Fabric of Union: Cotton, Federal Politics, and the Global Cotton Trade* (Baltimore: Johns Hopkins University Press, 2009), 47.

41. Ray Brighton, *Port of Portsmouth Ships and the Cotton Trade, 1783–1829* (Portsmouth, NH: Portsmouth Marine Society, 2002), 53–54; John F. Parrott, Affidavit of December 8, 1813; and Parrott to Alexander J. Dallas, May 28, 1819, Box 1, Folder 1; John F. Parrott to Hannah Parrott, June 24, 1809, Box 1, Folder 6, John Fabyan Parrott Papers, NHHS; State of New Hampshire, *Act to Incorporate the Union Insurance Company, Passed June 22, 1815* (Portsmouth: Beck & Foster, 1816).

42. Wm Lithgow & al. Inhabts of Lincoln C's to erect a Light House at Seguin [n.d. 1786], in *History of the State of Maine*, ed. James Phinney Baxter (Portland: Fred L. Tower, 1916), 21:198.

43. Entry of August 10, 1787, Diary of Henry Packer Dering; and Orange Webb to Henry Packer Dering, June 12, 1793; William Eldridge to Dering, December 19, 1792; Correspondence, 1792–1795, Henry Packer Dering Papers, NYPL; Pitkin, *Three Centuries of Custom Houses*, 109–10.

44. 1 *Statutes at Large* 29 at 160, 168, 169.

45. Circular to Collectors of Customs, December 18, 1789, Treasury Circulars, Reel 2; Higginson to Hamilton, November 11, 1789, *PAH*, 5:508; Dalzell, "Taxation with Representation," 192.

46. Dalzell, "Taxation with Representation," 199; David Gelston to Joshua Sands, August 27, 1802, Gelston Papers, Box 1, Folder 1; David Gelston, Acct Current 3d Quarter 1804, Gelston Papers, Box 17, Folder 1, G. W. Blunt Library, Mystic Seaport.

47. Dalzell, "Taxation with Representation," 203–4; Thomas Bee, *Reports of Cases Adjudged in the District Court of South Carolina* (Philadelphia: William Farrand, 1810), 140; Maeva Marcus et al., "Hazlehurst v. United States," in *Documentary History of the Supreme Court of the United States, 1789–1800*, ed. Marcus (New York: Columbia University Press, 1985–), 8:272, 273 (hereafter cited as *DHSCUS*).

48. Dalzell, "Taxation with Representation," 194–95; Sharp Delany to Alexander Hamilton, December 24, 1789, *PAH*, 6:32.

49. Port of Philadelphia, Bonds in Suit, 1807–1844, RG 36, #1081E, NARA-Phila; Dalzell, "Taxation with Representation," 196. Despite his fine account of events in Delany's custom house, Dalzell wrongly conveys the impression that Delany failed to prosecute any and all overdue bonds. See the Philadelphia *General Advertiser*, March 20, 1792, 1. Bond of November 13, 1792 (Gordon Barker), Bermuda Hundred Customs Accounts.

50. T. H. Breen, *Tobacco Culture: The Mentality of the Great Tidewater Planters on the Eve of the American Revolution* (Princeton, NJ: Princeton University Press, 1985), 135; Kenneth Morgan, *Slavery and the British Empire: From Africa to America* (New York: Oxford University Press, 2007), 64. On the role of credit in the merchant com-

munities' business practices in the revolutionary era and early republic, see Doerflinger, *Vigorous Spirit of Enterprise*; Jacob M. Price, *Capital and Credit in British Overseas Trade: The View from the Chesapeake, 1700–1776* (Cambridge, MA: Harvard University Press, 1980).

51. Jonathan Ira Levy, *Freaks of Fortune: The Emerging World of Capitalism and Risk in America* (Cambridge, MA: Harvard University Press, 2012), 22.

52. Benjamin Lincoln to John Steele, October 3, 1796; Smith, *Borderland Smuggling*, 44.

53. Alexander Hamilton, Circular to Collectors of Customs, February 6, 1792, Treasury Circulars, Reel 2; Joseph Hiller to Christopher Gore, October 17, 1792, Spec. Ms. Coll. Baltimore, Columbia University Library (hereafter cited as Baltimore Customs Correspondence).

54. Bermuda Hundred Customs Accounts; Craig Muldrew, *The Economy of Obligation: The Culture of Credit and Social Relations in Early Modern England* (New York: Palgrave, 1998); Bruce H. Mann, *Republic of Debtors: Bankruptcy in the Age of American Independence* (Cambridge, MA: Harvard University Press, 2002).

55. Hamilton, "Operations of the Act Laying Duties on Imports," *ASP-Fi* 1:380.

56. Alexander Hamilton, "Public Funds: Revenue, Income, Appropriations, and Expenditures, 1791–1792," February 14, 1793, *ASP-Fi* 1:219. *Historical Statistics of the United States* estimates revenue between 1789 and 1791 to have been $4,399,000. The same source provides a precise number for every year thereafter, beginning with $3,443,000 in 1792. John J. Wallis, ed., *Historical Statistics of the United States*, ed. Susan B. Carter et al. (New York: Cambridge University Press, 2006–), Table Ea588–593 (hereafter, *Historical Statistics*).

57. *Pennsylvania Packet*, October 5, 1789; *Cumberland Gazette*, January 18, 1789, 2; September 11, 1789; *Federal Gazette*, October 24, 1789, 2.

58. Dalzell, "Taxation with Representation."

59. Greene, "Colonial History and National History," 246.

60. Hulsebosch, *Constituting Empire*, 201.

61. Hamilton, Circular to Collectors of Customs, June 11, 1792, Treasury Circulars, Reel 2.

62. Alexander Hamilton, Circular to Collectors of Customs, October 25, 1792, Treasury Circulars, Reel 2.

63. Dalzell, "Taxation with Representation," 216–18; Olney to Alexander Hamilton, November 3, 1788, Reel 4, Hamilton Papers.

64. Jeremiah Olney to Edward Dexter, November 7, 1792; Edward Dexter to Jeremiah Olney, November 7, 1792; Arthur Fenner to Theodore Foster, December 30, 1792; *DHSCUS*, 8:577–78, 578–79, 583; Dalzell, "Taxation with Representation," 225.

65. Memorial of the Merchants of Providence, January 31, 1793, Jeremiah Olney Papers, Reel 1, Box 1, Folder 10, RIHS; Dalzell, "Taxation with Representation," 230–31.

66. Jeremiah Olney to William Channing, August 20, 1792, quoted in Dalzell, "Taxation with Representation," 225.

67. Alexander Hamilton to Jeremiah Olney, April 2, 1793, *PAH*, 16:277.

68. Jeremiah Olney to Charles Lee, August 26, 1796, *DHSCUS*, 8:619; Marcus et al., "Olney v. Arnold; Olney v. Dexter," *DHSCUS*, 8:575; Mary Sarah Bilder, *The Transat-*

lantic Constitution: Colonial Legal Culture and the Empire (Cambridge, MA: Harvard University Press, 2004), 194; Robert P. Frankel Jr., "Judicial Beginnings: The Supreme Court in the 1790s," *History Compass* 4, no. 6 (2006): 1009–1110.

69. Alexander Hamilton to George Washington, September 8, 1792, *PAH*, 12:344–46; 1 *Statutes at Large* 199 (1791).

70. Thomas P. Slaughter, *The Whiskey Rebellion: Frontier Epilogue to the American Revolution* (New York: Oxford University Press, 1986), 123; Tully No. III, August 28, 1794, *PAH*,17:160; Hamilton to Washington, September 19, 1794, *PAH*, 17:254–55.

71. Hamilton to Henry Lee, October 20, 1794, *PAH*, 17:331.

72. Hamilton to the President and Directors of the Bank of the United States, September 24, 1794, *PAH*, 17:264.

73. Tully No. III, August 28, 1794, *PAH*:17:160.

74. Mary K. Bonsteel Tachau, "A New Look at the Whiskey Rebellion," in *The Whiskey Rebellion: Past and Present Perspectives*, ed. Steven R. Boyd (Westport, CT: Greenwood Press, 1985), 99.

75. Andrew Shankman, "'A New Thing on Earth': Alexander Hamilton, Pro-Manufacturing Republicans, and the Democratization of American Political Economy," *JER* 23, no. 3 (2003): 326; Elkins and McKitrick, *Age of Federalism*, 116; J. Willard Hurst, *Law and the Conditions of Freedom in the Nineteenth-Century United States* (Madison: University of Wisconsin Press, 1956).

BALTIMORE, 1808

1. Baltimore *Federal Republican & Commercial Gazette*, October 21, 1808, 3.

2. James McCulloch to Albert Gallatin, April 19, 1808, April 19, 1808, Port of Baltimore, Letter Book/Record of Letters, 1806–1809, Series 1143, RG 36, NARA-Phila (hereafter cited as Baltimore Customs Letter Book); Whitman H. Ridgeway, *Community Leadership in Maryland, 1790–1840: A Comparative Analysis of Power in Society* (Chapel Hill: University of North Carolina Press, 1979), 81.

3. List of Public Property Received From the Representatives of Robert Purviance Late Collector of Baltimore on the 25 Octo 1806, Baltimore Customs Letter Book; John Bruce, Deputy Collector, to McLam Turner, Petersburg, November 11, 1806, Baltimore Customs Letter Book.

4. Brice to Unknown, August 29, 1807, Baltimore Customs Letter Book.

5. John Darby to Albert Gallatin, July 2, 1808; Albert Gallatin to James H. McCulloch, October 10, 1808, Baltimore Customs Correspondence.

6. Gallatin to McCulloch, October 24, 1808, Baltimore Customs Correspondence; McCulloch to Gallatin, January 3, 1809, M178, RG 36, Roll 3, NARA.

CHAPTER 4

1. Wallis, *Historical Statistics*, Table Ea588–593. The statistical increase in American commerce in these years is most clearly explained in the work of Douglass C. North, *The Economic Growth of the United States, 1790–1861* (Englewood Cliffs, NJ: Prentice-Hall, 1961), 53.

2. Rachel Hope Cleves, *The Reign of Terror in America: Visions of Violence from Anti-Jacobinism to Antislavery* (New York: Cambridge University Press, 2012); Seth Cotlar, *Tom Paine's America: The Rise and Fall of Transatlantic Radicalism in the Early Republic* (Charlottesville: University of Virginia Press, 2011).

3. Istvan Hont, "The Rhapsody of Public Debt: David Hume and Voluntary State Bankruptcy," in *Political Discourse in Early Modern Britain*, ed. Nicholas Phillipson and Quentin Skinner (New York: Cambridge University Press, 1993), 347–48.

4. Thomas Jefferson, Fourth Annual Message to Congress, *Annals of Congress*, 8th Cong., 2nd Sess. (Sen.), (November 8, 1804), 11. Jefferson's language of the "well-ordered society" invoked a common-law tradition of governmental police for the protection of the health and safety of the people. See Novak, *People's Welfare*.

5. George Washington, Neutrality Proclamation, *Columbian Centinal*, May 4, 1793; Elkins and McKitrick, *Age of Federalism*, 338–39, 353; William R. Casto, *Foreign Affairs and the Constitution in the Age of Fighting Sail* (Columbia: University of South Carolina Press, 2006), 31–34; Stanley L. Engerman, *Naval Blockades in Peace and War: An Economic History since 1750* (New York: Cambridge University Press, 2006), 67–68.

6. John Adams' 1776 Model Treaty likely informed Washington's thought on the matter. David M. Golove and Daniel J. Hulsebosch, "Civilized Nation: The Early American Constitution, the Law of Nations, and the Pursuit of International Recognition," *New York University Law Review* 85 (2010): 976. On Adams diplomatic thought, see James H. Hutson, *John Adams and the Diplomacy of the American Revolution* (Lexington: University Press of Kentucky, 1980).

7. Christopher Gore to Tobias Lear, July 28, 1793, Folder 1, Tobias Lear Papers, LC; Jacob G. Koch to Averhoff von Scheven, April 11, 1796, Box 3, Folder 3, Papers of Jacob Gerhard Koch, LC (hereafter cited as Koch Papers); Fichter, *So Great a Proffit*, 57; Cathy D. Matson, "The Revolution, the Constitution, and the New Nation," in *Cambridge Economic History of the United States* (New York: Cambridge University Press, 2000), 1:398.

8. Michelle Craig McDonald, "The Chance of the Moment: Coffee and the New West Indies Commodities Trade," *WMQ* 62, no. 3 (July 2005): 465; Brooke Hunter, "Wheat, War, and the American Economy during the Age of Revolution," ibid., 516–17; James Alexander Dun, "'What Avenues of Commerce, Will You, Americans, not Explore!' Commercial Philadelphia's Vantage Point onto the Early Haitian Revolution," ibid., 476; Kariann Akemi Yokota, *Unbecoming British: How Revolutionary America Became a Postcolonial Nation* (New York: Oxford University Press, 2011); Joanna Cohen, "'Millions of Luxurious Citizens': Consumption and Citizenship in the Urban Northeast, 1800–1865" (PhD diss., University of Pennsylvania, 2009).

9. Alexander Hamilton, "Public Credit," January 21, 1795, *ASP-Fi* 1:320; "Receipts and Public Debt," April 17, 1810, *ASP-Fi* 1:423–24.

10. William H. Bergmann, *The American National State and the Early West* (New York: Cambridge University Press, 2012), 134–35; Balogh, *Revolution Out of Sight*, 95–111.

11. Treaty of Amity and Commerce Between the United States of America and His Most Christian Majesty, February 6, 1778, 8 *Statutes at Large* 12 (1778), 20, 22, 24, 26, 28.

12. Duffy, *Soldiers, Sugar, and Seapower*, 107; Fulwar Skipwith, Summary of the

French Decrees, Box 12, French Proclamations, Causten-Pickett Papers; George A. King, *The French Spoliation Claims* (Washington, DC: Government Printing Office, 1916), 7–8.

13. Gould, "Zones of Law," 487–88.

14. *Daily Advertiser*, July 1, 1793, 2; August 12, 1793, 2.

15. *Moxon et al. v. The Fanny*, 17 F. Cas. 942 (1793); Affidavit of James Cavan and James Kennedy, March 26, 1798, Folder 2, Records Relating to Captures, 1789–1801 (Alexandria), French Spoliation Claims, #E1265, RG 36, Archives I. The affidavits belong to James Porter, n.d. [ca. 1797]; William Hall, March 9, 1798; and William Hodgson, March 6, 1798, ibid.

16. "Statement of the Tonnage of American vessels entered into the ports of the United States in the years . . . 1790, and . . . 1794 . . . ," January 22, 1796, *ASP-Commerce and Navigation* 1:330.

17. Bailyn, *New England Merchants*, 153; Koot, *Empire at the Periphery*, 119–25; Matson, *Merchants & Empire*.

18. 1 *Statutes at Large* 381, 381–84 (1794).

19. Alexander Hamilton, Circular to Collectors of Customs, June 17, 1794, Treasury Circulars, Reel 2.

20. Jeremiah Olney to Alexander Hamilton, March 31, 1794, M178, Roll 29.

21. William Stinchcombe, "Talleyrand and the American Negotiations of 1797–1798," *JAH* 62, no. 3 (1975): 581; Benjamin Lincoln to John Steele, May 3, 1796, Benjamin Lincoln Letterbook, Reel 9. French seizures are documented in Affidavit of William Hodgson, March 6, 1798, Folder 2, French Spoliation Records-Alexandria, RG 36, Archives I; Charles Cotesworth Pinckney to Henry William DeSaussure, November 4, 1797, reprinted in John LaFayette Brittain, "Two Recently Discovered Letters of Charles Cotesworth Pinckney: Another Glimpse into the Mind of an Eighteenth-Century Man of Affairs," *South Carolina Historical Magazine* 76, no. 1 (1975): 18–19.

22. Alexander J. Dallas, ed., *The Opinion of Judge Cooper, on the Effect of a Sentence of a Foreign Court of Admiralty* (Philadelphia: P. Byrne, 1810), xi, x–xi; Certificate of the New York Insurance Company [ship *Ohio*], May 26, 1798; Memorandum of Imperfect Certificates for Merchandise Exported from the District of the City of New York, with their Remarks, n.d. [1798 or 1799]; Marginalia on Protest of Abraham S. Hallett [ship *Favourite*], September 16, 1801, Folder Protests of Masters (F-O); John Steele to Joshua Sands, May 28, 1799, Folder Protests of Masters (P-W), French Spoliation Records-New York.

23. The joint resolution of Congress of March 26, 1794, created an embargo for thirty days. Two subsequent resolutions extended the embargo. See Resolutions of March 26, 1794, April 2, 1794, and April 18, 1794, 1 *Statutes at Large* 400–401. James Roger Sharp, *American Politics in the Early Republic: The New Nation in Crisis* (New Haven, CT: Yale University Press, 1993), 115.

24. Alexander Hamilton, Circular to Collectors of Customs, March 26, 1794, Treasury Circulars, Reel 2; Cabinet Meeting, Opinion on the Best Mode of Executing the Embargo, March 26, 1794, *PAH*, 16:198.

25. Otho Holland Williams to Alexander Hamilton, June 5, 1794, *PAH*, 16:462; William Ellery to Alexander Hamilton, April 14, 1794, *PAH*, 16:256. Interestingly, one of the merchants accused of violating the embargo was none other than Welcome Arnold,

Providence collector of custom and Jeremiah Olney's main antagonist. A more general indictment of American merchants is found in Alexander Hamilton to George Washington, May 1, 1794, *PAH*, 16:366–67.

26. *New-York Gazette*, March 29, 1794, 3; Philadelphia *Gazette and Universal Daily Advertiser*, March 31, 1794, 3; *Spooner's Vermont Journal*, April 28, 1794; *General Advertiser*, May 6, 1794, 3.

27. Philadelphia *Gazette*, May 8, 1794, 3; Salem *Gazette*, May 13, 1794, 3; Connecticut *Gazette*, May 15, 1794, 3; Massachusetts *Mercury*, May 20, 1794, 3.

28. Gould, "Zones of Law," 475; Jack Coggins, *Ships and Seamen of the American Revolution* (1969; New York: Dover, 2002), 74; Sidney G. Morse, "The Yankee Privateersmen of 1776," *New England Quarterly* 17, no. 1 (1944): 71–86; List of All Vessels Cleared Outward at this Port of Annapolis Between the first day of February 1780 and the fifth day of January 1781 . . . , Letters Received by the Collector (Annapolis), RG 36, Entry 1219A, NARA-Phila.

29. The sharp decline in the number of armed vessels in Baltimore between 1780 and 1786 is seen in Port of Baltimore, Records of Arrivals and Clearances, 1780–1939, Vol. 8, RG 36, #1149, NARA-Phila. Newspaper advertisements suggest that shipowners, states, and even Congress tried to sell their naval armaments after the war. See *Independent Chronicle*, January 3, 1782, 2; *Pennsylvania Packet*, May 2, 1782, 1; *North-American Intelligencer*, August 25, 1784, 2; *American Mercury*, September 13, 1784, 4.

30. Jerome R. Garitee, *The Republic's Private Navy: The American Privateering Business as Practiced by Baltimore during the War of 1812* (Middletown, CT: Wesleyan University Press, 1977), 118; Brian Lavery, *The Arming and Fitting of English Ships of War, 1600–1815* (London: Conway Maritime Press, 1987), 126–34. An instance of supply by public vendue is *Baltimore Daily Intelligencer*, December 21, 1793, 4.

31. Edward Preble, quoted in Christopher McKee, *Edward Preble: A Naval Biography, 1761–1807* (1972; Annapolis: United States Naval Institute, 1972), 46, 48; Bee, *Reports of Cases*, 71.

32. Benjamin Moodie to Phineas Bond, December 17, 1794, reprinted in *DHSCUS*, 7:77; Bee, *Reports of Cases*, 71; McKee, *Edward Preble*, 48; Oliver Wolcott Jr. to Sharp Delany, November 16, 1795, Reel 8, Wolcott Papers.

33. Wolcott to Delany, November 16, 1795; 1 Statutes at Large 381, 383 (1794); Charleston *City Gazette and Daily Advertiser*, July 22, 1794.

34. Cabinet Meeting, Proposed Rules Governing Belligerents, August 3, 1793, *PAH*, 15:168–69; Wolcott, Circular to Collectors of Customs, October 6, 1794, M735, Reel 2; Hamilton to Holmes, September 4, 1794, *PAH*, 17:194.

35. *Talbot v. Jansen*, 3 U.S. 133 (August 22, 1795).

36. Wolcott to Delany, November 16, 1795; Oliver Wolcott Jr. to William Heth, November 24, 1797, Wolcott Papers (emphasis in original).

37. Justice James Iredell's Notes of Arguments, *Moodie v. Ship Mermaid*, *DHSCUS*, 7:94.

38. Oliver Wolcott Jr., Circular to Collectors of Customs, April 8, 1797, *ASP-C&N* 1:811.

39. Alexander Hamilton to Oliver Wolcott Jr., April 13, 1797, Reel 1, Wolcott Papers; Frederick C. Leiner, *Millions for Defense: The Subscription Warships of 1798*

(Annapolis: Naval Institute Press, 2000), 20, 122, 125, 141, 149; Benjamin Stoddard to James Sheafe, July 16, 1798, quoted ibid., 30.

40. *Gazette of the United States*, January 1, 1798, 3; *Massachusetts Mercury*, April 10, 1798, 2.

41. Harrison Gray Otis to William Heath, March 30, 1798, reprinted in the *Massachusetts Spy: Or, the Worcester Gazette*, April 25, 1798, 1. Adams transmitted the instructions lifting the ban on "vessels of the United States from sailing in an armed condition" through a Treasury Department circular to the collector of customs. See Wolcott, Circular to Collectors of Customs, March 21, 1798, in *ASP-C&N* 1:811.

42. 1 *Statutes at Large* 572, 573 (1798). Between July 1798 and December 1800, the New York Custom house issued an average of six letters of marque per month, with the highest traffic occurring in January 1799 (22). Merchant Thomas Buchanan, described by historian Joseph Scoville as a "king among merchants" in New York, received the most letters of marque with five. Bonds for Letters of Marque, 1789–1801, RG 56, #948, Archives I. Joseph Alfred Scoville, *Old Merchants of New York City* (New York: Carleton, 1864), 45.

43. *Bas v. Tingy*, 4 U.S. (4 Dall.) 37, 45–46 (1800).

44. 1 *Statutes at Large* 565 (1798).

45. Wolcott to Richard Harrison, June 21, 1799, reprinted in *DHSCUS*, 8:327 (emphasis in original).

46. Wolcott to Samuel Smith, January 23, 1800, Reel 3, Wolcott Papers.

47. Wolcott, Report to the President of U.S., July 13, 1800, Reel 3, Wolcott Papers; Extract of a Letter from a merchant in Boston, February 4, 1798, to Nicholas Gilman in Philadelphia, Reel 2, Wolcott Papers. Wolcott was also beginning to lose trust in customs officials to handle public funds. See Oliver Wolcott Jr., Report of March 10, 1798, Reel 11; Wolcott to Jedediah Huntington, November 22, 1798, Reel 11; Wolcott to Lamb, February 17, 1797, Reel 11; Report of July 24, 1799, Reel 11, Wolcott Papers.

48. Peter S. Onuf, *Jefferson's Empire: The Language of American Nationhood* (Charlottesville: University of Virginia Press, 2000); Peter S. Onuf and Peter Thompson, ed., *State and Citizen: British America and the Early United States* (Charlottesville: University of Virginia Press, 2013); James E. Lewis, *American Union and the Problem of Neighborhood: The United States and the Collapse of the Spanish Empire, 1783–1829* (Chapel Hill: University of North Carolina Press, 1998); Johann N. Neem, *Creating a Nation of Joiners: Democracy and Civil Society in Early National Massachusetts* (Cambridge, MA: Harvard University Press, 2008), 4–5.

49. Johann N. Neem, "Developing Freedom: Thomas Jefferson, the State, and Human Capability," *Studies in American Political Development* 27, no. 1 (2013): 40.

50. Drew R. McCoy, *The Elusive Republic: Political Economy in Jeffersonian America* (New York: W.W. Norton, 1980), 144–47; Crowley, *Privileges of Independence*, 110–55; John R. Nelson, *Liberty and Property: Political Economy and Policymaking in the New Nation, 1789–1812* (Baltimore: Johns Hopkins University Press, 1987), 66–79.

51. Prince, *Federalists*, 15, 275.

52. Thomas Jefferson, Memorandum on Customs Collectors, May 1793, Thomas Jefferson Papers, Series 1, General Correspondence, LOC (emphasis added); Prince, *Federalists*, 9–10; Freeman, *Affairs of Honor*, 98–99.

53. Albert Gallatin, *A Sketch of the Finances of the United States* (New York: William A. Davis, 1796), 23; Tench Coxe to Thomas Jefferson, January 10, 1801, in *The Papers of Thomas Jefferson*, ed. Barbara Oberg et al. (Princeton, NJ: Princeton University Press, 1950–2014), 33:425 (hereafter, *PTJ*). The *Aurora* reprinted in the *Philadelphia Gazette*, February 6, 1801, 3; Enrolling and Licensing Vessels in the Coasting Trade and Fisheries, 1 *Statutes at Large* 305 (1793).

54. Marcus, ed., *DHSCUS*, 8:391–95; *Priestman v. United States*, 4 U.S. 28 (1800). Gallatin to Jefferson, June 9, 1801, *PTJ*, 34:279. See also Jefferson to Levi Lincoln, June 12, 1801; and Lincoln, Opinion on the *Betsy Cathcart*, July 3, 1801, *PTJ*, 34:320–21, 497–503.

55. Jefferson to Gideon Granger, August 13, 1800, *PTJ*, 32:96; Jefferson to Caesar A. Rodney, December 21, 1800, *PTJ*, 33:336–37; Onuf, *Jefferson's Empire*, 100; Charles Pinckney to James Madison, May 26, 1801, in *The Papers of James Madison, Secretary of State Series*, ed. Robert J. Brugger et al. (Charlottesville: University Press of Virginia, 1986), 1:230.

56. Carl E. Prince, "The Passing of the Aristocracy: Jefferson's Removal of the Federalists, 1801–1805," *JAH* 57, no. 3 (1970): 570; Carl Russell Fish, *The Civil Service and the Patronage* (Cambridge, MA: Harvard University Press, 1904), 33; Remonstrance of the New Haven Merchants, June 18, 1801, *PTJ*, 34: 381–83; Thomas Jefferson to the New Haven merchants, July 12, 1801, *PTJ*, 34:554–56; Stephen R. Grossbart and David Waldstreicher, "Abraham Bishop's Vocation; or, the Mediation of Jeffersonian Politics," *JER* 18, no. 4 (1998): 617–57.

57. Aaron Burr to Albert Gallatin, April 24, 1801, in *Political Correspondence and Public Papers of Aaron Burr*, ed. Mary-Jo Kline (Princeton, NJ: Princeton University Press, 1983), 1:570, 534–38; Jefferson, Notes on New York Patronage, n.d. [after February 17, 1801], *PTJ*, 34:11; Gelston & Saltonstall Letter Book, 1791 May–1793 May, NYHS.

58. Edling, *Hercules in the Cradle*, 115; Douglas Bradburn, *The Citizenship Revolution: Politics and the Creation of the American Union, 1774–1804* (Charlottesville: University of Virginia Press, 2009), 276–77.

59. John R. Howe Jr., "Republican Thought and the Political Violence of the 1790s," *American Quarterly* 19, no. 2 (1967): 150.

60. *Annals of Congress*, 8th Cong., 2nd Sess. (February 23, 1805), 1205; Albert Gallatin, Report on Collection of Internal Revenues, July 28, 1801, *PTJ*, 34:651–55; Edward Livingston to Albert Gallatin, *Gallatin Papers*, 4:767; *PTJ*, 33:330, 331–32n.

61. J. E. Winston, "How the Louisiana Purchase Was Financed," *Louisiana Historical Quarterly* 12, no. 2 (1929): 200.

62. Jefferson, Fourth Annual Message to Congress, *Annals of Congress*, 8th Cong., 2nd Sess. (November 8, 1804), 11; Arthur Scherr, *Thomas Jefferson's Haitian Policy: Myths and Realities* (Lanham, MD: Lexington Books, 2011), 339.

63. Gallatin to Jefferson, n.d. [1804], *Writings of Albert Gallatin*, 1:211; Ronald Angelo Johnson, *Diplomacy in Black and White: John Adams, Toussaint Louverture, and Their Atlantic World Alliance* (Athens: University of Georgia Press, 2014).

64. Laurent Dubois, *Avengers of the New World: The Story of the Haitian Revolution* (Cambridge, MA: Harvard University Press, 2004) 251; Marietta Marie LeBreton, "A History of the Territory of Orleans, 1803–1812" (PhD diss., Louisiana State University, 1969), 257.

65. Albert Gallatin to Samuel Latham Mitchill, January 3, 1805, Reel 10, Gallatin Papers. Albert Gallatin to Thomas Jefferson, July 2, 1804, *Writings of Albert Gallatin*, 1:194–96, 197, 198; Scherr, *Jefferson's Haiti Policy*, 316.

66. Diary of Henry Packer Dering, Dering Papers; Dun, "'What Avenues'," 479; McDonald, "Chance of the Moment," 459–60.

67. Fulwar Skipwith, American Claims not Submitted . . . , March 14, 1802, Box 9, Causten-Pickett Papers, LOC; Tim Matthewson, "George Washington's Policy toward the Haitian Revolution," *Diplomatic History* 3, no. 3 (1979): 325; Tim Matthewson, *A Proslavery Foreign Policy: Haitian-American Relations during the Early Republic* (Westport, CT: Praeger, 2003), 45.

68. Unknown [mutil.] to Charles C. Rogers & Co., March 28, 1796, Correspondence 1796–1818–1827, # 895, RG 36, NARA-NY; Rayford Logan, *Diplomatic Relations of the United States with Haiti, 1776–1891* (Chapel Hill: University of North Carolina Press, 1941), 126–27, 129. In Philadelphia, the Haiti trade grew steadily from 1794 to 1796 before slackening gradually by 1798. Between 1799 and 1805, the trade steadily declined. Dun, "'What Avenues,'" 478; Arthur Scherr, "Arms and Men: The Diplomacy of the US Weapons Traffic with Saint-Domingue under Adams and Jefferson," *International History Review* 35, no. 3 (2013): 603.

69. C. L. R. James, *The Black Jacobins: Toussaint L'Ouverture and the San Domingo Revolution* (New York: Vintage, 1963), 245, 262.

70. Tobias Lear to James Madison, July 20, 1801, July 25, 1801, and July 27, 1801, in *Papers of James Madison*, 1:445–46, 478, and 483.

71. Tobias Lear to James Madison, February 16, 1802; February 26, 1802; February 27, 1802; and March 2, 1802, in *The Papers of James Madison, Secretary of State Series*, ed. Mary A. Hackett et al. (Charlottesville: University Press of Virginia, 1993), 2:499–500, 519, 519–20, 522; Louis Andre Pichon to James Madison, March 17, 1802, ibid., 42; Speech of William McCreery, *Annals of Congress*, 8th Cong., 2nd Sess. (December 13, 1804), 818.

72. James Madison to Louis Pichon, March 25, 1802, in *Papers of James Madison, Secretary of States Series*, 3:68–69. See Logan, *Diplomatic Relations*, 139, and more generally, 129–30, 137–39. According to one account, Jefferson pledged to channel American commerce to France "and to reduce Toussaint to starvation" on the condition that France remain at peace with Great Britain. Carl Ludwig Lokke, "Jefferson and the Leclerc Expedition," *AHR* 33, no. 2 (January 1928): 324. Scherr (*Jefferson's Haiti Policy*, 342) interprets this a bit differently that "Madison and Jefferson generally ignored Pichon's complaints."

73. Anthony Merry to James Madison, August 31, 1804; Louis Pichon to James Madison, June 6, 1804, quoted in Logan, *Diplomatic Relations*, 163–64; Louis Pichon to James Madison, May 7, 1804, *ASP-FR* 2:607.

74. George Barnewell to James Madison, September 6, 1804, *ASP-FR* 2:607; *Dennis v. The Lear*, 7 F. Cas. 476, 477 (November 1805).

75. No. 160, Maryland Insurance Company, Box 32, Folder 1, Causten-Pickett Papers.

76. Caleb Cushing, "Saint Domingo Cases" [n.d.], Box 1, Folder "St. Domingo Cases," Causten-Pickett Papers, LOC-MSS; Killen & Williams to Robert and Alexander

McKim, January 23, 1804, Fulwar Skipwith Correspondence, L-Q, Box 8, Causten-Pickett Papers.

77. Alexander McKim to Samuel Sterret and Mark Pringle, May 7, 1806, Baltimore Insurance Company Correspondence, Box 19, Causten-Pickett Papers.

78. Peter Muhlenberg to Albert Gallatin, June 4, 1804, reprinted in Albert Gallatin to Thomas Jefferson, June 7, 1807, Reel 9, Gallatin Papers; and reprinted in Scherr, *Jefferson's Haitian Policy*, 384.

79. Muhlenberg used a similarly creative approach while collecting internal duties in 1802. Charlotte Crane, *"Pennington v. Coxe*: A Glimpse at the Federal Government at the End of the Federalist Era," *Virginia Tax Review* 23 (2003): 430–36.

80. Albert Gallatin to Thomas Jefferson, July 2, 1804, *Writings of Albert Gallatin*, 1:198; Joshua Michelangelo Stein, "The Right to Violence: Assault Prosecution in New York, 1760–1840" (PhD diss., University of California, Los Angeles, 2009), 48–59; Stein, "Privatizing Violence: A Transformation in the Jurisprudence of Assault," *Law and History Review* 30, no. 2 (2012), 443–47.

81. Gallatin to Jefferson, June 7, 1804, *Writings of Gallatin*, 1:194–95; Muhlenberg to Gallatin, quoted in Gallatin to Jefferson, July 2, 1805, ibid., 1:198–99.

82. Friend to Truth and Justice [pseud.], *Examination of the Memorial of the Owners and Underwriters of the American Ship the New Jersey . . .* (Philadelphia: s.n., 1805); Petition of Philip Nicklin & Robert E. Griffith, November 16, 1804, Philadelphia Forfeiture Appeals, RG 36, Entry 42-E-1-7-1.6, NARA-Phila.

83. *United States v. Peters* (1795), 3 U.S. 121, 131; *United States v. Worrall*, 2 U.S. 384, 400 (1798); Kathryn T. Preyer, "Jurisdiction to Punish: Federal Authority, Federalism and the Common Law of Crimes in the Early Republic," *Law and History Review* 4, no. 2 (1986): 232; Richard Peters to Timothy Pickering, December 5, 1807, Box 1, Folder 3, Papers of Timothy Pickering, MHS.

84. Peters to Pickering, December 8, 1806, Box 1, Folder 3, Pickering Papers.

85. *Annals of Congress*, 8th Cong., 2nd Sess. (November 8, 1804), 11; Scherr, *Jefferson's Haiti Policy*, 409–36. Gallatin's influence is seen in Albert Gallatin to Thomas Jefferson, October [n.d.] 1804, *Writings of Albert Gallatin*, 1:211. Thomas Jefferson to Thomas Paine, June 5, 1805, *Writings of Thomas Jefferson*, ed. Albert Ellery Bergh (Washington, DC: Thomas Jefferson Memorial Association, 1907), 11:81.

86. *Annals of Congress*, 8th Cong., 2nd Sess., 723 (draft bill; Clay); 812 (Eppes), 820 (Eppes), 834 (Jackson) (December 13 and 14, 1804).

87. *Annals of Congress*, 8th Cong., 2nd Sess., 812, 826.

88. William Plumer, *William Plumer's Memorandum of Proceedings in the United States, 1803–1807*, ed. Everett S. Brown (New York: DaCapo Press, 1969), 188, 189; Memorial of the New York Chamber of Commerce, December 21, 1804, reprinted in *ASP-C&N* 1:582.

89. Donald R. Hickey, "America's Response to the Slave Revolt in Haiti, 1791–1806," *JER* 2, no. 4 (1982): 373; Frank A. Cassell, *Merchant Congressman in the Young Republic* (Madison: University of Wisconsin Press, 1971), 118–19, 119; 2 *Statutes at Large* 342 (March 3, 1805).

90. 9 *Annals of Congress* 28–29 (December 20, 1805); Proclamation of Louis Ferrand, June 6, 1805, *ASP-FR* 2:728.

91. 4 June 1805 *Voltaire*, Foreign Outward Cargo Manifests, January 1805 to June 1805, Entry 1059, RG 36, NARA-Phila. My thanks to Dr. Michelle Mormul for drawing my attention to this document. For a general overview of Girard's commercial prowess and the voyage of the *Voltaire*, see Albert J. Gares, "Stephen Girard's West Indian Trade, 1789–1812," *Pennsylvania Magazine of History and Biography* 72, no. 4 (1948): 311–42.

92. Jefferson to Paine, June 5, 1805; *Rose v. Himely*, 20 F. Cas. 1179, 1181 (1805).

93. *Annals of Congress*, 9th Cong., 1st Sess. (December 20, 1805), 28–29. Peter Linebaugh, "All the Atlantic Mountains Shook," *Labor/La Travailleur* 10, no. 1 (1982): 119. Notably, the Federalists, despite cultivating close ties with Toussaint L'Ouverture during the Quasi-War, had worried about the possible effects of Haitian freedom on American slavery. Hickey, "America's Response to the Slave Revolt in Haiti," 375–76.

94. Plumer, *Plumer's Memorandum*, 379. Jefferson expressed his fears about fraying relations with France in his annual message to Congress, *Annals of Congress*, 9th Cong., 1st Sess. (December 10, 1805), 18–19; J. Holland Rose, "British West India Commerce as a Factor in the Napoleonic War," *Cambridge Historical Journal* 31, no. 1 (1929): 39.

95. Samuel Latham Mitchill to Catherine Mitchill, n.d. [1806?], Samuel Latham Mitchill Papers, 1802–1815, Clements Library, University of Michigan (emphasis added).

96. *Annals of Congress* (February 25, 1806), 510.

97. David Gelston to Albert Gallatin, January 12, 1807, Box 5, Folder 5, Gelston Papers: Gabriel Christie to McLam Turner, November 11, 1806, Baltimore Customs Letter Book.

98. Hickey, "America's Response to the Slave Revolt in Haiti," 378; David Gelston to Albert Gallatin, January 12, 1807, Box 5, Folder 5; Gelston to Nathaniel Sanford, January 20, 1807, Box 15, Folder 6, Gelston Papers.

99. Plumer, *Plumer's Memorandum*, 387.

100. Hickey, "America's Response to the Slave Revolt in Haiti," 378.

101. Hamilton to Olney, April 2, 1793.

102. Noble E. Cunningham Jr., *Jefferson v. Hamilton: Confrontations That Shaped a Nation* (New York: Macmillan, 2000); John M. Murrin et al., *Liberty, Equality, Power: A History of the American People to 1877* (New York: Cengage Learning, 2008), 220–21.

CHAPTER 5

1. Onuf, *Jefferson's Empire*, 94; McCoy, *Elusive Republic*, 211–19.

2. Donald R. Hickey, *The War of 1812: A Forgotten Conflict* (Urbana: University of Illinois Press, 1989), 19–24; Reginald Horsman, *Causes of the War of 1812* (Philadelphia: University of Pennsylvania Press, 1962). For accounts of the different measures, see Herbert Heaton, "Non-Importation, 1806–1812," *Journal of Economic History* 1, no. 2 (Nov. 1941): 178–98; Robert Mannix, "The Embargo: Its Administration, Impact, and Enforcement" (PhD diss., New York University 1975); Burton Spivak, *Jefferson's English Crisis: Commerce, Embargo, and the Republican Revolution* (Charlottesville: University Press of Virginia, 1979); Donald R. Hickey, "American Trade Restrictions during the War of 1812," *JAH* 68, no. 3 (1981): 517–38.

3. Bradford Perkins, "Sir William Scott and the *Essex*," *WMQ* 13, no. 2 (1956): 171.

4. Eliga Gould, "The Making of an Atlantic State System: Britain and the United

States, 1795–1825," in *Britain and America Go to War: The Impact of War and Warfare in Anglo-America, 1754–1815* (Gainesville: University Press of Florida, 2004), 251; "Sentence of the Vice-Admiralty Court of Nassau, New Providence, in the Case of the Brix Essex, Joseph Orne Master," reprinted in Perkins, "Sir William Scott and the *Essex*," 177–78; Zach Banker to Stephen Zacharie, September 10, 1803, Box 13, Miscellaneous Correspondence, Causten-Pickett Papers; Hickey, *War of 1812*, 12–16; also Bradford Perkins, *Prologue to War: England and the United States, 1805–1812* (Berkeley: University of California Press), 1–139.

5. Matthew Taylor Raffety, *The Republic Afloat: Law, Honor, and Citizenship in Maritime America* (Chicago: University of Chicago Press, 2013) 176–78; Brunsman, *Evil Necessity*, 246–47. See also Kevin Costello, "Habeas Corpus and Military and Naval Impressment, 1756–1816," *Journal of Legal History* 29, no. 2 (2008): 240; James Madison, Report to United States House of Representatives, March 5, 1806, *Annals of Congress*, 9th Cong., 1st Sess. (March 8, 1806), 635; 1 Statutes at Large 477 (1796); 2 Statutes at Large 203 (1803).

6. Raffety, *Republic Afloat*, 158–59: see also Thomas Pinckney, List of Representations Made to Lord Grenville, 1792–1796, n.d. [1796?], Box 15, Folder 1796-July, Charles Cotesworth Pinckney Papers, LOC.

7. Raffety, *Republic Afloat*, 175–77.

8. 2 Statutes at Large 379 (April 18, 1806); 2 Statutes at Large 246 (March 2, 1807); 2 Statutes at Large 195 (1815). The slave trade prohibition partially stemmed from a different constitutional basis than the commerce power. Article 1, section 9, gave Congress the authority to tax imported slaves at the rate of $10 per slave. It also permitted prohibition of the foreign slave trade on January 1, 1808, which became the operative date of the statute enacted in 1807.

9. Hickey, *War of 1812*, 19–24; Gordon S. Wood, *Empire of Liberty: A History of the Early Republic, 1789–1815* (New York: Oxford University Press, 2009), 648–58; Robert W. Tucker and David C. Hendrickson, *Empire of Liberty: The Statecraft of Thomas Jefferson* (New York: Oxford University Press, 1990), 204.

10. 2 Statutes at Large 379 at 380 (1806); 2 Statutes at Large 528 at 530 (1809); 2 Statutes at Large 451 at 452. See also the supplementary Embargo Act of March 12, 1808, 2 Statutes at Large 473 at 474, for clarification of the duties of the "collector of the port" with regard to these bonds. 2 Statutes at Large 506 (1809); 2 Statutes at Large 759 at 762 (1812).

11. 2 Statutes at Large 451 at 452 (1807); 3 Statutes at Large 98 (1814); 2 Statutes at Large 490 (1808). 2 Statutes at Large 411 (1806) gave the president the power to suspend the nonimportation law of 1806 at his will. 3 Statutes at Large 195 at 200 (1815).

12. The House Committee on Commerce and Manufactures justified the Embargo of 1808–9 as only the latest iteration of a string of commercial restrictions dating back to 1794. H.R. 10A-C2.1, Report of Mr. Newton from the Committee on Commerce and Manufactures, to whom was referred on the 4th instant, the petition of sundry merchants and traders in the city of Philadelphia, January 11, 1808, M1711, Roll 1, Unbound Records of the U.S. House of Representatives, 10th Congress, 1807–1809, RG233, NARA-DC.

13. William Lewis to David Lewis, April 30, 1808, Box 2, Folder 65, David Lewis Papers, LCP; J. H. Rose, "Napoleon and English Commerce," *English Historical*

Review 8, no. 32 (1893): 714–15; Lawrence S. Kaplan, "Jefferson, the Napoleonic Wars, and the Balance of Power," *WMQ* 14, no. 2 (1957): 203; Lance E. Davis and Stanley Engerman, *Naval Blockades in Peace and War: An Economic History since 1750* (New York: Cambridge University Press, 2006), 25–52; Gavin Daly, "English Smugglers, the Channel, and the Napoleonic Wars, 1800–1814," *Journal of British Studies* 46, no. 1 (2007): 30–46; Daly, "Napoleon and the 'City of Smugglers,' 1810–1814," *Historical Journal* 50, no. 2 (2007): 333–52.

14. Steven Watts, *Romance of Real Life: Charles Brockden Brown and the Origins of American Culture* (Baltimore: Johns Hopkins University Press, 1994) 195–97; Thomas Cooper, *Political Arithmetic*, in *Political Writings of Thomas Cooper*, ed. Udo Thiel (Sterling, VA: Thoemmes Press, 2001), 33; McCoy, *Elusive Republic*, 166–73; H.R. 10A-C2.1, Report of Mr. Newton from the Committee on Commerce and Manufactures, January 11, 1808, M1711, Roll 1. Yet it would be wrong to label the Republican Party as anticommerce. See McCoy, *Elusive Republic*, 211–15. Lawrence A. Peskin, "Conspiratorial Anglophobia and the War of 1812," *JAH* 98, no. 3 (2011): 654–55.

15. Laura Rigal, *The American Manufactory: Art, Labor, and the World of Things in the Early Republic* (Princeton, NJ: Princeton University Press, 1998), 15; Lawrence A. Peskin, *Manufacturing Revolution: The Intellectual Origins of Early American Industry* (Baltimore: Johns Hopkins University Press, 2003), 134; McCoy, *Elusive Republic*, 217–18, 226–29; Thomas Coles to Tench Coxe, March 30, 1812, Thomas Coles Letter Book, Ms. 360, RIHS; Cooke, *Tench Coxe*, 424; Ruhl J. Bartlett, "Industrial Survey, 1811," *Journal of the American Military Institute* 4, no. 4 (1940): 255.

16. Richard Cutts to Thomas Cutts, November 7, 1808, Box 1, Folder 7, Key-Cutts Papers, LOC; Cohen, "'Millions of Luxurious Citizens'," 92.

17. Thomas Jefferson to John Page, July 17, 1807, in *The Works of Thomas Jefferson in Twelve Volumes*, ed. Paul Leicester Ford (New York: G.P. Putnam's Sons, 1904–5), 10:470; Paul A. Gilje, *Free Trade and Sailors' Rights in the War of 1812* (New York: Cambridge University Press, 2013), 154–65; Robert E. Cray Jr., "Remembering the USS Chesapeake: The Politics of Maritime Death and Impressment," *JER* 25, no. 3 (Fall 2005), 445–74.

18. Wallis, "Federal Government Debt by Type, 1791–1970," Table Ea 650–661, in *Historical Statistics*, http://dx.doi.org/10.1017/ISBN-9780511132971.Ea584–678; Stabile, *Origins of American Public Finance*, 152.

19. Edwin G. Burrows and Mike Wallace, *Gotham: A History of New York City to 1898* (New York: Oxford University Press, 1999), 411; John Teackle to Charles Nicoll Bancker, January 9, 1808, Bancker Letters; H.R 10A-F3.3, Petition of the Merchants & Traders of Philadelphia, January 11, 1808, M1711, Roll 4; Charles Machin Memoir, 1807–1820, Clements Library, University of Michigan.

20. James McCulloh to Gabriel Duval, July 8, 1808, Port of Baltimore, Baltimore Customs Letter Book; *The Repertory*, January 1, 1808, 2. Extract of a letter from a gentleman in New York, *The Public Advertiser*, January 25, 1808, 2; Nathaniel Ruby, *A Serious Expostulation with the President & Congress* (Philadelphia: for the author, 1808), 4.

21. Henry Millen, "The Embargo, A Song Composed and Sung at Dover, July 4,

1808," reprinted in Brighton, *Port of Portsmouth*, x; Alexandria *Advertiser*, February 9, 1808, 3.

22. William Thomas, New Hampshire Fire and Marine Insurance Company, Sailing List, Portsmouth, N.H., 1807–1819, Shipping Papers Collection, Log Books, Etc., 1807–1866, Box 3, NHHS; Jeffrey A. Frankel, "The 1807–1809 Embargo against Great Britain," *Journal of Economic History* 42, no. 2 (June 1982): 297–98, 306. Frankel draws the conclusions that "the American government could and (by the end of the year) did enforce the Embargo to a much greater extent than was realized by contemporaries or by later historians"; and "the evidence points toward greater economic suffering on the part of Britain than the United States." Frankel, 301, 307. Though it is clear that the embargo had some impact on the British consumer market, it is equally clear that the embargo failed to achieve the goal of softening the British position on impressments and American commercial sovereignty. The ability of American smugglers to reach British markets no doubt played a role in limiting the impact of the embargo.

23. 2 *Statutes at Large* 380; 2 *Statutes at Large* 341–42; 2 *Statutes at Large* 506; 2 *Statutes at Large* 530.

24. Albert Gallatin to Thomas Jefferson, February 29, 1808, Reel 40, Jefferson Papers; LeBreton, "History of the Territory of Orleans," 247; *Poulson's American Daily Advertiser*, March 7, 1808, 3; James McCulloh to Albert Gallatin, April 22, 1808, Baltimore Customs Letter Book.

25. John Teackle to Charles Nicoll Banker, March 15, 1808, Bancker Papers.

26. Albert Gallatin to Thomas Jefferson, March 12, 1808; and April 1, 1808, Reel 40; May 5, 1808, and May 23, 1808, Reel 41, Jefferson Papers.

27. William Ellery to Charles Collins, November 10, 1808, Box 4, Folder: Letters-1808, Bristol/Warren Customs Correspondence, RIHS; John Darby to Albert Gallatin, July 2, 1808; Francis Cook to Joseph Wilson, February 2, 1809, Marblehead Customs House Records, 1789–1870, MSS 922, Baker Business Library Historical Collections.

28. Mashaw, "Reluctant Nationalists," 1651; Thomas Jefferson to Albert Gallatin, February 28, 1808, Reel 40, Jefferson Papers. See also Gallatin to Jefferson, December 18, 1808; and February 29, 1808, Reel 40, Jefferson Papers; Spivak, *Jefferson's English Crisis*, 163–64.

29. J. Brice to Unknown [Collector of the Port of Vienna], April 7, 1808; Brice to Unknown [Collector of the Port of Georgetown], April 11, 1808, Baltimore Customs Letter Book.

30. F. P. Prucha, *The Great Father: The United States Government and the American Indians* (Omaha: University of Nebraska Press, 1984), 121; Jacob Hitzheimer, "Extracts from the Diary of Jacob Hitzheimer, of Philadelphia, 1768–1798 (continued)," *Pennsylvania Magazine of History and Biography* 16, no. 2 (1892): 163; Robert F. Oaks, "Philadelphia Merchants and the First Continental Congress," *Pennsylvania History* 40, no. 2 (1973): 156 n. 25.

31. John Teackle to Charles Nicoll Bancker, February 27, 1808, and March 15, 1808, Bancker Letters; Gallatin to Steele, September 20, 1808, Port of Philadelphia, Letters Received 1808–1815, Vol. 1, RG 36, Entry 1049, NARA-Phila; William Duane to Thomas Jefferson, August 9, 1808, Reel 41, Jefferson Papers.

32. John Steele to Chandler Price, September 19, 1809, Port of Philadelphia, Letters Received from the District Attorney, 1808–1826, RG 36, #1049D, NARA-Phila.

33. Jefferson to Gallatin, December 7, 1808, Reel 42, Jefferson Papers.

34. Gallatin to Jefferson, May 10, 1808. Jefferson approved the idea, according to Jefferson to Gallatin, May 17, 1808, Reel 41, Jefferson Papers. James G. Cusick, *The Other War of 1812: The Patriot War and the American Invasion of Spanish East Florida* (Gainesville: University Press of Florida, 2003), 53.

35. Levi Lincoln to Thomas Jefferson, September 7, 1808, Reel 42, Jefferson Papers. Joshua Mitchell Smith, "The Rogues of 'Quoddy: Smuggling in the Maine New Brunswick Borderlands" (PhD diss., University of Maine, 2003), 262, and more generally on the Maine-Canada borderlands during the embargo, 251–83; Jefferson to James Sullivan, July 16, 1808, Reel 412; Gallatin to Jefferson, September 16, 1808, Reel 42, Jefferson Papers.

36. Albert Gallatin to John Steele, Gallatin to Steele, December 1, 1808, Port of Philadelphia, Letters Received 1808–1815, Vol. 1, RG 36, Entry 1049, NARA-Phila; Smith, "Rogues of Quoddy," 276.

37. David Gelston, Marginalia on List of Vessels Seized at the Port of New York, Box 16, Folder 13, Gelston Papers; Douglas Lamar-Jones, "'The Caprice of Juries': The Enforcement of the Jeffersonian Embargo in Massachusetts," *American Journal of Legal History* 24, no. 4 (1980): 326; Port of Philadelphia, Statement of Facts in Forfeiture Cases Appealed to the Secretary of the Treasury, 1792–1918, RG 36, Entry 42-E-1-7-1.6, NARA-Phila.

38. Albert Gallatin to Thomas Jefferson, July 29, 1808, Reel 41, Jefferson Papers. See also Gallatin to Jefferson, September 2, 1808, Reel 42; Gallatin to Jefferson, September 5, 1808, Reel 42.

39. Thomas Jefferson to Albert Gallatin, December 7, 1808, Reel 42, Jefferson Papers; Jefferson to Gallatin, December 5, Reel 42, Jefferson Papers.

40. Abraham Bishop to John Law, March 11, 1809, Bishop Papers, Yale University; Waldstreicher and Grossbart, "Abraham Bishop's Vocation"; Mattern, *Benjamin Lincoln*, 212–13.

41. McCoy, *Elusive Republic*, 211; Cassell, *Merchant Congressman in the Young Republic*; Ronald M. Baumann, "John Swanwick: Spokesman for 'Merchant-Republicanism' in Philadelphia, 1790–1798," *Pennsylvania Magazine of History and Biography* 97, no. 2 (Apr. 1973): 131–82.

42. 2 *Statutes at Large* 499 at 501 (1808).

43. Thomas Jefferson to Albert Gallatin, May 6, 1808, Reel 41, Jefferson Papers.

44. George L. Haskins, "Law versus Politics in the Early Years of the Marshall Court," *University of Pennsylvania Law Review* 130, no. 1 (Nov. 1981): 15; Albert Gallatin, Circular to Collectors of Customs, May 6, 1808, M735, Reel 2.

45. Affidavit of Adam Gilchrist and J. Sanford Barker, May 24, 1808, reprinted in *Ex parte Adam Gilchrist, & others vs. The Collector of the Port of Charleston*, reprinted in the *Monitor*, June 11, 1808, 3; Richard Marriotte Pugsley, *The Navigator, Or Mariners' Guide* (Jersey City: New Jersey Paint Works, 1918), 131; Lynn Harris, "South Carolina Shipyards: Labour, Logistics, Lumber, and Ladies," *Journal of Maritime Archaeology* 5, no. 1 (2010): 20.

46. Affidavit of Simon Theus, reprinted in *Ex parte Adam Gilchrist, & others vs. The Collector of the Port of Charleston*, reprinted in the *Monitor*, June 11, 1808, 3.

47. *United States v. The Hawke*, 26 F. Cas. 233 (1794).

48. Richard E. Ellis, *The Jeffersonian Crisis: Courts and Politics in the Young Republic* (New York: Oxford University Press, 1971), 238–39.

49. *Gilchrist v. Collector of Charleston*, 10 F. Cas. 355 at 356, 357. A good description of Johnson's logic is found in Thomas Jefferson to Charles Cotesworth Pinckney, July 18, 1808, Reel 41, Jefferson Papers.

50. *Gilchrist v. Collector of Charleston*, 10 F. Cas. 355 at 356; Mashaw, *Creating the Administrative Constitution*, 107.

51. Caesar A. Rodney to Thomas Jefferson, July 15, 1808, reprinted in *Gilchrist v. Collector of Charleston*, 10 F. Cas. 355 at 358–59; Mashaw, *Creating the Administrative Constitution*, 108.

52. *Gilchrist v. Collector of Charleston*, 10 F. Cas. 335 at 360.

53. Thomas Jefferson to Charles Cotesworth Pinckney, July 18, 1808, Reel 41, Jefferson Papers.

54. Albert Gallatin to Thomas Jefferson, October 13, 1808, Reel 42, Jefferson Papers.

55. Albert Gallatin to James McCulloch, October 14, 1808; October 24, 1808, Baltimore Customs Correspondence.

56. McCulloh to Gallatin, May 19, 1808, Baltimore Customs Letter Book; James McCulloch to Albert Gallatin, January 3, 1809, Reel 3, M178; McCulloh to Gallatin, November 9, 1808, Baltimore Customs Letter Book.

57. Lamar-Jones, "'Caprice of Juries,'" 310, 326, 328–29; William Ellery to Albert Gallatin, June 1, 1809, Reel 19, Gallatin Papers; Mashaw, *Creating the Administrative Constitution*, 108–12.

58. LeBreton, "History of the Territory of Orleans," 257; David Foster Long, *Nothing Too Daring: A Biography of Commodore David Porter, 1780–1843* (Annapolis: United States Naval Institute, 1970), 44; McCulloh to Allen McLane, June 21, 1808, Baltimore Customs Letter Book; Thomas Coles to Albert Gallatin, March 27, 1811, Reel 22, Gallatin Papers.

59. Joseph Whipple to Albert Gallatin, June 10, 1809, Reel 19; March 21, 1810, Reel 20; April 6, 1810, Reel 20, Gallatin Papers. See also John Shore to Albert Gallatin, February 26, 1810, Reel 20, Gallatin Papers. David Gelston to Albert Gallatin, November 20, 1811, quoted in Albert Gallatin to Samuel Smith, December 16, 1811, Reel 23, Gallatin Papers; Addin Lewis to Albert Gallatin, June 26, 1811, Lewis Family Papers, Box 1, Folder 1, MS 624, Yale University.

60. John Wells to David Gelston, April 28, 1809, Box 3, Folder 10, Gelston Papers.

61. *Bristol v. Burt*, 7 Johns. 254 (November 1810); Peter Sailly to Albert Gallatin, October 8, 1811, Reel 23, Gallatin Papers; *John M'Fadden versus Joseph Otis and Others*, 6 Mass. (6 Tyng) 323. The same court seems to have granted a new trial for Otis after he appealed a trespass verdict against him. Ibid. at 323. On the private indemnification bills, see James E. Pfander and Jonathan L. Hunt, "Public Wrongs and Private Bills: Indemnification and Private Accountability in the Early Republic," *New York University Law Review* 85 (2010): 1863–1931. On the use of common-law suits against imperial customs officials, see chapter 1.

62. David Gelston to Joseph McIlwaine, February 24, 1810, Box 1, Folder 6, Gelston Papers; *Gelston v. Johnson*, 3 N.J.L. 207 (February 1810).

63. Schooner *Courtney Norton* [Legal Memorandum], n.d., Box 20, Folder 15, Gelston Papers.

64. *Imlay v. Sands*, 1 Cai. R. 566 at 573 (February 1804); *Seaman v. Patten*, 2 Cai R. 312 at 314 (February 1805); *Woodham v. Gelston*, 1 Johns. 134 at 137 (February 1806).

65. *The Isabella*, 13 F. Cas. 161 at 163, 164 (April 1810); *The Enterprise*, 8 F. Cas. 732 at 734–35 (September 1810); *The William Gray*, 29 F. Cas. 1300 at 1302 (September 1810).

66. Smith, *Borderland Smuggling*, 63, 64; Worcester *Gazette*, May 18, 1808, 2; Jefferson to Gallatin, April 19, 1808, Reel 41, Jefferson Papers; John J. Duffy et al., *The Vermont Encyclopedia* (Burlington: University of Vermont Press, 2003), 153; H. N. Muller, "Smuggling into Canada: How the Champlain Valley Defied Jefferson's Embargo," *Vermont History* 38, no. 1 (1970): 5–21.

67. Abraham Bishop to Jonathan Law, March 11, 1809, Bishop Letterbook, MS352, Miscellaneous Manuscripts Collection, University Archives, Sterling Memorial Library, Yale University.

68. Nathan Sage to Albert Gallatin, November 15, 1811; Peter Sailly to Albert Gallatin, November 12, 1811, Reel 23, Gallatin Papers.

69. Hart Massey to Albert Gallatin, November 8, 1811; November 12, 1811, Reel 23; Hart Massey to Albert Gallatin, n.d. [1812?], Reel 24, Gallatin Papers. Notably, on the Gulf Coast, the army repeatedly refused to aid customs officials to enforce commercial restrictions. Addin Lewis to Albert Gallatin, December 24, 1811, Lewis Family Papers, Box 1, Folder 1, Yale University.

70. Hamilton to Olney, April 2, 1793, *PAH*, 16:277.

71. Jeremiah Olney to Albert Gallatin, January 25, 1809, Reel 23, M178, Archives II. See also Olney to Gallatin, December 13, 1808; and January 9, 1809, ibid.

72. William Ellery to William Stedman, February 8, 1809, William Ellery Papers, Box 1, Folder 1805–9, Mss 407, RIHS. See also Addin Lewis to Albert Gallatin, June 26, 1811, Lewis Family Papers, Box 1, Folder 1, Yale University.

73. 1 *Statutes* 755 (June 18, 1812); Richard W. Maas, "'Difficult to Relinquish Territory Which Had Been Conquered': Expansionism and the War of 1812," *Diplomatic History* 39, no. 1 (2015): 71; Troy Bickham, *The Weight of Vengeance: The United States, the British Empire, and the War of 1812* (New York: Oxford University Press, 2012), 27, 85–86.

74. *Annals*, 12th Cong., 1st Sess. (November 5, 1811), 13–14.

75. Gilje, *Free Trade and Sailors' Rights*, 157–70, 194–95; Cray, "Remembering the USS Chesapeake"; Bickham, *Weight of Vengeance*, 28–36.

76. 2 *Statutes at Large* 700 at 701 (April 4, 1812). A few days later, Congress also passed a nonexportation law. 2 *Statutes at Large* 700 (April 14, 1812); Hickey, *War of 1812*, 39.

77. Hickey, *War of 1812*, 170; Thomas H. Williams to Albert Gallatin, July 20, 1813; William Jones to Peter F. Dubourg, M178, Reel 16; William C. Davis, *Pirates Lafitte: The Treacherous World of the Corsairs of the Gulf* (New York: Harcourt, 2005), 126; Addin Lewis to Lt. Col. John W. Bawyer, March 7, 1813; Addin Lewis to George W. Campbell, August 8, 1814, Box 1, Folder 1, Lewis Papers; Smith, *Borderland Smuggling*,

87–89; H. N. Muller III, "'A Traiterous and Diabolical Traffic': The Commerce of the Champlain-Richelieu Corridor during the War of 1812," *Vermont History* 44, no. 2 (1976): 78–96; Charles Simms to Alexander J. Dallas, March 18, 1816, M178.

78. Hickey, "American Trade Restrictions," 522 n. 27; David Gelston to Albert Gallatin, April 28, 1812; Gelston to Gallatin, April 29, 1812; Gelston to Gallatin, May 5, 1812, Reel 1, M588, NARA; Dearborn to Lemuel Trescott, Collector Lubeck [Quoddy], April 26, 1815, RG 36, Collector's Letters, NARA-Boston; Reginald C. Stuart, *Civil-Military Relations during the War of 1812* (Santa Barbara: ABC CLIO, 2009), 105–6.

79. Herbert Sawyer, License to Robert Elwall, n.d., reprinted in *The Julia*, 14 F. Cas. 27 (May 1813), 28–29; 2 *Statutes at Large*, 778 at 781; Hickey, "American Trade Restrictions," 524. See also Smith, *Borderland Smuggling*, 89; Brian Arthur, *How Britain Won the War of 1812: The Royal Navy's Blockades of the United States, 1812–1815* (Rochester, NY: Boydell & Brewer, 2011), 39, 71, 141, 155; Jann M. Witt, "Smuggling and Blockade-Running during the Anglo-Danish War from 1807 to 1814," in *Revisiting Napoleon's Continental System: Local, Regional, and European Experiences*, ed. Katherine Aaslestad and Johan Joor (New York: Palgrave, 2015), 158–59; Alan Taylor, *Civil War of 1812* (New York: Knopf, 2010), 269–79, 290–92.

80. W. Freeman Galpin, "The American Grain Trade to the Spanish Penninsula, 1810–1814," *AHR* 28, no. 1 (1922): 25.

81. Maryland Memorandum Book, 1791–1817, LOC-MSS; Admiral Sir David Milne to Unknown, April 9, 1812, reprinted in Edgar Erskine Hume, "Letters Written during the War of 1812 by the British Naval Commander in American Waters (Sir David Milne)," *WMQ* 10, no. 4 (1930): 286; Gavin Daly, *The British Soldier in the Peninsular War: Encounters with Spain and Portugal, 1808–1814* (New York: Palgrave Macmillan, 2013), 118.

82. David Gelston to Albert Gallatin, June 30, 1813, Box 6, Folder 2, Gelston Papers; Paul A. Gilje, "The Baltimore Riots of 1812 and the Breakdown of the Anglo-American Mob Tradition," *Journal of Social History* 13, no. 4 (1980): 551; James H. McCulloh to Albert Gallatin, July 15, 1812, M178, Reel 3; Gallatin to McCulloh, July 21, 1812, M178, Reel 2.

83. On the British blockade policy and interaction with American vessels, see Arthur, *How Britain Won the War of 1812*, 25–26, 38–40, 70–73, 96–130.

84. Thomas Coles to William Jones, January 27, 1814; Thomas Coles Letterbook MS 360, RIHS; William Jones, Naval General Order, July 29, 1813, Letters Sent by the Secretary of the Navy to Officers, 1798–1868, M149, Reel 11, NARA; C. K. Gardner, "General Orders," August 5, 1813, *Niles Register* 4 (1813): 386. Albert Gallatin had left the Treasury Department to join the commission conducting peace negotiations with Great Britain. However, by this time, after over a decade at the helm of the Treasury, Gallatin felt that he had lost the support of Congress. See Thomas K. McGraw, *The Founders and Finance: How Hamilton, Gallatin, and Other Immigrants Forged a New Economy* (Cambridge, MA: Harvard University Press, 2012), 306–14.

85. William Jones to James McCulloh, June 21, 1813, M178, Reel 2; Levi Hollingsworth to William Thompson, July 23, 1813, and August 3, 1813, Hollingsworth Papers, Box 15, Folder 4, Clements Library, University of Michigan.

86. Protest of Abner Snow, Captain of the *Baltic Trader*, August 5, 1813, M125, Reel 30; William Barnewell to Charles Morris, August 4, 1813, ibid.

87. Customs revenue figures are drawn from Wallis, *Historical Statistics*, Table Ea588–593; Hickey, *War of 1812*, 215.

88. Edling, *Hercules in the Cradle*, 120, 124, 127, 132–35, 138–39; Hickey, *War of 1812*, 165–66.

89. Alan Taylor, *The Internal Enemy: Slavery and War in Virginia, 1772–1832* (New York: W.W. Norton, 2013), 322, 321, 323.

90. Anon. [Charleston, South Carolina] to Thomas Jefferson, June 1, 1808, Reel 41, Jefferson Papers; Jefferson to Gallatin, October 25, 1808, Reel 42, Jefferson Papers.

91. 2 *Statutes at Large* 506 at 509 (January 9, 1809); 3 *Statutes at Large* 88 at 91 (December 17, 1813); *The Columbian*, December 12, 1813, 3.

92. Samuel Smith to Albert Gallatin, November 18, 1811, Reel 23; Gallatin, Papers—Committee on Evasion, November, n.d. [1811], Reel 23, Gallatin Papers; Albert Gallatin, Evasions of the Non-Importation Act, November 26, 1811, *ASP-C&N* 1:873.

BOSTON, 1817

1. H. A.S. Dearborn to Alexander J. Dallas, June 29, 1816, Collectors Letters, NARA-Boston. On the location of Boston custom houses, see Pitkin, *Three Centuries of Custom Houses*, 70–72.

2. H. A. S. Dearborn to William H. Crawford, November 17, 1818, Collectors Letters, NARA-Boston.

3. Dearborn to Crawford, July 18, 1818; October 7, 1818; October 14, 1818; January 15, 1819; July 27, 1820; September 15, 1821; RG 36, Collector's Letters, NARA-Boston.

4. H. A. S. Dearborn to Richard Rush, October 16, 1825, RG 36, Collector's Letters, NARA-Boston.

CHAPTER 6

1. New York *Evening Post*, June 5, 1817, reprinted in *The Papers of James Monroe*, ed., Daniel Preston (Westport, CT: Greenwood Press, 2003), 1:103; H. A. S Dearborn to T. Aspinwall, July 11, 1817, H. A. S. Dearborn Papers, Clements Library, University of Michigan; Hartford *Times*, July 1, 1817, in *Papers of James Monroe*, 1:134; David Waldstreicher, *In the Midst of Perpetual Fetes: The Making of American Nationalism, 1776–1820* (Chapel Hill: University of North Carolina Press, 1997), 302; James Monroe, quoted in Waldstreicher, 302. Monroe's tour sought to replicate George Washington's of the early 1790s; Waldstreicher, 121. On the immortalization of George Washington in the early nineteenth century, see Francois Furstenberg, *In the Name of the Father: Washington's Legacy, Slavery, and the Making of a Nation* (New York: Penguin Press, 2006), 35–37. The self-consciously optimistic sensibility of these years is discussed by C. Edward Skeen, *1816: America Rising* (Lexington: University Press of Kentucky, 2003); and Joyce O. Appleby, *Inheriting the Revolution: The First Generation of Americans* (Cambridge, MA: Belknap Press of Harvard University Press, 2000).

2. Kyle G. Volk, *Moral Minorities and the Making of American Democracy* (New York: Oxford University Press, 2014); Edwards, *People and Their Peace*, 220–85; John Lauritz Larson, *Internal Improvement: National Public Works and the Promise of Popu-*

lar Government in the Early United States (Chapel Hill: University of North Carolina Press, 2001), 109-48; Harry L. Watson, *Liberty and Power: The Politics of Jacksonian America* (Boston: Hill and Wang, 1990); Hartog, *Private Property and Public Power*; Eric Monkkonen, *America Becomes Urban: The Development of U.S. Cities & Towns, 1780-1980* (Berkeley: University of California Press, 1988); Allen Steinberg, *The Transformation of Criminal Justice, Philadelphia, 1800-1880* (Chapel Hill: University of North Carolina Press, 1989); Novak, *People's Welfare*; Morton J. Horwitz, *The Transformation of American Law, 1780-1860* (Cambridge, MA: Harvard University Press, 1977).

3. Francis Paul Prucha, *Broadax and Bayonet: The Role of the United States Army in the Development of the Northwest, 1815-1860* (Madison: State Historical Society of Wisconsin, 1953); Gautham Rao, "The Federal *Posse Comitatus* Doctrine: Slavery, Compulsion, and Statecraft in Mid-Nineteenth Century America," *Law & History Review* 26, no. 1 (2008): 1-56; Rothman, *Slave Country*; Padraig Riley, *Slavery and the Democratic Conscience: Political Life in Jeffersonian America* (Philadelphia: University of Pennsylvania Press, 2015); Richard R. John, "Affairs of Office: The Executive Departments, the Election of 1828, and the Making of the Democratic Party," in *The Democratic Experiment*, ed. William J. Novak et al. (Princeton, NJ: Princeton University Press, 2003), 50-84; Heath J. Bowen, "Your Obedient Servant: Government Clerks, Officeseeking, and the Politics of Patronage in Antebellum Washington City" (PhD diss., Michigan State University, 2011); William E. Nelson, *The Roots of American Bureaucracy, 1830-1900* (Cambridge, MA: Harvard University Press, 1982).

4. Maurice G. Baxter, *Henry Clay and the American System* (Lexington: University of Kentucky Press, 1995); John R. Van Atta, "Western Lands and the Political Economy of Henry Clay's American System, 1819-1832," *JER* 21, no. 4 (2001): 633-65; Leonard Tabachnik, "Political Patronage and Ethnic Groups: Foreign-Born in the United States Customhouse Service, 1821-1861," *Civil War History* 17, no. 3 (1971): 222-31; William J. Hartman, "Politics and Patronage: The New York Custom House, 1852-1902" (PhD diss., Columbia University, 1952).

5. New York *Columbian*, June 6, 1817, reprinted in *Papers of James Monroe*, 1:105; Connecticut *Journal*, June 24, 1817, 1:120; John G. Swift, *Memoirs*, 159, excerpted ibid., 1:151; Monroe to the Committee of the Town of Providence, July 19, 1817, in *Papers of James Monroe*, 1:158.

6. McDonald, "Chance of the Moment."

7. Although the custom-house mob receded, mobs were a fairly common part of the texture of American politics during the Jacksonian era in particular. See David Grimsted, *American Mobbing, 1828-1861: Toward Civil War* (New York: Cambridge University Press, 1987); Leonard L. Richards, *Gentlemen of Property and Standing: Anti-Abolition Mobs in Jacksonian America* (New York: Oxford University Press, 1970).

8. Gould, "Making of an Atlantic State System," 258.

9. See, for instance, Cusick, *Other War of 1812*; David Head, "Slave Smuggling by Foreign Privateers: The Illegal Slave Trade and the Geopolitics of the Early Republic," *JER* 33, no. 3 (2013): 433-62; Arlyck, "Plaintiffs v. Privateers"; Richard G. Lowe, "American Seizure of Amelia Island," *Florida Historical Quarterly* 45, no. 1 (1966): 18-30; Lewis, *American Union*; J. H. Elliott, *Empires of the Atlantic World: Britain and Spain in America, 1492-1830* (New Haven, CT: Yale University Press, 2006).

10. Nathaniel Hawthorne, *The Scarlet Letter*, ed. Ross. C. Murfin (Boston: Bedford Books of St. Martin's Press, 1991), 23. This broad political economic shift is described by Schoen, *Fragile Fabric of Union*; Sam W. Haynes, *Unfinished Revolution: The Early American Republic in a British World* (Charlottesville: University of Virginia Press, 2010); Gould, *Among the Powers of the Earth*, 213; J. C. A. Stagg, *Mr. Madison's War: Politics, Diplomacy, and Warfare in the Early American Republic, 1783–1830* (Princeton, NJ: Princeton University Press, 1983), 513–17.

11. On the importance of the tariff, see Peter S. Onuf, "The Political Economy of Sectionalism: Tariff Controversies and Conflicting Conceptions of World Order," in *Congress and the Emergence of Sectionalism: From the Missouri Compromise to the Age of Jackson* (Athens: Ohio University Press, 2008), 47–74; Schoen, *Fragile Fabric of Union*; Peskin, *Manufacturing Revolution*, 207–22; William K. Bolt, "The Tariff in the Age of Jackson" (PhD diss., University of Tennessee, 2010); Daniel Peart, "Looking beyond Parties and Elections: The Making of United States Tariff Policy during the Early 1820s," *JER* 33, no. 1 (Spring 2013), 87–108; James L. Huston, *Calculating the Value of the Union: Slavery, Property Rights, and the Economic Origins of the Civil War* (Chapel Hill: University of North Carolina Press, 2003).

12. Schoen, *Fragile Fabric of Union*; Jonathan J. Pincus, *Pressure Groups & Politics in Antebellum Tariffs* (New York: Columbia University Press, 1977).

13. Wallis, *Historical Statistics*, Table Ea588–593.

14. Andrew Jackson to John Overton, June 16, 1827; June 24, 1827, *The Papers of Andrew Jackson*, ed. Sam B. Smith and Harriet Chappell Owsley (Knoxville: University of Tennessee Press, 1980–) 6:345, 346, and 6:345 (ed. note) (hereafter, *PAJ*); Jackson to James Hamilton Jr., June 29, 1828, *PAJ*, 6:476–77; John C. Calhoun to Jackson, July 10, 1828, *PAJ*, 6:481; Jackson, Inaugural Address, 1829, *PAJ*, 7:77; Jackson, Memorandum on Administration Policy, n.d. [1829], *PAJ*, 7:69–70; Wallis, *Historical Statistics*, Table Ea584–587.

15. Don R. Van Atta, *Securing the West: Politics, Public Lands, and the Fate of the Old Republic* (Baltimore: Johns Hopkins University Press, 2014), 17–84; Malcolm J. Rohrbaugh, *The Land Office Business: The Settlement and Administration of American Public Lands, 1789–1837* (New York: Oxford University Press, 1968), 42–50, 114–56, 221–70. Between 1789 and 1836 the federal government collected about $89.1 million in land sales compared to $682 million in customs duties.

16. Kornel Chang, *Pacific Connections: The Making of the U.S.-Canadian Borderlands* (Berkeley: University of California Press, 2010), 10. On the role of slavery in the growth of American capitalism, see Johnson, *River of Dark Dreams*.

17. November 1792, Customs Duty Bonds, Bermuda Hundred Customs Accounts; Robert E. Wright, *The Wealth of Nations Rediscovered: Integration and Expansion in American Financial Markets, 1790–1850* (New York: Cambridge University Press, 2002), 142.

18. Hamilton to Olney, April 2, 1793; Olney to Hamilton, June 21, 1791; Fenner to Foster, December 30, 1792, *DHSCUS*, 7:582–83; John Brown to Jeremiah Olney, March 7, 1795, U.S. Custom House Records, Box 1, Folder: Letters—1795, RIHS; Alexander Hamilton, Circular to Collectors of Customs, December 18, 1789.

19. Alexander Hamilton, Report on the Receipts and Expenditures of Public Monies to the End of the Year 1791, *PAH*, 13:39.

20. Dalzell, "Taxation with Representation," 204–6, 208–9.

21. Port of Baltimore, Index of Bonds in Suit, 1801–1856, RG 36, Entry 1178, NARA-Phila; *United States v. Potts*, 9 U.S. (9 Cranch) 284 (1809); Gabriel Christie to Gabriel Duvall, March 27, 1807, September 19, 1807, Baltimore Customs Letter Book; Addin Lewis to Albert Gallatin, June 26, 1811; James B. Wilkinson to Gabriel Duval, October 2, 1811, Lewis Family Papers, Box 1, Folder 1.

22. Wallis, *Historical Statistics*, Table Ea588–593, "Federal Government Revenue by Source, 1789–1939."

23. See Bruce Mann, *Republic of Debtors: Bankruptcy in the Age of American Independence* (Cambridge, MA: Harvard University Press, 2002).

24. Hickey, *War of 1812*, 303; William Jones to Alexander J. Dallas, September 15, 1814, George Mifflin Dallas Papers, Mss 1460A, HSP; Paul Studenski and Herman Edward Kroos, *Financial History of the United States* (New York: Beard Books, 2003), 80.

25. *ASP-Fi* 2:855; Caesar A. Rodney to Dallas, October 27, 1814, George Mifflin Dallas Papers, 1791–1880, Mss 1460A, HSP.

26. Leon M. Schur, "The Second Bank of the United States and the Inflation after the War of 1812," *Journal of Political Economy* 68, no. 2 (1960): 119; *Annals of Congress*, 14th Cong., 1st Sess. (1815), 1629–30, 1634–37; Norris W. Preyer, "Southern Support for the Tariff of 1816—A Reappraisal," *Journal of Southern History* 25, no. 3 (1959): 311; Mathew Carey, *Essays on Political Economy* (Philadelphia: H.C. Carey & I. Lea, 1822), 298.

27. Unsettled Balances, April 24, 1816, *ASP-Fi* 2:124.

28. Joseph Anderson to David Gelston, January 1, 1815, Box 8, Folder 1, Gelston Papers; Anderson to Gelston, November 18, 1815, Box 8, Folder 2, Gelston Papers.

29. Ralph and Thomas Haskins to William H. Crawford, November 26, 1817, 1/1, Papers of Ralph Haskins and the Haskins Family, Rauner Special Collections Library, Dartmouth College; Charles W. Greene to H. A. S. Dearborn, November 28, 1817, H. A. S. Dearborn Papers.

30. Bullock to Anderson, April 7, 1817; Crawford to Bullock, March 11, 1817; Bullock to Habersham, August 6, 1819; Bullock to William Gaston, October 29, 1819, A. S. Bullock Letterbook.

31. 3 *Statutes* 366 at 368 (1817) directed the comptroller of the Treasury to document unsettled balances that had been on the books for over three years.

32. Joseph Anderson, *Report of the Comptroller of the Treasury, of the Balances on the Books of the Register of the Treasury, Which Appear to Have Been Due More than Three Years . . .* (Washington, DC: W. De Krafft, 1818), 3, 5, 6, 7, 8, 9.

33. Clyde A. Haulman, *Virginia and the Panic of 1819: The First Great Depression and the Commonwealth* (New York: Pickering and Chatto, 2008), 28, and generally, 25–28.

34. Murray N. Rothbard, *The Panic of 1819: Reactions and Policies* (New York: Columbia University Press, 1962), 6, 17.

35. *Abstract of Bonds*, Part II, 86–103. On the debacle at the Philadelphia custom house, see Mary W. M. Hargreaves, *The Presidency of John Quincy Adams* (Lawrence: University Press of Kansas, 1985), 237.

36. *Abstract of Bonds, Part II*, 105.

37. William H. Crawford, *Letter from the Secretary of the Treasury . . . February 15, 1820* (Washington, DC: Gales and Seaton, 1820), 4; *Report of the Committee of Investigation . . . on the Subject of the Defalcations of Samuel Swartwout and Others . . .* (New York: Thomas Allen, 1838), 45; William H. Crawford, in *Message From the President of the United States, Transmitting . . . Abstracts of the bonds . . .* (Washington, DC: Gales and Seaton, 1820), 5.

38. 3 *Statutes at Large* 582 (1820).

39. *Annals of Congress*, 16th Cong., 1st Sess. (December 1819), 742–43; William Earl Weeks, *John Quincy Adams and American Global Empire* (Lexington: University of Kentucky Press, 1992).

40. *Annals of Congress*, 17th Cong., 1st Sess. (May 25, 1824).

41. Losses on Duty Bonds, *ASP-Fi* 2:148, 149–51.

42. Port of Baltimore, Index of Bonds in Suit, 1801–1856, RG 36, Entry 1178, NARA-Phila.

43. Bonds in Suit, RG 36, Series 1081E, NARA-Phila.

44. William H. Crawford, *Letter from the Secretary of the Treasury, Transmitting a Statement of the Loss Upon Bonds taken for Duties on Goods Imported The District of Philadelphia Since the 1st Jan. 1815* (Washington, DC: Gales & Seaton, 1825), 3; Jonathan Steele to William H. Crawford, January 26, 1825, ibid., 5, 82–15. The overdue bonds are listed in an oddly paginated section between Crawford's note and Steele's letter, 82-1 through 82-15.

45. Crawford, *Letter from the Secretary of the Treasury*, 12.

46. Andrew Jackson to Samuel Delucenna Ingham, n.d. [March 28, 1829], *PAJ*, 7:124; Samuel D. Ingham, Circular to Collectors of Customs, June 5, 1829, RG 21, Mobile-Correspondence, Box 2, Folder 1829, NARA-Atlanta.

47. John Elliot, Receipt of Customhouse Bond for Swanton Whitmore, September 21, 1830, Mobile-Correspondence Regarding Legal Matters, 1820–1904, Box 1, Folder 3, RG 36, Entry AC063101, NARA-Atlanta; John Smyth, Indictment in *United States v. Smith and King*, ibid., Box 1, Folder 1; Virgil Maxcy, Solicitor of the Treasury, to John Elliott, U.S. Attorney Mobile, October 30, 1830, ibid., Box 1, Folder 3; Virgil Maxcy to George W. Owen, February 22, 1831, Mobile-Correspondence, Box 2, Folder 1831.

48. Peter N. Green, Bath, to William King, Collector Bath, May 17, 1830, Box 23, Folder 12; J. L. Whitman, Boston, to William King, Collector Bath, June 19, 1830, Box 24, Folder 1, William King Papers, 1788–1834, Collection 165, Maine Historical Society, Portland, ME.

49. Benjamin F. Butler, "Indulgences on Custom-House Bonds," June 27, 1837, in *Official Opinions of the Attorneys General of the United States, Advising the President and Heads of Departments in Relation to their Official Duties . . .* , ed. Benjamin F. Hall (Washington, DC: Robert Farnum, 1852), 3:248.

50. *Annals of Congress*, 16th Cong., 1st Sess. (December 1819), 742–43. On the Adams-Onis Treaty, see Weeks, *Adams and American Global Empire*.

51. H. A. S. Dearborn to W. R. Lee, May 1, 1815; Dearborn to Joseph Anderson, January 2, 1816; Dearborn to Dallas, February 10, 1816; Collectors Letters, NARA-Boston. New York collector David Gelston had also identified false or altered invoices as a

problem in 1816. Joseph Anderson to David Gelston, July 12, 1816; Anderson to Gelston, July 23, 1816; Box 8, Folder 4, Gelston Papers.

52. Alexander James Dallas, Tariff of Duties on Imports, February 13, 1816, *ASP-Fi* 2:87, 91–92. Since suspension of hostilities with Great Britain, Dallas had suspected that "fictitious invoice[s]" were a major drain on federal revenue collection at the custom houses. See Dallas, Circular to Collectors of Customs, February 25, 1815, Treasury Circulars, Reel 2.

53. 1 *Statutes* 627 at 665–66 (1799).

54. John Brown and John LeBaron, Appraisement of Hemp in Ship Winnifred, December 8, 1810, U.S. Custom House Records, Box 4, Folder: Letters—1810, MSS 28 SG2: Bristol/Warren, RI, RIHS; Thomas Coles to Albert Gallatin, December 4, 1811; James McCulloh to Albert Gallatin, December 24, 1811; Reel 23, Gallatin Papers.

55. H. A. S. Dearborn to William H. Crawford, May 13, 1817; September 24, 1817, Collectors Letters, NARA-Boston.

56. Dearborn to Crawford, September 24, 1817; William H. Crawford, Circular to Collectors of Customs, October 8, 1817, Savannah-Letters Received, Box 3, Folder 1, RG 36, Entry AC062401, NARA-Atlanta.

57. Nathan Sanford, *Annals of Congress*, 15th Cong., 1st Sess. (December 16, 1817), 35, 37–38.

58. Ibid., 44–45, 46, 54, 55.

59. Peskin, *Manufacturing Revolution*, 210–16. See also Cooke, *Tench Coxe*, 502–8; and generally, F. W. Taussig, *The Tariff History of the United States* (New York: G.P. Putnam's Sons, 1910).

60. Dearborn to Crawford, May 13, 1817; September 24, 1817; November 17, 1817. Joanna Cohen, "'The Right to Purchase Is as Free as the Right to Sell': Defining Consumers as Citizens in the Auction-House Conflicts of the Early Republic," *JER* 30, no. 1 (2010): 25–62.

61. 3 *Statutes at Large* 433 (April 20, 1818), 434–35, 436, 438; R. Elberton Smith, *Customs Valuation in the United States: A Study in Tariff Administration* (Chicago: University of Chicago Press, 1948), 62–63; *United States v. Pitt*, 27 F. Cas. 541 at 543.

62. Marginalia on William H. Crawford to David Gelston, May 15, 1818, Box 6, Folder 9, Gelston Papers. The first appointees were William Dickinson and William Haslett (Baltimore); Ichobad Pratt and Abraham R. Lawrence (New York); William Little and Isaac Waters (Boston); Samuel Ross and Thomas Stewart (Philadelphia); Edward Mortimer and Andrew Smilie (Charleston). *Niles Weekly Register*, March 13, 1819, 49.

63. H. A. S. Dearborn to Messrs. William Little and Isaac Waters, Boston, May 22, 1818; Appraisers Office to H. A. S. Dearborn, February 23, 1819; Appraisers Office to H. A. S. Dearborn, April 5, 1823; Appraisers Office to Louis McLane, September 17, 1832; Appraisers Office to Levi Lincoln, July 7, 1830; Appraisers Office to Samuel Ingham, June 26, 1830, RG 36, Appraisers' Letters, NARA-Boston.

64. A. S. Bullock to William Crawford, Secretary of the Treasury, October 23, 1818, A.S. Bullock Letterbook, David M. Rubenstein Rare Book and Manuscript Library, Duke University; Storekeepers' Records of Receipts and Deliveries, 1819–1864, RG 36, #E931A, NARA-NY. See also Samuel D. Ingham to Samuel Swartwout, June 22, 1830; Samuel Swartwout to Louis McLane, September 30, 1831, M78, Reel 17.

65. Isaac Waters and William Little to Levi Lincoln, December 29, 1830, Appraisers Letters; N. Tracy to H. A. S. Dearborn, August 23, 1821, H. A. S. Dearborn Papers; Waters and Little to William H. Crawford, August 20, 1824, Appraisers Letters; William H. Crawford, Marginalia on Irving Smith & Holly to William H. Crawford, July 9, 1818, Gelston Papers 6/9. Gelston, it appears, even attempted to use the old method of customs appraisement as late as August 1819, much to the surprise of Dearborn. Dearborn to Gelston, August 24, 1819, Gelston Papers, 11/2.

66. Waters and Little to Lawrence and Pratt, November [n.d.] 1818, Appraisers Letters; Waters and Little to Ross and Stewart, August 13, 1819, Appraisers Letters; Waters and Little to Lawrence and Pratt, September 3, 1830, Appraisers Letters.

67. Waters and Little to Dearborn, June 30, 1819; Waters to Dearborn, January 29, 1827, Appraisers Letters; Dearborn to Daniel Webster, December 22, 1825, Collector's Letters. See also Dearborn to Nathaniel Silslea, December 31, 1827, Collector's Letters.

68. *Tappan et al. v. United States*, 23 F. Cas. 690 at 694 (1822).

69. Dearborn to Richard Rush, January 30, 1827, Collector's Letters; *United States v. Tappan*, 24 U.S. 419 at 426–27 (1826–27); Smith, *Customs Valuation in the United States*, 70; Dearborn to Rush, February 19, 1827, Collector's Letters.

70. Ingham to Samuel Swartwout, September 30, 1830, Reel 17, M178, NARA-NY.

71. Jackson and his allies had lambasted the John Quincy Adams administration's purported abuse of the patronage power at the expense of the "voice of the people," as John C. Calhoun put it. Calhoun to Andrew Jackson, June 4, 1826, *PAJ*, 6:177; Jackson to Thomas Patrick Moore, July 31, 1826, *PAJ*, 6:194.

72. Pitkin, *Three Centuries of Custom Houses*, provides a good overview of tenure in office from one port to another, though it is not comprehensive. For a broader perspective, see Leonard D. White, *The Jacksonians: A Study in Administrative History, 1829–1861* (New York: Macmillan, 1954), 176–77.

73. Jackson to John Coffee, May 12, 1828, *PAJ*, 6:457–58; Swartwout to Jackson, October 24, 1826, *PAJ*, 6:231. See also Jackson to John Branch, June 24, 1828, *PAJ*, 6:473–74.

74. Samuel Swartwout to Louis McLane, June 8, 1829, Reel 17, M178, NARA-NY; Sean Wilentz, *The Rise of American Democracy: Jefferson to Lincoln* (New York: W.W. Norton, 2005), 390; Benjamin Pierce to Andrew Jackson, January 12, 1829; Joseph Saul to Andrew Jackson, January 29, 1829, *PAJ*, 7:11, 23.

75. Joseph George Tregle, *Louisiana in the Age of Jackson: A Clash of Cultures and Personalities* (Baton Rouge: Louisiana State University Press, 1999), 420–21; Record of Testimony, February 11, 1834; *A. H. Smith v. Martin Gordon* (1834), Orleans Parish Court Records, Case #6879, City Archives, New Orleans Public Library; P. Rousseau, New Orleans, to Samuel Spotts, Surveyor New Orleans, April 3, 1833; Petition of the Merchants of New Orleans Against Martin Gordon, March [n.d.] 1832; Charges Against Customs Officers, Vol. 2, 1833–1861, RG 36, National Archives-College Park; Carl Kohn to Samuel Kohn, April 17, 1833, Carl Kohn Letterbook, MSS 269, Historic New Orleans Collection. See also Elisha Stilton, Canada Line, to William King, Collector Bath, January 4, 1832, Box 24, Folder 5 Correspondence 1830–1834, William King Papers.

76. Churchill Caldom Cambreleng to Andrew Jackson, April 15, 1829, *PAJ*, 7:156–57; Martin Van Buren to Andrew Jackson, April 23, 1829, *PAJ*, 7:178; Jackson to Morgan Lewis, n.d. [March 1829], *PAJ*, 7:134; Jackson to Ingham, n.d. [April 19 or 20], 1829, *PAJ*,

7:167; B. R. Brunson, *The Adventures of Samuel Swartwout in the Age of Jefferson and Jackson* (Lewiston, NY: Edwin Mellen Press, 1989), 61–62.

77. Swartwout to McLane, November 8, 1831; Swartwout to Ingham, June 20, 1829; Samuel D. Ingham to Samuel Swartwout, July 22, 1830; Louis McLane to Samuel Swartwout, August 25, 1830; September 10, 1833; Swartwout to McLane, March 31, 1833; Reel 17, M178, NARA-NY; James A. Hamilton to Samuel Swartwout, February 9, 1831, RG 36, Entry 895, NARA-NY.

78. Samuel Swartwout to William Duane, July 22, 1833; Henry Levely to Samuel Swartwout, July 30, 1833; William J. Duane to Henry Levely, n.d. [1833], Charges Against Customs Officers, Vol. 3, 1833–1861, NARA-College Park.

79. 5 *Statutes at Large* 347–48 (1839); Mashaw, *Creating the Administrative Constitution*, 214; *Report of the Committee of Investigation . . . on the Subject of the Defalcations of Samuel Swartwout and Others . . .* (New York: Thomas Allen, 1838), 28; Brunson, *Adventures of Samuel Swartwout*, 89–124.

80. Washington *Globe*, May 19, 1837, quoted by Brunson, *Adventures of Samuel Swartwout*, 83.

81. *Report of the Committee of Investigation*, 98; House Report 740, 24th Cong., 1st Sess. (June 7, 1836), 1, 7, 8, 31; 5 *Statutes at Large* 548 at 566 (1842); White, *Jacksonians*, 173.

82. Adams Bailey to James Swan, September 28, 1837; J. W. Breedlove to Levi Woodbury, October 20, 1837; William Ayer to Levi Woodbury, April 21, 1839; Anonymous to Levi Woodbury, December 28, 1838; John Daugh to Levi Woodbury, February 8, 1841; J. P. Mason to Andrew Jackson, December 11, 1834; Gabriel J. Floyd to Levi Woodbury, September 15, 1836; Samuel Penn Jr. to Levi Woodbury, May 14, 1836; Sugar Merchants of Boston to Levi Woodbury, May 22, 1833; Complaint of J. M Moriarty, n.d. [1840]; Letters Received Relating to Charges against Customs Officials, NARA-College Park.

EPILOGUE

1. Unknown to John R. Pringle, July 4, 1831, Ms. 11/322/21, South Carolina Historical Society, Charleston, South Carolina; Chauncey Samuel Boucher, *The Nullification Controversy in South Carolina* (Chicago: University of Chicago Press, 1916), 21; Lacy K. Ford Jr., *Origins of Southern Radicalism: The South Carolina Upcountry, 1800–1860* (New York: Oxford University Press, 1988), 132.

2. Henry Laurens to Clay & Habersham, October 26, 1767, in *The Papers of Henry Laurens*, ed. Philip M. Hamer (Columbia: University of South Carolina Press, 1968–2003), 4:377 (hereafter cited as *PHL*); Henry Laurens to James Habersham, September 5, 1767, *PHL*, 4:377.

3. Robert Barnwell Rhett, *Speech of Robert Barnwell Rhett, to his Constituents on the Ketcher River, at a Dinner* (Charleston: Burges & James, 1839).

4. *Niles Register* 34, June 28, 1828, 287–89, quoted in Robert Tinkler, *James Hamilton of South Carolina* (Baton Rouge: Louisiana State University Press, 2004), 91; William W. Freehling, *Prelude to Civil War: The Nullification Controversy in South Carolina, 1816–1836* (New York: Harper & Row, 1966).

5. On the Force Bill, see Freehling, *Prelude to Civil War*, 284–95.

6. Ruth M. Miller and Ann Taylor Andrus, *Charleston's Old Exchange Building: A Witness to American History* (Charleston: History Press, 2005), 49–58.

7. Louis McLane to J. R. Pringle, November 6, 1832, RG 56, M178, Reel 32, Archives II.

8. Ibid.; Freehling, *Prelude to Civil War*, 290.

9. McLane to Pringle, January 25, 1833, M178, Reel 32.

10. Freehling, *Prelude to Civil War*, 289–90.

11. On the history of federal statecraft during the Civil War and the late nineteenth century, see, among others, Richard Franklin Bensel, *Yankee Leviathan: The Origins of Central State Authority in America, 1859--1877* (New York: Cambridge University Press, 1990); Bensel, *The Political Economy of American Industrialization, 1877–1900* (New York: Cambridge University Press, 2000); Heather Cox Richardson, *The Greatest Nation of the Earth: Republican Economic Policies during the Civil War* (Cambridge, MA: Harvard University Press, 1997); Cohen, *Contraband*.

12. Salmon P. Chase to Abraham Lincoln, March [n.d.] 1861, Series 1, Lincoln Papers, LC. At least one critic warned that the floating custom house scheme would be attended with "insurmountable difficulties." James A. Hamilton to Chase, March 27, 1861, Reel 14, Chase Papers (UPI), LC.

13. Abraham Lincoln, Proclamation of a Blockade, April 19, 1861, in *The Collected Works of Abraham Lincoln*, ed. Roy P. Basler (New Brunswick, NJ: Rutgers University Press, 1953–55), 4:338–39; Abraham Lincoln, Proclamation of a Blockade, April 27, 1861, ibid., 4:346–47.

INDEX

Page numbers in italics indicate figures and tables.

accounting system, and federal custom houses, 75–76, 78–80, 95, 119
Adams, John, 115, 117, 121–22, 134, 237n6, 240n61
Adams, John Quincy, 172, 179–80, 182, 258n71
ad valorem duties, 186, 190
age of revolution, 50, 103, 107, 111, 168, 170. *See also specific revolutions*
Allen, James, 44
Allen, William, 44
American Board of Customs, 42–44, 93, 219n103
American capitalism, 168, 170–73
American Indians, 6, 13, 28, 106, 167–68, 171, 173, 208n31
American republic, 10, 12–13, 117, 119, 137, 171. *See also* federal authority; federal government; federalism; Federalists (Nationalists); republicanism; Republicans
American Revolution: British imperial custom houses and, 10–11, 21, 34–35, 45; commercial restrictions and, 45–46; corruption and, 11, 86; empire and, 21–22, 211n7; financing schemes and, 55–56, 222n14; marketplace and, 47; military service and, 6, 69–71; mobs and, 10–11, 19–20, 20, 22; national debt and, 54; Non-Importation agreements and, 45–46, 64; Non-Intercourse agreements and, 45–46; political economy and, 46; War of Independence and, 19, 54–55, 111, 162, 223n27

Ames, Fisher, 63, 227n64
Anderson, Joseph, 177–78
Appraisement Act of 1818, 186–90, 257n62, 258n65. *See also* fraudulent (false) manifests or invoices
armed forces, American, 54, 64, 70, 134, 155, 157, 160–61, 167–68, 176, 247n22, 250n69
armed merchant vessels: Atlantic marketplace and, 111, 116–17; commerce and, 127–28; Congress and, 104, 112, 115–17, 120, 126–30; Constitution and, 127–28; customs bonds and, 116, 124–29; customs officers and, 112–14, 116–17, 123–30; description of, 111; discretion of customs officers and, 113–14; federal government and, 115, 120–27, 129, 237n4, 240n61, 244n94; Federalists and, 104; France and, 112–13, 122–25, 128–29, 242n72, 244n94; Great Britain and, 112–13; Haitian trade and, 104, 120, 122–24, 126–33, 136; neutrality policy and, 112; Republicans and, 104; Treasury Department and, 112–14, 117, 129; West Indies trade and, 114, 116
Arnold, Welcome, 10, 95–97, 108, 155, 174, 238n25
Articles of Confederation, 1, 53, 59, 71
Astor, John Jacob, 193
Atlantic marketplace: age of revolution and, 103, 107, 111, 168, 170; armed merchant vessels and, 111, 116–17; capitalism and, 10, 14, 170; colonial America and,

261

Atlantic marketplace (*continued*)
45; commercial peoples and, 29–30; customs officers and, 10, 31, 50, 71, 81, 90; federal custom houses and, 50–51, 90; merchants and, 10, 29–30; negotiated authority and, 108

Attucks, Crispus, 19

Bailey, Adams, 195
Ballard, Robert, 69–70
Baltimore custom house, 101–2
Bancker, Charles Nicoll, 143
Bank of the United States, 55, 97–98, 115, 176
Barker, J. Sanford, 147–49
Barnes, David Leonard, 152
Barnewell, George, 123
Barrow, Thomas C., 66
Batte, Frederick, 50
Bee, Thomas, 112, 123, 148
Benezet, Daniel, 119
Benton, Henry, 195
Bermuda Hundred, 49–51, 70–71, 90, 113, 174, 220n5
Birchfield, Maurice, 32
Bishop, Abraham, 145, 155, 169
Bishop, Samuel, 118
black freedom, 104, 129, 244n93. *See also* slaves/slavery
black Haitian revolutionaries trade, 101, 104, 120–22, 124, 126–33, 136, 244n93
Bland, Giles, 27
blockades, 120, 159–60, 170
Board of Trade, 11, 21, 26, 30–31, 33, 37, 66, 68, 217n82
Boston Massacre, 19–20, 20, 22, 43, 163
Bowdoin, James, 69
Brackenridge, Hugh Henry, 137
Breen, T. H., 40, 45
Brewer, John, 211n10
British Empire. *See* Great Britain
British imperial custom houses: administration and, 28, 33, 67, 83; American Board of Customs and, 42–44, 219n103; American Revolution and, 10–11, 21, 34–35, 45; Boston Massacre memorialization and, 19–20, 20, 22, 43; commercial peoples and, 15–16, 32–33; commercial regulation and, 11, 19, 29–32, 215n57, 215n60; compensation system and, 27, 66–67; corruption and, 43; customs bonds and, 16, 23, 31–32, 36, 43, 67, 228n74; empire and, 11–12, 21–22, 211n7, 217n72; fiscal-military state and, 27–28, 213n39; history of, 7, 7, 27–28, 213n35, 213n39; imperial law enforcement and, 17, 19–23, 26, 28–37, 68, 211n15, 213n39, 214n46, 215n57, 215n60, 217n82; mobs and, 10–11, 16–17, 19, 37–38, 43–45, 253n7; Navigation Acts and, 11, 21; negotiated authority, 11–13, 15–17, 20, 29–34, 36–37, 39–40, 47, 76, 93, 95; Philadelphia and, 15–17; reform and, 29, 36, 38–40, 44–45, 47, 79–80; revenue and, 29, 33–35, 38–43, 218n90; smuggling and, 11, 15–16, 29, 33, 35–36, 39, 218n93; surveyors and, 33, 66, 162. *See also* colonial America

Brown, Charles Brockden, 137
Brown, John, 10, 95–96, 115, 155, 174, 185
Bullock, Archibald S., 177, 187–88
Burr, Aaron, 131, 193
Burrites, 118, 145
Butler, Benjamin F., 183
Butler, Peirce, 64

Calhoun, John C., 198, 258n71
Cambreleng, C. C., 192
Canada, 91, 144, 154, 157–58, 184, 248n35
Cap-Français, 107, 122–24
capitalism: American, 168, 170–73; Atlantic, 10, 14, 170; industrial, 86
capture theory, 11, 206n19
Carey, Mathew, 177, 186
central governmental institutions. *See* federalism; Federalists (Nationalists); limited central government
Chang, Kornel, 173
Christie, Gabriel, 176
Clark, Dora Mae, 42
Clark, Jeremiah, 177–78
Clay, Henry, 168
Clay, Joseph, 119, 127
Clifford, Thomas, 41, 46
Clintonites, 59, 72
Cohen, Patricia Cline, 77
Colbert, Jean-Baptiste, 55–57
Colden, Alexander, 33, 35–37
Coles, Thomas, 185
Collection Acts, 53, 64–67, 65, 81, 85, 184–85
Collins, Charles, 185
collusion captures, 116, 118, 170
colonial America: American Board of Customs and, 42–44, 219n103; Atlantic

marketplace and, 45; British revenue and, 29, 33–35, 38–43, 218n90; commerce and, 11, 21, 26–27, 45–46; commercial regulation and, 19–20, 29–34; commercial restrictions and, 45–46; customs duties and, 56–57, 223n27; law enforcement by Parliament and, 21–22, 36, 38, 42, 68; patronage and, 28, 30, 33; writs of assistance and, 44, 219n110. *See also* British imperial custom houses

commerce: armed merchant vessels and, 127–28; black Haitian revolutionaries and, 121–22; customs officials and, 11, 88, 90–91; empire and, 105; export market and, 23, 31, 57, 79, 98, 103, 135, 147, 250n76; federal custom houses and, 108–9; federal government and, 104–5, 110–11, 121–22, 130–32; Haitian Revolution and, 121–22; indirect trade and, 104, 108, 133; power and, 10–11, 136–37, 206n16; reexport trade and, 79, 133, 226n54; Republicans and, 137, 145–46, 246n14; states and, 11, 207n20; West Indies and, 21, 26, 31, 35, 39, 94, 105, 116, 121, 124

commercial peoples (merchant communities): Atlantic marketplace and, 29–30; British imperial custom houses and, 15–16, 32–33; credit and, 10–11, 25, 90–92, 157; customs officers and, 12–13, 87; description of, 10; embargoes and, 139–40; federal authority and, 136; law enforcement and, 84, 90, 104; marketplace and, 10; mobs and, 10–11, 19, 132, 154–56, 169–70, 206n18, 253n7; nationalism and, 133, 157; negotiated authority and, 76–77, 95–96, 98, 113, 131–33, 155–62, 179; politics and, 206n17; power and, 98, 119; public privately funded navy and, 114–15; Treasury Department and, 13. *See also* merchant capital; merchants

commercial regulation: Americanization of British, 53; British custom houses and, 11, 19–20, 22–23; British imperial custom houses and, 11, 19, 21, 29–32, 215n57, 215n60; colonial America and, 11, 19–20, 21, 26–27, 29–34, 45–46, 227n64; Congress and, 49, 134, 187; customs officers' discretion and, 113, 161, 169–70; discretion of customs officers and, 50, 81, 95, 108, 113–14, 131, 161, 169; federal government and, 55, 98, 119–20, 134, 136, 157, 198–99; Great Britain and, 11, 19–23, 26–27, 45–46, 53, 134, 227n64; marketplace and, 134–35; national revenue and, 199–200; neutrality policy and, 108; Nullification Crisis and, 197–200, *198*, 260n12; reform and, 164–65; slave market and, 4–5, 61, 135; smuggling and, 11, 21; states and, 198. *See also* tariffs

commercial restrictions: American Revolution and, 45–46; customs officers and, 135–36; customs officers' discretion and, 141–51, 161–62; federal authority and, 138; Federalists and, 136; France and, 120; Great Britain and, 45–46, 159–60; history of, 136, 245n12; nationalism and, 138; national sovereignty and, 132, 134, 157; Republicans and, 136–37, 246n14; wars and, 161. *See also* commercial regulation; embargoes

Congress, United States: armed merchant vessels and, 104, 112, 115–17, 120, 126–30, 129–30; bonds of value of scholarship and cargo and, 116; commercial regulation and, 49, 134, 187; customs bonds and, 68, 180–82; customs duties and, 61–64, 226n54, 228n78; customs officers and, 12; embargoes and, 110, 238n23; federal custom houses and, 1, 5, 8, *8*; federalism and, 54; financing schemes and, 55–56; fraudulent manifests or invoices and, 184–90, 257n62, 258n65; Hamilton and, 54, 222n9; negotiated authority and, 173; neutrality policy and, 104; ports of entry and, 66–67, 228n72; rotation system and, 179; tariffs and, 1, 8, 53, 64, 75; taxes and, 1, 97–98

Constitution, United States: armed merchant vessels, 127–28; Article I, Section 8, 61–62; Constitutional Convention and, 53, 59, 94, 124; fiscal-military state and, 13, 98; taxes and, 1, 53, 61–62

Continental Army, 54, 64, 70

Cooper, Thomas, 137

corruption, 11, 43, 86, 126, 195–96, 206n19

Court of Admiralty, New York, 63, 134

Coxe, Tench, 117, 138

Crawford, William Harris, 178–79, 185–86, 188, 191

credit: commercial peoples and, 10–11, 25, 90–92, 95, 157; federal government and, 54–55, 76–78, 80–81, 98, 161, 178; moral

credit (continued)
  crisis and, 174, 179–80, 183; national sovereignty and, 80; public credit and, 1, 55–56, 76, 81; republicanism and, 92; slave markets and, 91
Crowninshield, Jacob, 130, 146
customs bonds: armed merchant vessels and, 116; bonds for good behavior and, 124–29; British imperial custom houses and, 16, 23, 31–32, 36, 43, 67, 228n74; Congress and, 68; description of, 174; discretion of customs officers and, 174; embargoes and, 143–44; law enforcement and, 63–64, 143–44; legal procedures and, 68, 82, 84–85, 88–89, 96–97, 174–77, 180, 183; moral crisis and, 173–83, 255n31; negotiated authority and, 83–85, 87–92, 183, 234n49; Nullification Crisis and, 199; solicitor of the Treasury and, 182–83, 190; statistics and, 89. *See also* reform
customs duties, Europe, 4, 53–54, 56–57, 61, 66, 225n50. *See also* British imperial custom houses
customs duties, United States: British model and, 53–54, 61, 66, 225n50; Congress and, 61–62, 61–64, 226n54, 228n78; description of, 4, 61, 98, 225n49; federal government and, 60–61; merchant capital and, 1, 3, 86, 117, 203n2; national debt and, 6, 161, 168, 176, 178; national revenue and, 1, 2–3, 51, 53, 60–61, 75–77, 93, 98, 103, 105–6, 117, 160–61, 176–77, 224nn49–50, 235n96, 240n49; organizational revolution and, 61; proof of loss certificate and, 109; solicitor of the Treasury and, 182–83, 190; statistics and, 60–61, 103, 106, 119, 160, 171, 174, 254n15
customs officers: administration and, 64–66, 65, 83; applications and, 69–71, 229nn82–83; appraisers and, 188–90, 258n65; armed merchant vessels and, 112–14, 116–17, 123–30; Atlantic marketplace and, 10, 31, 50, 71, 81, 90; black Haitian revolutionaries trade and, 101, 120; British model and, 53–54, 66; characteristics and, 6, 54, 69, 83, 118, 229n81; commercial peoples and, 12–13, 87; commercial restrictions and, 135–36; compensation system and, 67–68, 86; Congress and, 12; "continued" men and, 71–72, 73, 230n91; corruption and, 195–96; embargoes and, 101–2, 110, 141–44, 151–56; embezzlement and, 194; federal authority and, 6, 50–51, 54, 69–70, 72, 87, 93, 101–2, 126, 149, 199; Federalists and, 54, 117–19, 228n79; Hamilton and, 49, 77, 83–84, 86; instructions from Hamilton and, 77, 83–84; Jefferson and, 69, 101, 118; law enforcement and, 49–50, 63, 68, 81–82, 84, 86–87, 95–96; mob violence against, 154–56; national sovereignty and, 76, 87; negotiated authority and, 11–13, 33, 51, 76–77, 83, 85, 87–96, 98–99, 104, 108–11, 131–33, 155–62, 168–69, 173; neutrality policy and, 103–5, 108–10; Nullification Crisis and, 199; personal liability for improper seizure and, 152–53; politics and, 54, 69, 71–72, 118–19, 145, 169–70, 190–96, 228n79; power and, 195–96; reforms and, 13; rotation system and, 179, 191–92, 195; smuggling and, 101, 142–43, 154–59, 170, 193, 195; statistics and, 69; Treasury Department and, 13; treaties and, 106. *See also* customs duties, United States; discretion of customs officers; *and specific individuals*

Dallas, Alexander J., 109, 126, 176–78, 184, 257n52
Dalzell, Frederick, 85, 95
Daugh, John, 195
Dearborn, Henry A. S., 158, 163–65, 167, 177, 184–91
debt, national. *See* national debt
Delany, Sharp, 6, 69–70, 73, 84, 90, 112–13, 118, 178, 234n49
Delesdernier, Lewis Frederick, 91, 144, 154
Dell, James, 195
Democrats, 192, 195
Dering, Henry Packer, 6, 88, 121
DeWolf, James, 185
Dexter, Edward, 95–96, 108
Dierks, Konstantin, 83, 229n82
Digges, Edward, 27
discretion of customs officers: ad valorem duties and, 186, 190; appraisements and, 188, 190, 258n65; armed merchant vessels and, 113–14; colonial America and, 11–12, 33–34, 42, 50; commercial regulation and, 50, 81, 95, 108, 113–14, 131, 161, 169; compensation for customs officers

and, 86; customs bonds overdue and, 174; description of, 12; embargoes and, 144, 146–51, 161–62; embezzlement and, 194; fraudulent manifests or invoices and, 185, 195; merchants and, 91–93, 102; political economy and, 90, 94, 104–5, 168, 195–96; reform and, 168–69, 173; smuggling and, 141–42; tariffs and, 190, 195; Treasury Department and, 102. *See also* customs officers

distance issue, and federal custom houses, 59–60, 70, 94

doctrine of continuous voyage, 133

Duane, William, 143, 193

Duer, William, 78

Dun, Alec, 121

Duval, Gabriel, 177

Edling, Max M., 221n2

Einhorn, Robin, 223n28

Elkins, Stanley, 81, 99

Ellery, William, 71, 142, 152, 156, 169

Elliot, Andrew, 41–42, 45

Elliot, John, 182–83

embargoes: 1794 and, 110, 238n23; 1806 and, 130; 1808–9 and, 101–2, 136, 141–42, 146, 157, 162, 245n11, 245n12; 1812 and, 135–36, 157; 1813 and, 160, 162; armed forces and, 155, 250n69; commercial peoples and, 139–40; customs bonds and, 143–44; customs officers and, 101–2, 110, 141–46, 151–56; detention of vessels and, 146–49, 153–54, 158–59; discretion of customs officers and, 144, 146–51, 161–62; economic effects of, 142, 247n22; Embargo Acts and, 135; federal authority and, 136, 141, 146, 148–51, 162, 245n11, 247n22; France and, 132–33; Great Britain and, 132–33; legal procedures for violation of, 101–2, 144–45, 148–54, 161–62, 249n61; manufacturing industry and, 138; merchants and, 103, 110, 139, 157, 238n25; mobs and, 154–56; national debt and, 139; national revenue and, 139; national sovereignty and, 132, 139, 247n22; presidential powers and, 136, 141, 146, 148–51, 162, 245n11; privateering and, 110; smuggling and, 140–45, 152–58, 247n22; trade with enemies and, 136, 157–60. *See also* commercial restrictions

embezzlement, and customs officers, 194

empire: American Revolution and, 21–22, 211n7; British imperial custom houses and, 11–12, 21–22, 211n7, 217n72; commerce and, 105; federal custom houses and, 11–13, 22, 49–51, 220n5; federal government and, 12, 105; fiscal-military state and, 22, 211n10; Great Britain and, 11, 22–23, 34; nationalism and, 12

Enemy Trade Act of 1812, 158–59

English Civil War, 25–26

Enrollment Act of 1789, 53, 86

Eppes, John, 127, 129

Europe: customs duties and, 4, 53–54, 56–57, 61, 66, 225n50; national debt and, 4, 56. *See also* West Indies; *and specific countries*

Eustis, William, 127

Eveleigh, Nicholas, 78–79

Exchequer, the, 11, 80

excise taxes, 11, 97–98, 177, 211n10, 225n50

export market, 23, 31, 57, 79, 98, 103, 135, 147, 250n76. *See also* reexport trade

false (fraudulent) manifests or invoices, 184–86, 189, 190, 195, 256n51, 257n52. *See also* Appraisement Act of 1818

farmers/farming communities, 25, 98–99, 117, 119, 137, 158, 211n11, 226n54

federal authority: commercial peoples and, 136; commercial restrictions and, 138; customs officers and, 6, 50–51, 54, 69–70, 72, 87, 93, 101–2, 126, 149, 199; embargoes and, 101–2, 136, 141, 146, 148–51, 162, 245n11, 247n22; marketplace and, 73–74

federal custom houses: administration and, 64–65, 65, 67–69, 72–73, 227n67; British model and, 53–54; critiques and, 54, 80, 117–19, 222n9; history of, 4–5, 5, 7, 8, 9, 10–14; physical structures and, 4–6, 5, 27, 82, 140, 172, 175, 198. *See also* customs bonds; customs officers

federal government: administrative history of, 55–56, 59–60, 225nn44–45; American Indians and, 6, 13, 28, 106, 167–68, 171, 208n31; armed merchant vessels and, 115, 120–23, 120–27, 129, 237n4, 240n61, 244n94; commerce and, 104–5, 110–11, 121–22, 130–32; commercial regulation and, 55, 98, 119–20, 134, 198–99; credit and, 54–55, 76–78, 80–81, 98, 161,

federal government (*continued*)
178; distance issues and, 59–60, 70, 94; empire and, 12, 105; federalism and, 1, 12–14, 53, 56, 75; financing schemes and, 55–56, 58–59; fiscal-military state and, 4–6, 13, 55–56, 75, 80–81; fiscal solvency and, 80, 97–98, 106, 137–39; law enforcement and, 58–59, 76, 95–96, 225n42, 225n45; limited central government and, 4, 14, 117–18, 123; marketplace and, 10–11; merchant capital and, 3, 11, 13; merchants and, 1, 3, 87, 99; national impost and, 53, 56–59, 62–63, 71, 223nn27–28, 226n54, 227n67; nation building and, 106, 117; neutrality policy and, 105, 116; political economy and, 80; power and, 13, 168, 200, 208n31; presidential powers and, 136, 141, 146, 148–51, 245n11; reforms and, 55–56; "Report on Public Credit" and, 76, 81; Whiskey Rebellion and, 97–98, 108. *See also* embargoes; national sovereignty; tariffs

federalism: Congress and, 54; federal government and, 1, 12–14, 53, 56, 75; fiscal-military state and, 55–56; Hamilton and, 1, 13–14, 53, 117; high federalism and, 87, 99; history of, 222n10. *See also* high federalism

Federalists (Nationalists): anti-Federalists and, 72; armed merchant vessels and, 104, 127; commercial restrictions and, 136; customs officers and, 54, 117–19, 145; federal custom houses and, 50; Haitian Revolution and, 244n93; negotiated authority and, 131, 136; neutrality policy and, 105; political economy and, 50; secession and, 161; taxes and, 53, 221n2

Ferrand, Louis, 128

fiscal-military state: Constitution and, 13, 98; empire and, 22; federal custom houses and, 6, 168; federal government and, 4–6, 13, 55–56, 75, 80–81, 98; federalism and, 55–56; Great Britain and, 22–25, 27–29, 212n19, 213n39; national sovereignty and, 4, 23–24

Fitzimmons, Thomas, 84

Floyd, Gabriel, 195

Fosdick, Nathaniel, 71, 73

France: armed merchant vessels and, 112–13, 122–25, 128–29, 242n72, 244n94; commercial restrictions and, 120; embargoes and, 132–33; financing schemes and, 55–57; naval vessels and, 106, 121, 124, 128; privateering and, 103, 106–7, 109; Quasi-War and, 115–16, 120–22, 244n93; treaties and, 106; XYZ affair and, 114. *See also* West Indies

Frankel, Jeffrey A., 141, 247n22

fraudulent (false) manifests or invoices, 184–86, 189, 190, 195, 256n51, 257n52. *See also* Appraisement Act of 1818

French Revolutionary Wars, 103–4, 107, 111

Gallatin, Albert, 102, 117–20, 138, 146–47, 160–62, 251n84

Games, Alison, 34

Gelston, David: appraisers and, 188, 258n65; customs officers appointments and, 89, 118; embargoes and, 130, 145, 152–54, 158–59; fraudulent manifests or invoices and, 256n51; negotiated authority and, 156; tenure and, 191

Genêt, Edmond-Charles, 106

Genêt affair of 1793, 106–7, 191

Gilchrist, Adam, 147–51, 149, 161–62

Gilchrist v. Collector of Charleston (1808), 148–51, 161–62

Girard, Stephen, 10, 128–29

Glorious Revolution, 21, 23, 28, 30, 39, 44, 80, 95

Goodrich, Elizur, 118

Gordon, Martin, 192, 195

Gore, Christopher, 107

Gracie, Archibald, 10, 174

Great Britain: armed merchant vessels and, 112–13; Board of Trade and, 11, 21, 26, 30–31, 33, 37, 66, 68; commercial regulation and, 11, 19–23, 26–27, 45–46, 53, 134, 227n64; commercial restrictions and, 45–46, 159–60; custom houses and laws and, 22–23, 27, 211nn14–15, 213n35; customs duties model and, 53–54, 61, 225n50; embargoes and, 132–33; empire and, 11, 22–23, 34; the Exchequer and, 11, 80; excise taxes and, 11, 211n10, 225n50; farmers and, 25, 124, 211n11; fiscal-military state and, 22–25, 27–29, 211nn10–11, 211nn14–15, 212n19, 213n39; imperial laws and, 19–23, 211n14; impressment and, 134, 157, 247n22; license trade and, 158–60; manufacturing industry and, 168; mob

power and, 10; national debt of, 34, 39; naval vessels and, 35, 37, 110, 121, 134, 138, 157, 158, 247n22; patronage and, 28, 30, 33; piracy and, 216n68; political economy and, 10–11, 80; ports of entry and, 67; privateering and, 103, 107, 109–10, 133–34; revenue from British imperial custom houses and, 22–23, 29, 33–35, 38–43, 218n90; and Rule of 1756, so-called, 133–34; smuggling and, 24–25, 212n26; trade with enemies and, 11, 38–39, 67, 133. *See also* British imperial custom houses; West Indies
Green, Peter, 183
Grenville, George, 16, 34, 38–39, 60
Griffith, Robert E., 125–26

Habersham, John, 87
Haiti (Saint-Domingue [St. Domingo]): black revolutionaries and, 101, 104, 120–22, 124, 126–33, 136, 244n93; commerce and, 104, 120–24, 126–33, 136, 143, 242n68; embargo of 1806, 130; Haitian Revolution and, 119, 121–22, 131–32, 244n93
Hall, George Abbott, 71, 73, 87
Hallowell, Benjamin, 41
Hamilton, Alexander: accounting system and, 76, 78–80, 95, 119; armed merchant vessels and, 112–14; Bank of the United States and, 55; custom house critiques and, 54, 80, 117, 119, 222n9; customs duties and, 60–61, 68–69, 174, 225n50; customs officers and, 49, 77, 83–84, 86, 191; death of, 131; distance issues and, 59–60, 94; federal custom houses administration and, 68–69, 117; federal government's credit and, 55, 77–78, 80, 98, 161; federalism and, 1, 13–14, 53, 56, 75, 117; financing schemes and, 55–56, 58–59; fiscal-military state and, 55–56, 75, 80–81; law enforcement and, 76, 95–96; legal procedures for overdue bonds and, 88–89; merchants and, 1, 3, 87, 99; national sovereignty and, 80–81; negotiated authority and, 76, 83–85, 93–97, 131, 155; political economic writings and, 1, 76, 80, 81; politics and, 191; "Report on Public Credit" and, 1, 76, 81; surveyors/supervisors and, 162; Whiskey Rebellion and, 97–98, 108

Harison, George, 38
Harris, Richard, 71
Harrison, B. I., 195–96
Haskins, Ralph, 177
Haskins, Thomas, 177
Hatton, John, 44
Haulman, Clyde A., 178
Hawthorne, Nathaniel, 6, 170–71
Hays, John, 155
Hazlehurst, Robert, 89
Heathcote, Caleb, 31–32
Heth, William, 49–51, 70–71, 90, 113, 174, 220n5
Hickey, Donald R., 128, 130, 157–58, 244n93
high federalism, 87, 99
Holmes, Isaac, 70, 89, 112–13, 175, 178
Huger, Benjamin, 177
Hulsebosch, Daniel, 27, 34
Hulton, Henry, 19–20, 39–40, 42–43
Huntington, Jedediah, 70–71

Iberian Peninsula, 158–60
Imlay v. Sands (1804), 153
impost duties. *See* customs duties
impressment, and naval vessels, 134, 157, 247n22
income tax, 177, 197, 200
Ingersol, Charles D., 181
Ingham, Samuel D., 182, 190
insurance, marine, 87, 105, 109, 124, 141, 174

Jackson, Andrew, 9, 9, 169, 171–72, 179, 182–83, 190–92, 253n7, 258n71
Jackson, John G., 127
Jay, John, 126
Jefferson, Thomas: armed merchant vessels and, 120–21, 124–27, 129, 237n4, 242n72, 244n94; commerce and, 121–22; commercial regulation and, 134, 136; custom house critiques and, 117–19; customs officers and, 69, 101, 118, 145–46, 191; detention of vessels and, 146–49; embargo of 1808–9 and, 101, 136, 141, 146, 245n11; limited central government and, 14, 117–18; national debt and, 139; nationalism and, 138; neutrality policy and, 119; presidential powers and, 136, 141, 146, 148–51, 162, 245n11; Revolution of 1800 and, 131, 188, 191; western settlement and, 117, 119–20, 172; yeoman agricultural republic and, 117, 119, 137

Johnson, William, 129, 148–50
Jones, William, 153, 160, 176
Jordan, Melatiah, 154
Judiciary Act of 1789, 68

Kennedy, Archibald, 38
King, William, 183
Kohn, Carl, 192

Lamar-Jones, Douglas, 152
Lamb, John, 6, 70, 72, 73, 89, 178
Lasher, John, 72, 73
Laurens, Henry, 37, 197
law enforcement: British imperial custom houses and, 17, 19–23, 26, 28–37, 68, 211n15, 213n39, 214n46, 215n57, 215n60, 217n82; British Treasury and, 17, 19, 21–22, 26, 28, 33, 35; commercial peoples and, 84, 90, 104; customs bonds and, 63–64, 143–44; customs officers and, 49–50, 63, 68, 81–82, 84, 86–87, 95–96; federal government and, 58–59, 225n42, 225n45; by Parliament in colonial America, 21–22, 36, 38, 42, 68; republicanism and, 60, 225n45; states and, 58, 62–63, 225n42. See also legal procedures
Lawrence, Abraham R., 189, 257n62
Lear, Tobias, 122
Lee, Arthur, 64, 227n64
Lee, Richard Henry, 69
legal procedures: Appraisement Act support and, 189–90; customs bonds overdue and, 68, 82, 84–85, 88–89, 96–97, 174–77, 180, 183; embargo violations and, 101–2, 144–45, 148–54, 152, 161–62, 249n61; smuggling and, 144–45. See also law enforcement; United States Supreme Court; and specific cases
Levely, Henry, 193
Levy, Jonathan, 91
Lewis, Addin, 176
license trade, 158–60
limited central government, 4, 14, 117–18, 123
Lincoln, Abraham, 200
Lincoln, Benjamin, 70–71, 85, 87, 91, 109, 145
Linebaugh, Peter, 129
Little, William, 187–89, 257n62
Livingston, Brockholst, 153–54
local waterfront peoples and governance. See commercial peoples (merchant communities); merchants
Logan, George, 128–30

Logan, Rayford, 122
Lords Commissioners of Trade and Plantations. See Board of Trade
Lords of the Treasury, 27, 42
Louisiana Purchase, 119–21

MacLay, William, 64, 227n67
"Macon's Bill Number 10" of 1810, 135
Madison, James: armed merchant vessels and, 123, 242n72; commercial regulation and, 136, 157; custom house critiques and, 80; customs duties and, 57, 61–62; limited central government and, 14; national debt and, 139; nationalism and, 138, 157; political economy and, 171; western settlement and, 172
Maier, Pauline S., 206n18
manufacturing industry, 137–39, 168, 171, 186
marketplace: American Revolution and, 47; commercial peoples and, 10; commercial regulation and, 134–35; consumer revolution and, 5–6; federal authority and, 73–74; federal government and, 10–11; negotiated authority and, 47; state boundary with, 11, 195–96, 207n20. See also Atlantic marketplace
Mason, Alphonso, 195–96
Massey, Nathaniel, 155–56
McCoy, Drew R., 137
McCulloch/McCulloh, James H., 101–2, 142, 144, 150–51, 159–60, 162, 178–80, 191
McIlvaine, William, 153
McKitrick, Eric, 81, 99
McLane, Louis, 199
McMaster, John, 154
McNiel, John, 195
merchant capital: customs duties and, 1, 3, 117, 168, 203n2; customs officials and, 86; federal government and, 3, 11, 13; national revenue and, 53, 77, 94, 99, 119, 171; political economy and, 11, 99; privateering and, 107, 121, 124, 238n15
merchant communities (commercial peoples). See commercial peoples (merchant communities)
merchants: as appraisers, 187, 257n62; Atlantic marketplace and, 10, 29–30; commercial regulation in colonial America and, 29–34; credit and, 10, 90–92, 95; description of, 10, 87–88; embargoes and, 103, 110, 139, 157, 238n25; Hamilton and,

1, 3, 87; insurance and, 87, 105, 109, 124, 141, 174; negotiated authority during colonial America and, 11–13, 15–17, 16, 20, 29–34, 36–37, 39–40, 47, 76; negotiated authority during federal government and, 11–13, 76–77, 83, 85, 87–96, 98–99, 104, 108–11, 125, 131, 155, 168–69, 173; neutrality policy and, 103–4, 105, 108–9; political economy and, 3; ports of entry and, 67–68; power and, 10, 206nn16–17; smuggling and, 103. *See also* commercial peoples (merchant communities); merchant capital
Miller, James, 191
Miller, Thomas, 27
Milne, David, 159
mobs: British imperial custom houses and, 10–11, 16–17, 19, 37–38, 43–45, 44–45, 253n7; commercial peoples and, 10–11, 19, 132, 154–56, 169–70, 206n18, 253n7
Molasses Act of 1733, 33, 38
Monroe, James, 167, 169, 171–72, 182, 189, 191
Moore, Daniel, 36
moral crisis: credit and, 174, 180, 183; customs bonds and, 173–83, 255n31; fraudulent manifests or invoices and, 184–86, 189, 195, 256n51, 257n52; nationalism and, 184; negotiated authority and, 13, 169, 173, 176; political patronage and, 168–69, 179; protectionism and, 184; state and marketplace boundary, 195–96
Morris, Robert, 53, 56–57
Moultrie, William, 229n83
Muhlenberg, John Peter, 124–27, 143
Murray, John, 127–28

Napoleonic Wars, 13, 103, 131, 133, 137, 139, 159, 167, 170
national debt: customs duties and, 6, 161, 168, 171, 176, 178; embargoes and, 139; financing schemes and, 54–57, 80, 139, 161, 222n14; history of, 54, 59; specie payments and, 176, 178; statistics and, 1, 139, 171–72, 176, 179–80; tariffs and, 168
national impost, 53, 56–59, 62–63, 71, 223nn27–28, 226n54, 227n67
nationalism, 12, 133–34, 138, 184, 186
Nationalists (Federalists). *See* Federalists (Nationalists)
national revenue: commercial regulation and, 195, 199–200; customs duties and, 199–200; crisis and, 1, 53–54; customs duties and, 1, 2–3, 51, 53, 60–61, 75–77, 93, 98, 103, 105–6, 117, 160–61, 176–77, 224nn49–50; 235n96, 240n49; distance issues and, 59–60, 70, 94; embargoes and, 139; federal custom houses and, 50, 120; merchant capital and, 53, 77, 94, 99, 119, 171; western settlement and, 119–20
national sovereignty: commercial restrictions and, 134; credit and, 80; custom houses and, 4; customs duties and, 4; customs officers and, 76, 87; embargoes and, 132, 139, 247n22; fiscal-military state and, 4, 23–24; revenue and, 1, 3, 80–81; Treasury's accounting system and, 80–81, 90. *See also* federal government
nation building, 106, 117, 119, 137–39, 167–68, 171, 176, 186. *See also* fiscal-military state
navies: America and, 160–61, 176, 247n22; France and, 106, 121, 124, 128; Great Britain and, 35, 37, 110, 121, 134, 138, 157, 158, 247n22
Navigation Acts, 11, 21, 23, 26–27, 45–46, 53, 134, 227n64
Necker, Jacques, 56–57
negotiated authority: Atlantic marketplace and, 108; benefits of, 29, 33–34, 90–92, 99; Board of Trade and, 11, 21; British imperial custom houses and, 11–13, 15–17, 20, 29–34, 36–37, 39–40, 47, 76, 93, 95; British Treasury and, 21; collusion captures and, 116, 118, 170; commercial peoples and, 76–77, 95–96, 98, 113, 131–33, 155–62; Congress and, 173; customs bonds and, 83–85, 87–92, 176, 183, 234n49; customs officers and, 11–13, 33, 51, 76–77, 83, 85, 87–96, 98–99, 104, 108–11, 131–33, 155–62, 168–69, 173; Federalists and, 131, 136; merchants during colonial America and, 11–13, 15–17, 20, 29–34, 36–37, 39–40, 47, 76; merchants during federal government and, 11–13, 76–77, 83, 85, 87–96, 98–99, 104, 108–11, 125, 131, 168–69, 173; moral crisis and, 13, 169, 173, 176; Parliament and, 21; political patronage and, 168–69; republicanism and, 86–87, 94; Republicans and, 131, 136, 161–62; smuggling and, 15–16, 20; Treasury Department and, 51, 76–77, 83–85, 92–97, 99, 113, 155, 173. *See also* discretion of customs officers

neutrality policy: armed merchant vessels and, 112; commercial regulation and, 108; Congress and, 104; customs officers and, 103–5, 108–10; federal government and, 105, 116; Federalists and, 105; Jefferson and, 119; merchants and, 103–4, 108–9; political economy and, 106; politics and, 106; trade with enemies and, 108–9
Neutrality Proclamation of 1793, 105–6, 108, 237n6
Nicklin, Philip, 125–26
Niles, Hezekiah, 186
Non-Importation Acts, 134–35, 141, 149, 152, 159, 245n11
Non-Importation agreements, 45–46, 64
Non-Intercourse Act of 1809, 135, 141
Non-Intercourse agreements, 45–46
Northey, Edward, 32
Nourse, Joseph, 78
Nullification Crisis, 197–200, *198*, 260n12

Olney, Jeremiah, 6, 70–71, 95–98, 108, 115, 155–56, 169, 174
Olney v. Arnold (1796), 97, 108
Onuf, Peter S., 118
organizational revolution, 61, 221n2
Otis, Harrison Gray, 115
Otis, Joseph, 73, 153, 249n61
Owen, George W., 182

Paine, Thomas, 57
Panic of 1819, 168, 173, 178, 181, 195, 199
Parliament: colonial law enforcement and, 21–22, 36, 38, 42, 68; corruption and, 86; negotiated authority and, 21, 33; ports of entry and, 66; powers and, 59. See also specific revenue acts
Parrott, John Fabyan, 87–88
patronage, 28, 30, 33, 168–69, 179, 191, 258n71
Pendleton, Edmund, 69
Pennington, William Sanford, 153
Perkins, Bradford, 134
Peskin, Lawrence A., 137
Peters, Richard, 126
Pettit, Charles, 36
Philadelphia's British imperial custom house, 15–17, 36–37, 41–44
Pichon, Louis, 122–23, 127, 242n72
Pinckney, Charles, 69
pirates, 30, 104, 111, 121
Pitt, Robert, 27

Pitt, William, 35
Plumer, William, 127
Pocock, J. G. A., 86
political economy: American Revolution and, 46; discretion of customs officers and, 90, 94, 104–5, 168, 195–96; farmers and, 98–99; federal custom houses and, 4, 6, 50; Federalists and, 50; Hamilton's writings and, 1, 76, 80; manufacturing industry and, 137–39, 171, 186; merchant capital and, 11, 99; merchants and, 3; neutrality policy and, 106; organizational revolution and, 61, 221n2; slave trade and, 171; tariffs and, 171; Treasury Department and, 90. See also federal custom houses; tariffs
politics: commercial peoples and, 206n17; customs officers and, 54, 69, 71–72, 118–19, 145, 169–70, 190–96, 228n79; neutrality policy and, 106; patronage and, 168–69, 179, 258n71; rotation system and, 179; Society of Cincinnati and, 49, 70–71, 124, 229n87; tariffs and, 171
Port Republicain, 122–24
Postal Service, United States, 82, *82*, 106, 193
power: commerce and, 10–11, 136–37; commercial peoples and, 10, 98, 119, 206nn16–17; customs officers and, 195–96; federal government and, 13, 168, 200, 208n31; mobs in Great Britain and, 10; Parliament and, 59; presidential powers during embargoes and, 136, 141, 146, 148–50, 148–51, 162, 245n11; states and, 13; Treasury Department and, 195–96. See also empire
Pratt, Ichobad, 189, 257n62
Preble, Edward, 111–12
presidents, and presidential powers during embargoes, 136, 141, 146, 148–51, 162, 245n11. See also specific individuals
Prince, Carl E., 228n79
Pringle, J. R., 199
privateering: description of, 103; embargoes and, 110; embargo of 1812 and, 135–36; France and, 103, 106–7, 109; Great Britain and, 103, 107, 109–10, 133–34; marque letters and, 115–16, 240n42; merchant capital and, 107, 121, 124, 238n15; Quasi-War and, 115–16; smuggling and, 103; War of Independence and, 111; West Indies and, 111–12

protectionism, 168, 171, 180, 184, 186, 226n54. *See also* tariffs
public credit, 1, 55–56, 76, 81

Quasi-War of 1798–1800, 115–16, 120–22, 244n93
Queen Anne's War, 31

Randall, John, 191
Randolph, Edward, 27–29, 35, 213n39, 214n46
reexport trade, 79, 133, 226n54. *See also* export market
reform: appraisers and, 186–90, 257n62, 258n65; British imperial custom houses and, 29, 36, 38–40, 44–45, 47, 79–80; commercial regulation and, 164–65; discretion of customs officers and, 168–69, 173; negotiated authority and, 13, 169, 173, 176
Registering Act of 1789, 53
Reid, John Phillip, 44
"Report on Public Credit," 1, 76, 81
republicanism: American republic and, 10, 12–13, 117, 119, 137, 171; credit and, 92; description of, 53; law enforcement and, 60, 225n45; limited government and, 4, 14, 117–18; negotiated authority and, 86–87, 94; Society of Cincinnati and, 71, 229n87; yeoman agricultural republic and, 117, 119, 137
Republicans: armed merchant vessels and, 104, 127; commerce and, 137, 145–46, 246n14; commercial restrictions and, 136–37, 246n14; custom houses critiques and, 117; customs officers and, 145; manufacturing industry and, 138; national debt reduction and, 171–72; negotiated authority and, 131, 136, 161–62; patronage and, 179, 191. *See also* republicanism
revenue, and British imperial custom houses, 22–23, 29, 33–35, 38–43, 218n90. *See also* national revenue
Revere, Paul, 19–20, 20, 22
Revolution of 1800, 131, 188, 191
Rhett, Robert Barnwell, 197
Robinson, John, 43
Rodney, Caesar, 149–50
Ross, John, 70, 73
Ross, Samuel, 189, 257n62
rotation system, 179, 191–92, 195
Rousby, Christopher, 27

Rule of 1756, so-called, 133–34
Rush, Richard, 177

Sailly, Peter, 155
Saint-Domingue (St. Domingo) [Haiti]. *See* Haiti (Saint-Domingue [St. Domingo])
Sands, Comfort, 58
Sands, Joshua, 89, 109, 118
Sanford, Nathan, 145, 153, 186
Sanford, William, 153
Seaman v. Patten (1805), 153
secession movements, 161, 167, 200
Second Amendment, 127–28
Sedgewick, Theodore, 67–68
Seven Years' War, 16, 19–21, 35–36, 38–40, 170, 211n7
Shays' Rebellion, 60
Shee, John, 143–44
Sherman, Robert, 63–64
Shippen, Edward, 62–63
Simons, James, 89, 115, 175
Skowronek, Stephen, 208n31
slaves/slavery: black Haitian revolutionaries and, 101, 104, 120–22, 124, 126–33, 136, 244n93; commercial regulation and, 4–5, 61, 135, 197–98, 245n8; credit and, 91; freedom and, 104, 129, 200, 244n93; Haitian Revolution and, 119, 121–22, 131–32, 244n93; political economy and, 173, 223n28; slave trade and, 170, 185, 245n8
Smith, Adam, 38, 225n49
Smith, Joshua, 144
Smith, Samuel , 146, 180, 183
smuggling: armed forces and, 155, 250n69; British imperial custom houses and, 11, 15–16, 29, 33, 35–36, 39, 218n93; British military forces and, 35; Canada and, 91, 144, 154, 157–58, 184, 248n35; customs duties and, 61–62, 225n49; customs officers and, 101, 142–43, 154–59, 170, 193, 195; discretion of customs officers and, 141–42; embargoes and, 140–45, 152–58, 247n22; Great Britain and, 24–25; legal procedures and, 144–45; license trade and, 158–60; merchants and, 103; mob violence and, 154–56; Navigation Acts and, 11, 21; privateering and, 103; protectionism and, 171; West Indies and, 16, 21, 33, 35, 37, 144
Society of Cincinnati, 49, 70–71, 124, 229n87
solicitor of the Treasury, 182–83, 190

272 INDEX

Sons of Liberty, 6, 41
specie payments, 176, 178
Spencer, George, 37–38
Stamp Act, 40–42, 45, 57, 156
states and municipalities: commerce and, 11, 207n20; law enforcement and, 58, 62–63, 225n42; marketplace boundary with, 11, 195–96, 207n20; national impost and, 57–58, 62–63, 71; Nullification Crisis and, 197–200, 260n12; power and, 13; state building and, 1, 167–68, 179
Steele, John, 109, 143, 178, 181, 191
Stein, Joshua M., 125
Stewart, Thomas, 189, 257n62
Story, Joseph, 189
St. Thomas, 31, 116, 130
Sugar Act of 1764, 21, 38–40
supervisors (surveyors), and custom houses, 23, 33, 65, 66, 162, 195–96
Supreme Court, United States, 89, 97, 113, 129, 148, 153, 189. *See also specific cases*
surveyors (supervisors), and custom houses, 23, 33, 65, 66, 162, 195–96
Swanwick, John, 146
Swartwout, Samuel, 192–94
Swift, John, 15–17, 16, 36–37, 41–44
Swift, Jonathan, 38

Tappan v. United States (1822), 189–90
tariffs: 1816 and, 177; 1824 and, 171; 1828 and, 190; 1842 and, 195; anti-tariff leaders and, 198; Congress and, 1, 8, 53, 64, 75; discretion of customs officers and, 190, 195; manufacturing industry and, 168, 171, 186; national debt and, 168; political economy and, 171; protectionism and, 168, 171, 180, 184, 186. *See also* commercial regulation; customs duties
taxes: Congress and, 1, 97–98; Constitution and, 1, 53, 61–62; excise taxes and, 11, 97–98, 177, 211n10, 225n50; Federalists and, 53, 221n2; Great Britain and, 11, 211n10, 225n50; income tax and, 177, 197, 200
Tea Act, 13, 45
Teackle, John, 142–43
Theus, Simon, 148–51, 161–62
Thompson, Edward Palmer, 10, 22
Tonnage Act of 1789, 84, 233n29
Toussaint L'Ouverture, 122, 242n72, 244n93

Townshend Revenue Act, 45, 206n18
trade with enemies, 11, 38–39, 67, 108–9, 133, 136, 157–60, 170
Treasury, British: accounting system and, 79–80; fiscal-military state and, 22–23, 211n11; law enforcement in British imperial custom houses and, 17, 19, 21–22, 26, 28, 33, 35; negotiated authority and, 21; reforms and, 79; smuggling and, 25
Treasury Board, 22, 75, 78
Treasury Department, United States: accounting system and, 75–76, 78–80, 95, 119; administration and, 78–80; armed merchant vessels and, 112–14, 117, 129; commercial peoples and, 13; Comptroller and, 95, 109, 177; credit and, 55, 77–78, 80, 98, 161, 178; customs bonds overdue and, 68, 175, 177, 180, 182; customs officers and, 13; embargo of 1808–9 and, 102; federal custom house history and, 5, 75; fiscal-military state and, 98; fraudulent manifests or invoices and, 184–85; Gallatin and, 102, 117–20, 138, 146–47, 160–62, 251n84; history of, 75–76; national sovereignty and, 76, 80–81, 90; negotiated authority and, 51, 76–77, 83–85, 92–97, 99, 113, 173; political economy and, 90; ports of entry and, 67–68; power and, 195–96; solicitor of the Treasury and, 182–83, 190; western settlement subsidies and, 106. *See also specific secretaries of the treasury*
Treaty of Amity and Commerce of 1778, 106
Treaty of Neutrality of 1687, 31
Tremble, David, 180
Truxes, Thomas, 37–38
Tucker, Thomas Tudor, 63
Tyng, Dudley, 115

Ubbelohde, Carl, 37
United States Postal Service, 82, 82, 106, 193
United States Supreme Court, 89, 97, 113, 129, 148, 153, 189. *See also specific cases*
United States Treasury Department. *See* Treasury Department, United States
United States v. The Hawke (1794), 148

Vice-Admiralty Courts, 39, 68
Virginia Port Bill of 1784, 58

Wadsworth, Jeremiah, 62, 71, 84–85, 87
Waldstreicher, David, 167
Wall, Richard, 178
Walpole, Robert, 21, 29–30, 33, 57
War of 1812, 136, 138, 156, 161, 167, 176, 178, 184, 198
War of Independence (American Revolutionary War), 19, 54–55, 64, 70, 111, 162, 223n27. *See also* American Revolution
Washington, George: commercial regulation and, 134; customs officers and, 6, 49, 54, 68–72, 73, 83, 230n91; embargoes and, 110; immortalization of, 167; military service and, 70; neutrality policy and, 105–6, 108, 237n6
Waters, Isaac, 187–89, 257n62
Webb, William, 88
Webster, Pelatiah, 56, 222n14
western settlement, 106, 117, 119, 167–68, 171–73, 176, 254n15
West Indies: armed merchant vessels and, 114, 116, 125; commerce and, 21, 26, 31, 35, 39, 94, 105, 116, 121, 124; privateering and, 111–12; smuggling and, 16, 21, 33, 35, 37, 144
Whately, Thomas, 39, 60
Whipple, Joseph, 87–88
Whiskey Rebellion, 97–98, 108
White, Alexander, 64
White, Richard, 206n19
Williams, Otho Holland, 64, 71, 73, 81–82, 84, 87, 89, 227n67
Wolcott, Oliver, Jr., 51, 78, 93, 112–14, 116, 119, 178, 240n49
Woodbury, Levi, 194
Woodham v. Gelston (1806), 153
writs of assistance, 44, 219n110

XYZ affair, 114

yeoman agricultural republic, 117, 119, 137
Young, Ammi Burnham, 82, *82*, 172, *172*

www.ingramcontent.com/pod-product-compliance
Lightning Source LLC
Chambersburg PA
CBHW022041290426
44109CB00014B/940